To Free the **Cinema**

To Free the Cinema

JONAS MEKAS &
THE NEW YORK
UNDERGROUND

Edited by
David E. James

PRINCETON UNIVERSITY PRESS

PRINCETON, NEW JERSEY

Published by Princeton University Press, 41
William Street,
Princeton, New Jersey 08540
In the United Kingdom: Princeton University
Press, Oxford

*Library of Congress Cataloging-in-Publication
Data*

To free the cinema : Jonas Mekas and the
New York underground / edited by David E.
James.
p.   cm.
Filmography:
Includes bibliographical references and
index.

ISBN 0-691-07894-7 (alk. paper) —
ISBN 0-691-02345-X
(pbk. : alk. paper)
1. Mekas, Jonas, 1922– —Criticism and
interpretation.
2. Experimental films—New York (N.Y.)
3. Motion picture industry—New York (N.Y.)
I. James, David E., 1945– .
PN1998.3.M44T6   1992
791.43'015—dc20   91-31685

This book has been composed in Linotron
Trump Medieval

Princeton University Press books are printed
on acid-free paper, and meet the guidelines
for permanence and durability of the
Committee on Production Guidelines for Book
Longevity of the Council on Library
Resources

Printed in the United States of America

10 9 8 7 6 5 4 3 2 1

10 9 8 7 6 5 4 3 2 1
(Pbk.)

*The stage of our work which
went by the motto, "Free the
Cinema," has been successfully completed. Now we are at
another stage, now the Aesthetic Dialogue will begin.*

—Jonas Mekas, Diaries, May 1970

Contents

Acknowledgments

WE GRATEFULLY acknowledge permission from the following to print copyrighted material: Jonas Mekas for frame enlargements from films by Jonas Mekas; for photographs of Adolfas and Jonas Mekas, of the Gramercy Arts Theatre, of the opening of Anthology Film Archives, and of the editors of *Film Culture;* and for all quotations from the poetry and diaries of Jonas Mekas. Robert Haller for the photograph of Jonas Mekas at his desk. Georges Borchardt, Inc. and John Ashbery for quotations from "A Wave" and "So Many Lives" from *A Wave* by John Ashbery, copyright © John Ashbery, 1981, 1982, 1983, 1984, reprinted by permission of Georges Borchardt, Inc., and the author. Anthology Film Archives for production stills from *Guns of the Trees* and photographs of the marquee of the Charles Theater and the Anthology Film Archives Film Selection Committee. Jonas Mekas and Vyt Bakaitis for all translations of the poetry of Jonas Mekas. Linda Thome for figure 11.1, "The Major Diary Films." Peter Moore for photographs of the Charles Theater during the Film-Makers' Festival, Robert Rauschenberg's *Map Room II*, Robert Whitman's *Prune Flat*, Charlotte Moorman being arrested, Philip Glass and Steve Reich, Jonas Mekas with Yoko Ono and John Lennon, George Maciunas's backyard, Richard Foreman's "Paris–New York Telephone Call," Peter Kubelka cooking, Richard Foreman's *Sophia = Wisdom, Part 3: The Cliffs*, George Maciunas and Nam June Paik, and Jonas Mekas at Anthology Film Archives, January 1991; all photographs in chapter 12 copyright © 1992 by Peter Moore. Charles Garrad for the photograph of the Museum of the Moving Image. Amy Greenfield for the photograph of the staff of Anthology Film Archives, 1980. Hollis Melton for photographs of the staff of Anthology Film Archives, 1990, and the drawing of Jonas Mekas by Jerome Hill.

We would also like to thank Robert Haller for assistance of many kinds, and Jane Lincoln Taylor for her creative, scrupulous, and generous editorial contributions.

To Free the **Cinema**

1. David E. James   Introduction

A RECENT BOOK on the arts in post-
war New York, designed for the coffee table, to be sure, but not
without scholarly pretensions, surveyed the city's achievements
and legacies in separate essays on its literature, its architecture, its
painting, its dance, its theater, its music, and its intellectual life.[1]
Not only was there no essay on film, but the only filmmakers mentioned in the index were Rudolph Burckhardt (for a still photograph), Andy Warhol and Red Grooms (for painting), Amiri Baraka
(for plays), Norman Mailer (for fiction), Meredith Monk and Yvonne
Rainer (for choreography), and Yoko Ono (for performance). To all
intents and purposes, the art form of the century had not been practiced in the century's capital.

Within film studies itself, this kind of occlusion is familiar; the
popular assumption of an unbridgeable gulf between the movies and
high art has been reflected in the academic assumption that nonin-
dustrial cinemas are by definition antipopulist. If film is the medium practiced in Studio City, then the medium practiced by artists
and Beats, Third World women and peace workers, in New York
cannot really be film. The blend of overfamiliarity with ignorance
that fuels these prejudices has for the past forty years surrounded
the efforts of all who have envisioned for film the aesthetic, social,
or cognitive functions claimed for painting or poetry, and who have
worked to establish the institutions in which such functions could

[1] Leonard Wallock, ed., *New York: Culture Capital of the World, 1940–1965* (New
York: Rizzoli, 1988). The present introduction is informed by William Alexander,
Film on the Left: American Documentary Film from 1931 to 1942 (Princeton:
Princeton University Press, 1981); Stephen J. Dobi, *Cinema 16: America's Largest
Film Society* (Ph.D. diss., New York University, 1984); J. Hoberman, "The Under-
ground," in J. Hoberman and Jonathan Rosenbaum, *Midnight Movies* (New York:
Harper and Row, 1983); Richard Koszarski, *The Astoria Studio and Its Fabulous
Films* (New York: Dover, 1983); Scott MacDonald, "Interview with Jonas Mekas,"
October 29 (Summer 1984): 82–116; P. Adams Sitney, ed., *Film Culture Reader* (New
York: Praeger, 1970); Lauren Rabinovitz, *Points of Resistance: Women, Power, and
Politics in the New York Avant-Garde Cinema, 1943–1971* (Chicago: University of
Illinois Press, 1989); P. Adams Sitney, ed., *The Essential Cinema: Essays on Films in
the Collection of Anthology Film Archives* (New York: Anthology Film Archives and
New York University Press, 1975); and Calvin Tomkins, "All Pockets Open," in *The
Scene: Reports on Post-Modern Art* (New York: Viking, 1976).

mature. These institutions—once powerful, now perhaps less vigorous—are part of a social history, the story of how significant numbers of people found in cinema the means to organize their aspirations. Yet through that social history there run also the personal histories of individuals who saw the social possibilities most clearly and seized them most forcefully. None has done so more than Jonas Mekas. The present collection begins to document his works and, through the optic they supply, to assist in the recovery and preservation of a history of filmmaking in New York that is rapidly being lost.

Film culture, of course, began in New York. The first movie ever publicly screened was at Koster and Bial's Music Hall, where Macy's now stands, and Edison, Biograph, Vitagraph, and other early production companies were all based in the city or its environs. Even after the trust battles of the first decade culminated in the move of the bulk of production to Hollywood, most of the administrative and research facilities remained in the city, as did almost all the documentary and much of the animated production. As late as 1929, almost one-quarter of all United States industrial filmmaking was done in New York, with the Famous Players–Lasky studio in what is now Astoria being the biggest and most important of those that remained or were opened in the twenties. The thirties saw a dramatic expansion of independent production and the growth of cinemas not simply outside Hollywood, but programmatically opposed to it. The elements of truly populist working-class cinema were inaugurated in the Workers Film and Photo League from 1930 to 1935 and in Nykino and Joris Ivens's Frontier Films, to establish another tradition, one almost obliterated in the fifties but then revived by Émile de Antonio and by the New York and Third World Newsreels. Far from being without film culture, the city to which Jonas Mekas came was the country's—and perhaps the century's—center of independent cinema.

Together with his brother Adolfas, Mekas arrived in New York on 29 October 1949, having spent the previous four years in displaced-persons camps in Western Europe. The brothers were refugees, Lithuanians from Semeniškiai, a village some twenty miles from the Latvian border. Born on Christmas Eve 1922, Jonas spent his childhood on the family farm looking after livestock and working in the fields. After being graduated from primary school in 1936, he became an agricultural laborer in a neighboring village, where he saw his first movies. He continued his belated education in local schools, moving to the nearby town of Biržai, and in 1938 he attempted to enter high school. Too old already for the beginning grades, he spent the winter and spring of 1939–1940 catching up, gaining admission shortly before the Soviet Union annexed Lithuania. Two years later, with the Soviets expelled by the German army, he began to work for a local newspaper, contributing at the same time to an anti-Nazi underground paper—resistance work that eventually forced him underground to escape arrest.

With forged papers, he and Adolfas boarded a train for Vienna, intending to study at the university. But their train was joined to another carrying Russian and Polish prisoners to a forced-labor camp near Hamburg, where they too were interned. After a failed attempt to escape to Denmark, they ended up on a farm near Flensburg, where they remained until the end of the war. Subsequently, a series of DP camps led finally to Wiesbaden and to study at the University of Mainz. In the camps, movies were common, and Jonas recalls being particularly impressed by German postwar neorealism, the films of Käutner, Baky, Liebeneiner, and others now forgotten. He continued his own writing, edited the camp newspaper and an avant-garde literary magazine for Lithuanian exiles, and published a collection of his own literary sketches and prose poems. In 1948 a book of his poems, *Semeniškių idilės* (*Idylls of Semeniškiai*), and a story in a short-story collection were published. The following year the brothers moved again, to the DP camp at Schwaebisch Gmuend. They left that for America, and on their third evening here they attended a screening of *The Cabinet of Dr. Caligari* and *The Fall of the House of Usher* sponsored by the New York Film Society and programmed by Rudolph Arnheim.

Living in the Williamsburg section of Brooklyn, the brothers found factory jobs, but they immediately began reading about films and planning their own, about the DPs and against war in general. They attended the early-evening screenings at the Museum of Modern Art (then in the middle of a three-year cycle, "The Film Till Now") and made contact with Hans Richter, who was at the time teaching at City College. They submitted scripts with equal lack of success to Hollywood and to such independent directors as Flaherty, and also began to make their own films. Jonas bought a Bolex and soon was using all his factory earnings to document the DP communities in New York and other cities. From that point on, his life was (and continues to be) totally occupied with film, with all branches of cinema.

The history of independent-film exhibition in New York goes back at least to 1932, to the first Film Forum (founded by Tom Brandon and Sidney Howard, mostly to show leftist films and others that had not passed the censor) and the New York Film Society

1.1 Adolfas Mekas and Jonas Mekas, 1955.

(founded by Julien Levy to show foreign films). The Museum of Modern Art established its film library and began screenings in 1935 (including in its first season a talk by Fernand Léger on "Painting and Advance Guard Film" and the showing of his work); in 1939, with the opening of the new museum building on West Fifty-Third Street, regularly scheduled public screenings began, which have continued to the present day. Postwar exhibition outside MOMA was sparked first by Maya Deren's popular showings of her own films at the Provincetown Playhouse in Greenwich Village in 1946–1947, roughly at the same time as the Art in Cinema screenings at the San Francisco Museum of Art, started by Frank Stauffacher and Richard Foster. The Deren screenings were attended by another European immigrant, who was so inspired by them that he began a screening society of his own. Cinema 16, founded by Amos Vogel and his wife, Marcia, lasted from 1947 to 1963; it educated a generation of cinéastes and provided the initial public presentation of the emerging American independent film.

Apart from a disastrous early occasion when a blizzard prevented the audience from attending a heavily invested show, Cinema 16 was an instant success, with 2,600 members by 1949 and 7,000 at its height, and evening attendances of 3,000 not uncommon. Organized as a film society in order to avoid censorship and to establish a financial base separate from the vagaries of individual admissions, Cinema 16 showed mixed programs in which experimental and art films were included with scientific, instructional, and documentary films and foreign features. It premiered many important films, including *Shadows* and *Pull My Daisy*, as well as Mekas's own *Guns of the Trees* in 1961. In collaboration with the Creative Film Foundation, a nonprofit organization established by Maya Deren in 1955 to make grants to independent filmmakers, Cinema 16 presented Creative Cinema Awards for documentary and avant-garde films annually from 1956 to 1961, and Vogel also began a distribution arm for the avant-garde, publishing his *Catalogue of the Experimental Film*, which included works by Sidney Peterson, the Whitney brothers, Gregory Markopoulos, Norman McLaren, Stan Brakhage, Willard Maas, Jordan Belson, and Kenneth Anger. But, like the programs themselves, the collection was exclusive, reflecting both Vogel's aesthetic values and his belief that the independent cinema was institutionally best served by principled selection rather than by indiscriminate promotion.

Mekas himself attended Cinema 16 screenings (he claimed in fact to have attended them all), and though his differences of opinion with Vogel about the advancement of the avant-garde subsequently soured their personal relationship, Cinema 16 was more influential than any other single enterprise in creating the environment in which Mekas's own work would prosper. Like Vogel, Mekas began to arrange screenings, but his first major project took up the journalism of his youth in Lithuania and the DP camps.

Film Culture, soon subtitled "America's Independent Motion Picture Magazine," first appeared in January 1955 with an editorial board consisting of Mekas and his brother, George Fenin, Louis Brigante, and Edouard de Laurot. In his first editorial, Mekas proclaimed the need for "a searching revaluation of the aesthetic standards obtaining both among film-makers and audiences and for a thorough revision of the prevalent attitude to the function of cinema"; that function, he asserted, was neither entertainment nor the production of commodities, both of which had combined to blunt public recognition of the "full significance of filmic art." While it was oriented toward Europe, from the beginning *Film Culture* gave sympathetic critical attention to American film, and eventually seminal work on Hollywood appeared there, most notably Andrew Sarris's "Notes on the Auteur Theory in 1962" and "The American Cinema" (appearing in 1963 in nos. 27 and 28 respectively). This tolerance did not extend to the avant-garde; an early issue contained Mekas's immediately notorious attack, "The Experimental Film in

America," in which he lambasted the "adolescent character," a pu-
tative "conspiracy of homosexuality," the "lack of creative inspiration," and the "technical crudity and thematic narrowness" variously to be found in the work of young filmmakers including Stan
Brakhage, Gregory Markopoulos, Curtis Harrington, and Kenneth
Anger. Mekas himself later termed this a "Saint-Augustine-before-
the conversion piece," and the religious metaphor is entirely appropriate, for within a few years he was the fiercest advocate of what
he had come to see as a new and distinctively American film culture, and an entirely new sense of its political significance.

All Mekas's early film projects were undertaken with a view to
reforming the mass-market, studio-produced feature film. Not only
was a mass audience essential to his political objectives of enlisting
film in the fight against war, but industrial production was intrinsic
to any cinema of which he could then conceive. Consequently, his
ideal through the late fifties was a reformed industrial cinema modeled on a proto-auteurist reading of prewar European film and the
postwar European art film. The turning point in his life in cinema—
and it is a crisis enacted in all the different fields of cinema in
which he was involved—was his realization that the Americaniza-
tion of these traditions faced distinctively American differences in
the production systems and the relation of these production systems to American life; capitalist cinema was so structurally incapable of responding to the realities of American life that a generation of cinephiles would be obliged to reinvent the medium in a
way that had not previously been imagined. As the possibility and
indeed the progress of these transformations became clear to him,
Mekas abandoned the idea of reforming commercial practice, and
instead espoused the radical decentralization of production, the reclamation of the apparatus by previously dispossessed social groups,
and a whole register of formal vocabularies that facilitated unprecedented expressive functions. These new independent cinemas
would take their terms of reference from the metaphor of poetry,
the exemplary and summary form of disaffiliated cultural practice.

For Mekas, the possibilities of such a cultural revolt were revealed virtually simultaneously from several angles. The increased
knowledge of the realities of both industrial and independent production and the greater understanding of the avant-garde that he
acquired after he began writing a weekly film column for the *Village Voice* in 1958 convinced him of the folly of expecting anything
from what, in one of the first of these columns, published on 4 February 1959, he termed "the conventional, dead, official cinema."
Given this atrophy, the only hope was for a total anarchic outbreak:

"There is no other way to break the frozen cinematic conventions than through a complete derangement of the official cinematic senses." As the necessity of this change became clear, *Film Culture* became the voice of the avant-garde, and Mekas its greatest and indefatigable champion. By the early sixties, his attitudes were also informed by his own experience in production.

During the fifties Mekas had on a number of occasions attempted to edit the documentary footage he had been collecting since soon after he arrived of the émigré Lithuanian communities. But such early films, tentatively titled *Grand Street* and *Silent Journey*, had never been completed, and indeed had been hardly more effective than the scripts he and Adolfas sent unsolicited to Hollywood. As the ineffectuality of these projects became apparent, the brothers decided to try independent production, each alternately helping the other. In the spring of 1960, Jonas began shooting a feature, *Guns of the Trees,* from his own script. Difficulties with police harassment, with fund-raising, and especially with Edouard de Laurot, whom he had admitted as codirector, made that experience unsatisfactory. Though the film won the first prize at the Second International Free Cinema Festival at Porretta Terme, Italy, in 1962, Mekas was never happy with it, and never again did he assay a similar project. But if, more than anything else, it convinced him of the need for total personal control over the artwork itself, it also showed him that such authorship was practically possible only in the context of a collective cinematic infrastructure.

Since the war there had been several attempts to organize the independent film community in New York, most of them fueled by the energy and initiative of Maya Deren. In response to her vision of an extensive artists' support system, the Film Artists Society was founded in 1953. Subsequently renamed the Independent Film Makers Association, it continued to meet monthly until 1956, while her Creative Film Foundation attempted to secure grants for independent filmmakers from 1955 to 1961. Renewing this heritage and working with Lewis Allen, a stage and film producer, Mekas called together a group of people interested in independent production, including filmmakers (Lionel Rogosin, Peter Bogdanovich, Robert Frank, Alfred Leslie, Shirley Clarke, Gregory Markopoulos, and Edward Bland), actors (Ben Carruthers, Argus Speare Juilliard), and distributors and producers (Émile de Antonio, Lewis Allen, Daniel Talbot, Walter Gutman, and David Stone). These cinéastes, self-styled "The Group," issued a "First Statement" (*Film Culture* 22–23 [1961]), which asserted that "the official cinema all over the world is running out of breath. It is morally corrupt, aesthetically obsolete, thematically superficial, temperamentally boring. Even the seemingly worthwhile films, those that lay claim to high moral and aesthetic standards and have been accepted as such by critics and the public alike, reveal the decay of the Product Film." Decrying the interference of producers and censors alike, the Group committed itself to cinema as "a personal expression," and planned new forms of financing, a festival to represent the new cinema, and a cooperative distribution center. Though most of these never materialized in the form envisioned, the distribution center did.

The Film-Makers' Cooperative came into being on 18 January 1962. Unlike previous attempts to organize an independent film distribution center (the Independent Film Makers Association and Cinema 16), the Co-op was nonexclusive, nondiscriminatory, and governed by the filmmakers themselves. It accepted all films submitted to it, and at no point in its administrative procedures were aesthetic or other qualitative judgments admitted. (Ironically, this decision not to discriminate, partially motivated by Amos Vogel's refusal to show Brakhage's *Anticipation of the Night* at Cinema 16, precipitated Brakhage's temporary withdrawal from the Co-op in 1967.) All the rental fees were to be returned to the filmmakers except the 25 percent retained to cover working costs and the salaries of the paid staff. In 1967 an attempt was made to develop a commercial arm, the Film-Makers' Distribution Center, but this was abandoned after two years. By 1989, the Co-op's catalogue listed more than 2,500 titles by 650 filmmakers, and reported renting in 1987 1,100 films to 500 museums, universities, media centers, and corporations.

Together with Mekas's ongoing journalistic enterprises, the Co-op created a network of filmmakers and information that transformed the independent cinema, for now films were easily available for rental from a single distribution center rather than separately and laboriously from individual filmmakers. Mekas began to arrange screenings with a new energy: first weekend midnight programs at the Charles Theater on Avenue B and East Twelfth Street in 1961, and subsequently at the Bleecker Street Cinema and the Gramercy Arts in 1963. The underground was coming into full flower and an unprecedented social visibility, not to say notoriety, with works in which the tradition of social realism associated with New York was rapidly giving way to bizarre sexual extravaganzas: the films of Ron Rice, Ken Jacobs, and especially Jack Smith, soon followed by Andy Warhol's early films—what, in a *Village Voice* column, Mekas had called "Baudelairean Cinema": "A world of flowers of evil, of illuminations, or torn and tortured flesh; a poetry which is at once beautiful and terrible, good and evil, delicate and dirty." Jack Smith's *Flaming Creatures*, first screened by Mekas at the Experimental Film Festival at Knokke–Le Zoute in Belgium in 1963, where it caused a riot, and then in the spring of 1964 in New York, when Mekas was arrested on obscenity charges for screening it along with Genet's *Chant d'amour*, announced the new movement and the attempts to repress it, convincing Mekas of the need for an outlet for independent film more responsive to the filmmakers themselves.

To this end, he organized the Film-Makers' Cinematheque. Like previous efforts, this was initially peripatetic, opening at the New Yorker in November 1964, moving to the Maidman, the City Hall Cinema, and other locations, and eventually settling at the Forty-

1.2 Gramercy Arts Theatre, February 1964. Location of Film-Makers' Showcase run by the Co-op, 1963–1964. *Scorpio Rising, Twice a Man, Chumlum, Sleep, Kiss, Little Stabs at Happiness,* and *Flaming Creatures* were premiered here.

First Street Theater. In September 1966, Andy Warhol's *Chelsea Girls* opened. Its financial success—eventually it moved to a "real" theater, the Regency on Seventy-Second Street, where it grossed three hundred thousand dollars in six months—and the degree of public attention it received made it possible to imagine the viable commercial distribution of underground films.

With Shirley Clarke and Lionel Rogosin, Mekas organized the Film-Makers' Distribution Center to serve what they hoped would be a circuit of art theaters showing at least the feature-length works of the avant-garde. But a combination of factors, including Warhol's decision to distribute his own work, the increasing appropriation of underground devices and subject matter by commercial films, and disapproval and factionalism within the purist wing of the avant-garde, confounded the project. At the same time, increasing losses forced Mekas to discontinue the cinematheque at the Forty-First Street Theater. He managed to reopen it in 1968, in what he hoped would be a permanent location in an artists' cooperative building at 80 Wooster Street. Police harassment ended these hopes, forcing it to temporary homes at the Methodist Church on West Fourth Street, the Bleecker Street Cinema, the Elgin, the Gotham Art; even the Gallery of Modern Art kept the cinematheque alive for a while. But when the Film-Makers' Distribution Center was forced to close, leaving Mekas personally liable for eighty thousand dollars in debts, the cinematheque ended too.

With the failure of these projects, Mekas reorganized his energies around what he felt to be the most pressing need: a permanent home where the classic works of film could be shown on a regular basis. Jerome Hill, P. Adams Sitney, Peter Kubelka, Stan Brakhage, and Mekas himself drew up plans for such a museum, to be called Anthology Film Archives. A selection committee made up of James Broughton, Ken Kelman, Peter Kubelka, Jonas Mekas, and P. Adams Sitney were to establish "The Essential Cinema," a permanent collection of "the monuments of cinematic art." Unlike Mekas's previous screenings, the Anthology was from the beginning critical and discriminatory. Its initial manifesto began:

> The cinematheques of the world generally collect and show the multiple manifestations of film: as document, history, industry, mass communication. *Anthology Film Archives* is the first film museum exclusively devoted to the *film as an art*. What are the essentials of cinema? The creation of *Anthology Film Archives* has been an ambitious attempt to provide answers to these questions; the first of which is physical—to construct a theater in which films can be seen under the best conditions;

and the second critical—to define the art of film in terms of selected works which indicate its essences and its perimeters.

The manifesto continued to sketch the planned repertory presentation of its one hundred programs in approximately monthly cycles, the theater's black, hooded, and blindered seats, especially designed by Peter Kubelka to ensure maximum concentration on the films themselves, and the selection committee's procedures.

Anthology Film Archives opened on 1 December 1970 at Joseph Papp's Public Theater. After the death of Jerome Hill, its most generous sponsor, in 1974, it relocated to a less auspicious venue at 80 Wooster Street, where, in addition to screenings of the repertory, preservation work was commenced. In 1974 video programming began, with weekly exhibitions curated initially by Shigeko Kubota and later by Robert Harris; gradually the video facilities were expanded, and by 1982 they included multichannel and interactive installations.

1.3 The opening of Anthology Film Archives, 1970: Hollis Frampton, Jonas Mekas, Flo Jacobs, Ken Jacobs.

The exclusivity of Anthology's programming was from the first controversial, and it became more so as the historical moment sedimented in the initial selection gave way to new filmmakers and other agendas. But although this concerned Mekas enough that he attempted to intersperse the cycles of the Essential Cinema with works by new filmmakers, his and the board's commitment to their canon never wavered. In any case, by the late sixties independent film culture was solidly established in the city, with many of the new concerns holding their own screenings. Going into the seventies, there was a variety of organizations for independent film on both a grass-roots level and in more established institutions. Ken and Flo Jacobs had started the Millennium Film Workshop at St. Mark's Church, and in the fall of 1966 they had begun regular one-person screenings that, under the direction of Howard Guttenplan since 1969, continue to the present. The Film Forum, cofounded in 1970 by Peter Feinstein and Sandy Miller, was devoted to independents and new work, but it supplemented the avant-garde with showings of political documentaries, animations, and narrative art films. Somewhat as a reaction against what was felt to be the premature canonization of the Essential Cinema, in 1973 the Collective for Living Cinema began screenings of the works of filmmakers who had matured since Anthology's selection, along with marginalized American studio films and foreign features. In 1969 the Museum of Modern Art started its Cineprobe series, focused specifically on the avant-garde, with weekly presentations by new independent filmmakers who were present to discuss their work. The Whitney Museum of American Art had begun its New American Filmmakers series in 1971, and in 1975 film and then in 1979 video were added to the Biennials. The American Federation of the Arts, begun in 1909 to exhibit and circulate paintings, added various media programs in the early seventies. Beginning in 1972 it distributed individual films from the Whitney's New American Filmmakers series, and it began organizing its own traveling exhibitions, the first of which was "A History of the American Avant-Garde" in 1976; it also distributed the Whitney Biennial films after 1979, and in 1983 added video.

This support for the avant-garde freed Anthology to concentrate on its own mission. As the collection of films and books grew, it became clear that the Wooster Street facilities were inadequate. In late 1979, having acquired from the city a disused courthouse at the intersection of Second Avenue and East Second Street (it had for a time been used by Millennium for its film workshop), Anthology closed, to devote all its resources to fund-raising and to renovating the new building. When Anthology reopened in October 1988, the new facility contained two theaters, the Courthouse Theater (225 seats) and the Maya Deren Theater (66 seats), each equipped with 35 mm, 16 mm, 8 mm, and video projectors, together with a reference library, a film preservation department, a gallery, and offices. Screenings of the repertory collection of the Essential Cinema have been supplemented by programs of new films and retrospectives of the works of filmmakers (beginning with Alexander Kluge), bridging the catholic openness of Mekas's early screenings and the exclusiveness of Anthology's previous incarnation. In addition to its own

1.4 Jonas Mekas at his desk, circa 1978.

screenings, Anthology has hosted other groups and organizations. In the fall of 1989, for example, in addition to holding its own programs of the Essential Cinema, retrospectives and other programs of the avant-garde, and a series, "The American Narrative Film, Its Roots and Flowers" curated by Andrew Sarris, Anthology acted as a temporary screening space for the Millennium Film Workshop and festivals of films from Canada, Germany, and the Philippines, and hosted conferences on gay and lesbian films and on video art. As a result, some weeks it was open every day, and some days it presented as many as six or eight programs. If the independent cinema has a home, this is it.

In this necessarily brief cadastral survey of Mekas's public works, what has gradually fallen from sight is his own films. For so long the servant of other filmmakers and other cinemas, he appeared to set the pattern for such disregard, and it has never been easy to hold his films in a common focus with his other activities. But, in ways whose full implications are only slowly becoming clear, the films are summary of his other achievements, their reinvention of film the surest track of his liberation of cinema. If it is anywhere appropriate to think of cultural activity as heroic, it is so in respect to them.

2. Paul Arthur — Routines of Emancipation: Alternative Cinema in the Ideology and Politics of the Sixties

The only obligation which I have a right to assume is to do at any time what I think right.
—Thoreau, "Civil Disobedience"

I prayed to be relieved of all routines.
—Jonas Mekas, Diaries, 1964

The combination of centralized authority and direct democracy is subject to infinite variations.
—Marcuse, *One-Dimensional Man*

SEIZING THE TIME

Archaic as it may seem, cinema was once imagined as an emblem, harbinger, and social vehicle of the transfiguration of time; a phenomenology of an eternal present made image. To whatever degree this utopian promise is already inscribed in the work of Vertov, Epstein, and others, its consummate expression and true home is in the American culture of the 1960s. In the broadest terms, an elaborated myth of "presentness"—empowering the new while repudiating the old—was held in multiple arenas of social struggle as a precondition as well as a consequence of change: a paradox that casts the period in the same rhetorical cloak as countless other moments of historical upheaval. Directives aimed at the discovery of new, unalienated modes of conducting everyday life in a subjectively foregrounded present were issued in a barrage of ethical, political, and aesthetic versions from practically every station on the compass of opposition: recall in passing such slogans as "today is the first day of the rest of your life," "be here now," "if you really believe it, do it," or in the deathless lyric of the Chambers Brothers, "time has *come* today."

The movies were a perfect setup, a process whereby material was converted into light, a hub around which metaphors of temporality, consciousness (collective and individual), motion, and representation accumulated and were then redeployed in a calculus of politicized rhetoric and direct action. Although it was never supposed that this medium would be the principal agent of transformation, cinema was given a supporting role by many and a vanguard role by some. In the charged reciprocity between art and life, movies suffused reality, which in turn acquired a cinematic gloss. Events unspooled on a mental screen, movies were a journey in time, interior and external trips conjured or became occasions for movies,[1] and although the revolution might be theater, it was clearly scripted with the optics and cadences of classical montage.

Behind the visionary vernacular lurked a cluster of ideas about film just then surfacing in academic discourse. What appeared on-screen was held to have an undeniable immediacy of impact, an address continuously couched in the present tense. The scale and fluidity of the image beckoned the fantastic, the transcendence of artificial limits, while its surface registered an exacting or "indexical" correspondence to the world. Direct and oblique, familiar and strange—these terms rotated ceaselessly through efforts to figure exigencies of the moment as the shadow play of a new historical subject. More concretely, a growing recognition of commercial cinema's complex machinery of desire and ideological interpellation was counterbalanced by the prospects of a domesticated technology universally available to personal needs and the spontaneous framing of commonplace, "inconsequential" activities. In a tactical maneuver aimed squarely, if inaccurately, at the obliteration of authority, immutable distinctions between amateur recording and commodity production were blurred in the fantasy of film's liberatory potential.

Unprecedented affluence in white middle-class society helped secure a privileged association of movies with the space of subjectivity. The same economic conditions that fueled the emergence of student protest and counterculture movements sanctioned a per-

---

[1] A metaphoric relation between a spiritual journey, especially one involving cross-country travel, and cinematic narrative is a key premise of Ken Kesey's "Merry Pranksters" as celebrated by Tom Wolfe in *The Electric Kool-Aid Acid Test* (1968), and figures as well in Allen Ginsberg's collection *The Fall of America* (1972) and Don DeLillo's novel *Americana* (1971). For more on the conflation of movies with altered consciousness, see James 1989, 137–39. I have tried in this essay to acknowledge James's important insights into the relation between avant-garde film and the counterculture while advancing a somewhat different analytic perspective.

ception of filmmaking as an amalgamation of work and play. For the first time an entire generation—haunted by images of childhood already preserved on celluloid—was able consciously and realistically to harbor the ambition to become "moviemakers," believing this epithet to be both inherently progressive and open to myriad redefinitions.[2] Implicitly adopting a stance in league with Marcuse's notion of "everyone a producer," a broad sociological cohort made cinema a touchstone for its presumed accessibility and demonstrable public reach.

To many observers, film's radical potential was embodied precisely in the promise of a highly visible, collective, noncommercial mastery of the apparatus. The process of witnessing, of recording, *as* a means of political representation, persons, attitudes, and events traditionally excluded from commercial channels was not simply propaedeutic but virtually commensurate with social empowerment.[3] Even a staunch defender of the status quo opposed to any democratization of film as a social practice found it hard to resist exaggerated claims of effectiveness. Excoriating *Easy Rider* for its celebration of drugs, Diana Trilling was forced to conclude that "no art exerts more moral influence than the films, and for the present generation . . . more than personal character is being formed by our film-makers: a culture, a society, even a polity" (Trilling 1969, 240).

Trilling is speaking of and for mass culture, not the utopian designs of an alternative system. But if Hollywood was identified during the sixties as an armature of social and economic order, a dominant vehicle of bourgeois values, the capacity of movies as a *ritual experience* to induce antiauthoritarian attitudes is equally evident. An adolescent mark of group solidarity, movies were consumed outside the home (unlike, for example, recorded music), were the

[2] During this period, Hollywood was the beneficiary of a new crop of writer-directors, many of whom had made amateur movies as children and gone on to train in the then-proliferating university film programs. A small number of independent filmmakers (e.g., John Cassavetes, Robert Downey, Curtis Harrington, and Andy Warhol) were able to effect a transition to commercial production. In a related development, in the "liberated" climate of the late sixties studios were motivated to tap both the technical expertise and the stylistic trappings of the avant-garde. See Zimmerman 1988 for a useful account of the intersecting ideological agendas of Hollywood and home movies.

[3] Annette Michelson was among the first to connect the avant-garde's diffusion of technology to a "radical aspiration": "One rejoices in the promise of . . . the generation of little Americans making science-fiction films after school in those backyards" (Michelson 1966, 421). Another version of this common scenario is found in Callenbach 1968, 8. Accepting many of the premises of Marshall McLuhan's then influential theories, promoters of independent film invariably stressed the conjunction of amateurism with resistance to political domination.

site of erotic adventures, broke territorial barriers of class and race, and offered a battery of dramatic characters and plots easily recoded into subcultural axioms (the cult misreading of *Casablanca* as a parable of radical individualism is a case in point). Here it was less the idea of cinema itself than specific patterns of consumption that served to undercut established values.

The ways in which moviegoing as the flip side of recording were threaded into the routines of daily life helped nurture a twin aspiration to reform Hollywood from the inside, replacing its repressive structures and social address with a "New Hollywood," and to challenge its status as popular commodity on its own turf through a loose network of independent production. These two finally untenable yet never totally abandoned projects constantly intersect a third possibility: radical disengagement from the pressures and rewards of commercial cinema in the form of avant-garde and documentary practices. These divergent approaches, each equipped with its own internal contradictions, were interdependent, each interpenetrated by the others.

The biographical legend called "Jonas Mekas" weaves its way through the multitextured landscape of sixties cinema like a thin sinew touching every fold, every recess. There is no single vantage from which to discern its fluid embrace. Different witnesses have couched the legend in the tireless passion and obstinacy of a religious seer or the makeshift ferocity of a guerrilla leader operating on many fronts at once. The sheer scope of Mekas's headlong activism, the number of dimensions within film culture with which he was engaged, is matched only by the range of voices and roles he assumed for himself—proselytizer, organizer, producer, publisher, documentarist, polemicist, friend and enemy, potentate and madman. It was, he says, in his "nature to do 100 things at the same time and work on 100 levels" (Diaries, 23 August 1964). And the conviction, at least initially, that everything was possible, that in the utopian tradition the good society could be created here and now through the exercise of individual and collective will, intrinsically aligned his enterprise with the philosophical currents animating the period.

Mekas was an unlikely candidate for the mantle of counterculture hero. A practically middle-aged Lithuanian émigré and fervent nationalist with a deep and abiding attachment to family virtues in an agrarian society, he was far from the fabled person "of this generation, bred in at least modest comfort, housed now in universities, looking uncomfortably to the world we inherit" adduced as the vanguard in the 1962 "Port Huron Statement" of the Students for a

Democratic Society (SDS) (Miller 1987, 329). Having digested relatively little of American mass culture and the values it transmits, he lacked the sense of betrayal shaping the activism of a younger generation. The felt burdens of alienation and the measures Mekas took to alleviate them took on meanings and implications not shared by even his closest collaborators. For instance, he harbored a flickering residue of orthodox religious belief that militated against the support of certain types of life-style experimentation swirling around him. His equal revulsion toward liberalism—stamped by the Allies' sellout of Lithuania at Yalta—and communism was necessarily of a different order from that of the New Left. "You don't have to be a communist to be anti-capitalist," he concluded. "It's enough to be a poet" (Diaries, 30 March 1960).

Despite unbridgeable gaps in personal history, especially the direct experience of political oppression, statements like that above hint at a common ground with the diffuse cadres of sixties rebellion; the tension between personal authenticity and commitment to social change, the aestheticizing of struggle. Given the desire to chart here the "100 levels" on which Mekas contributed to and was influenced by the forces of opposition, it is necessary to sound a double warning at the outset. First, Mekas's career in the sixties cannot be reduced to any unbroken aesthetic or political profile. Its determining features are complex and often avowedly self-contradictory. No single model of increasing radicalization or radicalization followed by disillusionment is appropriate. The usual roster of historical events proclaimed as catalysts for protest or creative innovation rarely coincide with shifts or intensifications in Mekas's campaigns. Moreover, different arenas of struggle such as filmmaking, organization building, and public discourse evince varying degrees of energy and commitment at any given juncture. Second, the temptation to establish concrete points of solidarity or mutual accord with other figures and oppositional movements cannot mask wide disparities in purpose and method—indeed, outright conflicts that in general annotate the correspondence between countercultural and political sectors of film and other practices.

Mekas remarks that his burgeoning interest in filmmaking in the late 1940s was forged from the notion of a universal language, cinema as a "tongue in which we could reach everybody" (Tomkins 1973, 36). Although he and his brother Adolfas wrote fictional scripts both before and after their flight from German displaced-persons camps to New York City, Jonas's progression from documentarist to feature director to avant-garde diarist—traced diegetically in his greatest work, *Lost, Lost, Lost*—can be read as a gradual repudiation of film's universalist mandate and the advocacy of small communities of interest, a gyrating fall from one village to another. In a context in which to "be of one's time" was virtually synonymous with "living in the moment," this evolution subtended an additional process. Taking an active role in the social turmoil around film in the sixties meant for Mekas the possibility of "forgetting," of subduing the past as painful memory, of inventing a new identity. As David James contends, "as the independent cinema became the vehicle of his psychic, artistic, social, and professional lives, it enabled him to integrate them all, assuage his alienation, and eventually find a second homeland" (James 1989, 100).

If we consider the signature style he developed for the film diary, we see that Mekas inscribes a structural tension between preservation and erasure, a clinging to and a repudiation of the past that inevitably colors the terms by which the immediate present is captured. This dialectic is, if not unique to Mekas's artistic project in the sixties, the more powerful for its origins in an extreme succession of social displacements. In his method of production, principal labor is displaced from the trappings of memory—the enactment of prescribed events, dialogues, themes, camera placements, movements—to the rapid and direct accumulation of quotidian fragments that all but freeze the play of retrospection.

Previously he had dismissed this form of recording as "sketches," camera exercises performed *in between* feature opportunities. But when he discovered the personal efficacy of the diary, it authorized a shift in visual language that complicated memory in the throes of recording, and, likewise, spectatorship. Scenes and takes, the image fixed in time and held in place by conventions of narrative coherence, are detonated by short single-frame bursts, twitches of hand-held movement. Events and objects seem constituted as much by what is elided, what happens between frames, as by what is offered briefly for perception. Fragmentation and incompleteness, then, emerge as stylistic tokens of commitment to the present and its consequent forging of a new social identity. This representation of events implies an open-endedness, a willingness to abandon preconceptions and to court irresolution, reformulating the signs of a unified self as camera gesture and a shuddering trace of physical idiosyncrasy.

In the spoken narration at the start of *Reminiscences of a Journey to Lithuania*, over footage of a stroll through the woods in 1959, Mekas recalls with pleasure not having to think about the previous decade, the war and its aftermath. It was, he says, a new beginning, the dawning of a process of assimilation: "There was a moment when I forgot my home." And then: "Hey, I escaped the ropes of time once more" (accompanied by a shot of a nooselike strand of rope dangling from a tree). An entry in his 1961 diary about a group of recent films strikes a note that reverberates constantly in his public pronouncements: "New is moral, it liberates, it frees. Today all old is corrupt, it drags man down, and I am putting my bets on the young and the new" (Diaries, 12 July 1961). Don't look back. Democracy is in the streets. Admittedly, this was a standard line in sixties radicalism of every stripe, yet it suggests one route by which Mekas found his biographical and aesthetic particularities reflected in the emerging counterculture.

The past imposes itself in various guises. What was sacrificed by leaving the discipline of feature-film directing, apart from the slim prospect of a mass audience, rehearses in a minor register an initial and far greater loss. The self-contained interaction of the movie set, with its specific though not ironclad jobs, its loose hierarchy, can evoke an extended family or ad hoc village. This sense of affiliation would be rediscovered not in filmmaking but in its ancillary networks. During much of the ensuing decade Mekas would complain of never finding time to edit his growing reservoir of footage. Having shifted his central focus decisively and on multiple levels to the public sphere, the solitary regime of editing and avant-garde postproduction must have stirred in him a raw ambivalence. Letting it all hang unfinished from the walls of various apartments protected his images from the "ropes of time." Indeed, in the completed diary films, aspects of memory (labeling, explanation, ironic comparison) are vested in procedures added after the moment of filming: collation, intertitling, narration, music.

For the "man who never wanted to leave his home"—the invocation to *Lost, Lost, Lost*—a glorious interval is spent careening between polarities of past and present, public and private, popular and elite, authority and disengagement, consolidation and direct action. The dilemma addressed here is summarized by Todd Gitlin as the typically sixties dynamic of "strategic" versus "expressive" political ends (Gitlin 1987, 6). Like the onslaughts of a younger, and in many ways alien, generation, Mekas fought a constant battle over how to turn the ecstatic moment into historical reality.

LET'S REMAIN DISORGANIZEDLY ORGANIZED

Toward the end of 1966, Mekas inserted into his written diaries a neatly drafted diagram resembling the flowchart of a major corporation, a "family tree" illustrating with their dates of inception the various parent and subsidiary branches of independent cinema then under his control. The chart includes the New American Cinema Group (1960), Film-Makers' Cooperative (1962), Film Culture Non-Profit Corporation (1963), Film-Makers' Cinematheque (1964), Film-Makers' Workshop (1964), Film-Makers' Lecture Bureau (1964), Friends of the New American Cinema (1964), and Film-Makers' Distribution Center (1966). It is an impressive list and a testament to the common political tactic by which simply naming a group or event validated its existence while disguising its actual clout in numbers or funds.

Yet Mekas's chart is far from inclusive. It would have required more vectors and separate boxes to encompass *Film Culture* magazine, founded in 1955, the Anti-Censorship Fund (a short-lived response to repeated police busts in 1964 of *Flaming Creatures* and other "obscenities"), and the New American Cinema Exposition (a series of programs that toured Europe in 1964 and 1967 under the stewardship of P. Adams Sitney and Barbara Rubin). Another branch could have been added for a host of failed proposals such as "Shoot Your Way Out with a Camera," a scheme to train two hundred minority children to make "diary-like, journalistic, or poetic films about their own lives, how they feel, how they live, what they see. . . . Make your film frames into bullets of truth" (Diaries, 2 October 1967). There is no space for countless alliances with commercial movie theaters and museums hosting the Film-Makers' Showcase and other avant-garde series (eighteen different venues between 1961 and 1969). Absent as well are traces of the close collaborations with groups such as the Poets' Theater, the Living Theater (with whom Mekas filmed *The Brig* in 1964, ceding to them all subsequent profits), and Newsreel, the documentary collective whose organization he helped facilitate, publicize, and provide with film stock. Nothing is said of the dozen or so distribution cooperatives that sprouted around the United States, Canada, and Europe, fertilized and partially supported by the New York Co-op. Nor is there a hint of the project that would consume the bulk of his energies at the tail end of the sixties, Anthology Film Archives (1969)—the repertory "museum" that grew directly out of the cinematheque's division in programming between avant-garde "classics" and new work. Extrapolated from this chart, the concentric circles of Mekas's engagement enfold an ever-greater arena of sixties activism. Emerson said that "an institution is the lengthened shadow of one man." Here the shadow is long indeed.

In the second report of the New American Cinema Group (1962), Mekas declares, "Let's remain disorganizedly organized"—a tactic intended both to guarantee maximum personal freedom and to disguise the real fragility of the network. It was, to borrow a phrase from activist Rennie Davis, "organizing with mirrors." Virtually the same tiny roster of participants appears at the core of every group, every public campaign. What needs to be explained is how this outline of marginalized empire actually functioned in the realm of concrete social and economic relations, and to what other tendencies and movements its infrastructural workings can be correlated. Precious few of the energies enumerated above have found their way into official histories of American avant-garde film. Ironically, the best source of information remains Mekas's private, unpublished diaries—encompassing some fifteen hundred pages for the years 1960–1970. They are in many respects a textual complement of his diary films, a heterogeneous mix comprising not only private musings, moral declarations, descriptions, and ideas for movies, but also newspaper clippings, quotations, memorandums, and an immense body of correspondence, often averaging three or four letters per day.

Appropriately, the relationship between diary materials and public manifestations is quite intricate. A diary entry might serve as a sketch for, or be recycled almost verbatim in, the "Movie Journal" column he wrote in the *Village Voice* between 1958 and 1971. Shards of insight about current trends were expanded in articles written for *Film Culture*. Film images of individual pages or Jonas at his typewriter show up in various films, while quotations cited in the diaries are transferred to intertitles. Certain revelatory passages return, years later, as voice-over narrations. For instance, *In Between* incorporates with slight alterations this moving assessment: "Again I thought about my splintered, fragmented single-framed world, with all monolithic ideas disappearing; a replica, a reflection of my own self, ego, as it slowly disappears, the consciousness that is becoming more and more open, with many centers" (Diaries, 21 April 1966). Finally, and most germane, ideal versions of projects are mapped out, revised, and then annotated in their day-to-day clashes. The diaries record the interaction between private imagination and attempts to realize it through the praxis of improvised organization.

Like other self-created activists of the period, Mekas stepped into a vacuum of public advocacy armed only with the ambition and resilience to create a visible "image" and then use that image to bind a loose skein of partners and attract new recruits. The social precepts to which he responded or with which he helped shape the burgeoning avant-garde movement required little true consensus and even less strict adherence. A bohemian individualism, an abiding faith in face-to-face negotiation and directly participatory decision making, governed both the policies of and the labor performed within denoted groups. An ambiance of voluntary decentralized power briefly allowed, as it did for political organizations such as the Student Nonviolent Coordinating Committee (SNCC) and the SDS, a suppression of conflicts between individual and group goals. With greater numbers and widening public visibility, such harmony proved increasingly hard to sustain.

Economically, the small amounts of cash flowing into and out of various institutions seems to have been treated roughly as communal largesse. No one, aside from theater managers and the secretary of the Co-op, collected a regular salary. Monies collected from rentals or theater admissions were routinely plowed back into other ventures or given to filmmakers on the basis of immediate need (often to pay lab fees for a new film), a mechanism that eventually resulted in misunderstandings and charges of favoritism. Mekas relied on several "angels" such as Jerome Hill and publisher Harry Gant to underwrite the costs of commercial space or the printing of *Film Culture*, but virtually all outside funding was garnered ad hoc. And given a strongly antibureaucratic, antigovernment bias, there was little effort to secure public funds or foundation grants. In a 1964 diatribe against the "sad state" of European experimental film, Mekas implored, "Let's keep our art free of any sponsorship, whoever the sponsor may be" (Mekas 1972b, 114). Years later a pragmatic concession would be made to the changing cultural climate, but for the bulk of the decade an obsession with autonomy and direct personal communication shaped fiscal policy—such as it was.

This approach shared with its politically motivated kin the advantages (and obvious disadvantages) of a constantly renewed sense of crisis, where demands for labor or money were disguised as individual and essentially ethical choices. Mekas's instinct for creating what C. Wright Mills had called "primary publics" was unerring, affording loosely composed groups the political undertone of classic democracy practiced in the face of "giant technology, monopoly capitalism, and the behemoth state" (Miller 1987, 83–84). It became at once a master organizing strategy and its own program for social rectification. In fact there existed few viable alternatives to this organizational model. If the aspiration underwriting independent filmmaking was to create social as well as economic options in production, distribution, and exhibition, the inscription of a personal stake in each maneuver and the concomitant of a fluid, responsive chain of command was essential. In an angry retort to rival Amos Vogel's accusations of irresponsible permissiveness, Mekas declared, "The policy of NO POLICY is also a policy" (Diaries, 25 August 1966). A familiar theme across the range of sixties radicalism, the "metaphysics of participation" functioned in a positive if fleeting context to mask increasing centralization of authority and its public expression.

To understand how power as the precipitate of social and economic structures was exercised through Mekas's advocacy of independent cinema and how its terms overlapped with strategies in parallel precincts, it is useful to examine the development and operations of the Film-Makers' Cooperative, the lodestar and most significant legacy of the avant-garde movement.[4] The formation of the New American Cinema Group in 1960 laid the groundwork for the Co-op in its strident rejection of the corrupt "Product Film" and the systems it enforced. The group's first manifesto rails against censorship and state licensing of films and stresses the need for new organs of distribution and exhibition: "It is time to blow the whole thing up" (Diaries, 28 September 1960). Despite sundry alliances with the traditions of narrative and social documentary held by the majority of its founders, the group dedicated its rebellious energies to the freeing of "personal expression" as the highest ideal of cinema. (See David James's introduction to this volume for more on the NACG.)

By the early sixties, Mekas's previous antagonism to the "adolescent character" of American experimental film (Mekas 1955, 15) was supplanted by a desire to merge the social awareness and spontaneity of the documentary, the popular appeal of dramatic narrative, and the solitary vision and formal boldness of the "film poem." Institutional patterns would have to mirror the potential convergences of many practices: the Film-Makers' Cinematheque was advanced as a "place where all factions of cinema will meet" (Diaries, 1 December 1965); and while *Film Culture* would decisively shift its focus after 1963 to the celebration of the avant-garde, it never totally reneged on a committment to mainstream concerns. The prospect of reconciliation and of cross-fertilization of aesthetic methods remained lodged in Mekas's sensibility even as he entered the experimental film orbit. Frustration at the disabling trials of feature production, the corrosive infighting among and defections of

---

[4] It is a pleasure to report that the New York Co-op was alive and well in 1990, continuing to operate according to the precepts of openness and direct participation on which it was founded. For the record, I am a member of its board of directors and a past president of that oversight body.

group members, and the tremendous creative outburst of unfettered modes of expression brought him to the front lines of anticommercial insurgency. However, the failure to achieve a semblance of integration echoes along the path of avant-garde organization and is rehearsed (and to some extent recuperated) within the formal antinomies of Mekas's mature films.

The Film-Makers' Cooperative was founded shortly after the death of Maya Deren, who had pioneered the involvement of film artists in the circulation of their work. At first, films were to be selected for inclusion by group members, but this stipulation was quickly dropped in favor of open submissions. Despite some unspoken guidelines, filmmakers were free to set their own rental prices, draft their own promotional materials, and control overall policy through direct vote. No special treatment was accorded any work regardless of style, content, or rentability. Only in 1966, after a spurt of growth, did the Co-op elect a representative board, and even then it functioned more like a casual advisory body. In five years membership expanded from roughly 20 to 234 artists (the 1989 catalogue lists 638 filmmakers). Initially, members and their films were a diverse lot: narrratives and documentaries (including early examples of direct cinema), experimental "shorts," animation, and glorified home movies. There was a scattering of women and several African-Americans among the filmmakers.

By mid-decade, Mekas's diaries indicate that the Co-op's small commercial offices rocked with the ecstatic, multifocused energy of an urban commune or a militant party headquarters. In addition to the business of rentals, *Film Culture* was edited in one corner, while artists such as Gregory Markopoulos, Ron Rice, and Naomi Levine worked around the clock splicing footage at an adjacent table. At night the offices served as a crash pad, dining hall, and impromptu screening room. Visiting filmmakers perceived it as a hub for the exchange of information, equipment, and ideas. Aside from constant monetary privation, the first real emergency erupted in 1964 over the issue of censorship. Anticipating a massive influx of tourists for the World's Fair, the New York City government decided to scour its cultural image by harassing or closing down clubs, coffeehouses and porn theaters. Jack Smith's *Flaming Creatures*—along with Genet's *Chant d'amour* and, later, other films—was caught in the net. Projectors and box-office receipts were seized and Mekas and theater staff members were arrested, jailed, and roughed up.

This generated a long series of skirmishes conducted in newspapers and journals, at the Third International Experimental Film Festival in Belgium (where Mekas and Barbara Rubin took over a projection booth to screen Smith's film), and finally in the courts; after several appeals, the Supreme Court voted narrowly not to hear the case, but the following year it handed down its infamous obscenity ruling pegged to "community standards."[5] In the interval, the Co-op office was recruited as a private exhibition venue and clearing-house for information and public protest. With its cachet of sexual deviancy, the *Flaming Creatures* affair placed avant-garde film on the cultural map, stimulating support from quarters previously oblivious or even hostile to the movement.

Coincidentally, this was the same moment in which the Berkeley Free Speech Movement gained national attention for its insistence on the right to disseminate political materials on campus. Mining a deep vein in American political philosophy, the early New Left discovered in the confrontation with administrative censorship a volatile issue, a set of tactics, a channel for publicity, and the trigger for an analysis of related social injustices. The suppression of Smith's languorous demolition of Hollywood-epic sexuality provided Mekas and his colleagues with a similar manual of arms. In personal terms, the experience of censorship and police harassment dredged up the specter of his and Adolfas's flight from their village under threat of Gestapo arrest—for publishing a clandestine newsletter—and the continuing oppression of his homeland under Stalinism. More recently, Jonas had been stopped repeatedly by police during the filming of *Guns of the Trees*, and censorship constituted a minor theme in the earliest issues of *Film Culture*. Mekas even described a hilarious 1961 encounter with an FBI agent eager to determine his financial support from Soviet citizens (Mekas 1972b, 41–45). Resistance to government authority fostered a binding in-group paranoia about police surveillance that later emerged as a dominant chord in leftist activism. The need to "travel light," to submerge one's activities in an "underground," reverberates through the sixties diaries and surfaces publicly in a number of "Movie Journal" columns.

Like other mentors of the counterculture such as his friends Allen Ginsberg and Julian Beck, whose first instincts were aesthetic rather than political, Mekas was forced to navigate between the promotion of independently produced art as replete experience and its use as an instrument of information, polemic, and agitation. Through the Co-op, writings, and related screening activities Mekas

[5] The best accounts of this catalytic incident are in Mekas 1972b, 111–72, and Tomkins 1973, 36–38.

championed documentary or satirical "protest films," as he called them, made by Stan Vanderbeek, Richard Preston, John Korty, Bruce Baillie, Edward Bland, and Mark Kennedy. His friendship with Judith Malina prompted him to film the antimilitarist vigils of the Mothers' Strike for Peace in the late fifties (they appear in *Walden* and *Lost, Lost, Lost*), just as close associations with Mailer, Ginsberg, and filmmaker-activists such as Barbara Rubin and Naomi Levine provided a rationale for shooting antiwar demonstrations in the mid-sixties. Mekas was, then, frequently an indirect participant in political protest, his active support of militancy deflected by the roles of documentarist or entrepreneur.

Nonetheless, his ambivalence could be set aside in the turmoil of specific events. After the 1968 police riot at the Democratic Convention, he argued for the appropriation of video technology to scrutinize and expose the venality of public officials (ibid., 319). His role in promulgating the radical Newsreel movement can be seen as a logical extension of repeated calls for the formation of politicized, noncommercial newsreel networks: "With our 8 mm cameras we can record the KKK and the life in prisons, the cruelty of man to man in Vietnam, the genocides and follycides and bring it all to the public consciousness" (Diaries, 19 April 1966). "There was," Mekas often maintained, "no disagreement between the avant-garde, experimental line and the political documentary line" (Mekas 1990).

In the late sixties, "protest films" were programmed alongside avant-garde works for theatrical and college audiences. The Co-op lent films for benefits held by the New York Civil Liberties Union and other organizations, and endorsed in word and deed several antiwar strikes. Although Mekas's nourishment of overtly political filmmaking caused friction with a number of prominent avant-gardists, the *Flaming Creatures* incident sealed the recognition that the lines between creative expression and political resistance could be breached by official malfeasance or eroded for strategic purposes.

Instances of unalloyed solidarity are, however, counterbalanced by a deep-seated mistrust of mass movements, organized protest, and the bureaucratic process. Like other convergences between political groups and the counterculture—rock music, experimental theater, and the underground press ducked in and out of collaboration with the SDS, National Mobilization, and other bodies—the divergent ideologies advocating societal change through the liberation of individual consciousness or through mass action coexisted uneasily. During anticensorship battles Mekas advocated mass picketing of commercial theaters showing licensed movies, but such efforts were not generally conducive to a style built on what

Hawthorne called "the magnetic chain of humanity." Responding to published criticism of the avant-garde for its lack of social commitment, he characteristically declared, "Down with barriers, borders, national interests, national parties, national movements." And when Barbara Rubin and Shirley Clarke got arrested at the Pentagon in 1967, he noted, "I am no longer with it, or with them" (Diaries, November 1967).

Fear of being swallowed up by large organizations beyond his—or beyond informal group—control, of having to adopt a measure of ideological discipline, kept Mekas from fully throwing his organizational and rhetorical energies into the accelerating culture of dissent. The sort of argument he used to prop up ideals of autonomy applied equally to alliances with the New Left and opportunities to direct avant-garde film to a wider and more diverse audience: "Once you use established channels you have to embrace their techniques of promotion and that will eventually affect the kinds of films you make. There is no end. You end up with a product everyone else makes" (Mekas 1990). With a Marcusean insight he saw the obvious dangers of co-optation, and it mattered little whether the dangers came from leftist institutions or mass culture.

Yet the lure of thrusting alternative cinema into public view, and by so doing enlarging its role in the socially redemptive transformation of consciousness, remained strong even after Mekas repudiated the independent feature. He could preach disengagement in one newspaper column: "Artists shouldn't waste a single drop of their lives fighting the old: we should continue and concentrate on the creation of the new, because the old will die by itself" (Mekas 1972b, 181), and then a week later argue that "the balance must be restored. There should be three or four theaters in Times Square playing *Normal Love*, Brakhage, Markopoulos, etc." (ibid., 182).

On several occasions he explored the possibility of placing 8 mm film prints in bookstores and, in 1970, considered a proposal from ESP Records (an innovative promoter of the most difficult black jazz music of the sixties) to distribute videotape copies in record stores (Diaries, 6 March 1970).[6] Mekas could nurture the vision of an al-

---

[6] In 1960, C. Wright Mills, who provided the New Left with its theory of power, urged intellectuals to "make the mass media the means of liberal—which is to say, liberating—education" and set an example by publishing his defense of Castro's revolution as a mass-market paperback. Debates over the potential to mobilize or affect public consciousness through channels of mass communication raged from the beginning to end of the decade. At one extreme is the Yippie assertion that the TV image is the very site of revolutionary work because that medium unavoidably transmits the values it records (Armstrong 1981, 118). With equal conviction, the founder

ternative system while at the same time, and without apparent contradiction, challenge entrenched power in the commercial industry. International film festivals were a persistent target for avant-garde infiltration, and daily movie reviewers were berated in print and privately for their lack of coverage. Taking a cue from Mao's Cultural Revolution, Mekas humorously proposed that student strikers "take over" the *New York Times* and Time-Life buildings and "demand a complete revamping of their cultural coverage, policies, and staffs" (Mekas 1972b, 340).

As avant-garde film pressed closer to the sources of (mostly local) notoriety and power, Mekas's principled support of democratic access—in the Co-op, "Movie Journal," and showcase screenings—was strained by the potential for publicity and preservation of the movement's aesthetic achievement. (This tension is movingly captured in the dynamics of the diary films.) The spread of institutional connections with their incumbent responsibilities widened the gap between what one can call the structural position of leadership and the rank and file. Because of his skill at and willingness to perform the mundane tasks that kept institutions from expiring, he accepted the curious bind of trying to order the fruitfully disordered. Memorandums to the Co-op are playfully signed "Minister of Defense," "Minister of Propaganda," and "Minister of Finance." He was aware that his public image conferred an invidious privilege, yet he perceived that, without a greater measure of regulation, the organs he had helped sustain would collapse. There is in the diaries a genuine perplexity about how to balance personal freedom with the demands of increasing authority. There is raw anger—"I am sick of playing the money father to all" (Diaries, 20 October 1963)—and the temptation to abdicate: "I am a fanatic and I can do much. But it is my fanaticism that is also my danger. I have become a force, a leader, even a saint. It is time to dissolve all forces and all illusions and all saints. Even art can enslave man, take them over, take away their freedom. . . . It is so easy to think that what you are doing is needed to serve the cause" (Diaries, June 1964).

Activist and key New York Newsreel member Norm Fruchter offers this salient analysis of the dilemma shared by Mekas and reluctant leaders of the New Left:

---

of a radical video group Armstrong cites argued that "no alternative cultural vision is going to succeed . . . until it develops its own alternate information structures, not just alternative content pumped across existing ones" (ibid., 132). Despite the dominance of a Frankfurt School position toward mass culture, there were continuous efforts at alliance even from those most instrumental in building alternative institutions.

Often [the] refusal to play responsible roles at the center of the organization was based on . . . genuine humility, the fear of authoritarian roles
and the perpetuation of hierarchy. . . . But just as often it was based on a
sense that such roles would alter the necessary balance between political
work and personal experience, a balance intuited as crucial to the new
life styles being developed. . . . The contradictions between SDS's articulated values and SDS's traditional organizational structures thus reflected and perpetuated ambivalences within the SDS leadership itself.
(Gitlin 1980, 157)

The lessons of overdiscipline and bureaucratization gleaned by
Mekas and by sixties militants from the failure of established progressive and socialist movements resulted in a constant round of
aggressivity and self-denial. As the stakes grew higher and management more complex, accusations of egotism, "revisionism," and
selling out grew more vocal.

The popular thesis in texts such as Abbie Hoffman's *Revolution
for the Hell of It* is that celebrity status in a media-dominated age
is a necessary tool of organizing and the concomitant of responsible
leadership (Hoffman 1968, 218–27). Mekas was never accorded the
kind of access given to image-savvy radicals, but this did not prevent intrafraternal ruptures. Their symptomatic tone is captured in
Amos Vogel's mean-spirited attack: "There are really two Jonases—
one very dedicated, the other a Machiavellian maneuverer, a history
rewriter, an attempted pope. He has two passions: film and power.
His greatest talent is to make people—some people—believe that he
is what he is not" (Tomkins 1973, 37).[7] Mekas's close friend Ken
Jacobs accused him of revoking the purity and buoyant freedom of
underground film by making the avant-garde "fashionable," by
"promoting a star system" in *Film Culture* and the "Movie Journal"
(Sitney 1974, 384), and Susan Sontag found his public pronouncements "shrill and often positively alienating" (Sontag 1964, 228).
What appears to have happened is that for a variety of reasons—
personal, principled, and otherwise—trusted associates as well as
outside competitors bought the rhetoric of imperious authority intended as a media charade. And there is no way of knowing just how
much it consumed its author.

Mekas's long-standing feud with Jack Smith is perhaps the most
bizarre yet illuminating example of the onus of leadership faced in

---

[7] There is insufficient reason here to examine the intricate history of personal friction between Mekas and Vogel, except to say that the tenor of Vogel's attacks was
often that of traditional Old Left politics railing against the younger generation's lack
of discipline and focus.

parallel situations by Mekas and the New Left. Mekas claims he has never understood why Smith "turned against" him (Mekas 1990). But the bases of the conflict are readily apparent: money and social power—the friction of directing a community adamantly opposed to the potential corruptions of commerce and centralized authority. In 1965 Smith accused Mekas of expropriating his Co-op rental fees, siphoning them into other accounts.[8] Several years later Smith charged Mekas with the theft of the negative of *Flaming Creatures* in order to keep the film in circulation under his control.[9]

Although he then allowed Mekas on several occasions to program his films in progress, Smith lashed out in a 1972 *Village Voice* article, comparing the generosity of programming at the Elgin Theater with Mekas's "stingy" policies. Smith called him a "praying mantis" and claimed that the Co-op had been transformed into a "pawnshop" (Ehrenstein 1984, 29). Less than a year later, Smith escalated his attack in another *Village Voice* piece, referring to Mekas as a "Golden Brassiere Publicity Mummy" who had "sponged off the baby-vomit of art, while taking the opportunity to slip the museum price tag of death around the neck of each" (ibid.).[10] Vicious references to Mekas in the guise of "Uncle Fishook" and other characters appeared in performance pieces by Smith, and a final salvo was launched in a 1978 interview with Sylvere Lotringer in *Semiotext(e)*. On the subject of Mekas's defense of *Flaming Creatures*, Smith asserts: "Uncle Fishook wanted to have something in court at the time, it being so fashionable . . . he could be made to look like a saint . . . when he was really kicking it to death" (Smith 1978, 192). Smith asserts that "it made his career; I ended up supporting him." With not entirely specious logic, he says, "What you do with it economically is what the meaning is" (ibid., 194).

The problem is that the Co-op became a "grotesque parody of Hollywood" with Mekas as its "capitalist" purveyor while he, Smith, remained an "anarchist" ("anarchy is the giving part of pol-

---

[8] Mekas's diaries mention similar accusations by other Co-op members and by Canyon Cinema members who had screened their films under Mekas's auspices. It appears likely that rentals and box-office receipts were at times handled in a loose fashion, but it is inconceivable that improper personal gain was the motive or demonstrable outcome.

[9] The legend of Smith's missing negative is another turbid story not, in this context, worth trying to reassemble. According to Mekas—and this is confirmed by others—the negative was after many years salvaged from a film-lab trash heap and returned to Smith.

[10] David Ehrenstein, to his discredit, repeats and even enhances Smith's charges without a word of skepticism or qualification in order to bolster his own insipid campaign against Mekas and the "avant-establishment" (Ehrenstein 1984, 15–34).

itics"). His "roomful" of completed films was being denied exhibition due to Mekas's restrictive agenda. As for his momentary celebrity, "I couldn't live with it. . . . This was the golden gift of Uncle Fishook to me. Please let him keep the blessings of publicity." Refusing to accept Lotringer's proposal that Mekas was only a representative of a more complex power, he declares: "Usually in life nothing is ever clearcut. How many people are lucky enough to have an archetypal villain for an adversary?" (ibid., 198, 202, 203).

Smith's outbursts recall William Blake's complaint, "Where any view of Money exists Art cannot be carried on, but War only." Mekas was befouled by commerce; his ambition to preserve not only his own career but the creative possibilities of a marginal culture through publicizing and constructing institutions[11] purloined the "freedom" of those who rejected absolutely the snares of organized leadership.[12] This was, finally, a family squabble, and Smith "turned" on the patriarchal figure most invested in succession. Thus the "prophet" of the personal and spontaneous in film was outflanked on the very terrain he had publicly delineated, flayed in his vision of social change as requiring material forms of perpetuation. Defending himself from a different attack, Mekas would exclaim, "My dogmatism is larger than their permissiveness" (Diaries, July 1970).

While the Smith feud is an extreme case, there were clashes of a similar order with Jacobs, Barbara Rubin, and others in what could be called the "anarchist" wing of the avant-garde. Conflicts erupted in turn with the opposite pole, those who favored greater selectivity, consolidation, or focus on popular (as opposed to populist) endeavors. In 1967, Stan Brakhage briefly withdrew his films from the Co-op precisely because it refused selection and, in his view, too many works "advertised violence, hatred, dope, self-centered love,

---

[11] Mekas was adept at turning his self-evident passion for collecting and preserving into a politically correct course, as in the following passage: "Who started the idea that the new, revolutionary, radical, underground culture is diametrically opposed to the old? I think the idea was invented by the enemies of processes of change. . . . Revolutionaries and underground are really restorers of culture, they are attacking the vulgarizations and misuses of culture, art, etc." (Mekas 1972b, 400).

[12] Todd Gitlin offers a detailed account of factional conflicts within SDS that are in many ways comparable to countercultural clashes between advocates of unconstrained, isolated activity and the strategic management of mass-movement dynamics. By the late sixties, at the apogee of SDS's size and power, a younger core of spokespersons from various ideological factions sought to discredit the original leadership base through accusations of "revisionism," "popularization," careerism, and counterrevolutionary policies (Gitlin 1987, esp. 237–40, 388; see also Miller 1987, 238–40).

nihilism" (Diaries, 2 August 1967). Brakhage too referred to the Co-op as a "mini-Hollywood," this time the avatar of "antiart." Mekas clung to the principle of open access but later worried that Brak-hage's argument for the promotion of a "select few" had merit after all (Diaries, 2 April 1968). It was in this period that plans for an "academy" of independent film were given serious attention, and after the usual tribulations Anthology Film Archives was founded in 1970. In typical fashion Mekas would work toward the incorpo-ration of radical art into stable institutions while upholding the theme of permanent cultural transformation.

THE RHETORIC OF LIBERATION

One year after the publication of *The Communist Manifesto*, Thoreau wrote his essay "Civil Disobedience," originally entitled "Resistance to Civil Government." Mekas does not recall when he first read this piece, but the importance of Thoreau—along with Whitman, Emerson, and other nineteenth-century American think-ers—to his writing, filmmaking, and moral sensibility is amply ev-ident. A privileged text in the political philosophy of Martin Luther King as well as factions of the New Left, "Civil Disobedience" of-fers a wealth of clues to the development in the sixties of Mekas's political assumptions and their manner of articulation.

Thoreau's argument, which is consistent with his other writings, is that unjust laws should be fought less through the abstractions of petitions and mass protests than through individual confrontation: "It is, after all, with men not parchment that I quarrel." A single citizen suffering the consequences of refusal becomes, for him, the founding "definition of a peaceable revolution, if any such is possi-ble." Any government authority not totally respectful of the indi-vidual must be rejected. Freedom, the "obligation . . . to do at any time what I think right," rather than democracy, seals the individ-ual's course of action.

Written in the first person, Thoreau's essay bears the cadences of an oral lecture. The language is direct, employing patterns of repe-tition of words and phrases and the figure of chiasmus, a crisscross-ing relation of signal terms: "Under a government which imprisons any unjustly, the true place for a just man is also a prison." As in Thoreau's journals, argument is balanced by passages of detailed de-scription of nature; the view of a puddle from his jail cell window links the idea of spiritual freedom to perceptual specificity. Without suggesting that a given text or rhetorical style can fully account for Mekas's political-aesthetic prescriptions, his assumption of the voice and prerogatives of radical individualism is grounded in a set of features analogous to those of Thoreau, hinged as always on a shifting functionality of private and public.

Mekas's discourse about film in the sixties is exemplary in part because it shares what Stanley Aronowitz identifies as the period's leading ideological theme: "The attempt to infuse life with a secular spiritual and moral content, to fill the quotidian with personal meaning and purpose" (Aronowitz 1984, 18). This entailed, among other things, the fashioning of a language that could integrate subjective feelings with an analysis of social ills, an appropriately indigenous speech woven from diverse strands of pragmatism, transcendentalism, utopian religious thought, and apocalyptic and "outsider" literary traditions.[13] The reformation of diction would lay the groundwork for a new political and social identity.

In a sweeping gesture, groups such as the SDS abjured concepts associated with Old Left or "European" thought: for instance, "revolution," "the proletariat," and so on barely appear in *The Port Huron Statement*. There was in this position something of a mistrust of rational argument, of language itself, and a corresponding belief in experience as an ideological benchmark.[14] Organizer Keith Lampe voiced a characteristic bias: "We emancipated primitives are free to do what we *feel* now because we understand that logic and proportion and consistency and even perspective are part of the old control system" (Albert and Albert 1984, 405). Or as Tom Hayden put it in an early dispute with the Old Left: "They *had* politics. We *were* politics" (Gitlin 1987, 134). Since "politics" in the inherited wisdom stood for all that was premeditated and rigid, it must be replaced by a faith in intuitive action. In a similar vein, Mekas would contend: "We want to liberate cinema from politics by putting it in the hands of the people"; "It's my soul that is my politics" (Diaries, October 1967, July 1968).[15]

[13] There has been considerable discussion of the literary and intellectual roots of New Left writing. See, for example Gitlin 1987, 26–27, 84–85; Miller 1987, 146–48.

[14] Entreaties such as Timothy Leary's "Get out of your mind and into your senses" are indicative of a broad tendency in the sixties to regard inherited rules of argument and exposition (logical sequence, evidence, appeals to authority) as aligned with established structures of power and repressive of the individual's firsthand experience. The animus against formal language is reflected by such diverse phenomena as lyricless rock music, the near-muteness of much experimental theater, and avant-garde film's almost complete severing of the image from human speech.

[15] A similar spirit inflected other precincts of the counterculture. *Rolling Stone* magazine founder Jan Wenner spoke for what he imagined as the "purity" of rock music at exactly the moment of its increasing politicization and interpenetration with mass protest: "Rock wants no part of today's social structure, especially in its

Adopting a posture toward authority commensurate with that of the New Left, Mekas rejected the provenance of European culture for its complicity in two world wars and the consequent erasure of cultural entities such as Lithuania (Diaries, 10 October 1960). He says he was "taken in" during the fifties by the orthodox Marxism of collaborator Edouard de Laurot, but abandoned this influence, and its aesthetic requisite of social realism, when the relationship collapsed in 1962 and Mekas edged closer to the avant-garde (Diaries, 12 July 1963). Nevertheless, he regularly employed political metaphors in framing the project of independent film: "What I want to achieve ideally with my film [*Guns of the Trees*]: is to overthrow the government. All governments. So we can start from the beginning" (Diaries, 11 August 1960). And both early and late he resorted to antipodes such as "capitalist" versus "revolutionary" views of art.

Such terms proved especially useful in response to those who spurned experimental film for its lack of social engagement while devoting their journalistic attention to commercial movies (Diaries, May 1967, May 1970).[16] A general tendency to link the counterculture with resistance to capitalism was augmented by an identification with the struggles of Third World countries for self-determination, a romantic self-justification figured in a rhetoric of guerrilla warfare, liberation, and underground cadres (Jameson 1984, 180–86). Here as well, Mekas blended into the cultural landscape by proposing parallels between Third World revolutionary practice and the incursions of alternative cinema (Diaries, 1 June 1962).[17] If he grudgingly lent support to militant protests, he wound up adopting similar slogans and methods of polarization. He even wrote a "New American Cinema Agit-Prop Notebook," a somewhat satirical ver-

---

most manifestly corrupt form, politics, even 'new left' politics" (Armstrong 1981, 124).

[16] Eventually, the avant-garde became almost synonymous with "art" in Mekas's politico-aesthetic pronouncements, and all art was inherently revolutionary in its "betterment of man, wakening up of his humanness. . . . Art is always anti–status quo, anti-imperialist, anti-capitalist, anti-dictatorship, and anti-private property" (Diaries, May 1970).

[17] Another avant-garde filmmaker who adapted liberationist ideology to the consequences of aesthetic renewal was Saul Levine, at one time a prominent member of the national branch of the SDS. In an interview for a campus newspaper, he defended Brakhage's work as the most radical filmic contribution to social change: "The kind of film I'm interested in is unmanipulative. It teaches people to be free" (Levine 1968). For another version of the identification with Third World movements, see the manifesto published in an early issue of *Cineaste* (Radical Education Project 1970, 2–3).

sion of the revolutionary instructional manuals flaunted by the underground press. With enough common cause, such as the trashing of the New York Film Festival, he might turn over "Movie Journal" to radical groups such as the New York Motherfuckers: "Up against the wall, bourgeois institutions, bourgeois culture, bourgeois life" (Mekas 1972b, 317).

The willingness to pose homologies with sixties radicalism oscillates in Mekas's writings, partly in response to the trajectory of escalating claims in adjacent arenas. The pressure of relentless social upheaval created within avant-garde film a tension between assertions of autonomy, of distance from the organized political sphere, and the expectation of a mutually enhancing solidarity. For instance, Mekas joined with film activists in opposing the impersonal, hierarchal power emblematized by the Hollywood industry. While this went against both his passion for certain auteurist spectacles and his sense of absolute alterity—"Hollywood is a cow, the avant-garde is a sheep. There can be no competition between them" (Mekas 1990)—he seemed to anticipate, and never get, a reciprocal endorsement of the avant-garde by leftist cultural organs.

One reason experimental film was written out of the official history of sixties radicalism may be found in a sub rosa admiration for the instrumentality of commercial cinema, a machinery totally disavowed by Mekas and his cohort. As early as 1960 he began to connect the excitement of new cinematic forms with a repudiation of "professionalism" and economic control. The "impoverishment" of means and techniques was calibrated as a sign of a cinematic rebirth that augured a more sweeping revolt against convention (Diaries, 28 July 1960). Filmmakers were lauded for working through "ignorance and confusion," having freed themselves from a "trust in clarity, in pre-planning where everything is predictable" (Diaries, 5 September 1960). Commenting on *Come Back Africa*, he set the tone for subsequent appraisals: "The very amateurism of the cast becomes part of the movie's truth and authenticity" (Mekas 1972b, 19). Since American cinéma vérité was found to contain the same liberating marks of rawness as avant-garde work, the crucial distinction was not in theme or narrative approach but in the ability of unfettered technique to register a passionate, subjective confrontation with reality.[18]

---

[18] The equation of improvisational form or dramatic action with a political ideal of direct confrontation was fairly common. Ernest Callenbach praises the cinéma vérité documentary for its refusal of an omniscient, authoritarian camera address (Callenbach 1968, 3), while Leo Braudy goes even further in an assessment of early Newsreel work: "The non-sync film becomes more radical than the sync because

The valorization of performance over clarity, structural elegance, or programmatic meaning is tied to the investment in sensory engagement, which in the sixties ran the gamut from the drug culture to rock concerts to guerrilla theater to oral poetry. For Mekas, almost any attempt to reduce the separation of image and viewer—and by extension art and life—seemed worthy of praise. He was an early and ardent supporter of "expanded cinema," of film-performance fusions, and he promoted the custom of filmmakers appearing in public with their work. Immediacy was held to be the single most important criterion of not only aesthetic truth but social effectiveness.

"This generation," he declared, "is by a dialectical necessity a generation of irresponsibility, disobedience . . . and these 'negative' characteristics should be encouraged" (Diaries, 4 August 1960). It is difficult at times to distinguish Mekas's sympathy for outlaw disobedience from his notion of political resistance. In 1960 he celebrated *Cry of Jazz*, made by two African-Americans, because of its anger at white society, and eight years later he announced that "the students of Columbia are the only ones in this city doing anything that can be called human" (Diaries, 22 November 1960, 4 June 1968). Harlem street gangs could embody the same "independent spirit" as emerging filmmakers: "Some disrespect for officialdom, parenthood. Society without thieves, robbers, hooligans, is a dying worthless society in which all theft and murder is legalized, done from above" (Diaries, 8 August 1960).

Increasingly explicit in the doctrine of the personal and the spontaneous was the repudiation of private property and its legal trappings. In a seven-page manifesto, "On Art and Politics," summarizing ten years of thinking about the avant-garde's place in the landscape of liberation, he attacks the shortsightedness of "radicals who speak against art [but should] really speak against the property and ownership of works of art" (Diaries, July 1970). Alternative film is crucially important because it works toward "the destruction of the phony privacy walls" (Mekas 1972b, 281). Hollywood, newspapers, the New York Film Festival were all on the side of property. Maintaining the nonexclusivity of an organization such as the Co-op was by this measure a blow against property relations (as, inci-

---

the sync suggests easy solutions, the effortless marriage of word and image." Newsreel proposes a "more open-ended" political result via the "radicalizing of aesthetic responses" (Braudy 1968, 49). One of Mekas's earliest and most comprehensive treatments of the link between spontaneous form and emancipation is found in "Notes on the New American Cinema" (Mekas 1962, 6–10).

dentally, was the decision by the SDS never to turn down a request for charter).

Like Jack Smith, Mekas viewed himself as an anarchist, and he wielded anarchy's inflammatory appeal in the promotion of independent film. A characteristic stance was that "through anarchy filmmaking has gained a new freedom" (ibid., 185). Since he equated anarchism with the vicissitudes of the outcast, the marginalized, anarchism assumed in his writings the status of simply that which sustains individual liberty against demands for collective order. This offhand appropriation of anarchism as aesthetic quality, as personal praxis, and as social design further complicted an already complex ambivalence toward violence. More than once Mekas decried the tactics of civil disobedience. The prospect, for instance, of serving a jail term in defense of *Flaming Creatures* was deemed counterproductive. Witnessing a protest over the building of Polaris submarines, he reported: "I think all those pacifists are schmucks. I wish they would do something violent instead. You cannot fight businessmen with passivity. Hit them on the head" (Diaries, 26 November 1960).

Yet alongside arguments for the necessity of direct rather than symbolic action, even when it entailed physical confrontation, are stinging condemnations of destructive impulses in both film and mass politics. Following a film showing he wrote to the Sisters and students of Sacred Heart College that "those who will be part of the destruction, they are helpless fools" (Diaries, January 1968). On a host of occasions he reminded himself and implored filmmakers not to "add to the ugliness" of society by making works that conveyed anger or divisiveness, recommending "celebration" of love and beauty over "protest" (Mekas 1972b, 318). The residue of a Christian ethics bleeds into pronouncements of militancy, and one frequently finds demands for action nestled alongside the credo of Saint Theresa of Avila that "however great the good, one may never do anything wrong, however small, to bring it about" (Diaries, November 1966). A long letter published in the hippie-oriented newspaper *Avatar* proposed spiritual solutions to questions of whether to enter the army, drop out, and so forth (Diaries, November 1967).

Ideological crosscurrents engendered by Mekas's effort to clarify the functions of advanced art in the juggernaut of rebellion point to a wider uneasiness within sixties counterculture. How is it possible to reconcile the self-affirmimg, redemptive thrust of the creative process with an unavoidable obligation to dismantle existing structures of individual domination? Should the subjective transmission of immediate responses, regardless of their source or import, *always* take precedence over long-range goals? Jerry Rubin, in a famous 1967 article in the *Berkeley Barb*, addressed this issue in directives for a gathering that could rally cultural and political radicals, a proposed fusion of the "I am" with the "I protest" (Armstrong 1981, 120). For Mekas such unsettled, and ultimately insoluble, questions at once bracketed and fueled everyday conflicts between leadership and egalitarianism, between conducting campaigns for the public acceptance of the avant-garde and nurturing a communal spirit built around an antiauthoritarian assertion of personal vision.

Marcuse postulated that "the imagination has become an instrument of progress" and that "to liberate the imagination . . . presupposes the repression of much that is now free and that perpetuates a repressive society" (Marcuse 1964, 250). Coexistent with utopian designs for an alternative system was the omnipresent recognition of limits to the exercise of imagination in a medium defined by its technological-industrial scaffolding. The formulation of an ideological position through which to advance social options for the individual in cinema virtually compelled the collision in Mekas's writings of a critique of liberal society and an insatiable desire for withdrawal. Every gesture toward consensus, toward tactical solidarity, was chastened by the moral requisites of independence. Saint Teresa met the Motherfuckers on the barren plain of estrangement.

COMMUNITAS

According to Fredric Jameson, it is a "social *symptom* that in the mid-60s, people felt it necessary to express their sense of the situation and their projected praxis in a reified political language of power, domination, authority, and antiauthoritarianism" (Jameson 1984, 184). For all his dedication to the fluid gemeinschaft tenets of social interaction, Mekas was fond of applying clear, if self-consciously fanciful, labels to those on the side of grace and those in league with corruption. People were "angels," "monks," "saints," or in an alternate idiom, "heroes," "Viet Cong," "fanatics." Or they were "devils," "bureaucrats," "capitalists." That such labels might be inverted on short notice is of less significance than their manner of dispensation, the philosophical dualism that underscores, and at times subverts, Mekas's imbrication with motifs of sixties rebellion. Alternative film and the movements with which it frequently conspired shared more than tactics, goals, or social practices.

With historical distance it is possible to extrapolate from documents and practices at least some of the terms that for Mekas held in place the promise, and in specific areas the realization, of community: a redemptive body strung between moral and political exigencies, between personal codes of authenticity and "doing good for others" (a litany permeating the diaries). Certain elements of this secular religion are obvious. The enactment of life as an aesthetic adventure conducted for its own sake secured the celebration of idiosyncrasy among the subcultural outcasts of avant-garde film. Doing one's own thing was an inviolate measure of opposition, of antistructure, even when it threatened to disrupt the precarious unity of group objectives. The principle of permissiveness accounts for, among other things, Mekas's swift recanting in the early sixties of his distaste for homosexuality and its impact on sexual representation in the avant-garde (Mekas 1959, 3). "First I thought I'd like to see all homosexuality and lesbianism go. . . . Now I understand that really it's our culture that has to go" (Diaries, January 1966).[19]

In accord with his rather ambivalent stance toward sexual license, the institution of marriage was rejected because it limited personal freedom and interfered with the commitment of the artist to his or her work (Diaries, 19 August 1960). Equally important was the implicit vow of voluntary poverty. Being on the cultural margins almost inevitably meant being on the economic margins, and while Mekas continually complained about material deprivations in his own life and that of his immediate circle, he was deeply suspicious of nearly every sign of affluence and tended to regard poverty as an index of virtue. In a similar vein, while it could be said that he himself bore the symptoms of a public logorrhea he rationalized verbal inarticulacy or declension in certain filmmakers as a natural result of heightened contact with the "truth" of the image. The appropriate arena for excess was that of performance, the collapse of social style into aesthetic production.

Unquestionably, much of what Mekas admired and attempted to consolidate was a direct inheritance of the Beat ethos.[20] The pursuit of spontaneous creative explosion was fiercely maintained as a critical standard of authenticity even as the stakes of public programs expanded. The model of disaffection proffered by the Beats had a corresponding effect on the development of the radical politics and the music of the sixties. It is said, for instance, that Tom Hayden

---

[19] Endorsing in 1964 the New York League for Sexual Freedom, he demanded "respect for individual liberty" and the repeal of all laws restricting what is done "voluntarily by adults in private" (including, by the way, laws hindering free contraception and abortion) (Diaries, 24 March 1964).

[20] Again, David James supplies a most thorough and authoritative analysis of the confluence of Beat and underground film cultures (James 1989, esp. 85–102).

tried, with others in his circle, to infuse the SDS prospectus for social change with Beat values of "spontaneity, imagination, passion, playfulness . . . the sensation of being on edge, at the limits of freedom" (Miller 1987, 147). Simon Frith, analyzing the decisive tension in rock music between "pop" and "art," asserts that San Francisco acid rock—and the entire thrust of Romantic individualism exemplified by Jim Morrison and the Doors—"was the sound of the Beatniks" (Frith 1984, 65).

In both cases, the key to an identification with a previous generation of social dissidents was the imagined reconciliation of individual with communal needs under the aegis of what Dick Hebdige defines as "subcultural." Anticipating the denizens of avant-garde film, the initial activism of the SDS, and the first glimmerings of sixties rock, the Beats "expressed a magical relation to a poverty which constructed . . . a divine essence, a state of grace, a sanctuary" (Hebdige 1979, 49). The presumed relation between the trappings of material disavowal and personal or social redemption came under increasing stress as challenges to established order produced new opportunities for legitimation. But the theme of bohemian emancipation resurfaced across a variety of efforts to attach a vanguard political significance to marginal-group activities. Beat refugee Gary Snyder delivered this message of accommodation:

> The joyous and voluntary poverty of Buddhism becomes a positive force. . . . The belief in a serene and generous fulfillment of natural loving impulses destroys ideologies which blind, maim, and repress points on the way to a kind of community which would amaze "moralists." . . . The mercy of the West has been social revolution; the mercy of the East has been individual insight into the basic self/void. We need both. (Snyder 1968, 432)

Recognition of the impossibility of reforming liberal society and the consequent utopian desire to construct an alternative arrangement that would *spontaneously* substitute a new set of values for the hopelessly corrupt order was not confined to white youth culture and politics.[21] But for organizations such as the SDS, the promise of a "sanctuary" was direct and often highly conscious. Todd Gitlin testifies that the movement was, more than anything else, "a living protest against isolation and fragmentation." "The SDS circle

---

[21] The opening statement by the SNCC proposed that "the redemptive community supersedes immoral social systems" (Albert and Albert 1984, 113). This vision is one source for subsequent demands by African-Americans for "community control" and autonomy within economic, political, and cultural spheres. For a powerful example of this commitment, see Malcolm X 1965, 126–32.

had founded a surrogate family, where for long stretches of time horizontal relations of trust replaced vertical relations of authority" (Gitlin 1987, 107). Another SDS leader, Paul Booth, refers to the tenor of a national convention as "group marriage": "We all got together and functioned as the priest" (Miller 1987, 239). Gitlin closes the circle of communitarian themes by suggesting that through feelings of solidarity with peoples trying to repossess their homelands, "we were straining to overcome our own sense of homelessness" (Gitlin 1987, 262).

Correlations between Mekas's personal involvement in and visionary guidance of avant-garde film and the communitarian ideals of adjacent movements permit a final observation drawn from a slightly different perspective. Anthropologist Victor Turner examined, over the course of his long career, the concept of *communitas* as a counterweight or antinomy to "social structure," the highly ordered and hierarchal set of symbols and events that govern interaction in tribal societies. In the late sixties he proposed links between communitas and the evolution of mendicant religious sects in the Middle Ages (Turner 1969, 143–48). A few years later, he extended the analysis to illuminate aspects of sixties counterculture. For hippies, as for monks and participants in tribal rituals, there is an attempt to establish "a timeless condition, an eternal now," in which structural adherence to segmented temporality is inapplicable, in which restrictive social roles are cast off and imagination reigns as the measure of knowledge and power. It is an attempt to duplicate, to make permanent, the freedoms mandated in rites of passage, especially the "liminal" stages of transformations in social identity.

Adducing a text on rock music published in the underground press, Turner isolated elements that align sixties culture with tribal and religious groups: the rejection of marriage; the endorsement of sexual license (of "polymorphous perversity"); improvisation and abstraction; the mobilization and union of discrete sensory experiences; the enforcement of face-to-face interaction; the leveling of conventional indicators of sexual difference through dress, ornamentation, and behavior (Turner 1974, 231–70). He asserts that the work of communitas as an "aesthetic of discovery" was inherent in the conditions of rapid and unceasing change in American society. He links a commitment to voluntary poverty with feelings of religious love; "cease to have and you are." The yearning for authenticity in individual existence feeds the potential power of the self-confirmed exile by casting separation as a critique of normative social order. "The difficulty," Turner concludes, "with these Edenic prescriptions is that men have to organize structurally in order to exist materially at all" (ibid., 266).

It is tempting to see in Mekas, the self-proclaimed "monk" of avant-garde cinema, the modality of religious aspiration outlined by Turner as a common thread among distinct social phenomena. Its compensatory function for "a man who never wanted to leave his country" cannot adequately be sounded. Yet by immersing himself in the openings created by the rupture of social order in the sixties, by translating constant pressures of estrangement into a manifold form of praxis, he was able to implant a spirit of community in a field where only ragged individualism had flourished before.

Bibliography

Albert, Judith Clavir, and Stewart Edward Albert, eds. 1984. *The Sixties Papers: Documents of a Rebellious Decade.* New York: Praeger.

Armstrong, David. 1981. *A Trumpet to Arms: Alternative Media in America.* Boston: J. P. Tarcher.

Aronowitz, Stanley. 1984. "When the Left Was New." In *Sixties without Apology,* 11–43. *See* Sayres et al. 1984.

Arthur, Paul. 1979. "*Quixote* and Its Contexts." *Film Culture* 67–69:32–56.

Braudy, Leo. 1968. "Newsreel: A Report." *Film Quarterly* 21, no. 2:48–51.

Briggs, Judith E. 1980. *Jonas Mekas.* Minneapolis: Film in the Cities.

Callenbach, Ernest. 1968. "Looking Backward." *Film Quarterly* 22, no. 1:1–10.

Cineaste Editors. 1988. "Editorial." *Cineaste* 16, no. 1–2:6, 86–87.

Ehrenstein, David. 1984. *Film: The Front Line, 1984.* Denver: Arden Press.

Frith, Simon. 1984. "Rock and the Politics of Memory." In *Sixties without Apology,* 59–69. *See* Sayres et al. 1984.

Gitlin, Todd. 1980. *The Whole World Is Watching.* Berkeley and Los Angeles: University of California Press.

———. 1987. *The Sixties: Years of Hope, Days of Rage.* New York: Bantam.

Goldstein, Richard. 1986. "Son of the Return of the Repressed." *Village Voice,* 8 March, "Thinking about the Sixties: A Special Section," 23–28.

Hebdige, Dick. 1979. *Subculture: The Meaning of Style.* London: Methuen.

Hoberman, J. 1985. "Karma Chameleons: Why the *Eighties* Started in 1961." *Village Voice Literary Supplement* (November): 1–13.

Hoffman, Abbie. 1968. *Revolution for the Hell of It* (excerpt). In *Sixties Papers*, 417–28. *See* Albert and Albert 1984.

James, David E. 1989. *Allegories of Cinema: American Film in the Sixties.* Princeton: Princeton University Press.

Jameson, Fredric. 1984. "Periodizing the Sixties." In *Sixties without Apology*, 178–208. *See* Sayres et al. 1984.

Klinkowitz, Jerome. 1980. *The American 1960s: Imaginative Acts in a Decade of Change.* Iowa City: Iowa State University Press.

Levine, Saul. 1968. "Interview." In *The Book of Saul*, ed. Marjorie Keller. New York: n.p., 1976.

Malcolm X. 1965. "The Ballot or the Bullet." In *Sixties Papers*, 126–32. *See* Albert and Albert 1984.

Marcuse, Herbert. 1964. *One-Dimensional Man.* Boston: Beacon Press.

Mekas, Jonas. 1955. "The Experimental Film in America." *Film Culture* 3:15–20.

———. 1959–1970. Diaries. Anthology Film Archives, New York.

———. 1959. "A Call for a New Generation of Film-Makers." *Film Culture* 19:1–4.

———. 1962. "Notes on the New American Cinema." *Film Culture* 24:6–16.

———. 1972a. "The Diary Film." In *Avant-Garde Film*, 190–98. *See* Sitney 1978.

———. 1972b. *Movie Journal: The Rise of a New American Cinema, 1959–1971.* New York: Macmillan.

———. 1990. Interview with the author, 8 February.

Michelson, Annette. 1966. "Film and the Radical Aspiration." In *Film Culture Reader*, 404–21. *See* Sitney 1970a.

Mierau, Maurice A. 1986. "Carnival and Jeremiad: Mailer's *Armies of the Night*." *Canadian Review of American Studies* 17, no. 3:317–26.

Miller, James. 1987. *"Democracy Is in the Streets": From Port Huron to the Siege of Chicago.* New York: Simon and Schuster.

Mills, C. Wright. 1956. *The Power Elite.* New York: Ballantine.

Newsreel. 1968. "Newsreel." *Film Quarterly* 21, no. 2:43–48.

Radical Education Project. 1970. "The Cineaste in Society." *Cineaste* 3, no. 3:2–3.

Renov, Michael. 1987. "Early Newsreel: The Construction of a Political Imaginary for the New Left." *Afterimage* 14, no. 7 (February): 12–15.

Rubin, Jerry. 1970. *Do It!* (excerpt). In *Sixties Papers*, 439–48. *See* Albert and Albert 1984.

Sayres, Sohnya, Anders Stephanson, Stanley Aronowitz, and Fredric Jameson, eds. 1984. *The Sixties without Apology.* Minneapolis: University of Minnesota Press.

Sitney, P. Adams, ed. 1970a. *Film Culture Reader.* New York: Praeger.

Sitney, P. Adams, ed. 1970b. "Introduction: A Reader's Guide to the American Avant-Garde Film." In *Film Culture Reader*, 3–11. *See* Sitney 1970a.

———. 1974. *Visionary Film*. New York: Oxford.

———, ed. 1978. *The Avant-Garde Film: A Reader of Theory and Criticism*. New York: New York University Press.

Skolnick, Jerome. 1969. *The Politics of Protest*. New York: Simon and Schuster.

Smith, Jack. 1978. "Uncle Fishook and the Sacred Baby Poo-poo of Art." *Semiotext(e)* 3, no. 2:192–203.

Snyder, Gary. 1968. "Buddhism and the Coming Revolution." In *Sixties Papers*, 431–33. *See* Albert and Albert 1984.

Sontag, Susan. 1964. "Jack Smith's *Flaming Creatures*." In *Against Interpretation*, 227–31. New York: Laurel, 1966.

Students for a Democratic Society. "The Port Huron Statement." In *"Democracy Is in the Streets,"* 329–74. *See* Miller 1987.

Tomkins, Calvin. 1973. "All Pockets Open." *New Yorker*, 6 January, 31–49.

Trilling, Diana. 1969. *"Easy Rider* and Its Critics." In *Mass Culture Revisited*, ed. Bernard Rosenberg and David Manning White, 233–44. New York: Van Nostrand Reinhold, 1971.

Turner, Victor. 1969. *The Ritual Process*. Chicago: Aldine.

———. 1974. *Dramas, Fields, and Metaphors*. Ithaca: Cornell University Press.

Zimmermann, Patricia R. 1988. "Hollywood, Home Movies, and Common Sense: Amateur Film as Aesthetic Dissemination and Social Control, 1950–1962." *Cinema Journal* 27, no.4 (Summer): 23–44.

3. George Kuchar   The Old Days

IN THE OLD DAYS, when I was younger, I first met Jonas Mekas at the loft where Ken Jacobs used to live and screen movies. He may still live there, I don't know, because I was always a part of the scene in front and never behind. In other words, I was kind of the snot-nosed guy from the Bronx and that was a whole other backwoods dimension in the twilight zone. Anyway, Jonas Mekas was standing in the back of the loft when my brother and I were screening our 8 mm movies way back then; way back in 1962 or so? He was way back there in the shadows with a corduroy suit on, I believe: a trim, brown, corduroy suit with a matching vest. You know, he always looked to me like Mr. Snatch (or is it Mr. Scratch?). Mr. Scratch is the other name for the Devil when he appears to country folk in human garb. He was always slim and animated and had a semi-grin on his face. The eyes were always going here and there and he appeared happy but I don't know if that is what it was like underneath. His brother was more like the other side of the mask: brooding like a snapping turtle. Yet his brother made happy pictures; at least the ones I saw were happy. In those old days, Jonas Mekas's columns in the *Village Voice* popped off the page with passion and that weird little line drawing of his profile . . . a visual logo that was completely the opposite of the one associated with Alfred Hitchcock and yet somehow just as menacing. He was one of the very few people writing about underground films in that period and so he had a lot of power and was feared, respected, and hated. That little, trim, animated man was responsible for bringing national and international attention to the underground film movement in those days. He was also the only person I know of who wrote a nice word about Hare Krishna people in one of his articles. Jonas Mekas, in those old days, was a powerful force to reckon with despite his size. I think even today he still has that fast and playful grin on his face. At least, I hear it in his voice, because I don't see him anymore: we are three thousand miles apart. In fact, we always were, even when I was living in New York. I have fond memories of him, though. He was constantly busy doing something and even when he was just standing around the guy was racked with neurotic or neurological mannerisms that kept him jumping. A Czechoslovakian jumping bean (at least I think that's where he's from). As you can see, I don't know much about him. All I do know is that he was kind to me even when he couldn't stand me and that was nice. People tell me that they used to hear P. Adams Sitney and him screaming at each other at Anthology Film Archives and that sounds nice too: at least it contradicts the rumors that the place is nothing but an elephant burial ground. The other day he called me up long-distance and asked a question. The long distance was still there but so was the smile in his voice at times. I hope that never fades.

4. John Pruitt   Jonas Mekas: A European Critic in America

And so this makes it that Henry James just went on doing what American literature had always done, the form was always the form of the contemporary English one, but the disembodied way of disconnecting something from anything and anything from something was the American one. The way it had of often all never having any living was an American one.

Some say that it is repression but no it is not repression it is a lack of connection, of there being no connection with living a daily living because there is none, that makes American writing what it always has been and what it will continue to become.
—Gertrude Stein, *Lectures in America*

On one side there is Hollywood; on the other side, are the experimental filmmakers. The middle, the largest area, the whole human reality, sung by the poets and painted on canvas from time immemorial—as the source of all art— is lying fallow.
—Jonas Mekas, "Experimental Film in America"

ANY OVERVIEW of Jonas Mekas's criticism must first confront the anomaly that this European exile, profoundly influenced by the polemics of Italian neorealism, would become the champion of the filmmakers Maya Deren, Stan Brakhage,

Kenneth Anger, and Michael Snow, artists who strove to detach
their works from the everyday social realities that played so large a
role in the major European films of the postwar period. The story of
Mekas's "conversion" is a crucial one because it reveals the complex, ambivalent nature of his critical stance and the continuity between his criticism and his filmmaking endeavors.

In 1955, Mekas and his associates founded *Film Culture* magazine, a review that contained substantial studies of past cinematic
achievements, but whose main thrust was to support worthy contemporary filmmaking, to help found a "New American Cinema"
in which the filmmakers would control their own work, free from
the Hollywood industry.

In order to replace meretriciousness with authenticity, there was
no question but that such a movement had to look to Europe, which
meant an all but complete rejection of the American avant-garde.
The lead article in the first issue, "Towards a Theory of Dynamic
Realism," was written by Edouard L. de Laurot, like Mekas a displaced European. His guiding assumption was that "dynamic realism" was not a mere slave to actuality, but rather actively engaged
social causes. After *Un chien Andalou*, de Laurot pointed out, Buñuel made *Land without Bread*, and after *Entr'acte*, René Clair
made *A nous la liberté*—that is to say, after formal experimentation, the European avant-garde "advanced" to a more mature social
vision. According to this progressivist view, American abstract surrealist experimenters were retrograde. Europe was waiting for
America to catch up, and *Film Culture* was to lead the way (de Laurot 1955). De Laurot's vision was compatible with that of most of
the regular early writers for *Film Culture*, who included Mekas
himself, George Fenin, Siegfried Kracauer, Lotte Eisner, Amos Vogel, Jay Leyda, and two who focused primarily on classic films, Andrew Sarris and Herman G. Weinberg. The contributors representing a more purely aesthetic stance were fewer: Parker Tyler, Rudolf
Arnheim, and Hans Richter—but of these three, only Tyler's articles made a particular point of championing Americans (e.g., Sidney
Peterson and Stan Brakhage) who might not easily fit the mold of
the engaged artist making independent features and documentaries.

The operative word in virtually all Mekas's editorials and critical
surveys of the late fifties is that slippery one: "realism." He recognized the Italian neorealist school as being the dominant movement
in postwar Europe, and through his understanding of its style he
interpreted most of what he found significant in contemporary filmmaking. In praising a new group of young British filmmakers he virtually recapitulated the point of view of Bazin or Zavattini:

In their harsh, black and white colors and direct documentary approach, they brought to the screen images of contemporary London, with its dance halls, its night streets, its playgrounds, its warehouses. The people in these films were real, not actors. They looked and acted and spoke and behaved and moved as their contemporaries did. And there was no phony glamorizing, no artificial tragedies. (Mekas 1960a, 2)

His perspective was consistent enough so that even in championing Robert Frank's *Pull My Daisy* in 1960, a film that had an aesthetic tint to it because it portrayed a New York milieu of poets, painters, and musicians, he was quick to offer the following qualification: "We know that Richter and Cocteau have used friends— painters and poets in their films. However, they used them in symbolic situations, moments. *Pull My Daisy* has nothing to do with any such literary symbols. The situations are everyday situations, with no other intentions" (ibid., 14).

As late as 1962, realism was still a leading criterion for him. His loosely historical survey of the New American Cinema asserted that it was founded on the New York realists and documentarists, such as James Agee, Helen Levitt, and Sydney Meyers. Attached to what in retrospect appears a far weaker brand of American filmmaking, Mekas had not yet discovered the strong point of American film. Symptomatic of his critical confusion with respect to the United States at this stage was his linking of Rossellini, Renoir, Hitchcock, and Hawks into one grand tradition from which he wanted new filmmakers to take their cues. No doubt he based his reflections on the pioneering work of *Cahiers du cinéma*, but one wonders if he realized how far apart in sensibility Hawks and Hitchcock were from Rossellini and Renoir. The realism of the latter two was firmly rooted in Europe and a distinct social milieu, while the films of Hawks and Hitchcock belonged to the insular, fantastic creations of Hollywood. *The Big Sleep* and *Vertigo* represented popular American Gothic at its best, their effectiveness a function of their unreality. Yet Mekas could praise Hawks and Hitchcock and still condemn the fifties Hollywood film in general by saying: "Nothing in these films is real; even death, the most powerful of realities, becomes mere decor, one more stone in the general mosaic of violence and force" (Mekas 1956, 1–2).

But in the United States, films in which "even death, the most powerful of realities, becomes mere decor" often have both greater formal integrity and a moral edge, while Hollywood's few attempts at realism have not been its strong suit. When Hollywood becomes socially concerned, its hypocrisy and fairy-tale formulas only become all the more obvious and offensive. So pervasive are the formulas that these films are virtually the same across the generations, and equally unconvincing as works of art—from *Mr. Smith Goes to Washington* (1939) to *The Best Years of Our Lives* (1946) to *On the Waterfront* (1954) to *Wall Street* (1987). In film there has never been a school of American realism to draw on as a strong tradition. Even the thirties school of American documentarists (vastly overrated, in my estimation, due to an insufficiently penetrating sociopolitical vision) seems to have been making fairy tales of sorts. For all their anti-Hollywood rhetoric, today most of these classic American documentaries come off as Hollywoodized versions of Soviet prototypes. It is still difficult for many intellectuals to acknowledge that Sternberg's *Scarlet Empress* could have had a greater influence in establishing a New American Cinema than Ralph Steiner and Willard van Dyke's *City*.

On the other side from Hollywood in Mekas's formulation were the so-called experimenters. Here too, Italian neorealism was the least appropriate lens through which to view the American avantgarde with any kind of sympathy. Predictably, in his first attempt at a critical appraisal of what he then called "experimental cinema," Mekas expressed his negative judgment in vitriolic fashion:

> Their protagonists seem to live under a strange spell. They do not appear to be part of the surrounding world, despite many naturalistic details that we find in these films. They are exalted, tormented, not related in any comprehensible way to society or place or family or any person. It is impossible to imagine these characters buying food or working in a shop or bringing up children or participating in any concrete manner in the activities of other men—they are not much more real than fictitious characters in space novels. In these films, touch with reality seems to be very feeble. Instead of a human being, we find a poetic version of a modern zombie: After all our efforts to make it alive, we find ourselves stuck with a corpse. (Mekas 1955, 16)

He saw as harmful precisely that "feeble touch with reality" that Gertrude Stein had once proposed as the positive characteristic of American art. Having been immersed in the political and social turmoil of Europe for ten years, and having arrived on the American scene a mere six years before, he was not yet in the position to understand his new homeland or to see its idiosyncrasies as possible virtues within its own tradition. In fact, he has more or less said as much, and subsequently referred to the essay as a "Saint-Augustine-before-the-conversion piece" (Mekas 1970, 26). The word "conversion," used somewhat ironically but nevertheless highly characteristic of his rhetoric, is misleading since it implies that Mekas's change of perspective was a sudden reversal. In fact, his acceptance of the American avant-garde was gradual and did not really signify the wholesale jettisoning of his former critical values.

Through the sixties and into the seventies, in his column for the *Village Voice*, there were numerous occasions when his loyalty to a realist tradition would come to the fore. In 1966, ruminating on the Vietnam War and ghetto disturbances, he called for a new 8 mm journalism: "Why should we leave all reporting to the press and TV?" (Mekas 1972, 236). In 1968, Mekas announced the creation of a "radical film newsreel service" (ibid., 305). In 1971, he reflected on the then-emerging video art and thought of it in terms so consistent with his 1955 tirade against the American avant-garde that one can almost consider his reaction a milder, more considered recapitulation of that essay: "On one hand we talk about our involvement in society, revolution, etc., we march and we protest and we go to Washington D.C., on the other hand we have this fantastic, miracle too which we could use to criticize, to record, to celebrate, or reveal society around us, to expose it to ourselves and others; instead we prefer to play abstract artists. I think it's pretentious."[1]

A realism in opposition to abstraction is clear enough, but it is surprising to see Mekas making virtually the same critical pronouncements no matter what kind of film was under discussion. The words "real" and "reality" were frequently employed simply to assess artistic effectiveness. To take one of many possible examples, in castigating some works of East European animation he declared that the works had "nothing to do either with visible reality nor the reality of our imaginations" (Mekas 1972, 286). On the other hand, he admired some recent children's animated films: "It's the realism, the poetic realism of these films that amazes me most" (ibid.).

In sticking so doggedly yet inconsistently to his particular terminology, Mekas was inevitably led to paradoxical pronouncements:

> Cornell's images are all very real. Even when they are taken from other movies, as in *Rose Hobart*, they seem to gain the quality of reality. The Hollywood unreality is transported into Cornellian unreality, which is very very real. Here is an evidence of the power of the artist to transform reality by choosing, by picking out only those details which correspond to some subtle inner movement or vision, or dream. No matter what he takes, be it a totally "artificial" reality, or bits of "actual" reality, he transforms them, bit by bit, into new unities, new things, boxes, collages, movies, with no other things on earth resembling them. (Ibid., 408)

[1] Jonas Mekas, "Movie Journal," *Village Voice*, 20 May 1971, 72.

In short, a real image is one that resembles nothing else; Mekas's term proves insufficient to account for a highly individualized vision that he nevertheless wants to acknowledge. Not unaware of the conceptual tension the term "realism" implied, Mekas could state that "whenever a work of art fails it fails formally," but form is nevertheless a secondary phenomenon, whose characteristics are shaped by "what details of reality are selected from the huge mass of reality and how they are put together."[2] Artistic style is really a form of perspective on a reality that has its own integrity prior to the creation of a work of art:

> Artists, that is, film-makers, always used real-life techniques in cinema. It's only a question of the emphasis, of the degree. And the emphasis, the degree, the angle always comes from the immediate (contemporary) needs of man. The theatre of Stanislavsky is based on the use of "real-life" experiences, too. All good acting is based on "real" experiences. But there are so many levels and aspects to this "real truth" in which we live. The emphasis, the styles keep changing. (Mekas 1972, 304)

The reality that the new filmmaker would document was a multifaceted one precisely because there were so many possible perspectives, and thus there was a corner reserved for those "film poets" who chose to record interiorized dramas. Pure abstraction, too, a *document* of mind and spiritual states in Mekas's formulation, was part of the total picture—but at first it was a small, ambiguous part. In 1959 Mekas wrote a long report to Europe on the state of new filmmaking in the United States for *Sight and Sound*, with much attention devoted to recent documentary and socially oriented films: Robert Frank and Alfred Leslie's *Pull My Daisy*, John Cassavetes' *Shadows*, Lionel Rogosin's *Come Back Africa*, and Edward Bland's *Cry of Jazz*. There is a brief but appreciative mention of *Desistfilm*, a Brakhage work that predates the other films under discussion and as such represents an earlier, less-radical style that hovers between an adolescent self-consciousness and a vague awareness of social rituals. In other words, Brakhage was squeezed into the survey as almost another new-wave director even though by then his work had taken off in another direction. Perhaps it was also in part the brevity of films like Brakhage's that earned them only a minor, if respectable, position. This is still the attitude of many mainstream critics today, who will grant the avant-garde credibility so long as it can be relegated to a secondary position—

---

[2] Jonas Mekas, *Village Voice*, 21 January 1971, 61.

usually that of an experimental training ground whose practitioners are waiting for a break into the big time.

But Mekas was more open-minded and more sensitive than even the better mainstream critics, and within a couple of years of his *Sight and Sound* article he was forced to recognize that the independent, realist feature film was not developing—that if that particular form were to continue it could only continue as a hapless compromise between art and industry. The dilemma was anticipated by the critical controversy over the first and second versions of *Shadows*. Cassavetes had reshot particular scenes, making it more commercially viable, and Mekas had seen this as a fatal betrayal—a kowtow to Hollywood. On the other hand, he saw that Brakhage and his fellow film poets such as Markopoulos, Breer, Smith, and Anger were not making compromises and were advancing their art. It was high time the primacy of their achievement was acknowledged. What in the late fifties had seemed like perhaps a minor element in the larger picture had revealed itself to have been the true dominant force all along. After Mekas sent out the call in *Film Culture* for the new American filmmakers, the people who answered the challenge were not the ones he had really expected. The fact that they were refining their particular brand of art regardless of whether he paid them attention or not only forced him to recognize that his adopted homeland had an indigenous tradition with which he had to reckon. He could not demand that American filmmakers do such and such; rather, he had to learn just what it was the best of them were doing and why they staunchly refused to conform to European models even though the European school of filmmaking was the center of attention for the majority of serious critics and intellectuals.

As a displaced European heavily involved in the American filmmaking scene, Mekas was in a privileged position to understand the schools of filmmaking on both sides of the Atlantic. While never wavering from his assertion that Markopoulos, Warhol, and the like represented *the* most important mode of American filmmaking, when he encountered the European critics of the American avant-garde he often defended the American style on *European* terms— namely, the issue of the social responsibility of the artist. As would be expected in such discussions, the term "reality" was never far away. In a particularly instructive interview, Mekas debated the French film critic Louis Marcorelles:

LM: This new cinema of Brazil, Canada, Hungary is definitely very socially rooted, engaged. It may not be so individualistic as the underground cinema. The fight that these film-makers are leading may seem to be divorced from the underground.

JM: It is not the question that they are engaged and we not. It is a question of different realities, of different concerns in each country. The artist in Brazil feels that his people are hungry; he feels that that is an important reality of his country; so he makes a film about bread. We feel that there is a different reality that is important in America today. . . .

LM: I personally feel that cinema should be highly socially responsible, in the Brechtian line. Cinema has to be located in a given time, even if it's poetry—in a given time, a given purpose.

JM: But that's what we are doing. In Brazil they have hunger problems. But here we have hunger of the soul. . . .

LM: I feel that the underground cinema is completely divorced from America.

JM: That is because you don't know what's the real reality of America that really asks to be brought out and developed. (Ibid., 239–40)

One could of course quibble with my point here by questioning how the word "reality" is actually being employed in the particular historical context (the mid-1960s) of my chosen example, and assert that Mekas is summoning to his aid what might be termed a naive "hippie ontology," perhaps inspired by the then-fashionable popular readings of Eastern philosophy. While there is no doubt that in the cult of drugs and Buddhism, "reality" was an ambiguous entity to say the least, Mekas's point of view at the time was nevertheless consistent with his earlier, "pre-sixties" concerns. Perhaps unconsciously there was just so far he could go in accepting the American cinema on its own terms.

The clearest case of what this meant with respect to the qualified nature of Mekas's "conversion" can be found in his famous appreciation of the earlier films of Andy Warhol. In writing on *Poor Little Rich Girl* in 1965, he went back to Italian neorealism for his measuring stick: "It was an old dream of Cesare Zavattini to make a film two hours long which would show two hours from the life of a woman, minute by minute. It was up to Andy Warhol to do it, to show that it could be done, and done beautifully" (ibid., 186). In the following year there were similar echoes in his impassioned defense of *The Chelsea Girls*: "No doubt most of the critics and 'normal' audiences will dismiss *The Chelsea Girls* as having nothing to do either with cinema or 'real' life." Mekas continued by emphasizing the centricity of the latter value: "The terror and hardness that we see in *The Chelsea Girls* is the same terror and hardness that is burning Vietnam; and it's the essence and blood of our culture, of our ways of living; This is the Great Society" (ibid., 257). A heavily politicized critic might have looked at *The Chelsea Girls* and taken Warhol to task for an inner directedness—an ironic detachment (even in the "Hanoi Hannah" sequences) from the political forces erupting in the United States. No doubt the Jonas Mekas of 1955 would have said something vehemently negative along those lines. If anything, *The Chelsea Girls* contains in more pronounced form those attributes of the American avant-garde that he had found positively distasteful in 1955. I find it worth emphasizing that in praising the film Mekas does not adopt, say, an orthodox modernist position, which might have focused on the evolution of cinematic language per se (e.g., Warhol's use of a double screen and the supposed random order of projecting the reels); rather, he finds in it the values he had sought and missed in the American film scene of the mid-fifties: an authenticity and a moral force.

Admittedly, one could make a case that *The Chelsea Girls* is a socially committed document, but frankly I find Zavattini and Warhol to be strange bedfellows indeed. To call a film symptomatic of a social problem is different from saying that it honestly confronts that problem, but Mekas comes close to saying that these are the same thing. That Mekas took a moral, humanistic stance in defending the film should come as no surprise, especially when one considers the turmoil then erupting in the United States. But the next cinema to which he lent his support was on its face more detached even than Warhol's films. Roughly a year after *The Chelsea Girls*, Michael Snow's *Wavelength* appeared, a film that appropriated Warhol's long-take and impersonal camera style—the style that, according to Mekas, had revealed a new, objective, real presence. But Snow willfully shut out the real, and others (Frampton, Gehr, and the like) followed. In engendering a new formalist (or "structuralist") cinema, *Wavelength* was the most important film of 1967; Vietnam made no appearance in it.

That was no accident, for the sociopolitical realities of the time threatened the premises of the avant-garde film movement. Nowhere is this more clear than in the work of Bruce Baillie, who made two particularly impressive films in the mid-sixties that were both political in nature and highly wrought formally: *Mass for the Dakota Sioux* (1963–1964) and *Quixote* (1965). But I find both works troubling, especially the latter, in which the issue of Vietnam creeps in at the end and the inevitable "sloganeering" tears apart the finer sensitivity of the earlier sections. Apparently, Baillie had enormous problems finding a final form for *Quixote*; the work went through a couple of revisions and as a completed work never left its maker fully satisfied. I am venturing that it was precisely the issue of so-called engaged film that caused Baillie some confusion. The following year, 1966, the Vietnam War was more of an issue than ever, and Baillie's art beat a retreat from the social scene into a more purely aesthetic realm, where he created two of his most perfectly realized efforts, *All My Life* and *Castro Street*.

Through the twenty or so years of Mekas's regular public writing, he never lost interest in the wide spectrum of film's manifestations. Even though he became almost entirely identified with the avant-garde, he continued to write about European film—to help reassess Rossellini's "Bergman" films, to celebrate Carl Dreyer—and to defend underappreciated filmmakers on the fringe of the American avant-garde, such as Ricky Leacock and Jerome Hill. In the mid-seventies he even interviewed John Cassavetes, despite the fact that Cassavetes' cinema had less and less to do with the American avant-garde. Mekas's quarrels with Andrew Sarris in the *Village Voice* took Sarris to task not for defending what the latter considered the best of Hollywood, but rather for writing about the kind of cinema he knew little about. In turn, Mekas maintained that there were certain films he did not cover, not because he did not like them, but because others like Sarris gave them sufficient attention. His insistence that the kind of filmmaking Brakhage represented was film "poetry," as opposed to the larger novelistic tradition of the feature narrative, affirmed the cultural continuity of a type of filmmaking that appeared "revolutionary" only to its detractors.

One of Mekas's most eloquent and extended defenses of the poetic film, written after his long relationship with the *Village Voice* was over and during a brief stint with the now-defunct *Soho Weekly News*, brought him to a point, finally, where it appeared he had actually found a way of defending American art on *its* terms—by finding a unique place to put it: "Most poetry, certain kinds and styles of prose, music, painting, etc. will remain restricted, personal, of interest only to those who are pulled to them from inner necessity. And it's the miracle of it all that the human spirit has so many different nooks and corners—including a little corner labeled 'Avant-garde Film'—where one can find privacy of one's soul."[3] Mekas's humanism will not allow him to be alone with his soul with quite the same detached absolutism of, say, Wallace Stevens, just as in

---

[3] Jonas Mekas, "Movie Journal," *Soho Weekly News*, 20 May 1976, 15.

Notes for Jerome he cannot walk alone among the hills on the French Mediterranean coast without recalling that Petrarch once strolled there too. Indeed, he seemed to say in his column that the very "aloneness" of a European was essentially a contradiction in terms: "The soul of a European is full of deep grooves, molds, forms of past cultures. He may even die with his grooves, without escaping them. That is his fate" (Mekas 1972, 27). And if the soul is never alone, then neither is a work of art. In his diaries Mekas quoted a fellow artist-in-exile, ironically one who also has been associated with an American avant-garde, abstract movement, and whose words presumably struck him particularly: "De Kooning: 'There's no way of looking at a work of art by itself; it's not self-evident—it needs a history, it needs a lot of talking about; it's part of a whole man's life' " (Mekas 1960b, 6 August). In plain language not unlike his own, much of the spirit of Jonas Mekas's film criticism, consistent over a thirty-five year period despite apparent bobbings and weavings, is summed up right there: its practical striving for representational completeness, its dogged refusal to lose sight of what he called "the whole human reality."

Bibliography

de Laurot, Edouard L. 1955. "Towards a Theory of Dynamic Realism." *Film Culture* 1:2–14.

Mekas, Jonas. 1955. "The Experimental Film in America." *Film Culture* 3:15–20.

———. 1956. "Editorial." *Film Culture* 10:1–2.

———. 1960a. "Cinema of the New Generation." *Film Culture* 21:1–20.

———. 1960b. Diaries. Anthology Film Archives, New York.

———. 1970. "Editorial Note." In *Film Culture Reader*, ed. P. Adams Sitney, 26. New York: Praeger.

———. 1972. *Movie Journal: The Rise of a New American Cinema, 1959–1971.* New York: Macmillan.

5. Tom Gunning   "Loved Him, Hated It": An Interview with Andrew Sarris

THE SUGGESTION *that I interview Andrew Sarris about his relation to Jonas Mekas brought together two such formative influences on my conception of cinema that I could not resist the opportunity. Sarris's writings on the auteur theory had converted my undergraduate passion for movies into a discovery of the unexpected power of the American commercial cinema. Later, when I was a graduate student, my studies with Annette Michelson and P. Adams Sitney revealed to me the challenges and rewards of the other voice I had basically ignored earlier: Jonas Mekas's advocacy of a radical American cinema existing outside the methods and concerns of commerce. This split has fascinated and provoked me ever since. I have never been able to forget that these nearly opposite forces were articulated in the same seminal journals,* Film Culture *and the* Village Voice, *and that Sarris and Mekas began their careers in criticism closely intertwined—in fact if not in theory. As a film historian I have learned to value the contingency of space and time as much as intellectual differentiations. Sarris here describes both. This interview was conducted at Sarris's New York City apartment on 10 March 1990. What follows is an edited version.*

Gunning: I guess we'll start with history, start at the beginning, start with *Film Culture* and your first meetings.

Sarris: The first time I met Jonas was in the winter of 1954–1955; I think it was the end of '54. The person who introduced us was a man named Roger Tilton who used to give a film course, a rather good course for that time. That was a time when there were very few people teaching film in New York. There was Robert Gessner at NYU and not too many others. It was in Tilton's course that I met Eugene Archer, a formative influence on my thinking at that time. In that period I had been in Columbia College from '46 to '51. I had just gotten out of the army. I had been in the army from '52 to '54. I got out really to complete my degree, get a master's, which

5.1 Editors of *Film Culture*. Back row: Andrew Sarris, Eugene Archer, George Fenin, Adolfas Mekas. Front row: Jonas Mekas, Edouard de Laurot. (The seventh editor, Arlene Croce, was not present for the photograph.)

I still have not gotten, in dramatic literature—dramatic arts, actually. But at this point I was going to Teacher's College of Columbia University; I just took this film course right out of the catalogue, just an extra course. I was expecting to complete some kind of graduate degree at Teacher's College, then maybe teach high school. I was in a low professional state. I had no experience in holding good jobs. Anyway, I met Eugene Archer at that time. He knew a lot about film. He knew more about it than I did; he was more fanatical than I.

And Tilton introduced me to Jonas toward the end of the term. Jonas wasn't a student there, he just knew Tilton. Jonas was looking for someone to help him edit this new magazine, *Film Culture*. One issue had already come out, the first issue. I began editing the second issue and I wrote my first review (a brutal pan of *The Country Girl*) in the second issue. I hadn't really published anything up to this time. So I got my first chance. It was a magazine that had all kinds of people supporting it. It had a huge list of donors.

At that point I didn't know where Jonas came from or who he

was, or what he was. He was just a person with a foreign accent; English was obviously not his first language. And he needed someone to help basically with grammar, to rewrite, because there was a strange group of foreign contributors. I remember there was someone from the Philippines who wrote this strange kind of English. There were also some big names in film history. I think there was something by Kracauer at one point. It was very badly written, and I was surprised because his basic texts are very well written. Obviously editors were helping him a lot with putting stuff in some order.

My first impression of Jonas was that he was a very affable, very friendly person. It was *Jonas*, you know. Jonas has changed less than anyone I knew from that time to this, now that's—what? 1954, that's thirty-six years. And Jonas is very much the same today as he was then. I think he's the same person. It's not that nothing has happened but that there's something, there's some inner core of Jonas that's irreducible. And he was very open about everything. There was no money for editing *Film Culture*, which I understood. But he gave me the opportunity to write.

Gunning: When you first met with Jonas and the magazine was discussed, was there any particular aesthetic attitude that you were told the magazine was going to have?

Sarris: Well, it was that we were serious. There wasn't much else around to compare. Jonas came up with the idea of the magazine, and the very title of the magazine—*Film Culture*—which reminded me of microbes under glass. I thought it was very pretentious, it was laying it on the line, saying "we are something special." It was not "Film Fun" or "Film Pleasure" or "Movies," it was *film*, it was a pretentious kind of thing. But there wasn't much serious consideration of film, pretentious or otherwise, at that time. I mean there were good people scattered around. But there was no institutional focus for it. And that's what Jonas represented. A lot of the people he represented were people from the New York community, documentary people. I remember Helen Levitt, James Agee. (Not the later Hollywood Agee, but the Agee of *The Quiet One*.) The aesthetic emerged out of the seriousness, out of experimental film, out of foreign art films.

The other people who were involved with *Film Culture* at that time, who were influential . . . well, Adolfas Mekas, Jonas's brother, was very influential. George Fenin, and there was a French writer, Edouard de Laurot, who had great influence on Jonas at that time, and who was very au courant with French criticism. Something funny, shortly thereafter—in the period of *Shadows*, I remember we went to see a French film, a Molinaro thriller, some melodrama, and Jonas came out and he said, "Oh, this is not as good as Sam Fuller." And that's the first time I heard Sam Fuller's name, Jonas's was the first mention. That's one of those things that always stuck in my mind. I'd never heard of Sam Fuller. And I don't think it was a direct response that Jonas had. I think de Laurot had read Luc Mollet in France and they were talking about Fuller. But even then I didn't pick up on this whole thing, on genres, on auteurs, on all this stuff. In '54, '55 I did not know about *Cahiers du cinéma*. I had never heard of André Bazin. De Laurot was always saying, "the French say this, and the French say that." But Jonas was not involved with the French directly.

Jonas was not articulating a magazine aesthetic. From the beginning he was articulating a film aesthetic. The odd thing about the magazine—from the beginning it was glossy. I think he had an instinct. . . . He wanted pictures, he didn't want just text. His strength was not in text. It was in pictorial ideas. And there was also a sense of innovation, of going to something new. He had all the antiquarians, Herman G. Weinberg with his column "Coffee, Brandy, and Cigars," which became a kind of comic fixture of the magazine, and the historical articles about Russian film, and so forth. But the heavy hitter at *Film Culture* was mostly de Laurot. And then Archer and I began to specialize in the American and the serious foreign film. We had complete freedom; we could write anything we wanted.

Gunning: So there was an immediate trust between Mekas and you?

Sarris: I was one of those people who had a hell of a time getting any copy in. Mekas was very patient. It was probably the best possible way for somebody like me to get started. Jonas had no editorial authority over me. He couldn't tell me what was good writing. He wasn't the traditional editor. I was the editor, and I edited manuscripts, and did the best I could. But I'm basically a very lazy editor in a way. I'm very fatalistic about it: "You'll find your way," serendipity, that kind of thing. So the magazine was very sloppy, slapdash; it was very unevenly written. Archer came along, who was a much more disciplined, much tighter writer, and he later wrote the big pieces for the magazine.

In 1955 to '56 I began to function as a film person, a person who was doing it, '57, '58. Then things began to change. I kept some relationship with Jonas through the fifties. But, of course, my biggest relation was with Archer. We were virtually collaborating on what would later become *The American Cinema* (but he dropped out)—a lot of the beginnings of it came out of that. But my attitude at that point was very much a hodgepodge of traditional attitudes, very social, very political.

Jonas—it was hard to establish what his politics were. We used to make jokes that he came on a submarine from Lithuania. I heard that he was the Lithuanian poet laureate. I still don't know anything about it. When he went back to Lithuania and did his film on it later, it was a revelation to me. He was a very mysterious person. Where he got started, how he got to know all these people who supported *Film Culture* at the beginning, how he got them just to sign their names, to become a spokesman for all these people. I think there was something in his personality that was open to everything.

There really was very little linking the different segments at the magazine. There were the political people, the antiquarian people, experimental people, there was the gay subculture, much less political than it is now. In fact Jonas wrote a very strong antigay manifesto at one point. I'm not sure Jonas actually wrote it. And through Jonas I began meeting a lot of these people in the underground, in the experimental area, Robert Breer, and Stan Brakhage, Ron Rice, and all these people. It all becomes a muddle after that. I had nothing to do with putting the magazine together. I would just turn in all the copy. And Jonas and various people assisting him would put it together. And also I never had any idea of who read it.

The one thing I want to make clear about Jonas is that I'm not qualified really to evaluate Jonas. If Jonas had never existed (or hadn't come on a submarine from Lithuania) I probably wouldn't be in film today. I had not done anything before, had only a vague interest in film, no real experience. I don't think I'd be here.

Gunning: Is that primarily in terms of just providing an opportunity for your writing, or is it more than that?

Sarris: No, no. In the beginning it was the *Film Culture* thing, that started it. But by 1960 I had pretty much finished my connection with Jonas. A lot of things happened in my life which were complicated. And my relationship with Archer was complicated. But in 1960 I had finally gotten a decent job. All these years my mother supported me, she had a business and supported me. I had really the worst kind of low-paying jobs, or no pay at all—just floundering around and not knowing where I was going, a very disorganized kind of existence. In 1960 I had a job, strangely, with the census. It was an interesting period of my life, very, very complicated. I got this job as a technical officer and it was a good job, paid more money than I'd ever been paid before. And I would have dropped out of the field of film, if I hadn't bumped into Jonas. By this time Archer had gone to Europe on a Fulbright (he started working on the *Times* before that, then he'd gone to Europe on a Fulbright), and he began writing me these long letters about the Cinematheque, about *Cahiers du cinéma*, and these theories. And also I met Richard Roud in '59, he was the first person to explain Bazin to me.

But I was sort of out of this field, and I bumped into Jonas, and he asked me to come to a filming session. He was shooting *Guns of the Trees*. I never took Jonas very seriously. I thought he was a strange person, but interesting—nice. I always got along with Jonas. But you know I didn't consider him the gateway to anything. I bumped into him and he says, "Come on over," someplace in Brooklyn, and he was shooting a scene and I would do a cameo in the scene. I would just come over really to look at it, but also to be in it. Peter Bogdanovich was working one of the cameras, and de Laurot was doing a lot of work, and Jonas was shooting it. I'm in that scene—it wound up on the cutting-room floor. All I did was stand by some books and look at some books with my finger pointing. It was like a parody of regular shooting, which is tedious enough. Here they spent all night for something I don't think ever got on the screen at all. But there were all these people.

And Jonas said, "I just started doing a column for this new publication, the *Village Voice*," which at that time was like a six- or eight-page throwaway, the kind you get at the supermarket. And he said, "Can you fill in for me for a couple of weeks?" This was the big thing that changed my life, even more than *Film Culture*. Without *Film Culture* this would have never happened, he would never say that to me if I hadn't written all those pieces. But the *Voice* changed my life without me knowing it. And I think part of the reason all these things happened with Jonas was that I never took them very seriously, and I was always very casual about them. If I had said, "Oh my God, this is my big chance, tomorrow I'm going to be a star," I think I would have frozen up and I would have bombed. I would have been so scared.

Jonas sent me in off the street to Jerry Tallmer at the *Voice*, who'd never seen me before in his life. I could have been some psychopath who had killed Jonas and decided to take over his column or something. Who knows? I walked in and Tallmer looked at me. Tallmer had written a column some months before I came on telling how a lot of people wrote that they were disgusted with Jonas—that he wasn't a real reviewer, he was so personal, you know the usual. . . .

It was already a contentious paper. Norman Mailer was bitching all the time about how they were ruining his copy in the *Voice*. Everybody was screaming at everyone else. It was near the end of the so-called Eisenhower period and so any kind of Villagey bohemian gesture was really *hot stuff*. It wasn't like the later sixties where it became commonplace. It was a fertile market.

Of course the last thing *I* was was a bohemian. I wasn't even within ten miles of the neighborhood. I knew the Village, I hung around the Village a little bit, but I wasn't that type. I don't know what I wanted . . . basically in life-style I just wanted to be successful, I wanted to be rich, meet all the interesting people in the world. I didn't want to flounder around with a personal vision or anything. So I walked into Tallmer with a review of *Psycho*, of all things, and he ran it and there was a tremendous reaction to it and I did other things, and I stayed.

Now this was '60. In '60 I did several pieces, got a lot of flack. In '61 I did one or two pieces. A lot of things happened. My brother died. This and that. And I went to Europe, I went to Cannes, why I don't know, I still don't know why. I had very little money, but I said, "I want to go to Cannes." And my mother said "OK." Then I spent almost a year in Paris, on my mother's money. And when I came back, I just walked in, Jerry Tallmer was walking out and I just walked in, because I had never taken it all that seriously—after leaving for eight months, I just walked in to start writing again. It was that kind of thing.

So I just walked in and Jonas and I started first of all doing columns together. And that was it. And I was back in the swim, and I was writing for other people. And then I did a couple of big articles for *Film Culture*. At that time it was going into this sort of smaller edition, more print-oriented, more text. It was always struggling for deadlines, articles for *Film Culture*. In the midst of doing heavens knows what—seeing two thousand movies, wasting most of my life. Occasionally getting a job and losing it (because I would see a couple of movies during my lunch hour). So I was a bit of a mess. These things that I was doing, for which I got no money in the beginning, were really building and accumulating, and then came Pauline Kael's attack on my articles on the auteur theory, the debates and all that. And then I began becoming established at the *Voice*, and then I began teaching; gradually things came to a boil.

I knew Jonas from '55 to '65. I mean, I was involved with him through that period. I always lent myself to anything that he suggested. But I always felt this guilt when he became particularly involved in New American Cinema, not *Shadows* so much but the Jack Smith period, his greatest notoriety.

Gunning: With his arrest for screening *Flaming Creatures*, and so on?

Sarris: Yeah, all that stuff. I wasn't part of that. It's guilt on my part that I didn't do more to help him, to help with his problems. My philosophy always was, (a) it wasn't my field, (b) if I couldn't say anything positive I wouldn't say anything negative.

Gunning: The *Cahiers* policy of only positive reviews?

Sarris: No, not *politique* really, it was just personal gratitude. I pushed Adolfas's film *Hallelujah the Hills* at the Montreal festival very strongly. And when I *could* make a real case for something, like Warhol's collaborator, Ronny Tavel (*The Life of Juanita Castro* and so on). I never signed in on the Paul Morrissey thing. Morrissey was an example of someone really smart and sharp, but really cynical. Whereas I felt Tavel had an interesting vision. Brakhage I could never get into. Jonas had become an umbrella figure for a whole movement because he was just completely open.

The whole thing with Jonas was that he wasn't a critical journalist. He was an evangelist. There is something in Jonas that is consistent, this marvelous consistency, the personality, the life, the career. And I think that Jonas's great virtue, or great achievement, is in demonstrating through himself that anything is possible. Jonas goes out and does things that no one had any reason to believe can exist. There is no demonstrable need for them. But he says, "We have to do this," and something happens. I'm the antithesis of that. I'm a disaster freak. I was pessimistic about his enterprises—and *my* position in them. I never felt they were going to lead anywhere. I always worried that I would never make a living, never reach anything. I wasn't quite good enough, I didn't work hard enough, I missed out somewhere. I was always filled with negative, dark feelings. And Jonas was, "Yes, we will do it." And nothing could stop him. And that's something I find awesome. And he was ridiculed frequently, but he endured. He has just endured, and that's what's extraordinary about him.

How important is he, in the ultimate measure of things; did he accomplish anything? It's hard to say. But I think one of the things he accomplished is—he demystified, he did his share in America to demystify the filmmaking process. I don't say that there would have been no independent cinema without him. I think what he did, he opened up the door for so many people, even people who looked down on what he was doing or represented. A lot of people suddenly realized, "Well, if this can be done, I can do something else." I think he opened up everything. In the long run it might be said that he opened up to too many people, and that he was much too generous, much too open. And there were people who didn't really have talent, or who really had to turn themselves inside out to get any attention. There wasn't enough rigor in his aesthetic—but there never is in anybody's.

I think his completely unconditional generosity—everyone came in contact with it—ultimately it's sort of saintly. He's like a guru from a religion I really have never practiced. There's a great deal in my aesthetic religion which is based on cruelty, rejection, and derision, and savagery, and foul humor, and jokes, and cynicism. Jonas has none of that. And he says every expression is sanctified, sacred. It's like a Franciscan aesthetic. And it's difficult to cope with it, but you can't reject it either.

Gunning: That period in the early sixties, the term "New American Cinema," when it combined a lot of different things, Cassavetes as well as the avant-garde—I'm curious what your relationship or attitude to that was.

Sarris: You couldn't find much in common. One question that always came up was money. Some people had money and some people didn't. There were the dilettantes who had individual wealth. Shirley Clarke, people like that, who could put up all the cash from their family money. Joe Strick, an industrialist. Others. . . . I was talking to Andy Warhol one time and he said, "Poor people like Ron Rice always ask me for money." Others were desperately poor. Brakhage was suffering, something frighteningly Christlike about him, suffering for his art, for which there was really not much interest. And the irony was that someone like Warhol used the art racket, the art world, to subsidize movies. Now movies are the one field where you can't fake it. The critics can't give value to things; the public gives value to it, critics don't. At one point Allen Ginsberg, I met him somewhere, said "How do you live? How do you survive?" People were for many years wondering how I managed to work in that world. I didn't come over as somebody who was on an endowment or a trust fund or anything. I was a grubby middle-class person. How did I go through so many years without being gainfully employed, without a job, without teaching? I lived on my mother, but that was neither here nor there, such as it was. Well, the money thing was always there.

The question was, how did Jonas manage? Where did he get his money? There were rumors about the CIA, this and that. Nobody could understand how he kept afloat. And people just kept afloat. And he kept a lot of other people afloat. And people just kept going on and on. Some of the people that we were dealing with were really rough trade, like Kenneth Anger, a violent, wild sexual radicalism kind of thing. In those years there were a lot of questions about that.

But as I said, I was on a different track. The strange thing with Jonas is that we never became personally estranged, even when we may never have seen each other for a long time. Our feelings were always warm toward each other. We knew that basically we were there for each other, we were loyal to each other. Jonas has never questioned any aspect of my aesthetic. Jonas operates by the individual, by the human being, not by what the human being professes. He believes genuinely in individuals singing their song. And he's like a master of ceremonies with all the acts on the same plane; they have the same spiritual value. And my thing was I was interested in American cinema, I had these strange ideas, and well, that was me. And he sees me as one entity, he sees Jack Smith as another entity, he sees Kenneth Anger as something else. And he just particularizes all these people. And these people are as different from each other as they are from the mainstream. But what brings them all together is they *are* doing things. They represent something.

Gunning: It's always struck me (Mekas, in fact, kind of refers to it once in a column in the sixties when he's jabbing you a little bit), that's there a rough similarity between the principles of the auteur theory as you particularly outline them, the idea of the personal filmmaker, and the ideals of Jonas's New American cinema—and also an obvious contrast.

Sarris: I'd say that the big cleavage between us is that Jonas puts a higher value on expression than on communication. I put a very high value on communication. I think you have to reach someone, there has to be an audience there. My rejection of most of the film avant-garde has to do with a fundamental rejection of the idea that movies have the same options that the fine arts—painting and sculpture—do. They don't. Painting and sculpture essentially are spatial and nontemporal. Temporal forms—music, drama, narrative, fiction, literature, cinema—these are time things. And to take time from people, you have to enrich them. You can't just repulse them. Now this is a very complicated argument. And the argument has taken different shapes, different forms, over the years.

Some of the people blamed me. I remember one filmmaker, Stan

Vanderbeek, I think. He got drunk and he said to me, "You killed this movement, destroyed it." Had I really destroyed the movement? If I had used the *Voice* as a vehicle to promote avant-garde film. . . . Now I'm not sure about that. I don't think I could have turned the tide, so to speak. I think things exist apart. It becomes complicated. Now Markopoulos, who is a really nasty, unpleasant person, who really plays hardball, really gets angry, vicious about things, because of this homosexual thing, this homophobic reaction—and who I found very dull, very precise. Somebody wrote a letter, I think one of these people, when *Last Year at Marienbad* was in vogue: "Congratulations to the New American Cinema, or *Last Year at Marienbad* would not have been possible." I interviewed Truffaut in Paris in 1961. Truffaut come out of a screening of a Robert Frank movie, *The Sin of Jesus*. And Truffaut came in and said, "That's the worst movie I've ever seen. I guess I'm just not an original sin boy," in French of course. I think Truffaut wrote something about, "We were very encouraged by *The Little Fugitive*" by Morris Engel. Engel then complained: "Why can't I get any more projects, I started the nouvelle vague, why don't you do something for me?" That kind of thing.

There was another thing. I wasn't as guilty of it as some people. People felt that the only alternative to Hollywood was Europe. The nouvelle vague, or before that, French films—anything foreign was superior to anything American. I didn't buy that entirely. I was in the art-house syndrome, I pushed various people from abroad more than I pushed the comparable alternatives over here. But the people abroad were making what I thought were movies, narrative film. What Jonas was promoting was not narrative—it was documentary or it was experimental. I'm still not convinced that there's that much to it.

Later the argument was refined. From de Laurot you went to the new theoreticians, the people concerned with film structure, like P. Adams Sitney. I had many arguments with Jonas about that. In the sense that there's a fallacy involved. The whole implication of the Bazinian thing is that cinema renews itself over time. It doesn't need formal renewal. It's self-renewing, because life changes, time changes. People talk about new forms, but it's new forms of relation to the content, the visual world which constantly changes, it's evanescent, it's impermanent, it's vanishing. I thought that the American avant-garde became frozen in the sense of the purely visual. I think its future would have been much more interesting if it had concentrated on the documentary aspect, finding new forms for documentary. I don't think it ever could compete with narrative.

The avant-garde had to understand that there were new mythologies created in narrative cinema. Instead you get someone like Markopoulos, who has all these dancing wood sprites, stuff from *The Faerie Queene* or whatever, or ancient mythology. They don't realize that there are new mythologies. That's the thing Cocteau recognized. In Cocteau the new messengers from hell were on motorcycles. This argument was raised a long time ago in France, where a lot of the French intellectuals in the twenties loved the slapstick comedians, the Americans, Chaplin and Keaton. They loved the commercial cinema, the pop cinema if you will, because it had this unconscious energy and created the new mythologies. And mythologies basically, what are they? They're things that people believe. They're not affectations. They serve some social function. There is a market. There's somebody there, there's an audience. Too much of the New American Cinema was: "This is me, and if you don't understand me, something's wrong with you."

So there was this tension all the time, but it wasn't between Jonas and me because we went our separate paths. Now there's one other point I want to make. I owe everything I am to Jonas, but for the most part we don't intersect at all. When I say that I'm grateful, I'm not saying that it's something that's continuous or that it's massive. I'm participating in this project simply to express my gratitude, and my warm feelings and my genuine admiration for the man. But not to indicate in any way that I can give an adequate definition of what I think is an enormous achievement, which I think others are much more qualified to judge. Perhaps no one person can ever judge it because he has touched so many people in one way or another.

But I think that Jonas is a very remarkable person in a lot of ways. I have tremendously warm feelings toward him. I know many good people in this world and he's one of the best people I've ever known and I really both admire and appreciate him. But we really came together in this accidental way. We're both in a different sense mavericks, people on the outside; we'll always be somewhat on the outside. But the main thing is, people survive. That's the best you can say. And I think our ultimate measure is beyond both of us, and somebody else will make the final judgment.

Gunning: I'm very interested in the muddle you're describing, how much the various elements which were in *Film Culture* were not necessarily meant to cohere in any sense. But there is another common denominator that's always struck me, even though I know the differences outweighed the common, shared elements. In the early sixties, when you began writing *The American Cinema*, to praise directors like Sam Fuller or Edgar G. Ulmer was a kind of provocation, even though I'm not saying that was your purpose. And that's something that was shared in a much more polemical and intentional way by the evolving New American Cinema: a sense of underground movies as provocation. I'm curious whether you see that as another kind of accidental overlapping or whether there was some shared area, or where you draw the boundaries?

Sarris: There was an atmosphere that was common to both things—the underground aspect, the covert aspect, the revolutionary aspect. In the one case you have people who are genuinely underground. Very many of them had subversive ideas of one type or another, either political, or social, or sexual, or behavioral, or formal, or artistic ideas. Then there was the second underground thing. It was the perception that a great many things that were considered disreputable, grubby, cheap, vulgar, were really much more interesting than that. And that there was something underneath all of this. The process of getting underneath is basically an intellectual process. It's a high-art process. It's not fandom, it's not just undisciplined enthusiasm. It's overturning something. And I think my generation, the people with whom I identify critically, people at *Cahiers*, people at *Movie*, were in their different ways overthrowing a very pious, proper, socially conscious, socially responsible—but really socially conservative—establishment, mostly a critical establishment. It's like when rock music came in, people said, "Well, what's new about that?" Well, what's new about it is that it just completely overturned everything else. It ended pop music in the way it had been; it destroyed it. The nouvelle vague did a lot of damage, the *Cahiers* people did a lot of damage, I did a lot of damage. You can't make an omelette without breaking a lot of eggs, and a lot of eggs were broken, a lot of eggs that didn't deserve to be broken, not that completely. Now I feel I want to return to film history everything that we dislodged.

Gunning: Such as?

Sarris: I think there is a case to be made at any given time for all kinds of things that were denigrated: Philco Playhouse, even this much overrated Broadway theater in the fifties, social consciousness, Marxist political consciousness. All these things, they were formulated perhaps in naive ways or they were foolish, but I never meant the traditional quality to disappear.

And I think one thing to say about Jonas in this context is that he wasn't overthrowing anything. He was less that kind. But I think some other people took up the cudgels. I was polemical. I'm much more of a dialectician than Jonas. I think everything that goes up, something else has to come down, that's natural. I have a very political instinct, much more so in a way than Jonas does. Jonas is a religious figure. I'm more political. I think that's the difference.

But I think yes, there was a correspondence. Roger Greenspun has pointed out the original cover for the American Cinema issue of *Film Culture*—it wasn't my idea for the cover—which everybody thinks is so brilliant.[1] The American Cineman, a still of the Goldwyn Girls, from *Roman Scandals*, being enslaved. It's so funny. A lot of the things were thought of by other people. I was always much more serious. But gradually I realized that you have to be a little funny, you have to be a little ironic about it. It was all so tentative, all so temporary, it wasn't meant to be so permanent. And it's a process, it's something that keeps on going. I think in a way what Jonas has done is kept going. Things go on and on and that's the important thing. It's not finding something and holding on to it, it's constant change, shedding skins. In that respect I think there was a subtle interpenetration between Jonas and me. But also this thing of being on the outside; it's common to both of us.

You know Jonas has an easier time raising funds. Because he takes something and says, "Look." And people say, "Oh yeah, that's not something you get on PBS. That's really different." It may be ghastly, it may be horrible, it may be amateurish, but it's something different. I can't do that. Because what I show, people say, "Well, is that all?" And I say "Yes, but it's more than you think." And people are less impressed with that, that there is more to all these things. I don't believe in kitsch. There's no such thing as intellectual subjects and nonintellectual subjects. There are intellectuals and nonintellectuals. If you're an intellectual everything is worth thinking about. It's also a Christian thing I have. You know a sparrow falls, it's taken notice of. Everything's in fact observed. And everything's connected to everything else, held together in some way.

So I think there is a relationship. And the fact that these two things happened to coexist, which at first seemed so strange, is not so strange; they were both revolutions of sorts. They had different goals, different objectives, but they had basically the same impetus: to change something, alter something, shake things up. And that's

[1] This was the special issue on American Directors, no. 28 (1963), which provided the basis for Sarris's later book *The American Cinema: Director and Directions, 1929–1968*. —T.G.

what Jonas and I in that upstairs room were launched on without knowing it, perhaps, without knowing the full dimensions of it, or how long it would last, where it would end, where it would go. I consider myself very lucky that I met Jonas, or that I met him again. I don't know where I would have gone without the *Voice*, or *Film Culture*. I cannot imagine my existence today without those two events and in both of them Jonas was central. What more could anyone owe anyone else?

Gunning: To bring up something that's maybe a little more difficult, and you may or may not have much to say about this. But you talked about you in a way thinking more politically and Jonas thinking in a certain way religiously. One thing I remember that's probably not one of the happiest moments between you two is the little cartoon that Jonas drew in *Film Culture* concerning *Far from Vietnam*. Do you remember it? You'd reviewed the film somewhat negatively, or critically, and he'd drawn a little cartoon of you, while people are being killed around you, sitting back and being concerned only with aesthetics.

Sarris: I don't remember that cartoon. I've never engaged in any debate with Jonas. I think Jonas has been with good reason vexed and exasperated with me, and I sort of blocked it out, I sort of ignored it. For one thing I have so many real enemies I don't need my ex-friends jumping on me. Jonas is very emotionally involved with a lot of things, a lot of people whom I hold in complete contempt. And Jonas sees things in them that I don't see, I don't value. But also I'm sort of cantankerous too. I would never do anything to hurt Jonas. At one point I wrote my declaration of independence from Jonas at the *Voice*. But I never undermined Jonas at the *Voice*. I was really very upset when Clay Felker, the new publisher, forced him out. That was not my doing. I was very upset. I'd done everything to prevent that, except the ultimate thing. I never said I'd quit. I never debated with Jonas, because from the very beginning I had a great advantage over him. I basically have a language advantage; I can do much more to him in words than he can do to me. When I attacked the New American Cinema in the *Voice*, some people wrote letters saying I'd like to see Andrew Sarris review *Guns of the Trees*, like I would find it fun to destroy Jonas, which I had no intention of doing. Jonas is entitled to take a few shots at me. I'll give him more shots than that, if he wants. I don't remember that cartoon, or I didn't see it, or I blocked it out.

Gunning: It was in *Film Culture*, I guess around the time the film came out.[2]

Sarris: Oh, it was in *Film Culture*. I'd stopped looking at *Film Culture* then. During Vietnam everybody said stupid things about everyone else, we were very emotional—an awful period.

Pauline Kael's attack on me was very difficult.[3] I couldn't adequately answer it because it was so garrulous and so inconsistent that if I started I'd begin sounding petulant. Pauline also attacked many other journalists in the same article. That's something else that handicapped me answering her. I didn't want to disassociate myself from Jonas. Say, "You can't accuse me of what *he* says." That's what the *Movie* people did. They said, "You can't blame us for what Sarris said." Which I think is a sort of ungracious thing to do to someone with whom you're vaguely allied. And I didn't want to say to Pauline about the guy that gave me my break, "You can't blame me for all that nonsense that Jonas spouts, that's not what I'm saying." So I didn't want to do that. The other problem, of course, the kind of thing only a woman can get away with, these homophobic innuendoes. It's so funny because she was up to her ears with homosexual associations, into the marital stage practically. It was so funny, so odd. And also I was very provincial, very unsophisticated, very vulnerable. And she had a kind of Berkeley hard edge, had a lot of experience, a lot of gruesome experience, of psychosexual wars.

I think that pretentious gloss that Jonas put on the whole enterprise at *Film Culture* in a strange way legitimized my writing in a way that a less pretentious format wouldn't have. Because there was so much pretentious writing, forensic writing, so much bullshit: academic and revolutionary, avant-garde crap, that all these poisonous academic people were exposed to the writing of mine who wouldn't have been otherwise.

And this was the big thing, that Pauline really won in terms of the mainstream. Her argument was embraced by so many people, she became so famous, so popular and everything. It was something that everybody sensed: "You're taking the fun out of the movies. You're taking them too seriously. I mean we like them, but we don't want to think about them." And that's very strong. It was

[2] No. 46 (1968). It is labeled as a column by Mekas that was rejected by the *Village Voice*, and is printed next to Sarris's original *Voice* review of *Far from Vietnam*. — T.G.

[3] The primary reference here is Kael's article "Circus and Squares" in *Film Quarterly* 16, no. 3 (1963), reprinted in Kael's anthology *I Lost It at the Movies*. —T.G.

something I found hard to conquer. Because I enjoy films, I enjoy movies, I enjoy the whole thing, but I don't want to argue "No, we must be serious." It would just be more of the same. So instead I just opted to elevate the stakes of the American cinema. To say well, this is it, there it is, I love fun, and a lot of things in it, but there it is. But there again Jonas gave me that format. The frisson of that cover of that special issue of *Film Culture* I did was something that I hadn't even figured out. It was something that I hadn't figured out at the time. The thing that makes it is that something called *Film Culture* shows this thing that has this ironic subtext—this still from *Roman Scandal*—and it really works. Because people are buoyant as they go into it. And then the writing is sort of allusive and floating and not too tight, not too congested, a lot of pictures of directors, a sense of things happening, a lot of activity—in a scholarly framework. There's a kind of seriousness to the overall context of it, and the content of it. And I've never given full credit to Jonas for that, creating that.

Gunning: Did Jonas actually select the cover picture?

Sarris: I don't remember who selected it. I have a feeling de Laurot selected that. I didn't. I didn't have that much imagination. It's brilliant now in retrospect. I suddenly realize how much it meant. Because it conveys a lot. Because most film enthusiasts are young males, and this wasn't exactly what they had in mind. This wasn't exactly the fun of movies. This was something a little silly. But it sort of typifies the conditions in which movies were made. And the appeal of movies—something silly, yet something strangely effective. And it was brilliant and I didn't appreciate it at the time.

Gunning: To pick up on another of these subterranean connections, I know that even in *The American Cinema* you disassociate yourself from the Maria Montez cult and the way some Hollywood images were used by the underground, but it seems to me there is some relation between your work and that aspect.

Sarris: I can appreciate Maria Montez and Rose Hobart. I understand that, I can buy that, more Rose Hobart than Maria Montez. I always preferred Yvonne DeCarlo because she was *real* ersatz. Maria Montez—Robert Siodmak has a nice quote about her, that she was a sort of Method actress before her time. When she was playing a princess she was all very haughty; if she was playing a slave girl you could just kick her around. She really got into the part.

Gunning: But there was a kind of common ground, as opposed to the critical establishment. The underground appreciated certain aspects of the American cinema. In a way your work allowed films of that sort to be seriously treated.

Sarris: What I did was I brought this French openness toward genre to America. The first wave of attacks on me was all this nonsense. The second wave of attacks was, "There's nothing original about it, so and so did it, these two Frenchmen did this book back here." Actually the model for the issue was an issue of *Cahiers* that did the American directors—not the categories, they didn't break it up in that sense. That was mine. But I never claimed to be original. I had been completely steeped in the whole Griersonian, Eisensteinian, all the basic film histories, all the basic pompous texts, and so forth—I knew all that stuff, I'd gone through Vachel Lindsay and all the best critics. They'd all influenced me. And all the gossip, the magazines, the inside stories. And we knew the movies backward and forward. And when we shook it all up, and thought about it, we said why is it that so little of anything serious is written in America, in English, about the things that really brought us into movies and keep us there. All these things are terrific and nobody says anything about it. Or the things that they say are so silly. Like Kracauer talking about *The Blue Angel*—talking about the corruption of the bourgeois by the fallen woman. All this bullshit, when that isn't what makes these things go. We were past that stage that the people attacking us were at. But one thing Jonas showed me, though, and perhaps I've taken from him in emulation, is that, boy, you can really take a lot of abuse in this world and still . . . Nietzsche says, "Anything that doesn't kill you strengthens you." And anything that didn't stop me in my tracks really made me a little stronger; at least it enabled me to cover my tracks.

Gunning: Looking at *Film Culture*, and also looking at the movements that have collected around Jonas through the years, the Film-Makers' Co-op, the Cinematheque, and Anthology Film Archives, I always thought about how much it forms a sort of New York film culture. There's always been an interesting relation that New York had to Hollywood, of trying to set up an independent center. And that one of the interests Jonas had, even though geographically it doesn't work out quite that simply, was in creating a New York school of film.

Sarris: I think the debate energized a sort of New York school, but it's a school that's hydra-headed, has a lot of different prongs. In the beginning when I was going down to Orchard Street where Jonas had his first offices, really in the slums, railroad apartment kind of thing, there was a feeling down there that it was sort of the fringe

of certain things. But then he began having benefits. I remember
social maven Elsa Maxwell presided at a benefit for *Film Culture* at
the Museum of Modern Art. And then you had the Museum of
Modern Art culture mavens. And later in the sixties you had the
Film Culture world and this potpourri of rich people interested in
the arts. So there was this New York thing. But a lot of it was eter-
nally—like the Cinema 16 crowd—prepared to be disillusioned or
disappointed or suspicious of pomposity. They had a panel of the
independent filmmakers and they had Dylan Thomas and Arthur
Miller. But Dylan Thomas was very conservative aesthetically. He
said "I saw a little movie with a cat running around; we should have
more of that." And everybody cheered and applauded. I remember
Wilfrid Sheed covered Jonas one time, a seminar where Jonas got up
to start speaking. And Sheed went very skeptically to this thing.
And he said, "Jonas made some sense." He began to think about
what Jonas was saying. And then one of these other guys got up, I
don't know if it was Sitney, one of the real hard-core ideologues.
Then we got the real stuff: "You're all excrement, bourgeois cow-
ards, you don't know what art is; you're all a bunch of Philistines."
This was the real stuff, what you came for. This was the period,
Jonas was in the period. You know, the Living Theater and all these
people were coming and saying, "You're all excrement, you're all a
bunch of. . . ." Everybody was eating it up and wanting more. So
there was this kind of New York thing, there was this ferment back
then.

My point of view was . . . I was movie-struck from an early age.
And the fact that Hollywood was so far away, there was something
enchanting about that. I wasn't alienated the way a lot of people
were. That's another reason that I stood out at the *Voice* and *Film
Culture*. I wasn't as angry and as envious as a lot of people there.
And people were fascinated by this. Because one thing about New
Yorkers, they're tired of each other. There are so many people who
share the same sensibility that it gets to be grating. Whereas I was
really out, I wasn't typically New York. I was sort of reacting
against it. And I got a lot of mileage at the *Voice* by puncturing
humanistic critics, humanistic platitudes. People were outraged.

Gunning: Provocation again?

Sarris: But I didn't set out to be provocative. It's just that I am genuinely centrist, genuinely provincial, sentimental, romantic. I'm
not abrasive; I don't want to blow everything up. I just want to get
into all these nice places. But I'm not really in the ultimate sense
opportunistic either, because I carry this feeling for sentiment to

the point of unpopularity. I defend things that everybody else is laughing at. I was outraged by the way people dismissed *The Umbrellas of Cherbourg*.

Where does Jonas fit into this New York sensibility? I think Jonas was a threat in a different way to it. He was unleashing something that a lot of these New York people couldn't be comfortable with. He was unleashing people who were outside the cultural mainstream, who were not on the boards. Jonas was in film first of all, which is not a New York art form. You can tell it's not a New York form. . . . Theater, which is our cottage industry, the *New York Times* will encourage almost any manifestation, however impractical. . . . Movies were not to be taken seriously. So Jonas proceeded to take them seriously.

One of the memorable things I remember about Jonas was when John Lindsay came along as mayor. And Jonas began lecturing him, talking about films in New York. What Lindsay meant by films in New York was Hollywood people shooting in New York. Jonas said "We've been shooting in New York for decades, why don't you recognize us?" It took a form of guts to do that in a formal . . .

Gunning: This was a person-to-person meeting?

Sarris: Person-to-person. And Lindsay, of course, he's about the last person to understand Stan Brakhage. And I just laughed, I had to turn away. I said, "Jonas, how could you, sit and try to tell *Lindsay* about Gregory Markopoulos?" But Jonas didn't say anything, he went ahead and did it. Congratulations. I mean, three cheers for Jonas. I would never do that. I'd be too cynical. Thinking, that obtuse politician, try to talk to *him* about culture? But Jonas. . . . "Talk about films in New York? I'm going to talk about films in New York," boom. Jonas keeps it straight. He's not cynical. That's really something remarkable. New York's the most provincial city in the world I think. And they're proud of their provincialism. It's not simply that it's all here; they think they've gone deeper into everything than anyone else. A rundown suburb of Europe, that's what we are, Eurocentric with a vengeance.

I don't know. I'm grateful to Jonas—I guess. I think the tragedy perhaps of the New American Cinema is that the people that Jonas nurtured weren't talented enough to break out.

Gunning: Do you think that was ever the intention, though?

Sarris: I don't know. You talk about the French avant-garde; Buñuel and Clair made it. Well, did they make it, or did they just use the avant-garde as a stepping-stone to the movie industry? I don't mean break out, I don't mean that they didn't become Steven Spielberg. . . . But I don't think that they created enough work that is really permanent. Does anybody look at Brakhage today?

Gunning: Well as you know, I do. I might add here, knowing your aesthetic position, that when I wanted to teach the course on American avant-garde film at Columbia, you were my main supporter, I mean along with John Belton, of course. There were a lot of people there really trying to prevent that from happening and you really made it happen. So, of course, I do have the attitude that this is important work.

Sarris: I think the avant-garde should be taught. But today, the students wouldn't like it. They're much more crass. I think times have changed.

Gunning: But, curiously, I'm teaching a course on the American avant-garde at Purchase.

Sarris: What's the reaction?

Gunning: It got a larger enrollment than my Hitchcock course. Of course this may have to do with how it fits into their schedules.

Sarris: They like the stuff.

Gunning: Yes. Of course, my worst moments are when they tell me, "We loved your lecture, but we couldn't stand the film."

Sarris: That's it, that's how I feel about Jonas, Love him, hated it. [Laughs.] Well, hate is a strong word, because there is something there, I think there is a field there. It's a field of study, it's there. It exists. As long as it exists, it should be understood, somewhat. I think in the whole process of film I've been involved with . . . to me now, I'm now going back to the thirties. In my cycle I got up to the sixties. I decided I don't want to go to the seventies and eighties—it's too soon for that. So I'm going back to the thirties. And my rationale for going back to the thirties is that I can talk about history. And if I talk about the sixties, all these things that were happening in the sixties, the avant-garde—in some way it's outside history. Whereas *The Graduate, Bonnie and Clyde* are in history. Now I think that is the problem I have, even on the academic level. On the ultimate formal artistic level that's still open. That hasn't been settled.

6. Marjorie Keller   The Apron Strings of Jonas Mekas

WOMEN'S DIARY literature and auto-biography, recently unearthed and reevaluated *as* literature, finds an uncanny likeness in Jonas Mekas's collected film diaries. The famous people fall away, as do the big events and important voices. Even the camera work—that choppy and sometimes raucous cascade of images—is inflected by association with the diaries kept out of economic and psychic necessity by women. While women have not been the only ones to keep meticulous records of personal life, nor to concentrate their energies on a retrospective look at the cumulative details of experience as they add up to a life, theirs has been the most consistent attempt to comprehend the world and the self metonymically. Mekas's cinema emerged at a moment in the historiography of literature that brought to light works so marginalized by dominant literary history that they had become invisible. The rise of the American avant-garde diary film coincided with this reevaluation, and it is possible to place the discoveries of one next to the achievement of the other to some avail. One finds that the appreciation of daily life as a proper subject for cinema provides another crucial, almost inevitable link between literature and film. Moreover, one can see evidence in Mekas's films of subject and style that breaks down what has been theorized as a gender-specific literature—that is, women's literature.

While in literature (and in most cinema) the difference between a diary and an autobiography is generally clear, there is a much more subtle melding of the two that goes on in Mekas's cinema. His diaries are really a retrospective compilation of accumulated footage, linked by commentary, narration, or intertitle. This is a common feature of women's autobiographical writing as well. One often reads diary entries interrupted by general comments, especially in travel diaries meant for those "back home" to read when the journey is completed and the manuscript can be mailed. An example can be found in Elizabeth Geer's touching remarks about the process of recording her life: "I could have written a great deal more if I had had the opportunity. Sometimes I would not get the chance to

In fond memory of Bernice Peterson, whose idea this was.

write for two or three days, and then would have to rise in the night when my babe and all hands were asleep, light a candle and write" (Jeffrey 1979, 26). The rush of daily life on the routes west left little time for contemplating the patterns and implications of events, or even for distinguishing events of consequence from inconsequential ones. Only in formalizing the document for presentation or preservation is the evaluative, summarizing urge obeyed.

It is particularly these and not the more literary diaries, autobiographies, and bildungsromans of Augustine, Stendahl, Flaubert, Rousseau, and Goethe that bear association with Mekas's cinema. One would like—probably Mekas himself would like—these masterpieces to be more of a source, more uniquely antecedent. One of the clues that Mekas's oeuvre is not in the Romantic autobiographical mode is that the moment of his incarnation as a filmmaker does not occur within the work as it does in many autobiographies. Taking as evidence the films themselves, one finds in the earliest footage and Mekas's later commentary the statement that "we" (he and his filmmaker-brother Adolfas) "bought a camera." This is far different from Rousseau's or Wordsworth's calling to literature. Implied in Mekas's comment is the idea that they already were filmmakers: the act of buying the camera was simply the acquisition of a new tool. Sometime between leaving home and arriving in America the transition had been made, and we are not privileged to witness it. In addition, just what kind of filmmaker Mekas was to be was not resolved immediately. Early issues of *Film Culture* and Mekas's first films testify to a different cinematic allegiance than the vocation announced during Mekas's later years as a film critic for the *Village Voice*.

Nor is Mekas's cinema the same kind of spiritual or epistemological quest as the works of Augustine or Descartes (despite Mekas's tongue-in-cheek homage in *Walden*: "I make home movies, therefore I am"); Augustine and Descartes also recount events in life, but to a purposeful or revelatory end. Theirs are much more calculated self-reflections. Their plans are announced and determined before the work begins. The weight of the different aspects of Mekas's films—shooting, editing, adding sound and titles—is more evenly spread. The present of events remains, even in these substantially retrospective works. This is a quality we have come to value in the more marginal diary/autobiographical literature of women as a sign of authenticity. "I was there," the refrain of *Lost, Lost, Lost*, is an assertion that distills the power of the form and provides the key to its appeal.

How specifically can one draw the parallel between Mekas and women diarists and autobiographers? Very specifically. There is evidence that from the earliest recorded "diary" by a woman, Julian of Norwich (1373), two important qualities that link Mekas with this tradition were in place: the nondramatic, nonheroic representation of the self, and the temporality of the fragment (Mason and Green 1979, xiv). For religious as well as domestic women, there is a strong tradition of balancing the service of God and man with the claims of writing. Anne Bradstreet's 1656 *Spiritual Autobiography* documents such an attempt. In the United States, diaries are often catalogues of loneliness (the theme of *Lost, Lost, Lost*). Finally, in at least one of the diaries of women during the migration west in the nineteenth century, that of Laura Downs Clark, the form served as a way to maintain contact with the "imagined company of women," particularly her mother, for whom she wrote (Culley 1985, 9). All these features are analogous to aspects of Mekas's endeavor as a film diarist–autobiographer, and are unique to him. There are other film diarists, to be sure, women as well as men, but none who so thoroughly concern themselves, however unconsciously, with the parallel tradition evolved through women's intimate journals.

There is no father in Mekas's films. (As far as I can determine, the only reference to his father in the films is in *Walden*, reel 1, in which we see a photograph of a man, presumably the elder Mekas.) There is a motherland in *Lost, Lost, Lost*, a mother in *Reminiscences of a Journey to Lithuania*, and a daughter in *Paradise Not Yet Lost (a/k/a Oona's Third Year)*. Except for the masculine presence of Mekas's own voice lamenting the loss of home in the earlier films and proclaiming the moral imperative of simple values in the later, one could imagine these as a woman's films. It is his self as the continuity between mother and daughter that is so unusual. Yes, one might imagine a son or daughter as fixed on the image and loss of a mother, but I know of no other case of a father being as much of a mother himself as Mekas in *Paradise Not Yet Lost*.

When seen in this context, the camera work takes on new meaning. Short bursts of images of daily life, were they shot by a woman, would carry two implications beyond the otherwise formal, aesthetic ones. (1) Shyness and reticence before the subject and an unwillingness to stare, behavior enforced in women's upbringing, are inscribed therein. (2) The grasping for bits of time in the midst of the events of the day is historically asserted as characteristic of women's creative rhythms. Domestic life has its temporal exigencies, and the artistic life is often wedged in between them. For Mekas, the domestic life until his marriage was entirely in bringing to life and nurturing a young film-art community. His films were (and still are to a large extent) made in the gaps. "I had to . . . become practically a midwife. I had to pull out, to hold, to protect all the beautiful things that I saw happening in the cinema. . . . So I kept running around my chickens, cackling, look look how beautiful my chickens are, more beautiful than anything else in the world, and everybody thinks they're ugly ducklings" (Mekas 1972, ix). Mekas is not the first to describe his social function in the arts and literature as a midwife. He takes the metaphor further, however, than his most noted literary precursor, Socrates, who felt it necessary to pull ideas from his students. Mekas is not content merely to help in the nascence of the young cinema. He describes himself as continuing to "mother" the brood (filmmakers and films alike). This aspect of his work has not stopped, even in the maturity of the avant-garde cinema, for Anthology Film Archives is nothing if not the home Mekas created and runs for the films in the tradition.

Whether one can radicalize Mekas's position into a feminist one is an open question. One might argue that his domestic life is not analogous to that of most women, and that entertaining and being entertained by rock stars, political celebrities, and fine artists does not usually make up the quotidian life of women. Further, identifying with women, especially mothers, can often be a form of domination: one usurps their existence by claiming it as one's own. While these criticisms can be leveled at Mekas, an alternative argument can be made using evidence from the diaries of literary and political women that they, in fact, conducted their domestic lives in a similar fashion. Further, there is little evidence of masculine domination in Mekas's representation of women beyond a fascination with certain feminine types.

In *Movie Journal* Mekas chooses as his cinematic *maîtresse* Marie Menken. It is through her that the link to the earlier diaristic tradition can be made. She is the cinematic mother of his genre and another figure whose achievement has been underappreciated. Her films resonate far beyond their quiet surfaces. *Notebook* stands as a portal opening up filmic spaces on their own terms. In the film she presents details of daily life as the jottings in a moving sketchbook, fragments of observation and cinematic creation—little mysteries. The titles of her films provide some clues—*Glimpse of a Garden*, *Arabesque for Kenneth Anger*, and *Notebook* itself all indicate a fleeting look, gesture, jotting. While Mekas makes more sustained and contemplative works, he nevertheless incorporates the fragmented, cutoff, or hurried registering of event or image in his camera work. His debt to Menken is large, although he is not alone in her wake. Brakhage, the maker of "an avant-garde home movie," had, too, paid homage to Menken: "It is the ideology, if you can call it that, of Marie's working processes which have influenced my work. She made me aware that I was freer than I knew" (Brakhage 1982, 93). Brakhage here valorizes freedom, by which he seems to mean aesthetic freedom. Menken opened a Williams-like poetic dailiness to film. Williams's attention to detail—poetry as a series of close-ups—is analogous to Menken's cinematic style, which Brakhage has radically extended. But one reads in Brakhage, too, a kind of Thoreauvian freedom of the individual, a condition easily questioned and dismissed by Mekas (despite his valorization of Thoreau's *Walden* in his film of the same name): "But shouldn't I simply be a humble servant of the filmmakers and do my duty, do at least some good to my fellow humans? Are you telling me that my freedom is more important than to serve men?" (Mekas 1972, x). This is a telling question, one that pertains both to aesthetic and to political freedom. Mekas is not one of the American avant-garde filmmakers known for radical formal achievement. The success of his work has been in the very personal nature of the material, presented with a stylistic freshness, but not with the kind of systematic rigor of his contemporaries. His achievement is measured equally by the genuineness of self-representation and the rich diversity of material registered as present history. Much of it has to do with fledgling independent filmmakers and organizations. Mekas's question, then, involves a partial definition of "freedom" as antithetical to his enterprise as a whole. Neither aesthetic nor social freedom can be separated from the question of how to "serve men." Taking Anne Bradstreet as the paradigm, this is a question found repeatedly in women's private self-examinations.[1] For the most daring of them it meant giving up domesticity entirely in favor of social and political service. For others it required a balance between the traditional work of women in the home, on the farm, and by extension, in the workplace when it was required to keep the home functioning. For only a very few was it ever a clear choice.

One finds a brilliant contrast to Brakhage, and a moving portrait in itself, in Mekas's memoir of Menken and description of her effect on his life:

> We used to sing some old Lithuanian songs together, some of which she still remembered, from her mother, and they were very lyrical. . . . The bits of songs that we used to sing together were about the flower garden, about *a young girl* tending her flower garden. . . . Eh, but you can sit in

[1] Numerous examples can be found in Moffat 1974 (esp. 5) and Culley 1985.

it, you can sit among the flowers of Marie Menken, and they'll fill you with sweetness and heavenly smells, and a certain rare happiness, a joy of life—yes, and maybe sadness, too, but it's all like sitting among flowers and seeing *your own life*.[2]

Mekas here doubles the role of Menken as a progenitor and as a version of himself "as a young girl." Menken's effect on his films, however, is much more encompassing than even this strong personal identification suggests. Near the opening of *Lost, Lost, Lost,* in footage from 1949, Mekas includes a shot of raindrops in a puddle, a standard cinematic trope for sadness. Menken used that very same shot in *Notebook* (circa 1945) as a redemptive image, the patterns of drops seen as infinitely expanding, playful circles. Mekas, champion of Menken, chose to include this image in 1976 in direct quotation. The fact that his shot has a melancholic context of the "displaced" does not lessen the degree of the debt. Further, throughout his films as throughout the diaries of women taken from their homes, the description of loneliness and the identification with certain natural phenomena (particularly rain) are common. The direct proclamations of a prospector's young wife in Denver, 1863 ("I was never so lonely and homesick in all my life") or a Nevada mother ("Lonely day . . . very lonesome . . . town dull and everything lonesome") (Armitage and Jameson 1987, 183) are not much different from the early lament of *Lost, Lost, Lost* in which Mekas is "crying from loneliness" and describes the "long lonely nights." This sad refrain is followed by "spring came slowly" and a picture of Mekas at a magnolia tree, forcing himself into the optimism of renewal. As if in echo of that spring, years later Mekas entitled an interlude in *Walden* "Flowers for Marie Menken."

The progress (one cannot call it plot) of *Lost, Lost, Lost* is the slow acceptance of a new state of being. It is a diary of transition and reconciliation. Its power stems from the discreet balance it strikes between alienation and intimacy. Images of people, children, animals, parks, city streets are glimpsed à la Menken to inspect for traces of "home." Mekas shoots strangers the way others shoot home movies—as if trying to imbue the movie with "home." The sound track functions as resistance in the form of a more distanced contemplation from a later time. It was added shortly before the film's release in 1976.

Mekas had released many hours of film before completing *Lost, Lost, Lost,* thereby putting the film in the position of a flashback for those who followed the diaries as they appeared. The later foot-

[2] Mekas 1972, 414 (italics added).

age functions as a kind of resolution to the problem of transition posed by *Lost, Lost, Lost*. Both *In Between* and *Walden* are more joyous films, celebrating friends and film personalities, beautiful young women, and nature everywhere. Enthusiasm pours from the films. Yet even within these highly energized works, one finds traces of the same longing camera hovering around other people's families, children, and homes. Within Mekas's chronology, it is as if he could center himself in the United States only to a degree. Even in his most fully engaged moments, the specter of the distant Lithuania and the family he left behind creeps in.

Lost, Lost, Lost moves chronologically from the period shortly after the Mekas brothers arrived in America to almost fifteen years later when Mekas was able to acknowledge that he was "putting down roots." Early in the film the camera most often remains on a tripod. Slowly, it is freed and is more and more frequently hand-held. Repeatedly throughout the first part of the work, Mekas films exile families at outings in the park, in places of work, and at ceremonies and meetings, in what seems to be an attempt to cleave to them as his own family. In Prospect Park in Brooklyn, Mekas studies the faces of people at a gathering of displaced persons as if to search them for traces of home (figs. 6.1 and 6.2). There are many women's faces and many babies, often photographed from near ground level, as if from a child's point of view.

6.1 *Lost, Lost, Lost*: Displaced persons, Prospect Park, Brooklyn.

6.2 *Lost, Lost, Lost*: Prospect Park, Brooklyn.

While this is a very personal strategy to reinforce his own identity during this "lost" period, it is also a political one (despite Mekas's disclaimer early in the film that he "did not have much to do with politics"). Mekas situates his portraiture of the many faces of the displaced persons within the context of the usurpation of the sovereignty of Lithuania and the other Baltic states by the Soviet Union. Everyone in the film, except Mekas himself sometimes, looks happy, as if the pain of exile is kept hidden in each countenance. Filmmaking becomes a way of asserting the identity of each of these otherwise invisible souls. When he proclaims on the sound track "I see you, I see your faces, each one is separate in the crowd," it is as if to rail against the anonymity forced on immigrants in the massive flood into New York since the nineteenth century. "I remember you. I was there" is Mekas's manifesto of solidarity addressed to his peers. Alternately, when he says "I hate big nations, big mountains, big wars . . . you always think that you are the only ones. The others do not matter. They should be part of you or speak your language," the "you" is the enemy. That enemy early in *Lost, Lost, Lost* is equally the Soviet Union and the United States. Mekas makes no distinction between the cause of his exile and the place that, however inadequately, embraced him. His resentment stems from the unwelcome embrace and pressure to "speak your language."

The end of the first part of the film signals the beginning of Mekas's accommodation to America. The shift in feeling is obliquely acknowledged through the narration: "I can be useful . . . by building myself and giving myself back to Lithuania" becomes "I must go on this road of no returning." The music changes as well. Until this point there has been an alternation between classical music (particularly Chopin) and Lithuanian folk music, keeping the European traditions central. Just before the "Diaries, Notes, and Sketches" section begins, the music changes to the popular American "Kiss of Fire." The intense longing and backward-looking thrust of the first ten years is channeled into a remembrance of lessened intensity balanced by the new pleasures of the 1960s.

"Rabbit Shit Haikus"—an interlude of vignettes on the set of Adolfas Mekas's *Hallelujah the Hills*—presents the new consciousness in the form of self-portraiture. In very brief shots, Mekas runs through the snow. On the sound track he chants, "The snow, the snow, the snow . . . the childhood, the childhood, the childhood." The cumulative effect is to invoke memory, as if this snow, here and now, is the snow of the past, and the memory is not dependent on returning to the site of childhood. It is joyful, however touched by loss. For the first time in the film, the loss is universalized. We all lose our childhoods and can all find traces of them in the present.

The cinematic style shifts simultaneously. Almost the entire first part of *Lost, Lost, Lost* is clearly focused and well exposed. Much of it is recorded on a tripod. With "Diaries, Notes, and Sketches" comes the much more fluid and staccato single-frame camera work that is characteristic of Mekas. Focus varies in scenes at the Film-Makers' Cooperative as figures approach the camera, trying, it seems, to climb inside the lens. Footage begins to be superimposed. Silhouettes are formed in high contrast with uncorrected backlighting. In the scenes at the Flaherty Film Seminar, Mekas includes footage of himself shot by Ken Jacobs and we see the filmmaker shrouded in a blanket, using the camera as a censer, making holy the flowers and grasses.

The ultimate recognition of his new life on its own terms centers on the renewal of memory. Once Mekas begins to have memories that succeed his arrival in America, the lament of *Lost, Lost, Lost* is finished. In the middle of reel 5 there is a strange interlude in which the narration changes from first to third person and provides a negative imperative. It occurs at the image of a woman's head. (I believe it is the filmmaker Barbara Rubin.) "He was looking at her hair . . . he had seen that hair before. . . . No, no he won't look back." In the context of the rest of the film, Mekas seems to mean that he had seen similar hair before he came to America, and he cautions himself not to fall into melancholy and nostalgia. But that warning is no longer necessary by the end of the film. He has accumulated enough experience of value to him in his exile so that life becomes bearable. The simple act of sitting on a bench triggers the thought: "Memories. Again I have memories. I have been here before."

It was years after he shot the material for *Lost, Lost, Lost* but only one year after editing it that he was able to go to Lithuania with two of the three most important women in his life, his wife, the photographer Hollis Melton, and his daughter Oona. The visit was to his home and to the third woman, his mother. He had been back once before, in 1971, and his visit was the occasion for his great film *Reminiscences of a Journey to Lithuania*. While *Reminiscences* is not the subject of discussion here, it too presents a significant portrait of his mother; at eighty-four she is seen as a vigorous mistress of her own home, equally resistant to the collectivization of Soviet-style farming and to modern plumbing.

The temporality of *Paradise Not Yet Lost (a/k/a Oona's Third Year)* (1979) is complex and exists on the levels of both intention and representation. Like Anne Bradstreet's *Spiritual Autobiography*, it is addressed to the author's children (here, Oona). It will only find its ideal audience when the child matures and can understand and benefit from the morality inscribed in the narration and the flow of images. At the same time, the film bridges generations by bringing the granddaughter to the grandmother and, through various allusions on the sound track, conflates the generations. Mekas himself is the link and becomes the pivotal figure for the women of the earlier and later generations. He is like both the mother and the young girl, and they are like him.

Paradise stands apart from Mekas's other diaries in its direct address on the sound track to an audience of one. Generally, the comment and narration in the diary films is self-absorbed and self-explanatory. Here Mekas is singularly "talking to you, Oona," advising against the pressures of society and cautioning against the loss of innocence.

An image recurrent throughout the diary films suddenly finds itself as the metonymical and philosophical center. The kitchen table is the hub of domestic life. In New York, traveling in America and Europe, and back home in Lithuania, Mekas sees again and again a circle of people gathered to prepare and eat. In Lithuania, Mekas's mother presides over these gatherings (fig. 6.3). Elsewhere the meals take many forms, but their repetition and emphasis with sound and

6.3 *Paradise Not Yet Lost*: Mother Mekas.

commentary reinforces their importance as representations of the site where more than bodies are fed. Mekas presides. The table is the forum for ideas and the passing along of ethical precepts. It is where life, once given, is lived.

My experience watching Jonas Mekas shoot film has been almost exclusively as a guest at his table. Dinner is prepared; children and guests gather. When there is a gap in the work to be done, or in a moment of sheer enthusiasm, Mekas will pick up his Bolex, ready right there, loaded with a film in the making, and rattle off frames, a few or many. If he is needed, the camera is put aside. When he wants to join a toast or a child's game, he might hand the camera to one of us to continue filming. Sometimes a tape recorder is left running unobtrusively on a bookcase when the conversation is particularly lively or serious about the nature of art, the spirit, Lithuania—the valued subjects of the household. Sometimes, as if to mark the occasion as not-to-be-missed, movie lights are added to the camera. Like an overzealous uncle at these times, Mekas makes sure his home movie is going to come out. More often, he is so circumspect with the camera that I do not notice when the shooting stops and he takes his seat again at the head of the table. He moves as if dancing between domestic life and artistic production.

In *Paradise,* Mekas is a child again at his mother's table, identifying himself with Oona there as well as in other acts in the film. She is sometimes identified with his work, as when he calls her "the diarist" after we see her writing in a book (fig. 6.4). Oona's mother is often the cinematographer, allowing Mekas to appear with his daughter. These fragments operate in a special way. The pervasive disembodied voice of the narrator finds its image and the often ponderous sound track finds a lighter counterpart in Mekas's own countenance and figure. He is alternately a ham and a passive subject, running around playfully or sitting serenely engaged in staring back at the camera eye.

Paradise poses the question of audience more radically than any other of his films. Within the loosely defined "diary" film, there is a general sense that these are public documents that use the diary form without its inherent private space, pressing themselves into the space of autobiography. The documentation of dailiness, the personal meditation on one's position in life, and the fragmentary style all signal the diary as a mode of literature and, since Menken, film. But one never surmises that these films were not made to be shown. They balance themselves with a great deal of grace between the *form* of a diary and the structured expression of artistic sensibility. This is perhaps partly a function of the temporality of film-

6.4 *Paradise Not Yet Lost: The diarist, Oona.*

making in which film footage often remains utterly private for many years before it is edited. *Paradise* sets the balance even more precariously, by insisting that "I am talking to you, Oona," either excluding the audience altogether or forcing it to identify itself, as Mekas does, with Oona. I do not believe there is another film in the American avant-garde (or outside it) that moves the spectator to such a choice. Within the thematically similar works that treat childhood, only Brakhage seeks to make himself and the audience see as a child does. But even there, there is a theoretical position of approximation and simulation. He does not expect us to *be* the child, only to attempt to see like one. In the work of Joseph Cornell, another mythologizer of childhood, we can witness his identification with the young girls who mediate the cinematic world he presents. He does not, however, ask us to do more than witness this one-to-one equation except, perhaps, when viewing works made specifically for an individual child or adult. In *Paradise*, to be included as audience, one must abandon oneself to the conflation of Mekas, Oona, and ourselves.

It is the desire to pass along to the next generation the lessons of this one that takes us back to the premise I posed initially. Mekas is of his time insofar as his image-bank is an active and ongoing record of life lived. There had not previously been such a thorough compilation of images of people and events as they touch one man. But these films were being shot and edited while other, similar projects were emerging in many tangential areas of study and research. Oral history projects like those of Studs Terkel; Folkways Records' gathering of songs and singers headed for extinction; labor, African-American, and women's history projects; storytelling conventions to preserve that dying art—all have emerged as significant parts of contemporary American intellectual life and culture during Mekas's career. All these efforts arose from shared desires to preserve soon-to-be-lost traditions for the collective benefit of the next generations. The consequence of this work has been broader, however, elevating neglected aspects of culture and history into visibility within our common heritage. Women's intimate writing has been carried along on this tide.

The autobiographies and published diaries that have surfaced were at first meant for the small audience of offspring who looked for guidance in life to the literary production of their mothers. In the light of the analysis within literary criticism and cinema studies over the last twenty years of images of women, representations of sexuality, and the debate over essentialism as a factor in women's artistic production, Mekas's diary films make him an aesthetic mother, and they can be seen as an anomaly, monkey wrench, or proof of the overwhelming but secret influence of historical women on the work of contemporary male film artists. Mekas crosses a boundary and lives in exile within the idiom of women. He resides, cinematically, very much alone. It has been his good fortune to choose a genre so little explored (by women as well as men) that has allowed him to position himself so dominantly. Yet the price has also been high. This book is the first substantial treatment of Mekas's more than seventeen hours of released film works. One can account for the critical neglect in part by acknowledging the marginality of the tradition as a whole. It is therefore ironic that the reassessment of women's diary literature is perhaps the next step that will allow Mekas's film achievement its full recognition.

Bibliography

Armitage, Susan, and Elizabeth Jameson, eds. 1987. *The Women's West.* Norman: University of Oklahoma Press.

Brakhage, Stan. 1982. *The Brakhage Scrapbook.* New Paltz, N.Y.: Documentext.

Culley, Margo, ed. 1985. *One Day at a Time.* New York: Feminist Press.

Jeffrey, Julie Roy. 1979. *Frontier Women: The Trans-Mississippi West, 1840–1880.* New York: Hill and Wang.

Mason, Mary Grimley, and Carol Hurd Green, eds. 1979. *Journeys: Autobiographical Writings by Women.* Boston: G. K. Hall.

Mekas, Jonas. 1972. *Movie Journal: The Rise of a New American Cinema, 1959–1971.* New York: Macmillan.

Moffat, Mary Jane. 1974. *Revelations.* New York: Vintage.

7. Rudy Burckhardt How I Think I Made Some of My Films

IN 1937 I bought a secondhand 16 mm movie camera, a Victor, for seventeen dollars. There were no film schools then so I began by filming the same things I had been photographing in the streets of New York.

You might call these short early films travelogues when made in an exotic place, or personal documentaries when made in New York, of people moving in the streets of midtown, inventing their own choreography in front of my camera. I intercut with stills or pans of buildings, storefronts, signs, and other details. No wide-angle lenses, no special camera angles. Not filmic in the sense of Eisenstein, who was very influential then.

But a still in a film is different from a photo, since it exists in time. It can appear for a fraction of a second, just long enough for the image to register, or it can linger for a while. A printed photo becomes a fact that cannot change. With a still in film you can never be sure: a wind might ripple through the image, a shadow or some other change occur. I still like stills.

After the war (and three inglorious years in the United States Army) I tried a more ambitious film, *The Climate of New York*, with text from poems by Edwin Denby and music specially written by William Flanagan. It showed buildings in various smoke and weather; morning crowds emerging from the subway, crossing every which way, intent on their destinations; Sunday in deserted Queens with quiet factory buildings, idle strollers, and children playing in empty lots; evening light behind silhouetted buildings; Times Square's many signs at night in Kodachrome color; down into the subway in black and white again; ending with the Brooklyn Bridge and downtown skyline in early morning. Still nothing for Samuel Goldwyn to worry about.

My favorite films in those days were by Buster Keaton, Robert Flaherty, René Clair, and Jean Vigo; Dziga Vertov's *Man with a Movie Camera* I only saw around 1960, so its influence must have been subcutaneous. With Helen Levitt and James Agee's *In the Street* I also felt a real affinity.

One day in 1955 Joseph Cornell called me and asked, "Do you

want to make a film with me?" We met in Union Square on a cloudy, cold Saturday afternoon in December. I brought my camera and he brought a few rolls of-black and-white film. A tripod he considered too technical, not direct enough. We began filming a turned-off fountain under a statue of a woman in flowing robes carrying a baby and leading another child by the hand. Underneath were reliefs of lizards, leaves, and butterflies. I had walked by there many times but never noticed it. We filmed an old man feeding pigeons, boys tumbling in the grass, a young girl running by, but mostly pigeons, starlings, and sparrows, on the ground or silhouetted among bare branches against a cloudy sky. "I'm a sucker for birds," he confided. Later, when we looked at the results, he was often disappointed: "Oh no, that's not what I had in mind." Only rarely did something please him, and a slow, wide smile would light up his face.

In the 1950s, 16 mm films were called experimental, independent, or creative. Maya Deren was showing her surreal, slow-motion films, and Stan Brakhage followed with his hand-held camera and inspired, fluent editing. Amos Vogel's Cinema 16 presented cultural films with elaborate program notes on Sunday mornings, instead of church. I was around but my films did not quite fit in.

Then came the hippie, anti-Hollywood, prosex revolution of the sixties when I was around fifty. I became a fellow traveler as my films were shown more widely and I received a good review from Jonas Mekas in the *Village Voice*, even while he was struggling against censorship and promoting far-out, wild films like Jack Smith's *Flaming Creatures*. Jonas Mekas's weekly column in the *Village Voice*—more often enthusuiastic than critical, and written in an open, conversational style—was widely read, and almost single-handedly he created an audience for underground films. Later, underground films were written about even in *Esquire*, and Kenneth Anger's *Scorpio Rising* became a big hit. Soon Hollywood was borrowing freewheeling camera movements and editing from the underground.

After *Wavelength* by Michael Snow, 16 mm art films then became conceptual, structural, strictly styled, often heavy-handed and humorless. They were written about in *Artform*, relegating my films again to the twilight zone of amateurish insignificance.

However, more recently, at an advanced age, I think my films have at last become avant-garde. They have also been diary or collage films. Without a plan, over a period of a year or two, I collect scenes and images wherever I happen to be, which is mostly New York and rural Maine in the summer. I do not need a tropical paradise anymore. Almost anything, if it is lively or funny or beautiful and has a clear mood, will fit in. If not, I can keep it around for the next film.

For a time Warren Sonbert's silent films, with their sharp, rhythmic editing, like twelve-tone music, almost convinced me my films should be silent as well, with their own inaudible interior music, but then his newest film, *Friendly Witness*, with a sound track of popular songs of the sixties and an overture by Gluck, happily worked together well. Sometimes I will find a piece of music and then set the images to go with its mood and movement. Johann Sebastian Bach's gorgeous keyboard fugues seem especially apt to give a film continuity and irresistible forward movement. And I would like to make a film to Elliott Carter's piano piece *Night Fantasies*.

Finally, here's a poem called *Movieland*. It starts off with some quotes from John Ashbery:

—You must then come up with something to say,
  Anything as long as it's no more than five minutes long—
—It's rapture that counts, and what little
  There is of it is seldom aboveboard
  That's its nature
  What we take our cue from—
—Not something so very strange, but then seeming ordinary
  Is strange too—

Strange	ordinary	ordinary	strange
commonplace	exciting	everyday	exotic
boring	déjà-vu	pedestrian	surreal
truly great	fantastic	a HIT	
	never Hollywood		
auteur	cinema	technically perfect	
angle	close-up	zoom	dolly
cut	dub	budget	
	in the can		

But all was strange.

8. J. Hoberman   The Forest and *The Trees*

FILM HISTORY is filled with would-be
rites of spring. When *Pull My Daisy* had its long-awaited premiere
on 11 November 1959 at the Cinema 16 film society in New York
on a bill with the revised version of John Cassavetes' *Shadows*,
Jonas Mekas used his *Village Voice* column to herald the dawn of a
new epoch in American cinema. Like the Living Theater's production of *The Connection* (championed in the *Voice* five months before), *Pull My Daisy* pointed "toward new directions, new ways out
of the frozen officialdom and midcentury senility of our arts."[1]

For Mekas, this half-hour movie—directed by photographer Robert Frank and painter Alfred Leslie from the third act of an unpro-
duced play by Jack Kerouac (who provided narration in "spontaneous prose"), produced for twenty thousand dollars by Wall Street
investors Jack Dreyfus and Walter Gutman, and featuring Beat poets
Allen Ginsberg, Peter Orlovsky, and Gregory Corso—represented
something more than the first flowering of some new aesthetic. *Pull
My Daisy* renewed the promise of the medium; it was a return to
origins, "to where the true cinema first began, to where Lumière
left off"; it was an implicit reproach to Porter, Griffith, and all those
who followed them, a reminder of the "sense of reality and immediacy that is cinema's first property" (Mekas 1972, 6). In short, *Pull
My Daisy* afforded Mekas—a thirty-seven-year-old Lithuanian immigrant who lived in poverty on Avenue B—license to wipe clean
the slate and reinvent the movies, virtually from scratch.

Pull My Daisy also suited Mekas's other needs. Not for the last
time would he hitch his wagon to an avant-garde star. Although a
rising second-generation abstract expressionist, Alfred Leslie was a
year away from inclusion in a show at the Museum of Modern Art,
while Grove Press would not publish *The Americans*, Frank's extraordinarily influential (and no less controversial) collection, until
January 1960. Still, many of the participants in *Pull My Daisy* were
already culture heroes, and the movement with which they were
associated had occasioned considerable media attention. In early
1959, a few weeks before the *New York Post* began a twelve-part

---

[1] Jonas Mekas, "November 18, 1959: *Pull My Daisy* and the Truth of Cinema," in
Mekas 1972, 5.

series on the "Beat Generation," Ginsburg and Corso were giving public poetry readings at the Gaslight, one of the half-dozen coffeehouses that had proliferated around Bleecker and MacDougal in Greenwich Village. As heralded by *Life's* seven-page spread "Squaresville U.S.A. vs. Beatsville," the autumn of 1959 was the season of the beatnik.[2] *Pull My Daisy* was even reviewed in *Time*— the magazine's fourth piece on the Beats that year ("Endsville" 1959).

But Mekas was not merely being fashionable. *Shadows* was a film that, using the language and ideas with which he now hailed *Pull My Daisy*, Mekas had championed for the past year as a cinematic breakthrough. Entirely reedited and restructured, the film's new version contained less than half the material used in the original; it was half again as long, and considerably more conventional. For Mekas, the evening of 11 November 1959 must have been at least as traumatic as exhilarating. Indeed, his diary entry for that day records a fearful dream: his world has fallen apart. He envisions the planet, half in flames, with great smoldering chunks fissuring off and falling into space.

> At this fateful night I realized that what I have to say, if I have anything to say, I'll be able to say it only as an artist. . . . My realization that I was betrayed by the second version of *Shadows* was the last stone [sic]. It helped me realize that what I was talking about, what I really saw in the first version of *Shadows*, nobody else really saw: I was pursuing my own ideal, my own dream. They didn't know what they had: a blind man's improvisation which depended on chance accidents.

In the short run, *Pull My Daisy* would take *Shadows's* place as the avatar of the new cinema. In the light of history, however, Mekas's extravagant and optimistic claims for both films suggest that

[2] True, the beatnik musical *The Nervous Set* bombed on Broadway, but *The Holy Barbarians,* Lawrence Lipton's quasi-sociological account of beat life in Venice, California, received the front page of the *New York Times Book Review.* Appropriating *Pull My Daisy's* original title, Albert Zugsmith's ridiculous *Beat Generation* opened in late October, as did *Bucket of Blood,* Roger Corman's low-budget satire of the Venice coffeehouse scene. The new CBS sitcom *The Many Loves of Dobie Gillis* brought a comic beatnik to prime-time TV. Indeed, five days after *Pull My Daisy's* premiere, Kerouac—who then had two LPs in release—appeared on the *Steve Allen Plymouth Show* reading selections from *On the Road* and *Visions of Cody.* The new attitude had even infiltrated the Museum of Modern Art; in his review of the show "Sixteen Americans" (which opened a month after *Pull My Daisy* and included Leslie), critic Robert Coates identified Richard Stankiewicz's welded-junk sculptures and Robert Rauschenberg's assemblages as defiantly "Beat [in their] emphasis on the castoff and the commonplace" (Coates 1960, 60).

restless excitement and apocalyptic yearning with which Americans greeted the end of the 1950s. ("Suddenly, it's 1960!" the automobile manufacturers had begun to proclaim as early as 1957.) Prosperity achieved, the impending decade was fraught with some other, as yet mysterious, promise.

New political extremists appeared to challenge the American consensus—the John Birch Society was founded in December 1958, Mike Wallace introduced television viewers to the "Black Muslims" in late 1959, an apocalyptic right-wing army known as the Minutemen appeared in 1960. These were perhaps the latter days; the *Twilight Zone* television series envisioned a postatomic "empty world" no less than three times during the course of its inaugural 1959–1960 season. New York's new governor, Nelson Rockefeller, had initiated a massive civil-defense campaign, predicated on the building of those private fallout shelters that suburban developers would, without irony, term "the family room of tomorrow."

And yet, with the cold war in temporary remission—bomb shelters, sputniks, and missiles notwithstanding—and grandfatherly Eisenhower poised to pass from the scene, there was a sense that for all the bland assurance and harmless enthusiasms of American life, the nation itself was on the brink of some epochal transformation—or cataclysm. Now, predicted Norman Mailer in his *Esquire* account of the 1960 Democratic Convention (itself the quintessential example of new-decade millennialism), "the incredible dullness wreaked upon the American landscape in Eisenhower's eight years . . . a tasteless, sexless, odorless sanctity in architecture, manners, modes, styles," was about to be drenched by that "subterranean river of untapped, ferocious, lonely, and romantic desires, that concentration of ecstasy and violence which is the dream life of the nation" (Mailer 1968, 34, 29).

As black college students staged sit-ins at segregated lunch counters throughout the South, beatniks were joined by folkniks and peaceniks, the spiritual (and actual) children of the Depression radicals. A paradigmatic event in the spring of 1960—as well as an unexpected success—was the 3 May demonstration against the city's annual civil-defense drill. Not just the usual band of War Resisters League and Catholic Worker activists, the ad hoc Civil Defense Protest Committee attracted six hundred supporters to City Hall Park, including such luminaries as Dwight Macdonald and Norman Mailer. There were twenty-six arrests and the event received extensive coverage in the *Voice* (complete with a Feiffer cartoon on the cover), as well as on the new listener-sponsored FM radio station, WBAI. The next week saw a follow-up demonstration at the Women's House of Detention in Greenwich Village. For some political observers, these two manifestations heralded the hoped-for radicalization of the Beats.[3]

Both demonstrations are documented, along with numerous others, in the fourth reel of Mekas's autobiographical epic *Lost, Lost, Lost* (1975). "I recorded it all, I don't know why," Mekas says in his plaintive voice-over. Perhaps he is being disingenuous. Perhaps he has forgotten. In the spring of 1960, his half-destroyed world was— at long last—being made over.

II

> *No feature of the* Village Voice *has stirred up more of a storm over the years than the "Movie Journal" customarily supplied in this space. . . . Jonas Mekas has an interesting talent for infuriating everybody, left, center, and right, avant and arrière, young and old, male and female, rich and poor, hip and square.*
>
> —Jerry Tallmer, "Movie Journal"

Less émigré than displaced person, Jonas Mekas arrived in the United States in late 1949. He left Brooklyn's Lithuanian enclave in 1953 and published the first issue of *Film Culture* in January 1955, but it was not until several years later, when he was living with his brother Adolfas on East Thirteenth Street, that he developed a public persona. In the passage "Life on Avenue B," *Lost, Lost, Lost* emphasizes the brothers' poverty and deprivation. But they were also part of (or at least adjacent to) a burgeoning bohemia—a nexus of Beat poets and coffeehouse troubadours, jazz musicians and Method actors, action painters and apostles of Wilhelm Reich, readers of Kierkegaard, itinerant bongo players, and earnest young students who wore black turtleneck sweaters to off-Broadway plays and foreign films.

It was then that Mekas was invited by Jerry Tallmer to contribute

---

[3] "They want a security that's more cosmic than what the average square wants," *Voice* writer Mary Perot Nichols theorized. "Beatniks are really very political in a strange way. I think there is a relationship between their rejection of politics and their concern over the H-Bomb. . . . The security the Beat person wants is knowing that he's not going to be annihilated in the next ten years" Fred McDarrah, *Kerouac and Friends: A Beat Generation Album* [New York: William Marrow, 1985], 206.

a regular movie column to the *Village Voice*, a neighborhood weekly that made its debut nine months after *Film Culture* and, after an uncertain beginning, had evolved into something resembling the boho paper of record. So it came to pass that, in addition to Allen Ginsberg's review of Jack Kerouac's new novel *The Dharma Bums* and a letter from Dwight Macdonald in praise of cartoonist Jules Feiffer (the *Voice*'s earliest and most resilient star), the 12 November 1958 issue featured the first installment of Jonas Mekas's "Movie Journal."

Reasonably consumer-friendly, the first "Movie Journal" singled out *Pather Panchali* as "still the most inspiring film to see in the Village."[4] That the column had an agenda was soon apparent. Mekas's praise for the Satyajit Ray film as plotless and unprofessional was merely a warm-up. By February 1959, he was calling for "less perfect but more free films" and paraphrasing Rimbaud: "There is no other way to break the frozen cinematic conventions than through a complete derangement of the official cinematic senses."[5] One aspect of this derangement involved opening oneself to a variety of movies. A few weeks after his manifesto, Mekas offered the following suggestions: "Go see [*The*] *Sheepman* if you want to see an intelligently written western; go to see *The Blob* if you want to see a movie that beat artists are crazy about; go to see Maya Deren's *Meshes of the Afternoon* . . . if you want to see a masterpiece."[6] Mekas had already praised Deren's *Very Eye of Night*; a week later, he described the scene at another Deren show: the Living Theater was "bursting with people, sitting everywhere, on the floor, standing by the walls, on the stairway."[7]

The spring's other public manifestations of the avant-garde film scene included Mekas's column in praise of Village resident Len Lye; Rudy Burckhardt's show at the Provincetown Playhouse; and the "Gryphon group" screening organized by Willard Maas at the Living Theater. The 6 May 1959 *Voice* ran a long letter from happenings artist Al Hansen attacking the Gryphon program, which included Stan Brakhage's *Window Water Baby Moving*. Maas's reply, published two weeks later, was no less polemical. Although Mekas, who ignored this contretemps, paid only intermittent attention to experimental cinema, "Movie Journal" appears to have had an im-

[4] Jonas Mekas, "Movie Journal," *Village Voice*, 12 November 1958, 8.

[5] Jonas Mekas, "February 4, 1959: Call for a Derangement of Cinematic Senses," in Mekas 1972, 1.

[6] Jonas Mekas, "Movie Journal," *Village Voice*, 18 February 1959, 8.

[7] Jonas Mekas, "February 25, 1959: Maya Deren and the Film Poem," in Mekas 1972, 3.

mediate effect on would be filmmakers. "Ron Rice called," Mekas noted in his diary. "He says he read my *Voice* column, got all excited, wants to make movies" (Mekas 1960b, 5 May 1959).

The early "Movie Journal," like the early *Film Culture*, was frankly eclectic, more inclined to praise than to decry. Orson Welles's *Touch of Evil* (a *Film Culture* cover) was repeatedly celebrated; Mekas defended Howard Hawks in general and *Rio Bravo* in particular, praised the Billy Wilder comedy *Some Like It Hot*, and proved surprisingly tolerant of Vincente Minnelli's *Gigi*. The column's adversarial nature did not crystallize until the 5 August *Voice*, where Mekas reported that Robert Frank—perhaps the Beat artist crazy for *The Blob*—had chastised him for his generosity toward Otto Preminger's *Anatomy of a Murder*. "My next review of a big Hollywood movie," Mekas promised, "will consist of adjectives only, such as a bad, horrible, boring, disgusting, stupid, ridiculous, etc., etc., interspersed with a few four-letter words. Our old generation of film-makers is so boringly bad and so outdated that all their current films, all unanimously acclaimed by New York reviewers, could be perfectly described by such a collection of adjectives."[8]

It seems hardly coincidental that this same column marks Mekas's first mention of the two films on which, as we have seen, he would pin his hopes—the original version of *Shadows* (already singled out as the winner of *Film Culture*'s first Independent Film Award) and *The Beat Generation* (soon to be retitled *Pull My Daisy*, and eventually to be awarded *Film Culture*'s second Independent Film Award).

Both films were products of specifically New York vanguards. Cassavetes, a young Method actor who appeared as a juvenile delinquent in Don Siegel's *Crime in the Streets* (1956) and an army deserter in Martin Ritt's *Edge of the City* (1957), had "improvised" his hour-long 16 mm featurette out of an acting workshop, exposing some thirty hours of film at a cost of fifteen thousand dollars. The drama of an interracial family was daring; the Times Square and Harlem settings were fresh; the Beat posturing of Ben Carruthers, as well as the jazz score, mainly by Charles Mingus, signified a hipster milieu. The movie was shot in mid-1957 and had its premiere in late 1958, just as Mekas inaugurated "Movie Journal."

Pull My Daisy, made in 35 mm, was programmatic in its celebration of a bohemian life-style. Its action confined almost entirely to a downtown loft, the film featured Ginsberg, Corso, and Orlovsky as themselves—declaiming verse, hanging out, smoking pot, goof-

[8] Jonas Mekas, "Movie Journal," *Village Voice*, 5 August 1959, 6.

ing on squares—with painters Larry Rivers and Alice Neel, composer David Amram (who also did the music), and actress Delphine Seyrig (who, married to Leslie's abstract-expressionist colleague Jack Youngerman, had come to New York to study the Method) in supporting roles.

During the summer of 1959, Mekas completed a survey for the British journal *Sight and Sound* on the state of what would eventually be called the New American Cinema. Citing a group of new filmmakers with "an open contempt for Hollywood," he singled out *Shadows* as the harbinger of this school: "Finished a year ago and screened here for a few midnight shows at the Paris Theater, [it] became a sensation overnight" (Mekas 1959, 119). Then there was *Pull My Daisy*—which Mekas erroneously believed to have been shot, like *Shadows*, without a script. This was "the first truly 'beat' film, in the sense that beat is an expression of the young generation's unconscious rejection of the middle-class way, the businessman's way; an outburst of spontaneity and improvisation as an unconscious opposition to the mechanisation of life" (ibid.). Other films mentioned were two recent documentaries, Lionel Rogosin's *Come Back Africa* and Edward Bland's *Cry of Jazz*, both dealing with institutionalized racism, and Stan Brakhage's 1954 *Desistfilm*.[9]

"All these films reveal an open ear and an open eye for timely, contemporary reality," Mekas wrote.

> They are similar in other respects: in their use of actual locations and direct lighting; their disrespect for plots and written scripts; their use of improvisation. And since their most passionate obsession is to capture life in its most free and spontaneous flight . . . these films could be described as a *spontaneous cinema*. This direction is intimately linked with the general feeling in other areas of life and art: with the ardour for rock and roll; the interest in Zen Buddhism; the development of abstract expressionism (action painting); the emergence of spontaneous prose and New Poetry—all a long-delayed reaction against puritanism and mechanisation of life. (Mekas 1959, 119).

[9] Mekas's inclusion of Brakhage is striking. Among other things, the *Sight and Sound* manifesto constituted an American vanguard in opposition to the prevailing establishment, namely those makers of poetic psychodramas who followed Maya Deren, were championed by Parker Tyler, and, some cases, associated with Willard Maas's "Gryphon" group—mainly Gregory Markopoulos, Charles Boultenhouse, and Curtis Harrington, but also Sidney Peterson, Kenneth Anger, and Brakhage. Mekas had attacked many of these filmmakers, most notoriously for their "conspiracy of homosexuality," four years earlier in *Film Culture 3*.

The *Sight and Sound* piece was Mekas's first attempt to construct and publicize an American new wave. That fall, he praised both François Truffaut's *400 Blows* and Claude Chabrol's *Cousins*; in the last *Voice* of 1959, he announced that, for the past two months, he had been working on his own script, *Guns of the Trees*.

III

The New American Cinema is not an esthetic but primarily an ethical movement. Before any esthetic can be built there are other, more important things to build: the New Man himself.
—Jonas Mekas, "Cinema of the New Generation"

What I want to achieve—ideally—with my film: is overthrow the government.
—Jonas Mekas, Diaries, 11 August 1960

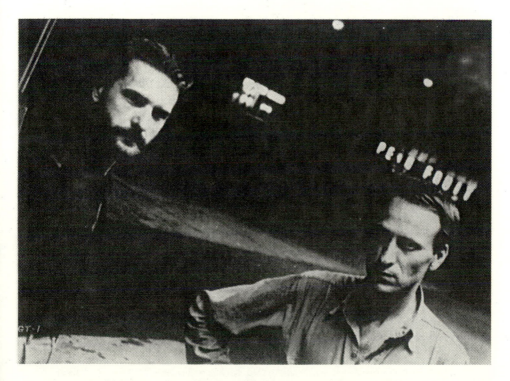

8.1 Adolfas Mekas and Jonas Mekas during the shooting of *Guns of the Trees*, 1960.

Even as Mekas wrote, the New York art world was showing signs of crazy new energy. The canvas was no longer sufficient. It was during the 1959–1960 season that painters began to stage "happenings," screen "underground movies," and sell plaster-of-Paris pie slices in Lower East Side storefronts. In April, Mekas announced the openings of the Bleecker Street Cinema and the New Yorker Theater, the former owned by documentary filmmaker Lionel Rogosin, the latter by occasional film critic Dan Talbot. (It is at the New Yorker that *Pull My Daisy* made its debut in a real movie theater on a bill with Orson Welles's *Magnificent Ambersons*. A decade later, the totemic image of this historic marquee would be emblazoned on the cover of *Film Culture Reader*.)

By the summer of 1960, when *Film Culture* 21 published Mekas's revised manifesto (which elaborated his *Sight and Sound* article by placing *Pull My Daisy* and the like in the context of the British "Free Cinema" and French nouvelle vague), he and *Film Culture* contributor Edouard de Laurot were shooting *Guns of the Trees*. The movie was the manifesto's celluloid corollary, a would be synthesis of *Shadows*'s "texture of dark lonely streets, bars and neon lights" (*Sight and Sound*) and *Pull My Daisy*'s Beat pad and spontaneous hijinks. The stars are Argus Speare Juilliard, Adolfas Mekas, Frances Stillman, and Ben Carruthers, the intense young actor, already being compared to Brando, who had "stolen" *Shadows* (and who agreed with Mekas that Cassavetes ruined the film with his second, "commercial cut").[10]

[10] The *Shadows* controversy was the first great debate of Mekas's career at the *Voice*. After publicly championing the one-hour version of *Shadows* shown at the Paris Theater in late 1958, befriending the filmmaker, and arranging for a subsequent series of screenings at the Ninety-Second Street YM-YWHA, Mekas disowned Cassavetes' virtual remake, attacking the film in the *Voice* (18 November 1959) and subsequently explaining (27 January 1960) that unnamed "distributors" had "succeeded in persuading Cassavetes to re-shoot and re-edit the film, to make it more suitable for the commercial theaters. The result was a bastardized, hybrid movie which had neither the spontaneity of the first version, nor the innocence, nor the freshness. It is this second version that the producers are now sending to festivals and trying to sell. . . . All the virtues which I am bestowing on *Shadows* concern the first version of the film and *only* this version." Between Mekas's two columns, the argument consumed the *Voice*'s letter page. Cassavetes and Cinema 16 programmer Amos Vogel wrote to defend the new *Shadows*; Carruthers wrote in support of Mekas. Before the *Voice* was ultimately closed to further statements, a final salvo was fired by Parker Tyler. In his "For *Shadows*, against *Pull My Daisy*" (Tyler 1962), Tyler praised *Shadows*'s "casual directness," while attacking *Pull My Daisy* as "a designing improvisation"—"arty" and "recherché" ("the scene witnessed by the camera eye is as old as the location of the Provincetown Theater"). If the original *Shadows* was actually more pragmatic than Mekas had imagined ("If we had a writer we would have used a script," Cassavetes told *Film Quarterly* in 1961), *Pull My*

More schematic than its models, *Guns of the Trees* is the story of two young couples—one white and gloomy (Stillman and Adolfas), the other black and life-affirming (Juilliard and Carruthers who, shades of *Shadows*, are, like Frances, called by their real names in the film)—both living under the shadow of the atomic bomb in New York City in 1960. The whole project has a Hegelian flavor: Carruthers meets Allen Ginsberg who, although never seen on screen, declaims a poetic sound track as Kerouac had in *Pull My Daisy*.

Mekas's was not the only ambitious independent feature to begin

8.2 On location for *Guns of the Trees*: Jonas Mekas (left); Frances Stillman and Adolfas Mekas (right).

Daisy was actually less so. Some years later, Leslie himself debunked the myth of *Pull My Daisy* as a "spontaneous documentary"—pointing out that the film employed a script, that a shooting schedule was planned, that the set was dressed, that each scene was rehearsed, marked, and slated. Moreover, Kerouac's narration (which he allegedly improvised off the cuff in a kind of intoxicated trance) was actually recorded four times—and these versions were edited together in the final mix. In short, the extreme informality that characterized *Pull My Daisy* was a deliberate and sophisticated aesthetic strategy (not unlike that illuminated by the identical abstract-expressionist canvases Leslie once polemically painted).

production. The former dancer Shirley Clarke was working on an adaptation of *The Connection;* in New Jersey, Robert Frank had started filming his *Pull My Daisy* follow-up, *The Sin of Jesus* (adapted from the story by Isaac Babel). Mekas took a leave from the *Voice,* entrusting "Movie Journal" to a number of guest columnists, notably Maya Deren and a young *Film Culture* associate, Andrew Sarris. (Sarris took advantage of this break to review *Psycho* and hail Alfred Hitchcock as "the most daring avant-garde filmmaker in America today";[11] Deren, who also criticized Mekas by implying that his praise of the French new wave was a self-serving manifestation of his own desire to make films, was included in a *Voice* survey on neighborhood response to the Democratic Convention, "Kennedy and the Intellectuals.")

That summer, when MGM's adaptation of Kerouac's *Subterraneans* opened to universal derision and Adlai Stevenson's youthful supporters were being termed "beatniks" (Hines 1960), there were intimations that the Beat Generation might become a full-scale counterculture. As noted in a detailed account of the scene in *Dissent,* warm weather brought "a horde of new teenage beats" to Greenwich Village (Polsky 1961, 352). The New York Fire Department raided a number of Village coffeehouses in June, while the *Voice* ran a three-part series on MacDougal Street as "beatnik mecca" and "fruitcake inferno."[12]

On Sunday afternoons, hundreds of folk singers, bongo thumpers, beatniks, tourists, and even locals would gather in concentric circles around the children's wading pool in Washington Square Park. The *New Yorker* came to check out the scene and found the streets "teeming" with "motorcycles, sports cars, Cadillacs, Larks, bicycles, tricycles, little kids, bigger kids, boy gangs, man gangs, girl gangs, young couples, loners, black-garbed Italian ladies in their seventies, panhandlers, book carriers, and Beats of various shapes, sizes, and natures" ("Life Line" 1960). It was a hot summer. Black and Italian teenagers repeatedly scuffled in Washington Square and, two weeks after publishing a plaintive account of antibeatnik persecution at the Newport Jazz Festival, the *Voice* articulated neighborhood fears of a "full-scale 'rumble' " in the park.[13]

[11] Andrew Sarris, "Movie Journal," the *Village Voice*, 11 August 1960, 8.

[12] J. R. Goddard, "Like Man, Where Do We Go from Here?" *Village Voice*, 7 April 1960, 3; J. R. Goddard, "MacDougal Street: Fruitcake Version of Inferno," *Village Voice*, 23 June 1960, 1; J. R. Goddard, "Run Beatnik, Run! to Mecca, 1960," *Village Voice*, 30 June 1960, 3.

[13] "Tension Boils Up in Square but Major Riot Averted," *Village Voice*, 28 July 1960, 1.

Meanwhile, *Guns of the Trees* was experiencing vicissitudes of its own. *Sunday Junction*, Mekas's first attempt at feature filmmaking—directed by Edouard de Laurot—had been abandoned back in 1957 because of "insufficient funds and constant bickering with the police" (Mekas 1959, 119). The making of *Guns of the Trees* entailed similar problems. Mekas's personal diary details all manner of harassment by an assortment of authorities. The filmmakers were accused of trespassing, of spying, of working without a license. On 14 July, Connecticut authorities detained them as "beatniks." It was as if the act of filming were in itself innately subversive. On 25 July, Mekas noted that "during the shooting on the beach, a group of truck drivers stopped their trucks and came to watch us work. One said: 'You are either communists or beatniks.' " At one point, the filmmakers were prevented from shooting on Fulton Street—the police considered them too close to the naval base in New York Harbor. On 25 September, Mekas noted that they were questioned and searched as part of the security surrounding Nikita Khrushchev's notorious shoe-pounding appearance at the United Nations.

Mekas was a sufficiently well-known figure for *Esquire*—which, having commissioned Mailer to cover the Democratic Convention, had entered its ace trend-spotting, "smiling through the apocalypse" phase—to express interest in publishing his shooting diary. (Later, however, the magazine rejected Mekas's notes as arcane, *Guns of the Trees* seeming nothing more than "a flash-in-the-pan beatnik film") (Mekas 1960b, 25 August 1960). Shooting continued into the fall, through the election and beyond. Equipment was stolen, cameras broken, money borrowed—mainly from Dan Talbot—and hunger drove Mekas and his crew to shoplift food from the supermarket. Nevertheless, one delirious "Movie Journal" column boldly predicted that "films will soon be made as easily as written poems, and almost as cheaply. They will be made everywhere and by everybody. The empires of professionalism and big budgets are crumbling. Every day I meet young men and women who sneak into town . . . with reels of film under their coats."[14]

There was also conflict on the set. In his 25 August diary entry, Mekas noted that de Laurot did not understand *Pull My Daisy* and had become an obstruction to *Guns of the Trees*. (On 3 April 1961 he noted that "since November, we have kept Edouard out. Whatever he touches turns into propaganda, stage, or shit.") He decried de Laurot's interference with the actors on the set: "I want Frances

[14] Jonas Mekas, "October 6, 1960: On Film Troubadours," in Mekas 1972, 20.

to be Frances, Benny to be Benny. . . . I want Frances to accept her
fate with a sad helpless submission, as she does in life, and as her
generation does" (Mekas 1960b, 7 November 1960). But Mekas too
seemed confused about his intentions. He wrote that Frances Stillman, who played the suicidal Beat chick, actually was a depressive:
"It is terrible how her part and her life are the same" (Mekas 1960b,
30 October 1960).

The movie wrapped at the end of November—but only temporar-
ily. That winter, while Mekas shot retakes and edited his footage on
Shirley Clarke's moviola (the first cut was some 160 minutes), the
New American Cinema Group voted to establish a distribution outlet, the Film-Makers' Cooperative. Although it took some time for
the Co-op to materialize, exhibition in New York was already expanding: the Bleecker Street Cinema was showing Maya Deren;
there were "independent experimental films" at the Aspects Gallery on East Tenth Street.

In March, Talbot took over the Charles Theater on Avenue B and
an even more subterranean figure, Ken Jacobs, placed an ad in the
Voice announcing a rough-cut screening of his beatnik epic-in-prog-
ress, *Star Spangled to Death*. (Jacobs's early films, made mainly on
Lower Manhattan streets, incorporated the sort of police intervention that plagued *Guns of the Trees*.) Still, "Movie Journal" lan-
guished for Mekas's lack of interest. Increasingly depressed, he
spent the spring tinkering with *Guns of the Trees*, adding material
filmed during the "folk music riot" on Sunday, 9 April, when New
York police battled banned folksingers and their supporters in
Washington Square, as well as during various protests against the
abortive, United States–sponsored invasion of Cuba.

There was another American invasion that spring. In May, *The
Connection* was shown in competition at the Cannes Film Festival.
Ginsberg, Corso, Orlovsky, and "all the 'beat' Americans in Europe
came to Cannes to support us," Shirley Clarke recalled. "Their
'look' was the hit of the festival. . . . The European press went wild
for this new American scene—'Les Beatniks' " (Ward 1982, 19–20).
In mid-June, *Guns of the Trees* had its world premiere at the Spoleto
Film Exposition—which was devoted entirely to the work of American independent filmmakers—on a bill with *Sunday*, a short documentary by Harvard undergraduate Dan Drasin about April's dis-
turbance in Washington Square.

"The mad, insane world has prevented me from finishing this
film," Mekas wrote in his diaries. "It will remain rough, a sketchbook of what I intended it to be, an unfinished poem, a madhouse
sutra, a cry. But I have decided that it should be seen, even in its

unborn form. There is not enough time" (Mekas 1960b, 3 April 1961).

IV
> *[The protagonists of* Guns of the Trees*]*
> *are conscious members of the*
> *generation of the Sixties for whom the*
> *revolution, in all aspects of the human*
> *enterprise which rocked the world from*
> *1905 to 1945, is remote history. Their*
> *world begins with Hiroshima and*
> *threatens to end in nuclear war. They*
> *grew up in a decade corroded by*
> *skepticism, fatalism and despair.*
> —Joseph Freeman, "Awakening of
> Spring: *Guns of the Trees*"

Guns of the Trees is by no means so rough as Mekas suggests. On the contrary, the film is nothing if not deliberate. Framed by shots of the filmmaker reading Shelley's "Prometheus Unbound," the narrative is rigorously overdetermined in its comparison of the two young couples. The white pair are petulantly self-important—Frances whining about the world's ugliness and moodily watching the rain; dour Adolfas, here given the name "Gregory," wondering why she killed herself or comparing himself to Fidel Castro (had Mailer not written of "revolutionaries in Cuba who look like beatniks"? [Mailer 1968, 19]). Ben and Argus, who later married in life as well as the movie, are, by contrast, children of nature.

This racial dialectic is the most open of any Beat movie (Ned Polsky was scarcely the first to note that "Negroes set much of the tone of beat life" [Polsky 1961, 348]), but no less simpleminded for being frank; Mekas buys the noble savage paradigm in toto. Untouched by angst (despite Ben's job as an insurance salesman), Ben and Argus frisk by the Brooklyn Bridge or in an abandoned train yard, sport on their mattress, and riff to Ray Charles. The couples are friends; the blacks try to help their unhappy counterparts. Argus advises Frances to "just live, baby." Ben, after ecstatically pounding on a set of drums, offers a stick to Gregory—who, in a paroxysm of white uptightness, goes catatonic and splits the scene. Argus is pregnant and, just as the entire film unfolds in the aftermath of Frances's suicide, a flash-forward reveals Ben and Argus with their child.

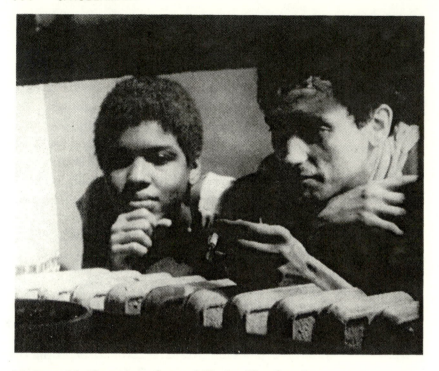

8.3 *Guns of the Trees*: Argus Speare Juilliard and Ben Carruthers.

Guns of the Trees is not overall as formulaic as its narrative structure. The fluid hand-held camera moves suggest early Brakhage (Mekas seems to have taken a good look at *Desistfilm*); the montage is dense and assured. "I attempted to break away from the last remnants of the traditional manner of story telling, using single, disconnected scenes as parts of an accumulative emotional fresco—like an action painter uses his splashes of paint," Mekas explained in *Film Culture* 24 (Mekas 1970, 97). Nor does *Guns of the Trees* lack documentary color. The narrative is played out in a series of automobile graveyards, city dumps, derelict harbors, downtown pads, and (for occasional contrast) unspoiled woods. Events are intermittently interrupted by the antics of two white-faced grotesques cavorting in a field and punctuated with shots of various marches, vigils, "Hands Off Cuba" parades, and antisegregation pickets.

Still, the movie has an impacted, inert quality. Straining to say everything, Mekas falls into grim self-parody. *Guns of the Trees* is not a work that illuminates its time so much as it implodes it. This corny but fascinating time capsule is an anthology of cultural motifs on the cusp of the sixties: police violence in Washington Square, loft parties with earnest banjo pickers, Allen Ginsberg reciting the "Sun Flower Sutra" ("I walked by the banks of the tin-can banana dock"), Ben drunkenly ranting about the execution of Caryl Chessman, Richard Nixon, and the general malaise of the nuclear era: "Let us drink to this beautiful, beautiful atom bomb. . . . We were born pure, goddamn it."

In the context of Mekas's oeuvre, *Guns of the Trees* is an extended digression between the third and fourth reels of *Lost, Lost, Lost.* (Perhaps this is how it should be shown—as a sort of dream that attempts to reconcile the conflicts of *Lost, Lost, Lost*'s waking life.) The autobiography repeats footage and themes from the narrative—the woods, the wasteland, and particularly the political demonstrations. The passage in *Lost, Lost, Lost* introduced by the title "On the Outskirts of New York" and accompanied by bits of Wagner's *Parsifal* might precipitate *Guns of the Trees'* hidden poetry. The movie is filled with veiled autobiographical references. The bar in which Ben's drunken outburst occurs is a Lithuanian dive on Union Street in Williamsburg—"the *verfluchte platz* [damned place] where Al and I spent two years of our lives," Mekas noted in his diary: "Old, dusty, sooty memories, factories, gypsy windows" (Mekas 1960b, 3 October 1960).

But if the Union Street bar was a *verfluchte platz, Guns of the Trees* proved a *verfluchte film.* The movie had its New York premiere in August 1961 at an invitation-only midnight screening at the Bleecker Street Cinema; the first public showings were at Cinema 16 in early December. The reception was brutal. In *Film Quarterly*, Ernest Callenbach called Mekas's film "sophomoric." Cecile Starr, who described it in her New York letter for *Sight and Sound*, reported that "for most people" *Guns of the Trees* is "nearly unbearable." (Still, she compared it favorably to Kubrick's *Fear and Desire.*)[15]

Dwight Macdonald was genially dismissive, writing in *Esquire* that "all that is spontaneous in *Pull My Daisy* is selfconscious here; Ginsberg is inferior to Kerouac as a narrator because he really is rhetorical while Kerouac is mock-rhetorical; here Ginsberg alternates with folk songs, the last refuge of the American left; he is too pompous and they are too simple" (Macdonald 1969, 318–19). A bit later, Pauline Kael weighed in in *The Massachussetts Review*, digressing from an attack on *Last Year at Marienbad* to term Mekas's film "embarrassingly paranoid" (Kael 1966, 170). Jerry Tallmer, who had the toughest job, reviewing *Guns of the Trees* in the *Voice*, was

---

[15] *Guns of the Trees* file, Theater Collection, New York Public Library.

the most diplomatic: Mekas's movie "has some of the virtues and all of the faults of its young, seeking, bewildered creator."[16] When Mekas observed four months later in the *Voice* that "the best of recent cinema is stupid (that includes *The Sin of Jesus* and *Guns of the Trees*),"[17] the paper published a letter accusing him of making a virtue of necessity.

The following summer in *Film Culture*, the venerable Joseph Freeman (who, thirty years before, had published a volume on the new Soviet art) extolled *Guns of the Trees* by setting its characters among those of the Western canon—Ivan Karamazov, Job, Hamlet, Candide, Emma Bovary, Anna Karenina, Hedda Gabler (Freeman, 1962). But, perhaps the best review the film received was from the FBI, which, after *Guns of the Trees'* Cinema 16 screening (had someone reported Ginsberg's line "I dreamt J. Edgar Hoover groped me"?), sent an agent to call on Mekas.

V

There was another "madhouse sutra" unveiled at Spoleto in July 1961—Ron Rice's *Flower Thief*, shot the previous summer on outdated, army-surplus film stock, in and around the Beat precincts of San Francisco's North Beach. Like *Guns of the Trees*, *The Flower Thief* took its inspiration from *Pull My Daisy*. Unlike *Guns of the Trees*, however, *The Flower Thief* was blatantly unscripted and essentially arbitrary, fearlessly regressive, haphazardly constructed, and filled with non sequiturs.

As a movie, *The Flower Thief* may be less talented, perhaps, than persistent, but Rice was fortunate to discover Taylor Mead and wise enough to make the Chaplinesque clowning and impulsive behavior of this wistful, infantile performer the film's center. Rice's locations (an abandoned construction site, a disheveled apartment, a beatnik coffeehouse)—were not so different from Mekas's, but appeared more bucolic, less freighted with symbolic baggage. Similarly, the casual ease with which Rice threw together an assortment of Mozart, blues, and children's records contrasts favorably with the inauthentic folk music Mekas used to score *Guns of the Trees*. That Rice recruited some third-rate coffeehouse ranter instead of Ginsberg to provide an exhoratory voice-over makes his film all the more disarming: "Holy, holy, holy methedrine!" and "Chinese civ-

---

[16] Jerry Tallmer, "Movie Journal," *Village Voice*, 10 August 1961, 9.
[17] Jonas Mekas, "Movie Journal," *Village Voice*, 14 December 1961, 8.

ilization built on opium! American [voice oozing contempt] . . . on Coca-Cola!"

In short, *The Flower Thief* was amiable rather than irate, relaxed and goofy even in its provocations—the mildly blasphemous spoofing of religious statues or the raising of the American flag at Iwo Jima, the daring flashes of bare skin, as when Mead moons the camera or a beatnik couple embraces in the shower. It would have been impossible for Mekas not to respond. "For the new American generation spontaneity serves an ethical purpose," he had written in *Film Culture* 21. "Spontaneity as liberation, as bliss, as a means of freeing one's self from the moral, social cliches, out-dated mores" (Mekas 1960a, 17). Mekas declared *The Flower Thief* "the craziest film ever made, a peak of spontaneous cinema and one of the five landmarks of the new American cinema."[18] (The others: the original *Shadows* and *Pull My Daisy*, of course, plus *The Sin of Jesus* and *Sunday*.)

A further-revised *Guns of the Trees* enjoyed a brief run at the Charles in February 1962, but it was *The Flower Thief* that broke attendance records and kept the Charles open during the summer of 1962—Rice's film, which was praised in the *New York Times*, attacked (along with Mekas's defense) in the *Voice* letters column, and cited by *Newsweek* as exemplifying an "American new wave" ("New Wave" 1962). (As if anticipating this, Ron Rice titled his nonnarrative follow-up *Senseless*, as in *Breathless*.) Mekas ended his review by predicting that "the right camp—those who talk about ideas, cinema—will say again that I am misleading the new American filmmaker, that I am leading him into the daisy fields of irrationality. But that is where the only beauty is left."[19]

The Flower Thief is not only quintessential Beat cinema, but a bridge to that more radical tendency that Mekas would begin to champion in the spring of 1963 as "Baudelairean cinema." This mode, however, was not for him. As a filmmaker, Mekas took a detour through *The Brig*, a cinéma vérité–style documentation of the Living Theater production, and his brother's new wave–inspired *Hallelujah the Hills* (originally *Hallelujah the Woods*), to assimilate the unpretentious cine-jottings of Marie Menken, the return to origins of early Warhol, and Ken Jacobs's anecdotal *Little Stabs at Happiness*. The latter lent its title to the most poignant of Mekas's manifestos, "Some Notes on the New Movies and Happiness" in which he asserted that "It is the so-called serious and engaged citi-

---

[18] Jonas Mekas, "Movie Journal," *Village Voice*, 14 September 1961, 10.
[19] Jonas Mekas, "Movie Journal," *Village Voice*, 19 July 1962, 11.

zen who stiffens the 'armors' of humanity by misleading man with false solutions and changes, by postponing man's realization of the fact that he, really, doesn't know the solutions and that he cannot know and cannot change anything, really" (Mekas 1965, 820–21).

Mekas's new aesthetic seemed the negation of *Guns of the Trees'* commitment: "My anger is not for sale, my anger is here to do some work," he wrote in program notes distributed at *Guns of the Trees* screenings. "Every poet wants to change the status quo of man's spirit, to wake up his consciousness, even if, in order to achieve it, he has to overthrow the government."[20] But it is the fulfillment of yearning that *Guns of the Trees* could never articulate. The image of ice floes breaking up on the Hudson that occurs in both *Guns of the Trees* and *Lost, Lost, Lost* could stand as the former's final shot.

For Mekas, *Guns of the Trees* was a necessary cul-de-sac. In his first column of 1962, he praised Menken's "film poetry free of obvious symbolism and artistic or literary influences."[21] Three weeks later, he wrote:

8.4 Marquee, Charles Theater, February 1962.

[20] Jonas Mekas, "While-U-Wait," leaflet, *Guns of the Trees* file, Film Study Center, Museum of Modern Art, New York.

[21] Jonas Mekas, "January 4, 1962: Praise to Marie Menken, the Film Poet," in Mekas 1972, 46.

Cinema is beginning to move. Cinema is becoming conscious of its steps. Cinema is no longer embarrassed by its own stammering, hesitations, side steps. Until now cinema could move only in a robotlike step, on preplanned tracks, indicated lines. Now it is beginning to move freely, by itself, according to its own wishes and whims, tracing its own steps. Cinema is doing away with theatrics, cinema is searching for its own truth, cinema is mumbling, like Marlon Brando, like James Dean. That's what this is all about: new times, new content, new language.[22]

These were new times. Soon Mekas himself would no longer be embarrassed. He too would abandon preplanned tracks, move freely, do away with theatrics, become spontaneous, put down his gun and light out for the trees.

Bibliography

Coates, Robert. 1960. "The Art Galleries: The 'Beat' Beat in Art." *New Yorker*, 2 January, 60–61.

"Endsville: Zen-Hur." 1959. *Time*, 14 December, 66.

Freeman, Joseph. 1962. "Awakening of Spring: *Guns of the Trees.*" *Film Culture* 25:26–30.

Hines, Leo. 1960. "Stevenson and the Beats." *Commonweal* 72, no. 19 (9 September): 465–67.

Kael, Pauline. 1966. "The Come-Dressed-as-the-Sick-Soul-of-Europe-Party." In *I Lost It at the Movies*. New York: Bantam.

"Life Line." 1960. *New Yorker*, 6 August, 21–23.

McDarrah, Fred. 1985. *Kerouac and Friends: A Beat Generation Album*. New York: William Morrow.

Macdonald, Dwight. 1969. "Some Animadversions on the Art Film." In *Dwight Macdonald on Movies*. Englewood Cliffs, N.J.: Prentice-Hall.

Mailer, Norman. 1968. "Superman Comes to the Supermarket." In *The Idol and the Octopus*. New York: Putnam.

Mekas, Jonas. 1959. "New York Letter: Towards a Spontaneous Cinema." *Sight and Sound* 28, no. 3–4:118–21.

———. 1960a. "Cinema of the New Generation." *Film Culture* 21:1–20.

———. 1960b. Diaries. Anthology Film Archives, New York.

[22] Jonas Mekas, "January 25, 1962: The Changing Language of Cinema," in Mekas 1972, 49.

Mekas, Jonas. 1965. "Notes on Some New Movies and Happiness." In *Film Culture Reader*, 317–25. *See* Sitney 1970.

————. 1970. "Notes on the New American Cinema." In *Film Culture Reader*, 87–107. *See* Sitney 1970.

————. 1972. *Movie Journal: The Rise of a New American Cinema, 1959–1971*. New York: Macmillan.

"New Wave, U.S.A." 1962. *Newsweek*, 30 July, 76.

Polsky, Ned. 1961. "The Village Beat Scene: Summer 1960." *Dissent* 8, no. 3 (Summer): 339–59.

Sitney, P. Adams, ed. 1970. *Film Culture Reader*. New York: Praeger.

Tyler, Parker. 1962. "For *Shadows*, against *Pull My Daisy*." *Film Culture* 24:24–33.

Ward, Melinda. 1982. "Shirley Clarke: An Interview." In *The American New Wave: 1958–1967*, 18–25. Minneapolis: Walker Art Center.

9. Vyt Bakaitis

Notes on Displacement: The Poems and Diary Films of Jonas Mekas

THE YEAR 1955, when Jonas Mekas was largely preoccupied with launching the first issue of *Film Culture*, also saw the New York publication of his first book of poems, *Semeniškių idilės* (*The Idylls of Semeniškiai*) (Mekas 1955).[1] The work had been published seven years earlier in postwar Germany, although in a much abbreviated, mimeographed version, due to material shortages and the restrictions on book production then prevailing (Mekas 1948). Its expanded second edition earned him the Vincas Krėvė Prize, sponsored by the loosely knit North American community of exiled Lithuanian writers. This prestigious award, presented to Mekas in a simple ceremony in Montreal in 1957, only confirmed what had become evident during the preceding decade: that its author ranked among the leading poets writing in Lithuanian, a vital albeit minor language central to an ancient East European culture settled along the Baltic Sea. There is a certain irony in the fact that when the book finally came to be published in his native Lithuania in 1971, this "home" edition for the first time included the complete set of *Idylls*, restoring sections that, essentially for considerations of space, had been kept out of both previously printed versions (Mekas 1971, 9–68).

Counting the *Idylls*, Mekas has published six separate books of poems under the imprint and aegis of several Lithuanian-language publishers, the last two by the author himself. The other titles—in order of issue—are: *Gėlių kalbėjimas* (*Flower Talk*) (Mekas 1961); *Pavieniai žodžiai* (*Words Apart*), (Mekas 1967); *Poezija* (*Poetry*) (Mekas 1971); *Reminiscensijos* (*Reminiscences*) (Mekas 1972); and *Dienoraščiai, 1970–1982* (*Datebook 1970–1982*) (Mekas 1985). All were written in Lithuanian and to date have been available only in Lithuanian-language editions, although a few poems excerpted from the earlier books have cropped up sporadically over the years in versions prepared by various translators for fugitive periodicals and an-

[1] Some of the verse translations in this chapter have had prior publication in *Beatitude*, *City Lights Review*, *Literary Review*, and *Translation*.

thologies now out of print. This situation is soon to change, for there is a consolidated edition of English translations of Mekas's poems currently in production.[2]

Overall, his poems constitute as significant and diverse a body of work as his films. While his work as a poet precedes and parallels his film career, there are enough similarities even beyond recurring themes and titles to allow comparisons to be drawn, the only telling point of exclusion being the admittedly large one of language. His poems and diary films are both organized responses to the primacy of experience as fundamentally perceived, according to Rimbaud's phrase, "under the eye of childhood." But the poems rely entirely on the resources and strategies of a plain language, composed in flowing cadences that absorb and transcend the easy repetitions of ordinary speech. Words conveying significant details or lyric associations often carry for emphasis the specific dialect textures and local usages from the immediate region of Mekas's childhood, some hitherto unassimilated into formal writing. The diary films, on the other hand, while extending and developing the process of poetic rumination, for the most part use language in voice-overs or title-cards in a secondary, essentially complementary mode. But even here, the halting, idiosyncratic, sometimes unplaceable English of Mekas's voice-overs lends his spoken words the weight and manner of authentic personality, a kind of local color by default.

Two rare but notable types of formal variation link the poetic and the cinematic, as elements augmenting each other by conscious imitation. The most playful example of one occurs in the sequence of Rabbit Shit Haikus from *Lost, Lost, Lost,* with the invoked verse form rendered implicitly as a cadence in briskly edited close-ups of a wintry landscape. The other is the outright poetic statement, given perhaps most significantly in the following title-card from *In Between*:

A king with a few soldiers
returns from war to find his
own palaces burned. He is
loaded with gifts. He stands
and cries, or just looks,
without dismounting
from the horse. Then he makes

---

[2] As yet untitled, though scheduled for publication (New York: Black Thistle Press, 1992), the projected book is the source for all English versions of the Mekas poems quoted herein, with the exception of the lines from *Reminiscensijos*; these are from a complete translation, titled "Reminiscences," by Vyt Bakaitis and Roland Grybauskas (Mekas 1988). All the rest are by the author of this essay.

a gesture to the others, in
silence, and they continue riding.

By itself, this is already a concise parable of mutability, and in its immediate context, it lends itself to being read as yet another excerpt from an author typically preoccupied with keeping his "notes and sketches" intact, "in the rough," really, within the larger structure. But it also suggests a larger (perhaps also an "ideal," and therefore unrealizable) scenario; "He stands and cries, or just looks" is equally valid as a compressed statement of the futility of grief and as a director's shorthand, preliminary to cueing a reaction shot. The film then closes with footage of an isolated young banjo picker's long wordless blues solo indoors, while the evening sun comes down on his city.

There are two other typical, though considerably less frequent, instances of language directly allied to Mekas's films. On-site voice recordings, for one, serve as approximate overlays, out of sync with the accompanying footage, and range from brief added touches of atmosphere (random street-cries) or characterization (particular vocal inflections, most notable for introducing the author's mother, speaking in Lithuanian) to extended excerpts of unrehearsed conversation. For the other, occurring less often, there are the close-up scans of incomplete textual passages, such as the glancing scrutiny of lines from Mekas's diary in typescript or from a printed edition of Thoreau's *Walden*. Related in style to the latter, although it is spoken rather than seen, is the instance of Mekas reading from John of the Cross to accompany the Millbrook footage in *Walden*; his delivery is unusually strained, almost the tentative reading of a beginner, laboring to glean a spiritual lesson in the context of hallucinatory-drug research.

Yet such distinctions between the workings of film and poetry remain procedural, since the forms pursue parallel processes of systematic notation in sorting the evidence of a mind's swirling activity around the fulcrum of memory—or rather, "tiny fragments, memories" as a title-card in *Paradise Not Yet Lost* suggests. The diary films and poems are all tied to the same knot of tensions. They all aggregate ever more remotely coalescing particles and link them to a nucleus. Yet simultaneously, each work also carries its metaphor of paradise to counter the grittiness of actuality; each text seeks to illuminate and sustain the currency of the author's earliest experience.

Often the films take up and recapitulate the concerns of the poems. The crucial theme for both is a jarring, aggravated sense of homelessness that gnaws in Mekas's work with the all-absorbing persistence of an unhealed wound. In its keenest sense, this local and personal deprivation registers as a series of offsetting shocks, at once social and moral, cultural and communal, divergent incongruities that prompt a desperate and constantly renewed search for self-definition. The act of "asking / where / I / am // and / what / I / am" (*Words Apart*, 2.1.46–52)[3] becomes a self-perpetuating crisis that always begs resolution; as the overall predicament evolves from moment to moment, with new demands for assurances of existence to counter the increasing odds against it, any resolution proves ambiguous at best.

> I learned my geography
> from war
> maps.
>
> Human anatomy
> I came to grasp
> from
> accounts of
> concentration camps.   (*Datebook*, 28)

The menace of history, enlarged in this century through mass deportations and executions, only confirms an ever more drastic need for hope. Poetry is one version of such hope, however diminished its effective range for public discourse may have become. Indeed, Czeslaw Milosz has proposed that its inherent restriction to the field of individual conscience, within the wreckage that accumulates from shifts in technologies and ideologies, leaves poetry in the unique situation of extending hope. In *The Witness of Poetry* (Milosz 1983), Milosz delineates the provenance of this proposition in several individually advanced programs of rebellion developed in European Romanticism, starting with William Blake's, which constitute a visionary tradition, one that would restore a spiritual dimension to human possibility by drawing on whatever spontaneity is still accessible and as yet unexhausted; Whitman is his American example. Such poetry keeps the imagination allied to memory, in trust for the collectivity of human experience, even at ground zero. However, there are certain clear parallels in modern art: the "fragments" T. S. Eliot "shored against [his] ruin" and the transforming ambiguity surviving the bleaker post-1945 landscape reflected in Samuel Beckett's texts (Beckett 1977).

---

[3] Line references are intended to accord with their Lithuanian-language originals in the editions cited above.

Mekas's displacement arises from the fact of his literal uprooted-
ness and the consequent irretrievable loss of both clear-eyed childhood vision and communal stability. Yet he has never given up the
Romantic expectation of finding illumination in the mystery of ordinary everyday awareness. To survive in the world means somehow to live in it. An actual "here and now" is the given of Mekas's
work, yet it aspires to a total reclamation.

I
look for
new
forms
which
would
let me
let me
disclose
the whole
memory
of my
experience.   (*Words Apart*, 2.2.1–13)

Such nostalgia carries great risk, recalling Basil Bunting's line: "It
is easier to die than to remember" (Bunting 1978, 42). This recovery
of the hard particulars of circumstance from the verge of sentimental dissolution suggests grief doubling back on itself. Yet for all the
personal quandary or spiritual qualm, the gain is evident throughout Mekas's work in persuasive instances of exemplary ordinariness, quickened at each modest reiteration with a palpable tenacity.

It's just
this image

just this
river
-willow
a bird swings

just this
burning
sun
in the lips
of a stream

just this.   (*Words Apart*, 1.4)

That poetry certifies an ideal of regeneration beyond resistance to oppression is a commonplace of Romantic poetics; its crux abides in what Charles Olson called "the root act" (Olson 1966, 13), an undeniable undercurrent of moral rage that, once it is tapped, becomes as forceful and articulate as springwater surfacing.

> But I'll say no,
> from basic principle,
> like salt. 						*(Datebook,* 10.9–12)

The interludes that celebrate vigils of such redemptive protest kept by the "women for peace" in *Walden* and *Lost, Lost, Lost* corroborate the earlier tributes to village women, which form central paeans in the *Idylls.* Each restatement patiently extends a sustaining immanence. Instruction regarding method is given in the course of an elaborate montage that chronicles an aborted journey to a Flaherty symposium by some "monks of cinema" in *Lost, Lost, Lost.* The mock-ritual and elegant goofing, in which the monks and their muses greet the dawning day, contain a spell of gestural abstraction that registers onscreen as an arching blur of lawn and sky. An inserted shot by Ken Jacobs of this stylized frolic reveals that Mekas achieved his exposure by sweeping his camera at arm's length back and forth before him. His gesture here duplicates the seasoned armswing with which he handles a scythe, in the brief moments of mowing depicted in *Reminiscences of a Journey to Lithuania.*

By a minute elaboration of gleaned particulars, much like the "100 Glimpses of Lithuania" in the film *Reminiscences,* scenes and images recollected in the poems are made to seem like shudders before eternity. Against the impositions of mortality and fate (the dust "falling everywhere" in the first part of *Walden)* the poet invokes his "childhood / sunlight classics." A similar spirit underlies the colorful montage of Mediterranean theatrics that contrasts actors from the Living Theater, engaged in simple physical exercises, with barnyard animals strutting and posing nearby, in *Notes for Jerome.*

While the values Mekas proclaims and celebrates are Romantic and idealist, his formal procedures are modernist. His diary films and the poems after *Words Apart* all depend on modernist compression and fragmentation, with the films showing a remarkable structural kinship to Ezra Pound's *Cantos.* Both employ an open-ended, ongoing, and epic life's-journey vastness of scope to register a disjointed, grainy disaffection with "a botched civilization," and both interject a vernacular voice.

"*Laukas*: a field as wide as childhood." This title-card from *Rem-*

iniscences also defines the poet's field of vision, which first takes in and then supplants the stultifying condition of exile. "The perfecting micrology of the artist" (in F. W. Schlegel's apt phrase) provides a defined topography that, if it needs a name, already has the name of his home village: Semeniškiai. (In Lithuanian, the word derives from "a locus for clan or family," and therefore, literally, the home place, which is at least as precisely targeted as the bearings "latitude 55 deg 31 min N, longitude 25 deg 3 min E" for the same location, first coordinated for the United States Army Topographic Command, and subsequently made available to interested researchers at American public libraries, courtesy of the Central Intelligence Agency.)

Mad Europe hurt him into poetry, to paraphrase Auden on Yeats. A signal instance of how Mekas's displacement informs his sensibility occurs in the following excerpt from *In Between*: "Oh Salvador Dali, what made you into a clown?" (Pause.) "Being away from the roots . . . that's what made me into a clown." Far from representing an actual exchange, this ballad-style report delivered entirely in the author's off-camera, improvisatory voice holds to a formula standard for several folk traditions. It accompanies footage of Dali spraying cream on a classically posed female model, standing outdoors in a city square before a discreetly distanced audience. Yet immediately startling as the commentary is, the brusque accusation remains unclear until a change of scene brings on the following voice-over explanation from Mekas: "I had never enough to eat, in those days. I lived on hamburgers and grilled cheese sandwiches. I thought I belonged to a generation who never ate enough. Whenever I was in a situation of being able to eat, I played a fool." This time the visual accompaniment shows Mekas himself with mock exuberance cutting into a thick steak and vigorously chewing each bite, as though the earlier stern judge had now condemned him to play the clown. The gallant Pierrot or dapper Chaplin who tips his exquisite pain into comic relief with each pratfall is here invoked in an ironic self-appraisal as a holy fool.

There is a groundswell of nostalgia to each obsessive reference to the theme of community in *Idylls*, which Mekas wrote over the winter of 1947–1948, but the surface of the work in the main does not show this. Mekas is a poet with a physical sense of place, and the cyclical structure of these free-form bucolics evolves variations on the theme of seasonal change in the countryside and the corresponding rituals of farm work. At least two large ambiguities traverse this design: the accrual of a seemingly random selection of impressions to suggest the timeliness of rural, communal life, and the wider resonances of sensuous local details. The source (in the original-language versions, at least) is an underlying enthusiasm that links clarity of detail with virtuosic elaborations of common speech.

Old is rain gushing down shrubstems,
and cockgrouse drumming in red midsummer dawn.
Old is our talk of this.

And of the fields, yellowing barley and oats,
and cowherd fires wetblown in lonesome autumn.
Of potato digs,
heavy summer heat,
white glare and sleigh-din down an unending winter road.
Of heavy timber hauls, the fallow to be cleared,
red brick ovens, the outlying limerock.
And—by the evening lamps, in autumn, while fields turn gray—
of wagonloads ready for tomorrow's market,
the roads, in October, washed out and swamped,
the potato digs drenched.

Old is our life here, long generations
pacing the fields off, wearing down plowland,
each foot of earth able to speak, still breathing of fathers!
Out of these cool stone wells
they drew water for their returning herds,
and when the flooring in the house wore down,
or the back wall quietly started to crumble,
they went out to the same pits to dig up yellow clay
and dragged fresh sand back from the same fields.
And even with us gone
there will be others, sitting out on blue fieldstones,
mowing the overgrown meadows, plowing these plains,
and when they come in at the end of their day and sit down to the
    tables,
each table, each clay jug,
each beam in the wall will speak,
and they will have the sandbanks to remember, glowing wide open,
the ryefields swaying in the wind,
the sad songs of our women from the far side of a flax field,
and one smell, the first time in a new parlor,
a scent of fresh moss!

Oh, old is the flowering clover,
horses snorting in the summer night,
rollers, harrows and plows scouring tillage,
the heavy millstones stumbling,

and women weeding the rows, their kerchiefs glimmering white.
Old is rain gushing down shrubstems,
and cockgrouse drumming in red midsummer dawn.
Old is our talk of all this.

(*Idylls*, 1)

The initial stress on senescence keynotes a litany of loss that nevertheless rises on the urgency of its lament to an exuberant close. As it gradually shifts toward more dynamic vistas, the poem simply announces what is to be the lifeline for the rest of the book: "And even with us gone / there will be others." A series of elegies recalls a traditional way of life and its ritual chores determined by the recurring seasons:

So even now,
way back where days fade beyond return from the horizon,
I still see you, the women of my childhood.

(*Idylls*, 13.59–61)

Fate is centrally linked to natural process in this vision:

as though each pace is bound to take forever,
a farmer walks in step with his fate:
the wind heaves, and his overcoat swerves
just like the crouching alder bush.

(*Idylls*, 26.24–27)

Composed in the dead of winter of 1950–1951, while Mekas was living in a bleak neighborhood in Brooklyn, the extended poem *Reminiscences* is a meditation on the poet's experience of the immediate postwar years in Germany. Against a general background of the hopelessness and ruin caused by total war, it again finds a model for meaning in seasonal cycles. The work of salvage and recovery develops into an elegy for the short-lived, makeshift refugee communities in displaced-persons camps under United Nations supervision, where Mekas stayed for over three years before crossing the Atlantic to New York; he remembers the frail experiments in communality they afforded ("one room, / one fate" [*Reminiscences*, 4.59–60]) and the fledgling affections ("those sweet / friendships" [*Reminiscences*, 2.50–51]) they inspired.

Tell me, Leonora, were you thinking of home that time?
Looking off at pale level coastlines
and green horizons, that evening—/The upper deck
full of people, some dancing, someone singing
and playing banjo, we stood by the railing
and listened to the music, looking out at the flaming
bend of the Palisades to take in this dizzying, mystic
and painful American night,
so lulling and hypnotic in its relentless grip,
one drowning pull to wear memories down,
tear away at longings, times past, as it goes dragging
clear up into itself, to its core/
while someone kept on playing banjo
there was singing and dancing, with the fiery
bend of the Palisades burning, and the nightlights on in New York/—

Now wasn't each place,
each stop a look, and each and every instant
home?
Wasn't it painful, each time we split up,
and wasn't that home?

Or was it all just binding ties,
just binding ties and separations?

Don't ask. It's not as if I had any way of telling.
Hungry and thirsty still, with eyes just as eager,
unquenchable, drinking each new horizon in,
each face and river, all the squares and bridges,
with the same ties to everything, still the same
pain and torment in letting go:

so go on falling down, white
snow of times gone by, while I keep going
on and on, wherever my travels take me, to whatever strange
new horizons, cities and people—
the same pangs reviving, each time I let go.

Now go on falling down, white
snow of times gone by, while I keep on
going wherever my journeys lead, to whatever strange
new horizons, cities and people—

moving on and on, each time
without knowing what for, or where to—
not knowing, and not knowing—just the heart

pushing on, eyes squinting into the distance
for each blue smoke trail, each
new tree and face:

but no
it's not that tree, not the blue of that sky,
no not the face,
no not the smoke.

Sorrow, sorrow, sorrow.

(*Reminiscences*, 8.74 to end)

The poem is clearly Romantic in its central ambition to reclaim a child's-eye view of exile, with an ear keen to register a corresponding scale of intonations ("childhood / the one voice your friends had in common" [*Reminiscences*, 2.30–31]) even while struggling to stay free of the lure of obsessive nostalgia, a chronic and symptomatic tendency to view the past as "one big Sunday / drenched in sun" (*Reminiscences*, 7.21–22). The plain articulation of ordinariness is deliberate. Place names are all specific, either to Germany or to America. Yet it is worth noting that while following very closely the course of nostalgia, the poem never alludes to the poet's childhood.

The voice of memory is carefully modulated to suit the unifying identity, for the "I" is representative, communal. Yet the idiom stays conversational and subdued throughout ("talking low among ourselves" [*Reminiscences*, 7.86]), even when it rises for occasional apostrophes, such as the one to the city to which the poet in his exile ultimately comes:

You, New York, with your ringing glass hands
immersed in soft cloudbanks one
endless rain, with your harsh
interminable streets, your longing
wound around every one of my hours

(*Reminiscences*, 8.36–40)

Flower Talk, published in 1961, takes the form of a continuous but undated lyrical diary. It is patterned on the discovery and progress of first love, and still structured, like the two earlier books, on the more abstract model of a calendar, with scrupulously observed changes in seasons and emotions. The book is remarkable for dwelling on the particulars of human intimacy, in a way the films never do, unless it is in the affection that informs his lingering close-ups of nature.

Flowers in dying
return to earth,
touching our faces
with fragrant breath.

Each tulip,
each mica flake
has its own face:

each thing
you touch
affects you
afresh.   (*Flower Talk*, 1.1)

The sequence is almost too studied as it begins, with brief spare
stanzas of potent intimation; then it gains interest and energy at the
cooling of ardor and the distancing that ensues. There is a closing
coda that has a glorious and independent recapitulation that confirms the plain intention of the book:

I don't know, whether it was
the sun had done it,
the rain or wind,
but I really missed
both snow and whiteness.

While listening to showers
rinsing the pink
fresh chestnut buds
and the high brook running
downhill in rivulets,
I missed the snow
and whiteness.

Now while the yards
fill out with sound,
the red-cheeked
farmgirls string their wash
out in the wind,
then leaning back
stay on to watch
fresh yellow willow banks.

For love is in the wind,
and love is in the water:
turning warm in spring,
freezing over in autumn.

Yet I, I don't know why,
whether the sun
had done it,
the rain or wind,
I really missed both
snow and whiteness.

This wet wind blows the wash
will blow again, I know;
just as the same old rain
rains in the chestnuts now.
Though love the snow took off with
will not be back,
asleep deep in snow
as words and heart are.
I watched it rain just now:
the first spring rain
dancing at my open door!
Someone I never noticed before

rushed by in the downpour,
and looking just lovely,
even smiled in at me.

So love is in the wind,
and in the water too,
turning warm in spring,
freezing over in autumn,
and yet I still don't know
why, whether it was the sun,
the rain or wind
had done it,
I really miss both
snow and whiteness.   (*Flower Talk*, 5.4)

Words Apart, first published in 1967, is ostensibly Mekas's most
tentative work to date, melding the actual and quotidian with the
enervating demands of memory. The strict minimalist format (no
more than one word per line in the original) is announced in the
title, and as the poem proceeds through its five parts somewhat in
the manner of a person struggling to free himself of a bad stammer,
there is a growing sense of strong formal confidence and suppleness.
As an experiment, it is akin to the "new man" footage incorporated
in *Lost, Lost, Lost,* which was filmed at about the same time.

So
I
revert,
again
and again,
in an attempt,
in my attempt
to wrench
the mystery
out
from
the core
of myself,

trapped
inside
an un
-breach
-able
isolation,

stray
-ing
deeper
and
deep
-er
in.

In
rock
I
found
my
source
solid
stiff,
waiting.   (*Words Apart*, 2.3.1–35)

This style of rigorously imposed line breaks, with stammered en-
jambments and repetitions, underscores a hammered import on
which each word seems to insist. It is a direct counterpart to the
single-frame, stop-shutter camera style Mekas devised for the film
diaries. Both styles imply a strategically ironic stance for the au-

thor-diarist in relation to his evasive, unyielding material; invariably, his subject matter stays beyond his grasp. His handling of the diary form, whether filmic or poetic, thus becomes a map of his own stubborn pursuit, describing in the process the staggering journey any closely examined life actually takes.

Also notable is the first introduction of self-consciously cultural references into the literal frame, not least in the following instance where the perspective of a postcard sunset (bearing direct relation to the "Cassis" interlude in *Walden*) is widened to include a Homeric reference.

As day
ends,
heartbeat's
stable.

Here
lies
the wine
red
sea.

(*Words Apart*, 4.19.9–17)

While the collected *Poetry*, published in Vilnius in 1971, was largely retrospective, it did include previously unpublished sequences, for the most part unvaried in either structure or substance from the work so far discussed. One verse, however, has the following unique statement of aesthetic intention, which as a motto may stand for the films as well:

There is the word,
and music
of the word.

And there are
things,
dreams
and
images.

I choose
one thing,
the thing
itself
is

poetry,
dream
and
reality:

ars
poetica.   (*Poetry*, "I Walk Alone," 3.2)

Datebook, 1970–1982 is his first attempt at discontinuous form for
a single book-length poem. It coalesces into a further refinement of
the stop-shutter exposures for single-frame sequences he produced
on film, though the line units here are generally longer, with at least
two words per line.

pastures of the past
wrenching hands apart
midnight rivers   (*Datebook*, 17.1–3)

There is in addition the novelty of ironic self-evaluation ("some
kind of born / dissident; / worse yet, / an anarchist!" [*Datebook*,
10.13–18]) with wry asides on what he perceives to be his own signature idiosyncrasies ("one of Schiller's Romantic leads, / a touch
sullen, / a touch sad" [*Datebook*, 11.15–17]). Yet on the whole, despite a periodic easing of manner, the book delineates a progres-
sively deepening isolation. The paradox at the close rings both fatalistic and defiant. Reduced to an inconsolable isolation ("all alone
/ with your / Lithuanian words" [*Datebook*, 76.21–23]), the
stranded survivor still finds himself as restless as an insomniac pacing the night, half-aching for oblivion yet vitally alert for the least
sign of daybreak.

late at night
drinking wine
think of friends
late at night

late city night
outside the window
words force a wedge
this late at night

late at night
think of friends
drink the wine
late at night

heart sore and how
memory quakes
this late at night
the wine I drink   (*Datebook*, 52)

"Hey, I escaped the ropes of time, once more!" the author's voice
intones at the close of the "American woods" prelude to *Reminiscences;* and the connecting image he provides onscreen is of a
frayed strand of broken rope, dangling from a branch.

Bibliography

Beckett, Samuel. 1977. "Imagination Dead Imagine." In *I Can't Go On, I'll
    Go On*, 551–54. New York: Grove Press/Evergreen.
Bunting, Basil. 1978. *Collected Poems*. London: Oxford University Press.
Mekas, Jonas. 1948. *Semeniškių idilės*. Kassel: Žvilgsniai.
———. 1955. *Semeniškių idilės*. Brooklyn: Aidai.
———. 1961. *Gėlių kalbėjimas*. Chicago: Santara.
———. 1967. *Pavieniai žodžiai*. Chicago: AM Fondas.
———. 1971. *Poezija*. Vilnius: Vaga.
———. 1972. *Reminiscensijos*. New York: Fluxus.
———. 1985. *Dienoraščiai, 1970–1982*. New York: Žvilgsniai.
———. 1988. "Reminiscences." Trans. Vyt Bakaitis and Roland Grybaus-
    kas. *City Lights Review* no. 2, 101–19. San Francisco: City Lights Books.
Milosz, Czeslaw. 1983. *The Witness of Poetry*. Cambridge: Harvard Univer-
    sity Press.
Olson, Charles. 1966. *Selected Writings*. New York: New Directions.

10. Richard Foreman   During the Second Half of the Sixties

DURING the second half of the sixties, when I was spending anywhere from four to seven nights a week at the Film-Makers' Cinematheque, not only was a vast quantity of film discovered and shown, but a significant number of theatrical events were staged, many of them created by filmmakers and artists specifically for performance occasions offered by Jonas Mekas at what was officially a movie theater.

The big event during that time, as I recall, was the Expanded Cinema Festival that took place at the Astor Place location. (The Cinematheque seemed to be moving every few months.) My memory is dim, and some of the events I can recollect more or less fully, others not at all—even some of those I remember as having had a strong impact on me at the time. I remember, for instance, being quite impressed with an event created by Dick Higgins, though I have no recollection of the event itself. (I do remember more accurately a piece of his staged around that same time at a boxing arena in Brooklyn or Queens, entitled *The Tart*, in which a variety of characterological types paraded around the ring amidst snatches of music and what seemed like a few appropriately assigned lines.) Then there was a Ken Jacobs event, of which I remember only some sort of projection over a New York skyline—I believe Jacobs or one of his assistants was holding a small 8 mm projector and throwing a bobbing image against the front curtain of the stage—but I can remember none of the more performative aspects of the piece.

It was either at that, or at a later festival, that I saw several images from a Rauschenberg piece (a man walking on tall platform shoes, picking up glowing tubes of some sort; another moment in which someone collected tires; someone on a couch with doves). But that event clearly belonged to the world of Happenings—prevalent at the time, but I had no experience of them, since I was spending all my free time at the Cinematheque.

What impressed me most—what has stayed in my memory most clearly—were the events, the "theater pieces," that in one way or another partook of the aesthetic of Jack Smith. These were either created by friends of Smith, with his influence clearly discernible, or ones in which he appeared and dominated the proceedings with the rhythm of his performance, or the single piece of his own presented at the Expanded Cinema Festival.

As has been publicly acknowledged by all concerned, Smith was a major influence on much of the experimental theater that emerged in the seventies. The two strands of the ridiculous—Charles Ludlam and John Vacarro—as well as the work of Robert Wilson and my own work clearly owe much to Smith's example and inspiration. I suspect that the power of his films probably inclined us all to a consideration of his (at first) more problematic theatrical work. (In my case, the first viewing of *Flaming Creatures* was perhaps the most overwhelming aesthetic experience of my life. I have not seen the film for many years, and have no idea if it would still affect me as it did then, but through fifteen re-viewings over a period of a few months, its impact on me did not lessen. To me, it was a Blakean vision come into three-dimensional, concrete life, and in that sense "theatrical" in the true sense of the word.)

The single Smith theater event I viewed at the time took place at the same Expanded Cinema Festival. (In later years I attended half a dozen or so of Smith's famous midnight performances in his loft, but I have no idea whether these were already occurring at the time of the Expanded Cinema event.) The piece I saw had something to do with Atlantis—a favorite Smith theme. In fact, the only aspect of the event I really recall was two women of some weight, stuffed into a single (polka-dot?) dress, who were playing Siamese twins; I think I recall them at some point struggling to a couch. The only other thing I recall was that most of my friends (other Cinematheque regulars) were more lavish in their praise of this particular event than I was. I had other favorites at the festival—including the more musically oriented events of La Monte Young and Angus McLease, but more of that in a moment. Does my limited recollection of any of these events, including those of the great Jack Smith, mean that these theatrical events were less important and crucial and aesthetically potent than I believed them to be?

I think not. I maintain this even though, for ten years or so preceding this period of regular Cinematheque attendance, I had been regularly attending almost every "official" play presented in the New York theater, on and off Broadway, and to this day I have more precise memories of those more normal theatrical events than I do of the events I saw at the Cinematheque. Even at that time, most of those plays I saw on and off Broadway were, in my opinion, of minuscule aesthetic value—of less value than what I saw at the Cinematheque. In addition, I regularly noticed a strange phenomenon.

I would attend, say, a hit Broadway play that had received reviews proclaiming it an important contribution to the ranks of Western drama, and I would sit in the theater, registering moment by moment a kind of untruthfulness to the rhythms of life and perception and experience as I knew them in my own life—and leave the theater convinced I had just experienced bad art that on a basic level did not tell the truth about what life was like on this planet. But a day or two later I would invariably notice that my rage at the stupidity and artistic crudity of the play in question had fallen into the background of my ongoing life, and what I retained from the play in question was a series of images—free-floating pictures accompanied by a certain emotional "tone"—and this totally nonrigorous collection of "tonal memories" seemed not nearly so contemptible as the play itself, from which they issued as a kind of perfume, distilled by memory. In fact, I found that in examining only these memories of the play, I somehow felt in the act of recollection that the play in question, which had truly offended and nauseated me in the theater, with its simplifications and stupidities and falsehoods, now seemed to take its place on the scale approximately where the mass of critical opinion (for which I had relative contempt) placed it.

I concluded (and I still conclude) that most people attending a play are somehow (though it is a mental experience taking place in present time) viewing it as if through that same mental screen that in my case was a screen erected by memory only. In other words, a kind of secondhand viewing takes place in which the viewer does not really attend to the specific density of each moment, with its multiple layers of reference and association, but rather focuses on the imagined and possible outcome of the narrative line—the possible filling of some mythic form that the viewer brings as his own private anticipation to the theatrical event. This bringing into play of mythically oriented anticipation really, I believe, puts the viewer into a sort of light hypnotic trance, making him not-present at the events of the play (the language, the light, the sound, the textures, the counterpoint of idea on idea), and so the viewer does not *see* what is happening onstage, but only *experiences* in a semiconscious state the rush of the river of narrative to its inevitable end-state—a memory trace, much like the memory trace I experienced the next day when "recollecting" the play in a way that brought my memory, generally speaking, into line with the critical opinion of the play that most other viewers experienced in the act of watching it.

I must emphasize that I in no way forgot that while experiencing the play, and through the rest of that day until I fell asleep, I consciously believed that play to be a thin, defective, and deceitful thing. But the next day I seemed to add a second level of experience, the memory of the play, to the first level of experience, which a day later I could only call the memory of what went on in me while *experiencing* the play (as opposed to the memory of the play itself).

I maintain that the theatrical events I experienced at the Cinematheque uniquely introduced me to a world of theater where the issues herein alluded to were clarified in very specific form. These events, which I find much harder to remember than the theater plays I attended during the same epoch, were experienced by me as events of more aesthetic worth, of greater seriousness and human truth, than the Broadway plays of the time. I believe that through the years they have proved hard for me to remember specifically because they dared, as has all important twentieth-century art, to evoke, render, and embody that vast area of our conscious and unconscious experience that the socially given forms in which we live have not named or categorized. The Broadway play arranged ideas and events, moods and sentiments already existing as recognizable gestalts in our mental organization—while the events I saw at the Cinematheque, like all true art, put onstage particular energies that matched no existing mental forms already existing as habit within our consciousness. Society had not preprogrammed us for the stage art on display at the Cinematheque in those days.

The theater is always the art form that is most behind the times, aesthetically speaking. I think this is so because the theater, in a sense, most resembles life itself. It is an art of three dimensions, dealing with concrete bodies and objects before us on the stage, with language issuing from those bodies—the stage, indeed, as a little envelope in which a piece of life as we experience it in our social interaction seems to exist.

Other art forms, being more partial in their reference and evocation of the spectrum of human experience, have, I maintain, a somewhat more direct route to those possibilities of structure and feeling that are *not* part of the conditioning we wear as glasses through which we view the world. To place inside our heads a new psychic rhythm or structure through paint or sound alone, for instance, means to encounter the resistance of habit on only one sensory level. But the theater must attack habit on all sensory levels at once, so it seems to me no wonder that the resistance to innovation is greater in theater.

The "memory-elusive" events at the Cinematheque were indeed the first events of theater I had seen that tried to function as other arts did, and made theatrically concrete reality that nevertheless partook of the elusiveness of mental structuring not yet habituated in our common consciousness.

I recall in later years, in response to my own plays (so clearly influenced by the aesthetic of the Cinematheque) hearing of a critic who privately explained, "Those Foreman plays, I don't know—when you are there watching them, they seem very strong, but the next day I can't remember what it was really all about." I of course felt that this was high praise—though not offered as such—for it meant that for this one critic at least, I had managed to touch deep roots (when you are watching them, a strong experience) that were part of this critic's being he had not yet been able to pull up into the conscious realm of his personality ("the next day, I can't remember"). I look on this elusive evocation of the mentally "non-handleable" as the proper activity of art, and first experienced that as palpable theatrical possibility at events that took place not in a normal theater, but at the Film-Makers' Cinematheque. I was introduced to the notion that art is not the reinforcement, through emotional intensification, of what you already know (what you know, being, nine times out of ten, probably just a bad habit you have acquired); it is rather a bath in a kind of consciousness you have potentially within yourself but which—not having discovered how to use it—you find yourself unable to hold onto on your own, even though with the help of the art experience you find it energizing and illuminating when you are in it.

Less hard to recall than the Jack Smith play itself was the Jack Smith performance in an event that was credited to filmmaker Jerry Joffren. Smith was, of course, a performer in many underground films, with a persona quite indescribable, based on the exploration of the ultimate potential within us for allowing human effort, will, and purpose to be deflected and brought to a kind of transcendent, oscillating standstill by the minutiae of every moment lived in the course of "trying to perform." To watch Jack Smith perform was to watch human behavior turn into granular stasis, in which every moment of being seemed, somehow, to contain the seed of unthinkable possibility. It was endlessly fascinating. In the Joffren piece, Jack extended the wait between lines of dialogue to five, ten, twenty minutes, believe it or not—with a further believe it or not: the wait was exhilarating. Report had it that it was at Jack's urging that the dialogue was extended in this way, something I take on faith since it seems central to the style and aesthetic he manifested in other circumstances. I recall, for instance, an occasion when I had been invited to attend an early rehearsal, of Robert Wilson's *Life and Times of Sigmund Freud*, in certain versions of which Jack appeared, and Wilson, unhappy at the end of the rehearsal, asking Jack for his thoughts, and Jack responding, in the extended nasal drawl that was so much his own, "it has to be . . . sadder, Bob, it's not saaad enough . . . make it . . . slow . . . er, much slow . . . er, just much slow . . . er."

That extended slowness, combined with the continual (and somewhat calculated) going wrong of every performance, brought the audience into a state of present attention that is precisely what other theater avoided in order to affect (i.e., manipulate) its audience. The theater generally hypnotizes; it pulls one into a dream that imitates a place in which the spectator would like to be. (Even Wilson falls into this habit.) The theater of Smith, along with other manifestations that took place in those days of Cinematheque performance, avoided that through building into the performance various "confounding" devices—in Smith's case the great slowness informed by a feeling that "everything was going wrong," which made it hard for the audience to remember what was happening at the same time that it was fascinated by what was, indeed, happening in a time rhythm that both spectator and performer were experiencing in sync.

It is interesting to me that the two events I *do* remember more clearly from that festival were musical events—Angus McLease's and La Monte Young's—both of which used loud, repetitive, drone-like sound against slowly shifting onstage textures (in Young's case, slowly shifting projected slide patterns created by his partner, Marian Zazeela). There is no question in my mind that the aesthetic operating here was similar to that in Smith's work in that it also introduced us to material that altered the scale of perception, replacing the mythic level of narrative or thematic development with the microscopic level of moment-attending (implying that the seed of the moment held the energy of all possible future flow-into-form). But because the form, dominated by sound in this case, was more abstract, it allowed the mind to deal with categorizing its effects in a way more assimilable by memory. The theatrical event, I maintain, "baffled" the conscious mind because the moves within its form were closer to the kinds of moves the mind normally makes in negotiating daily life; yet it confounded those move-patterns in a way that was not so much opposite as irrelevant, and so became less available to similarly conditioned memory.

In short, then, I believe that a good number of the theatrical events presented at Mekas's Cinematheque pointed the way to a theater that can only marginally be realized at any historical time, a theater that functions as art functions, directly on the consciousness, and the way that consciousness operates, rather than a theater as illustrative psychology, mythology, or sociology. But it is a theater that nurtures, at all times, the dreams of those few young theater artists who are most insightful and exact in the ability to dredge up from the mind what the social beast has not found useful in its struggle to suppress the real evolution of consciousness and the spirit. Unfortunately the theater, as a collective art (without the partial escape from collective rule available to cinema through the continued existence of the film itself through the years), is a difficult arena in which to sustain such a hard-won and delicate vision. So the young vanish, or change, and as might be expected, the brief appearances of such a theater, rather than flowing into the evolutionary current of theatrical history, tend to remain beacons flashing for only some of us, an aesthetic truth for which the theater as it seems it must always be—a creature of absolute public accountability—has not, alas, shown much aptitude or interest.

11. David E. James   Film Diary/Diary Film: Practice and Product in *Walden*

The amateur is—he will be perhaps—
the counter-bourgeois artist.
—Roland Barthes, *Barthes by Barthes*

Let us set up our Camera also, and let
the sun paint the people.
—Ralph Waldo Emerson, "Lecture on
the Times"

SINCE P. Adams Sitney's pioneering (and still unassimilated) *Visionary Film*, it has been clear that a major phylum of the American cinema found its main frame of reference in the aesthetic field initially mapped by the English Romantic poets, either in its original form or as mediated through the native tradition of literary transcendentalism. From these were inherited both the prototypical situation of the modern artist (the artist *as such*) and the categories of artistic practice: the work of art as an organic unity, formally autonomous and created in either a community of other artists or rural solitude, proposed as the palliative for the alienation of demythologized modernity in general and industrial culture in particular. For nearly two hundred years, the opposition of art to commerce in terms of this kind recurred in the ideologies of modernism, even when the two were recognized as being complementary, the sundered halves of a lost whole. Historically, the cultural dislocation this division represents has been addressed in two ways: by the creation of aesthetically autonomous works of art in which alienation is objectified, and by assaults on the autonomy of the aesthetic itself (and so upon category of art as a pivotal term within bourgeois ideology) toward the end of recreating the integrated praxis of life that preceded its rationalization. Beginning with Romanticism and other anti-Enlightenment reactions, the former produced the high modernist avant-garde, while the latter may be thought of as an antimodernist avant-garde, with (as Peter Bürger has shown) Dada its exemplary moment. Theoretically the two projects were incompatible, each the object of the other's attack, but in fact they were often imbricated; even in Dada, the attempt to return art to the praxis of life passed into its opposite, the creation of beauty, however much beauty was redefined in the process.

Given the overwhelming hegemony of the industrial and specifically the capitalist use of film, the creation of autonomous art in this medium has been difficult enough; the rationalization of the filmmaking process itself, its dependence on advanced technology, and its integration with other forms of manufacture has made its return to life all but inconceivable. Given the totality of the present penetration of commodity culture, modes that at first sight seem to herald a truly popular practice often turn out to be administered reservations within the industrial system as a whole, where its conditions are internalized. Home movies, for instance, are surrounded by advertising, instruction manuals, and the like, which seek to return them to the codes of the commercial feature. This containment of the amateur within the industrial frames the hesitation of Barthes's remarks above, but also exposes his idealism. For while all notions of a utopian cinema must begin from the possibility of production outside and against commodity relations, any real counterbourgeois practice must oppose bourgeois society's most fundamental distinction, that between industrial and amateur, between labor and the leisure that renews it.

The lifework of Jonas Mekas, who was displaced from rural Lithuania by World War II and who since then has been an immigrant in New York, has proposed such a utopian cinema. His negotiations with film were determined by several overlapping and mutually inflecting schema: the way he lived modernism's master narrative, the history of the displacement of the organic and rural by the industrial and the urban; his attempt to salvage an identity from within the confrontation of United States and Soviet imperialism; the continual passage back and forth in his work between writing and film, by which the resources of one have regularly been drawn into the other; and his commitment to a truly populist cinema. His engagement in these scenes has been so complete that, if not the resolution, then certainly the precipitate of the historical tensions they embody has been a magisterial and unprecedented oeuvre. It culminated in a series of "diary films," whose immense theoretical significance is only beginning to be glimpsed from behind the obdurate ambition that motivates them. Given the complexity of the issues compacted in this oeuvre, no one vocabulary can be sufficient to it. The present heuristic approach divides it into a double gesture, formally distinguishing between the different implications of the *film diary* and the *diary film*.

Swinging across the pun on "film" itself as designating alternatively a medium of activity and a completed artifact, the metamorphosis of Mekas's film diary into his diary films is summary of the conditions by which an antibourgeois cultural practice negotiates its context in bourgeois society. Just as much as a written one, a diary made in film privileges the author, the process and moment of composition, and the inorganic assembly of disarticulate, heterogenous parts rather than any aesthetic whole. It is a private event (the coded or locked diary) where consumption, especially consumption by others, is illicit: a pure use value. But a diary film finds itself in an economy of *films*, an economy that privileges the completed artifact as a whole, the moment of projection, the spectating public, and, in some form or other, exchange value. As he turned his innovations in the former into the latter, Mekas's antimodernist project came into being within the social conditions of the modernist avant-garde cinema. The tensions between his film diary and the diary films he subsequently edited from it—each considered as a text with specific formal properties situated between the social activities that produce it and the equally specific social relations it sets in play—span his intervention in cinema. The one inaugurated functions for the apparatus that radically refused both the industrial and the orthodox avant-garde uses of it, with the extravagances, deficiencies, and contradictions of the new (non)genre challenging the hegemonic forms of the medium. The other returned to a public context, entailing compromises, yet also occasioning new possibilities.

Among Mekas's films, *Walden* will be the special object of attention here since, as the first of the films in the mature mode, it is the place where the film diary was first edited into a diary film. The conditions of this transaction further allow us to respond to the full weight of the film's title, to address it as having a specific rather than a vague self-aggrandizing reference to a classic moment in American dissent. The invocation of Thoreau directs us to the point where the tensions between a private and a public culture are first elaborated, if not at the beginning of a specifically American experience, then certainly at its "Renaissance." [1] There is, moreover, a clear parallel between, on the one hand, Thoreau's journal, unpublished during his lifetime though clearly written with readers in

[1] The significance of this era in American literature was first announced by F. O. Matthiessen's *American Renaissance* (Matthiessen 1941).

mind, and the published form of a rewritten selection from it as
Walden, and, on the other, Mekas's film diary and his making public edited selections from it as a diary film, also called *Walden*.

THE FILM DIARY   *A journal, a book that shall contain a*
                                  record of all your joy, your ecstasy.
                                  —Thoreau, *Journal*, 13 July 1852

The relations between Mekas's *Walden* and its eponymous ancestor
are, as we shall see, multiple and complex, but subtending them all
is their common affirmation of the priority of autobiography. But
while Thoreau's request of every writer for "a simple and sincere
account of his own life, and not merely what he has heard of other
men's lives" (Thoreau 1971, 3) can refer to many such productions
in literature, transposed to film it confronts the virtual absence of
autobiography in the history of the medium.[2] Mekas has on several
occasions described the circumstances of his break with this history, and of his subsequent preoccupation with what was then a
new kind of film. Since completing *The Brig* in 1964, he had been
diverted from attempts to make his own independent features by
many different efforts on behalf of other filmmakers and the institutions of the alternative American cinemas: *Film Culture*, Film-
Makers' Cinematheque, Film-Makers' Cooperative, and eventually
Anthology Film Archives. During this time, he continued his habit
of photographing occasional fragments of his daily life as opportunity allowed, a habit he had begun soon after arriving in New York
in 1949. He had always understood this activity as preparatory only,

[2] Studies of film and autobiography (which essentially begin in the late seventies)
were, almost at their inception, misdirected by an unfortunate essay, Elizabeth
Bruss's "Eye for I." Arguing that "there is no real cinematic equivalent for autobiography," Bruss (1980) brought an obsolete notion of the autobiographical subject—
"a self existing independently of any particular style of expression and logically prior
to all literary genres and even to language itself" (298)—to bear on an uninformed
supposition that film language had no way of inscribing authorship, "no way of dis-
criminating a shot of the director from a shot of any other, indifferent individual"
(305). Like academic film scholarship in general, hers was ignorant of both nonin-
dustrial cinema and nonacademic scholarship, notably P. Adams Sitney's seminal
"Autobiography in Avant-Garde Film" (1977). For a sufficient critique of Bruss, see
Lejeune, "Cinéma et autobiographie" (1987). The various debates about the extratex-
tual status of the autobiographical subject are well summarized in Eakin, *Fictions in
Autobiography* (1985), especially 181–278. The equally extensive writing on the contingency of the autobiographical subject on post-Enlightenment humanism begins,
in its modern form, in Georges Gusdorf, "Conditions and Limits of Autobiography"
(1956).

a means of sustaining familiarity with the medium until such time
as it could be properly reengaged:

> I didn't have any long stretches of time to prepare a script, then to take
> months to shoot, then to edit, etc. I had only bits of time which allowed
> me to shoot only bits of film. All my personal work became like notes. I
> thought I should do whatever I can today, because if I don't, I may not
> find any other free time for weeks. If I can film one minute—I film one
> minute. If I can film ten seconds—I film ten seconds. I take what I can,
> from desperation. But for a long time I didn't look at the footage I was
> collecting that way. I thought what I was actually doing was practising. I
> was preparing myself, or trying to keep in touch with my camera, so that
> when the day would come when I'll have time, then I would make a
> "real" film. (Mekas 1978, 191)

Over some period—and it must have been all but complete by 1969
when, after a fire nearly destroyed the accumulated work of the previous five years, he prepared for public view a "first draft edition"
of *Diaries, Notes, and Sketches, Also Known as Walden*—his attitude to this footage was transformed. What before he had seen as
private, provisional, and exergual was now recognized as its own
justification and its own telos. What before had been the residue of
a continual postponement now came into focus as itself. Where before he had thought himself as only practicing until such time as he
could make feature films about "other men's lives," now he realized
that photographing the fragments of his own life was his practice of
film. Practicing, retrospectively and henceforth, found itself as
praxis.

Such discoveries were everywhere in sixties culture. Robert Rauschenberg's work in the gap between art and life announced the collapse of the aesthetic autonomy of abstract expressionism and heralded a decade of parallel projects, the use of natural movements in
dance, for example, or theater in which publicly performed plays
were extrapolated from the personal interaction of the players. Literature of all kinds similarly renegotiated its relation to the experience of the writer: in nonfiction novels where the novelist became
the protagonist even more overtly than in the autobiographical novels of the beat era; in various confessional poetries; and even in a
new valorization of the poet's journal in modes ranging from poetry
differentiated from journals as such by only a hairline asymptote
(Allen Ginsberg's *Fall of America*, Robert Lowell's *Notebook 1967–
68*), to the publication of daybooks themselves by Robert Creely and
Ed Dorn in 1972.[3]

---

[3] Ginsberg published journals themselves (e.g., *Indian Journals*) and, after *The Fall*

This context supplied the new importance of the diary in American culture at large. If the received attitude to the form had been summarized in W. H. Auden's remark in his poem "The Horatians" that "most / make no memorable impact / except on your friends and dogs," after the late sixties the diary was increasingly valorized as a literary practice of self-discovery, self-renovation, even as the place where a self might be constructed. The political ambiguities of the inflated claims of various forms of the "New Diary" are real, implicit indeed in the entire history of the genre as a function of Enlightenment subjectivity.[4] But that the modern diary is not inevitably so solipsistic is proven by women's diary writing in the seventies, where introspection and self-awareness were understood as individual participation in a collective historical recovery. The politics of the diary were consequently heavily invested by women, eventually to the point where its open-ended, nonhierarchical, impermanent form could be proposed as intrinsically feminist, defined against its completed, teleologically ordered, permanent, and hence masculinist sibling, the autobiography proper (e.g., DuPlessis 1985, 141). In film, the "femininity" of the genre was suggested by the tradition of fictional feature films (directed by men) involving distraught female "diarists": *Diary of a Lost Girl* (G. W. Pabst, 1929), *Diary of a Chambermaid* (Jean Renoir, 1946; Luis Buñuel, 1965), *Diary of a Mad Housewife* (Frank Perry, 1970) and so on.[5] Indeed,

---

of America in 1972, poetry that consisted of edited transcripts of journals dictated into a tape recorder while traveling. Commonly credited with influencing Lowell toward the increased colloquiality of his late work and possibly toward the publication of *Notebook, 1967–1968,* he also influenced Mekas, appearing in several films and reading on the sound track of *Guns of the Trees.*

[4] The therapeutic promises of what became known as *The New Diary* (Rainer 1978) amounted to vernacular reenactment of contemporary poststructuralist models of the construction of self in language; their most notorious commercializations are commonly thought to be Dr. Ira Progroff's Intensive Journal workshops and seminars. See Mallon 1984, 87–91. For the emergence of the diary as a genre in the Enlightenment and its associations with Puritan self-examination, see Fothergill 1974, 11–37, and Nussbaum 1988, 129–33.

[5] Though a feature recreation, George Stevens's *Diary of Anne Frank* (1959) was based on real life. The major fictional diary films that do feature male protagonists, are *Diary of a Country Priest* (Robert Bresson, 1951) and *Shinjuku dorobo nikki* (*Diary of a Shinjuku Thief*) (Nagisa Oshima, 1970). Even when, as in the case of *Anne Frank,* these features are derived from actual diaries, the term "diary" has no generic force beyond that of indicating a personal story. The major exceptions are, again, *Shinjuku dorobo nikki,* which, although its chief protagonist is male employs the mix of fantasy and reality and other conventions of the *nikki,* a form of women's diary common in Japanese literature during the Heian Era, and *David Holzman's Diary* (Jim McBride, 1967), which, in all but its self-contradictory ending, is a consistent imitation of a diary. These and other fictional diary films, including Godard's

as women became increasingly active as filmmakers after the early seventies, some form of the film diary proper, which had to all intents and purposes been invented by Marie Menken, proved viable for filmmakers as diverse as Chantal Ackerman, Storm de Hirsch, Sue Friedrich, Marjorie Keller, Yvonne Rainer, Amalie Rothschild, Carolee Schneemann, and Claudia Weill.[6] In several notable instances in the seventies, when the avant-garde modes developed in the sixties had generally lost their authority, the film diary also offered men a model praxis, with the work of Andrew Noren, Robert Huot, Howard Guttenplan, Ed Pincus, and Jonas Mekas the most considerable.[7] This efflorescence should be understood historically as simultaneously a contraction of the utopian politics of the sixties independent cinemas and an ongoing affirmation of an anti-industrial and anti-aestheticist cinema. Coinciding with the disintegration of the oppositional countercultures and the underground films they had sustained, it reflects the internalization of social aspirations (which only feminism was able to maintain as a public project), yet it afforded a means of mobilizing a subjectivity, otherwise stranded between the impersonal rationality of structural film, on the one hand, and on the other, the preoccupation of the field of subjectivity by people of color, women, and gays.

Ur-forms of the film diary had been fundamental in the American avant-garde cinemas. It may well be that, as Mekas claims, "until 1960 or so, no filmmaker was really filming his or her own life" (MacDonald 1984, 89), but by the middle of the decade personal, domestic filmmaking—home movies and film diaries[8]—supplied a

---

Vivre sa vie (1922) and Stanton Kaye's *Georg* (1964), may best be understood in parallel with novels written in the form of diaries; these have been historically surveyed by Abbot (1984) and by Martens (1985). In March 1973, the Museum of Modern Art presented a series of screenings called "The Diary Film" that reflected a very loose definition of the genre, including not only *Walden* and other examples of what I here argue are diary films proper, but also fictional diaries (*Vivre sa vie*, *Diary of a Country Priest*), films made from literary diaries (Robert Katz's *Daybooks of Edward Weston*), and examples of other chronicle forms.

[6] Rainer's *Man Who Envied Women* (1986), for example, has been called "a virtual home-movie of the Western intellectual Left in recent years" (Storr 1986, 159).

[7] On Huot's, see MacDonald 1980; on Guttenplan's, see Sanderson 1977.

[8] Since I contend that film diaries as a genre emerged as an adaptation of the stylistics and social functions of home movies, I have generally in this essay elided the differences between them, except for noting the processes of adaptation. A fuller taxonomy would attend to differences between the genres in respect to authorship (home movies are usually familial rather than individual), stylistics (their greater conventionality), and modes of distribution. Other cognate forms such as the film letter should also be noted. On the home movie as genre, see especially Camper 1986 and Chalfden 1975.

matrix of seminal practices: as models of style, as raw material for formal manipulation, as a referential or enabling concept, or even as home movies, as in Taylor Mead's *My Home Movies* (1964). The otherwise very different oeuvres of Ken Jacobs and Warren Sonbert indicate what could be mined from the lode. But, going into the seventies, footage collected on a day-to-day basis and re-presented as such—as a film, rather than a point of departure for a film—achieved a new authority.[9]

These contexts could only have encouraged a well-established propensity in Mekas. Since leaving Lithuania he had kept a written journal; much of his poetry is in a diaristic, documentary mode; and he had already appropriated the genre as a metaphor for what was for many years his most visible intervention in cinema, the weekly *Village Voice* column "Movie Journal" (itself often reproduced from his "tape recorded diaries": Mekas 1972, 101), which had been preceded for a short time in 1955 by his "Film Diary" in the *Intro Bulletin*. "Movie Journal" was not reviewing in the conventional sense (which he always bitterly disparaged) but a polemical and impassioned record of his personal musings and activities around the independent cinema, including accounts of his own filmmaking and promotional work for the avant-garde. For almost twenty years (1958–1976), the movie journal *about* film and the one *in* film were pursued side by side, and if the values expressed in the former are more completely manifest in the latter than in any other films, the discoveries he made in his own filming informed the criteria expressed in the writing.[10]

While specific sub- or parageneric groupings allow for taxonomy and genealogy, each person's diary is virtually sui generis; we will agree that "a diary is what a person writes when he says, 'I am writing my diary'" (Fothergill 1974, 3).[11] "Writing my diary" is, however, more specific as a mode of literary production, implying—though not requiring—single authorship; serial, spontaneous composition of some regularity; an identity, not only of author, narrator,

[9] So, in 1977, P. Adams Sitney thought the diary film to be "a vastly important genre today" (Sitney 1977, 103), even as he noted that it "draws upon the pure lyric, and often becomes indistinguishable from it" (104), and Scott MacDonald in 1980 proposed that the diary film was "a major genre . . . developing in the 1970s" (MacDonald 1980, 297).

[10] Mekas has claimed that his written and his film diaries are "almost identical"; "I only changed my tools" (MacDonald 1984, 94).

[11] For a list of subgeneric forms, see Fothergill 1974, 14. In Fothergill's terms, *Walden* may be thought of as a combination of a journal of travel and a journal of conscience.

and protagonist, but also of reader,[12] that at least makes possible a privileged veridicality in the relationship between text and history; and at least an initial existence outside the commodity relations of most other forms of writing.[13] The respective material properties of writing and film differently inflect the scene and possibilities of composition in the two mediums, allowing the film diary new functions, a different relation to time, and a different relation to subjectivity.

For the written diary, events and their recording are typically separate, but in film they coincide. Thoreau, who took his diary with him and composed it "in its own season & out of doors or in its own locality wherever it may be" (Cameron 1985, 86) was exceptional; more commonly the verbal diary's tense is that of the past perfect, recollections of events and states of mind that have passed. The only *present* it can record is that of the moment of composition and reflexive commentary on writing: "So I make my first entry today" (Thoreau 1981, 5). Image and audio recording, by contrast, cannot escape the present and the present tense, for filming can only capture events as they happen. This material difference leads to different contents; being independent of action, words can describe any event, no matter how extraordinary or unexpected, inopportune or impossible. Conversely, significant exceptions aside (the Zapruder footage and, increasingly, amateur video footage of unplanned news events), a movie camera is most conveniently deployed on mundane events or prearranged social rituals (the staging of a commercial movie is paradigmatic), from which the camera operator has a degree of distance. Pepys's accounts of his spontaneous sexual adventures, for example, do not interrupt or determine the exploits themselves, but when Andrew Noren's or Robert Huot's own copulation appears in their film diaries, they trace a subject divided in situ between performance and recording. Such a division, or doubling, is ubiquitous in film diaries, and when the diarist in-

[12] Lejeune employs the notion that autobiography proper may be distinguished from autobiographical fiction by virtue of the "pact" implicit in the title page of the former that author, narrator, and protagonist are identical (Lejeune 1989, 14). My extension of this identity as a definition of the diary to include the reader is possible only in the case of unpublished diaries. By analogy, it also distinguishes the film diary from the diary film.

[13] These conditions are not essential. Some diaries (e.g., those of Lewis and Clark, and the brothers de Goncourt) have multiple authorship, and poststructural linguistics has disabused us of the idea of a unified subjectivity existing prior to its production in and as text; some of the most celebrated diaries from Pepys on reveal erratic composition and extensive rewritings; and the diary's privacy may, of course, occasion self-serving subjectivity as much as truth.

cludes photography shot by others—as Mekas frequently does—it marks a parallel dispersion of authorship. The discursivity of writing similarly allows authorial subjectivity—the direct statement of feelings—but also reflection on and interpretation of the recorded events, easily turning *histoire* into *discours*; since the subject of shooting is less clearly constituted than the "I" of verbal enunciation, the conditions of representing the author and of inscribing subjectivity are somewhat different. The film diary must go to greater lengths to include the author (shooting mirror images or shadows, or having some other person handle the camera); otherwise authorship must be inscribed in style.

Mekas was the first fully to articulate this combination of imperatives—the need to respond immediately with the camera *to* and *in* the present, and the need to subjectivize that recording—as the essential conditions of the film diary, and the first fully to turn them to advantage, and eventually to invest filmic attention to daily life with religious significance.

As he thought it possible simultaneously to record the phenomenal world in a way consonant with what we take for the unique ontology of the medium, and to express the subjectivity that verbal discursivity and composition after the fact allows the written diary, Mekas came to understand filming as an emotional, technical, and above all visual discipline:

> To keep a film (camera) diary, is to react (with your camera) immediately, now, this instant: either you get it down now, or you don't get it at all. To go back and shoot it later, it would mean restaging, be it events or feelings. To get it now, as it happens, demands the total mastery of one's tools (in this case, Bolex): it has to register the reality to which I react and also it has to register my state of feeling (and all the memories) as I react. Which also means, that I had to do all the structuring (editing) right there, during the shooting, in the camera. All the footage you'll see in the Diaries is exactly as it came out from the camera. (*Film-Makers' Cooperative Catalogue* 1989, 362)

The claim that the edited diaries preserve only spontaneous composition is misleading. Even *Walden*, the occasion of these remarks, omits much of the material shot during the period it covers, while later films (especially *He Stands in a Desert*) modify chronology explicitly and extensively; all the films contain interpolated titles, and even if the rejection of editing is taken to refer only to intrasequential editing, the added music and voice-overs substantially inflect the visuals. Despite these caveats (which together define the diary film), it is clear that what is essentially at stake in the film diary lies in the moment of shooting.

The reconceptualization of shooting as an autotelic act defines it against its instrumentality in securing footage for prearranged scenarios or for later manipulation; instead it becomes a meditational attention to everyday life. This aim allows Mekas's project to be seen as the recapitulation in film of Romantic modernism in painting, that is, impressionism. In both cases, the representation of spontaneous sight, summarily figured as the *glance*, is combined with an attempt to represent modern life, and as we shall see below parallel contradictions are entailed.[14] Initially the record of a life seen and lived deliberately, the film diary becomes the vehicle of that deliberate seeing and living, and eventually the life-praxis of shooting is transcendentally invested as a means of redeeming life itself. The credo is announced as a parody of the Cartesian cogito in one of the first voice-overs in *Walden:* "I make home movies— therefore I live. I live—therefore I make home movies." In a title in *He Stands in a Desert* that quotes from Kafka's *Diary*, prayer is proposed as the proper analogue: "Schreiben als form des Gebetes." The emergence of this aesthetic in the "Movie Journal" and the form it takes in the diary footage that remains in *Walden* may briefly be sketched, together with its inevitable contradictions.

The formal qualities of the new mode are first detected as aberrations of the codes of the industrial feature, as amateurish mistakes.[15] As Mekas in the early sixties gradually abandoned his hope

---

[14] Within impressionist theory, this desire is expressed by a opposition between sensation (the retinal impression) and perception (interpretation), and is commonly figured as the sight of a man born blind who suddenly gains sight. The locus classicus of the film version of this is Brakhages's notion of "untutored vision"—vision not filtered through verbal categories, like that of a baby. The same desire is ubiquitous among the impressionists, in Cezanne's desire to see like a child, for example, and in Monet, who invoked the figure of the once-blind man. Charles F. Stuckey (1984) has traced the motif to Ruskin's *Elements of Drawing* and its recommendation to the "recovery of what we may call the *innocence of the eye*; that is to say, of a sort of childish perception of these flat stains of color, merely as such, without consciousness of what they signify—as a blind man would see them if suddenly gifted by sight" (108).

[15] There are direct parallels between "home movies" and "films" and "snapshots" and "photographs," and the aesthetics of snapshots similarly refer to aberrations from the conventions of photography. Thus, among the "characteristics which make up the snapshot vernacular" (49), King (1986) lists a titled horizon, unconventional cropping, eccentric framing, blurring, excessive light, and the shadow of the photographer. The efflorescence of the diary film in the seventies may be correlated with the vogue for such "New Photographers" as Garry Winogrand, Lee Friedlander, Nancy

for a reformed narrative cinema modeled on the European new waves, amateur filmmaking acquired a new status.[16] The kinds of infractions associated with it were recognized as a fully articulate vocabulary with intrinsic ethical implications: glimpses of daily life became more important than comprehensively narrated fictions; a fragmentary, insubstantial, and imperfect "lyrical" image was preferred over a realistic, full, and self-present image, and rudimentary 16 or 8 mm equipment was valorized over studio-quality apparatus. Linking aesthetics to demotic political aspirations, Mekas was able to envisage a great proletarian cultural revolution in and through film. For example, from 1964:

> All pleasures have become perverted, on the border of self-destruction. The words "amateur" (from "love") and "home" are used to describe something bad.
>
> But I could tell you that some of the most beautiful movie poetry will be revealed, someday, in the 8 mm. home-movie footage—simple poetry, with children in the grass and babies on mothers' hands, and with all that embarrassment and goofing around in front of the camera. (Mekas 1972, 131)

> The camera now picks up glimpses, fragments of objects and people, and creates fleeting impressions, of both objects and actions, in the manner of the action painters. A new spiritualized reality of motion and light is created on the screen. (Ibid., 191)[17]

This theory of cinema was elaborated in the *Voice* columns through the mid-sixties, with 1964 being the crucial year in its formulation. It was certainly complete and informing Mekas's own practice by June 1965, when he photographed the Living Theater's production of Kenneth Brown's *Brig*. While this is not itself a diary film—and it is his last major work that is not—his shooting of it in a continuous take (interrupted only for magazine changes) obliged him to

---

Rexroth, and William DeLappa, who imitated the effects of amateur photographers. See King 1986, 161.

[16] Maya Deren's tracing of the etymology of "amateur" to the Latin for "lover" (which Brakhage regularly invoked) allowed her to point to the superior versatility of rudimentary equipment and its greater responsiveness to "the complex system of supports, joints, muscles and nerves which is the human body" (Deren 1965, 46).

[17] For other examples, see especially the "Movie Journals" of 11 May 1960, 4 October 1962, 25 October 1962, 18 April 1963, 9 April 1964, 23 April 1964, 14 May 1964, 17 December 1964, 24 June 1965, 22 July 1965, 7 December 1967, and 17 July 1969. By this time *Walden* had been exhibited, and the diary film as a genre fully conceptualized; replacing the home movie as the model of proper praxis, it was subsequently invoked in its own terms, even in consideration of other diary filmmakers—for example, Andrew Noren (15 January 1970).

respond immediately to the play in the continuous present of his perception of it.

The inscription of such a "spiritualized reality of motion and light" demanded a virtuoso mastery of the hand-held Bolex and the turning to expressive functions effects of exposure, framing, and shutter speed that, outside the underground, were thought to be nonrealistic and thus nongrammatical. These resources had been most extensively and coherently developed by Brakhage (who had performed for the underground the same synthesizing and totalizing of previous innovations that Griffith had done for the Hollywood narrative), yet within this vocabulary Mekas established a precise idiolect. Its dominant trope is synecdoche; the overall thematic assumption that his individual life might be of general import is reenacted spatially, in a preoccupation with close-ups, not necessarily framed within master shots, and temporally, in single-framing.

The short bursts of photography and especially the single-framing by which Mekas takes note(s) of the loveliness of daily life characteristically involve swift modulations of focus and exposure that transform the colors and contours of a natural object or scene—painting with the sun, precisely. The constantly voyaging camera creates a continuous stream of visual aperçus, alighting on one epiphany after another—a face, a cup of coffee, a cactus, a foot, a dog scratching itself, another face, a movie camera. It is almost impossible to give a sense in words of these sights, but the following, in its detailed sensuousness and nuanced movement around different takes on a visual scene, comes close:

> The sun came out into a clear space in the horizon and fell on the east of the pond and the hillside, and this sudden blaze of light on the still very fresh green leaves was a wonderful contrast with the previous and still surrounding darkness. . . . The outline of each shrub and tree was more or less distinct downy, or silvery, crescent, where the light was reflected from the under side of the most downy, or newest leaves. (Thoreau, *Journal*, 28 August 1860, quoted in Cameron 1985, 12)

Echoing Thoreau's claim that in his journal he writes "only of the things I love. My affection for any aspect of the world" (Cameron 1985, 50), Mekas's voice-over in *Walden* explains his procedures as a "celebration" of what he sees.

The radical disjunction single-framing produces between the sights from which the film derives and those it subsequently makes available marks the limits of the documentary or representational mode within the film diary; if, as another *Walden* voice-over claims, "cinema lies between the frames," then the more hyperbolically distended the gaps between the frames become, the more powerful is the celebratory cinema they generate. The perception recorded in the diary is not then true to the optics of the eye, but is rather medium-specific and so technologically—and ideologically—mediated. Following neoformalist principles that go back through Maya Deren's (1960) belief that film "must cease merely to record realities that owe nothing of their actual existence to the film instrument" (167) to Vertov's Kino-Eye,[18] art is understood as defamiliarization, not the record of visual sensation but the transformation of it. Indeed, at crucial points, when it would be most logical for seeing to spring free from the mediation of the camera, the latter is most insisted on. *Movie Journal* recommends that, when you do not have any film, you pretend you do and keep shooting, still looking through the lens. The final aim is not the transcendence of the camera but rather the identification of the human subject with the apparatus; thus Ed Emshwiller is celebrated for wanting "to become a camera himself" (Mekas 1972, 387). Nor even is the eye a necessary participant, for Mekas himself often shoots from waist level or otherwise without looking through the viewfinder.

Such a project is coherent within a constructivist aesthetic like Vertov's, where it is part of a general program of industrialization. But it fundamentally contradicts the organicism that otherwise informs Mekas's philosophy, occasioning moments of blindness, contradictions that cannot be made articulate and explicit in his theory, but that cannot be entirely concealed in his practice; eventually and inevitably they force the film diary into the diary film. The several contexts in which these contradictions operate may best be approached via the role of his Lithuanian childhood in the structure of Mekas's life and thought.

As we shall see, the summary narrative of the diary films is the attempt to regain Lithuania, a mission that has several components whose isomorphism and fungibility supply the massive energy of Mekas's myth. The myth has a psychoanalytic component—the recovery of the mother; a social component—the recovery of the organic village community; an environmental component—the recovery of the rural scene; and a philosophico-aesthetic component—the recovery of a cultural practice appropriate to these. The

---

[18] The many similarities between Vertov and Mekas—their commitment to film journalism, their common interest in in-camera editing, their preference for the camera eye over the human eye, their commitment to the unscripted documentation of everyday life, and so on, end with Mekas's inclusion of titles, a practice that for Vertov represented an unwarranted admittance of the nonfilmic.

metaphor for such a practice cannot finally be that of the high modernist avant-garde, which was constructed, both logically and historically, in antithetical complementarity to industrial culture; instead it has to be the antimodernist, anti-aestheticist avant-garde—the moment of Dada—proposed as a return *before* industrialization and *before* the reified Kantian- Coleridgean hypostatization of art. It had—and this formulation was made as early as 1960—to "transcend art," to be "completely noncritical, and be anti-art, anti-cinema" (Mekas 1972, 15–16); for this the most appropriate metaphor is "folk art":

> The day is close when the 8 mm home-movie footage will be collected and appreciated as beautiful folk art, like songs and the lyric poetry that was created by the people. Blind as we are, it will take us a few more years to see it, but some people see it already. They see the beauty of sunsets taken by a Bronx woman when she passed through the Arizona desert; travelogue footage, awkward footage that will suddenly sing with an unexpected rapture; the Brooklyn Bridge footage; the spring cherry blossoms footage; the Coney Island footage; the Orchard street footage— time is laying a veil of poetry over them. (Mekas 1972, 83)[19]

Here the metaphor of the poet is residually present, and bourgeois aesthetics still traced in the emphasis that home-movies-as-folk-art will be *collected*; nevertheless, the passage rejects, not just the film industry, but also its complement, the avant-garde, and espouses a practice that would replace both and in that regain the time before their bifurcation. This is the film diary's fundamental aporia. Mekas was trying to use an apparatus of mechanical reproduction, itself entirely integrated into modern industrial production in general, to celebrate a myth of preindustrial, organic society and its values.

One history of modernism is of course a history of the different representational capabilities of its different mediums; while for over a hundred years after the industrial revolution Romantic and post-Romantic poetry in English was unable to treat industrialization or even urbanization, film has been understood as inherently (not merely historically) privileged in this task. Attempting to conjoin the organicism and somatic sensitivity of the one with the mechanism of the other in the painting of modern life, Mekas found himself in the position of the impressionist painters.

---

[19] Mekas did not himself make the shift to 8 mm, although, stimulated by the development of sophisticated super-8 cameras in the seventies and the rapid rise in film costs after then, Huot, Guttenplan, and most other diarists did.

The impressionist desire to picture urban leisure, new forms of mass culture, bohemian life, and fashion appears virtually unchanged in Mekas's films, with the recurrence to the picnic in the city park summary of them. His attempt to discover Lithuania in Manhattan, however, specifically parallels Monet's attempt to paint the modern landscape. For a brief time in the first half of the 1870s, living in the industrializing and rapidly expanding Parisian suburb of Argenteuil, Monet managed to paint landscapes that included the signs of modernization, generally in views of Argenteuil, and crucially in the railroad that was turning it into a dormitory for Paris.[20] His strategy was either to represent the urban landscape under snow, that is, in a "renaturalized" form, or to include a train within a rural scene;[21] *The Train in the Snow* (1875) conjoins both strategies. Soon the social tensions were too great for such assimilation, and Monet left for less-developed environments, eventually his garden and lily ponds. Mekas found the same solutions: with odd exceptions like a shot of workers leaving a factory at the beginning of *He Stands in a Desert* (whose reference to Lumière in any case deflects it back to film history and away from the real world), modern industry is generally outside his purview, and in *Reminiscences of a Journey to Lithuania* he declares his absolute lack of interest in the technological progress made under sovietization, his desire to see only the Lithuania of his childhood, and states his incomprehension of Mayakovsky's and Sandburg's faith in industry. But, as his daily life constantly brings him up against the mechanical reconstruction of the city, modernity is preeminently present in trains or covered by snow. *Walden* contains four major train journeys, from whose vantage point the natural elements appear in coruscating beauty, while the noise of the New York subway, ubiquitous on the sound track, usually sounds like the wind of spring that blows through the film as a whole. New York, when it is not the scene of bucolic splendor, is most often seen under snow, for like Thoreau, Mekas is a "self-appointed inspector of snow storms."[22]

A function jointly of the lure of his rural childhood and his bohemian life in New York, Mekas's inability fully to engage moder-

[20] For an exemplary exposition of these tensions, see Tucker 1982.

[21] For example, respectively, *The Vineyards in the Snow* (1873), *Snow at Argenteuil I* (1874), *Croix blanche* (1875), *Snow at Argenteuil II* (1875), and *Boulevard Saint-Denis* (1875); and *The Highway Bridge under Repair* (1972), *The Railroad Bridge Viewed from the Port* (1873), *The Highway Bridge at Argenteuil* (1874), and *The Promenade with the Railroad Bridge* (1874).

[22] C.f. Mekas, "There is practically no snow in New York; all my New York notebooks are filled with snow" (Mekas 1978, 191).

nity in his diary means finally and ironically that it may not recover Lithuania. For that to be accomplished, the film diary's containment in the present perception of the individual had to be extended into a mode of greater discursivity, one capable of social extension and of dealing with the past—the diary film. Here, in revision, the object of sight was not daily life, but fragments of film; the inscription of subjectivity took the form, not of somatically attuned single-framing and iris manipulation in in-camera editing, but of cutting and adding titles and sound tracks in the editing room. In place of the film diary's cancellation of social relations, the new practice created around itself a community, however small, continuous with the one it represented.

THE DIARY FILM

> *The* past *cannot be* presented.
> —Thoreau, *A Week on the Concord and Merrimack Rivers*

If Mekas's mature film practice was made possible when he realized the aesthetic and ethical priority of his film diary over any feature-film project he might undertake, his decision to introduce edited selections of it as autonomous works of art—as *films*—into the public institutions of the cinema, even the less formal and relatively unalienated institutions of the avant-garde, entailed a reverse movement. The one decision rejected film's history as a public event so as to use it to enrich private perception; the other confronted the public with an autobiographical film, and eventually a corpus of autobiographical films, whose extreme subjectivity and unprecedented formal complexity pose similarly extreme and unprecedented difficulties for spectator and commentator alike, reenacting within the avant-garde the avant-garde's own resistance to the industrial cinema. Whatever personal motives influenced the decision to shift from practice to product in this way, they are not separable from the political questions of the form a genuinely oppositional cinema might take. His voice-over claim in *He Stands in a Desert* that it is "a political film" may link it to the antiwar films of his earliest ambitions, but it also manifests a very different notion of politics.

Mekas's decision to produce a film artifact must at first appear as a compromise of the diary's commitment to presentness, to the process of perception, to the antiartifactual use of the medium, and to all these as the means of the renovation of the individual. The contrary decisions of other filmmakers with analogous projects are illuminating: Jack Smith's drastic refusal to allow his work a public existence, for example, was an act not against Hollywood, but against what he saw as the institutionalization of the avant-garde, and especially Mekas's role in it. On the other hand, in remaking and in fact extending in public his diary's formal innovations, its utopianism, and its recalcitrance, Mekas made cinema perform new functions for himself and transformed its social possibilities. The contradictions of this double gesture inhabit and determine *Walden*; they turn us again to Thoreau, but this time to a pattern of similarities and dissimilarities, determined partially by the material conditions of their respective mediums and partially by the particular way Mekas found a home in America.

The formalist argument that the most essential and authentic literary works of the American transcendentalists were their journals—an argument that has been made not only for Thoreau and Emerson, but also for Bronson Alcott, Margaret Fuller, and Charles King Newcomb[23]—also has a social dimension. The "deliberately unsystematic, irregular, almost dilatory relation to calendrical time" of the Concord "cottage industry" of journal keeping has been understood as both "a partial rejection of American tempo" and "a partial rejection of American mechanical and mercantile capitalism" (Rosenwald 1985, 89). In this respect and in the refusal of conventionally validated literary genres, transcendentalist journal writing refused the prevailing mode of literary production and consumption. Cutting across the distinction between private and public discourses, the habit of sharing and circulating journals actually resisted the growing commodification of writing, as well as implying a more general resistance to the commodity-based social relations of bourgeois society at large. It sustained a semipublic literary sphere, outside art and commerce alike, existing between the private realm of the individual conscience and the public realm of commercially published books. The sign of transcendentalism's utopian social project, the interdependence of the personal and the public in this literary sphere, was also the means of its implementation. The same issues are at stake in Mekas's work, modernized and translated from journal and literary sphere to diary film and cinema.

Though it was never a financial success in his lifetime, Thoreau's

---

[23] This argument is made by Lawrence Rosenwald (1985), who has reread Emerson in the light of Harold Bloom's contention that "Emerson's journals are his authentic work," made in refutation of a tradition from Henry James to F. O. Matthiessen that Emerson's works were "not composed at all." For a parallel argument that Thoreau's *Journal* is his greatest work, see Cameron 1985.

Walden—a completed aesthetic object that was publicly marketed—turned its back on the utopian Concord practice. A century later, Mekas reinvented that practice in making a film outside previous genres. Had he made a commodity object equivalent to Thoreau's, one in any real sense marketable outside the community of his diary's frame of reference—a feature-length condensation of the diary, for example (like Jerome Hill's *Film Portrait*), or an acted story of his life—then his *Walden* would indeed have resembled that of Thoreau. As it is, though it is available for public rental or even purchase, in several respects it more closely resembles Thoreau's journals than his *Walden*. The resistance to public consumption that keeps it essentially within the community of friends who are represented in it—across both the aestheticist avant-garde and the commercial industry, and counter to the different kinds of reification they each entail—reflects the terms of Mekas's engagement with the medium itself.

Stanley Cavell has pointed to the peculiar parallel between writing and living in Thoreau, by which the actions described in *Walden* metaphorically restage the act of writing:

> Each calling—what the writer . . . means by a "field" of action or labor—is isomorphic with every other. This is why building a house and hoeing and writing and reading (and we could add, walking and preparing food and receiving visitors and hammering a nail and surveying the ice) are allegories and measures of one another. All and only true building is edifying. All and only edifying actions are fit for human habitation. Otherwise they do not earn life. If your action, in its field, cannot stand such measurement, it is a sign that the field is not yours. This is the writer's assurance that his writing is not a substitute for life, but his way of prosecuting it. (Cavell 1972, 60)

The argument that *Walden* is the house whose building sustained Thoreau's life applies equally to Mekas's work. As his home movie, *Walden* is at once his movie and his home, "not a substitute for life, but his way of living it." But the peculiar problem of home for Mekas, the double valence produced by the split between the old Lithuanian and the new American home, makes his movie version of it especially complex in its negotiation of the past into the present reality, and crucially of its attempt to re-present the past. His are perforce negative home movies, movies that begin from the fact of the absence of home. Thoreau's demand for autobiography specifies it as "some such account as he would send to his kindred from a distant land" (Thoreau 1971, 3), and clearly Mekas's *Walden* is such a letter from exile. Spanning the period when exile becomes the only home that as an immigrant he will ever have, even as it traces the replacement of one home by another, it confronts the irretrievability of the original home. This incessant dialogue with loss, and the provisionality and supplementarity of all recompense, are inscribed in the film's formal properties and in the story it is made to tell.

Since Thoreau's art was writing, he was able to integrate into a singular, continuous text both his original diary entries and his retrospective elaborations of them to produce a book. In it, the traces of the revisions are sealed over in typesetting, and the formal discontinuities are subsumed in the teleology of the narrative of the stay in the woods and the return to civilization. But for Mekas, the fragments of the past exist as pieces of film that cannot be internally modified, that cannot be made continuous with the present revision of them. Where the film diary was constrained within the present of immediate perception, the diary film confronts its own present with the assembled fragments of a time now lost, of loss itself, of a past that can neither ontologically nor filmically be "presented." The review of the traces and the commentary on them must, like all autobiographical acts, be the "revelation of the present situation of the autobiographer [rather] than the uncovering of his past" (Eakin 1985, 56). Obdurately inaccessible in their own time, the preserved pieces of film are discursively inassimilable; editing can only add material that will clarify the present perception of them, but which, in its inevitable heterogeneity and discontinuity, will also register the unbridgeable gap between then and now.

The superimposition of these temporally disjunct layers of perception produces a macaronic assembly of mixed representational modes. The problem, endemic in autobiography, of the relationship of the speaking subject with the subject of the speech—the Mekas who represents against the Mekas who is represented—is doubled in the confrontation of the temporally divided versions of each. The multiple estrangements are sedimented in the dialogic interplay of irreconcilable subjectivities, each constituted in a different textual system. Comprising diaries, notes, and sketches, *Walden* contains unedited raw footage, works edited and released as separate films, and material of all intermediate degrees of reworking.[24] Where the

---

[24] *Walden* includes *Hare Krishna, Notes on the Circus,* and *Cassis,* all short films edited in 1966, without integrating them into the new whole. The passage from "diary" to "film" in these instances recalls the revision by which in transcendentalist practice a given piece of material was at different times journal entry, lecture, and essay. A contrary instance is *Lost, Lost, Lost,* which also includes many different shooting styles and fragments of unfinished films, but which organizes the succes-

pure visual practice of the film diary privileged a single sense and a single textual system, the diary film subjects the original images to sounds and disjunct visual material.[25] Thus although it eschews both script and synchronized dialogue, the usual ways of organizing film with words, *Walden* is everywhere inhabited and traversed by writing: by the initial appropriation of a literary genre as model; by the inclusion of photographed titles and recorded voices; by photographs of pages from Thoreau; and by Mekas's own voice-over commentary. (Eventually it will appear as unalloyed words in the published form of section-by-section verbal transcriptions.) To these are added old live-recorded conversations and music, new music, and other sounds. The final work is then irreducibly heteroglossaic, the singular iconicity of the diary dispersed; though it frames all other discourses, the authorial commentary is incapable of entirely subsuming them, or even placing them in a hierarchy under its control.

Reflecting the displacement that separates the time of shooting from that of editing, the separation of the two subjectivities confronts present consciousness with its frightening autonomy and obliges it to create fictions of the past. Consequently, the narrative sequence assembled in the films significantly restructures the chronology of Mekas's life; in formalist terms, "story" (the historical sequence of Mekas's life, as this sequence is inexorably sedimented in the film diary) is turned into "plot" (the sequence of events in any given film and in the films as a whole as they constitute a sequence). The conditions of this rewriting are themselves subject to time, as well as being determined by the history of the evolution of Mekas's own sense of what his diary films could accommodate, and so they change from film to film. Figure 11.1 gives some indication of the temporal complexity involved, though not of the diary material that has been excluded from the released films. As the time between the past and the present in which its remains are contemplated varies, so the terms of the possible dialogue between photographer and editor shift. The greater that distance, the greater the sense of loss and the greater the sense of the irretrievability of time; as the editing follows more closely on the shooting, time's ravages are felt proportionately less. The images of *Walden*, only recently recorded at the time it was edited, pose entirely different questions than the late-1940s footage in *Lost, Lost, Lost*, not edited until

sion of stylistic modes within the teleology of the mature diary style. See James 1989, 114–18. After he edited *Walden*, all the footage Mekas shot has been diaristic in nature, so later films do not include such radically heterogenous material.

[25] C.f. "While in *Walden* Thoreau is concerned with the discovery of sound . . . in the *Journal* he explores the complexities of vision" (Cameron 1985, 14).

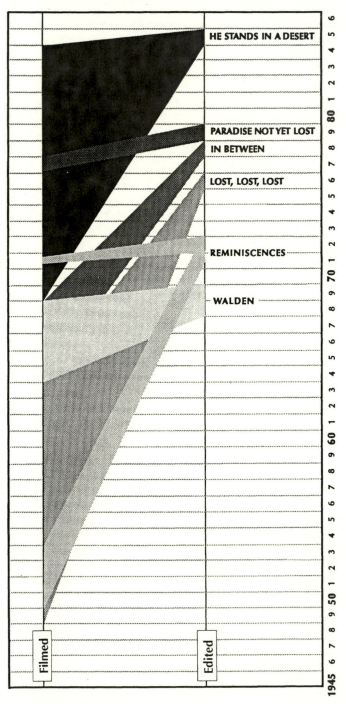

HE STANDS IN A DESERT

PARADISE NOT YET LOST

IN BETWEEN

LOST, LOST, LOST

REMINISCENCES

WALDEN

Filmed

Edited

1945 6 7 8 9 50 1 2 3 4 5 6 7 8 9 60 1 2 3 4 5 6 7 8 9 70 1 2 3 4 5 6 7 8 9 80 1 2 3 4 5 6

JONAS MEKAS: The Major Diary Films

11.1 Jonas Mekas: The Major Diary Films.

thirty years later. These variations supply the narrative drama of the sequence as a whole, and within that the drama of each individual film. The social issues here may best be approached via the metanarrative of the diary films as a whole, especially as it is first formulated in *Walden*.

Writers commonly note how in retrospect their diaries reveal patterns not visible at the time of writing; Virginia Woolf, for example, found it curious that in rereading hers she "went for things put in haphazard, and found the significance to lie where I never saw it at the time" (Woolf 1953, 14). Mekas has himself noted similar discoveries (MacDonald 1984, 96), made late at night and often many years later when for himself only he reviews his diary. In the added voice-overs and titles, he comments on the preserved images, finding in them a myth of the trauma of loss of the childhood gemeinschaft and its recovery in art and the community of artists; it is the secularized, interiorized myth of Christianity, most fully elaborated in Wordsworth's *Prelude*, though omnipresent in Romanticism.[26] Mekas first and fully articulates the myth in *Walden*, with subsequent works playing variations on the structure it establishes, displacing it into different temporal ranges, or focusing on particular stages. *Lost, Lost, Lost* confronts a double loss, that of Lithuania and that of the early years in New York, but, despite the reluctance of the voice-over, it also sketches the early stages of the recovery— the founding of *Film Culture* and the filmmaking community represented by Ken Jacobs and Barbara Rubin. In *Reminiscences of a Journey to Lithuania*, he again confronts footage from the early fifties, but juxtaposes it to material collected on his return to Lithuania. Though he is there restored to his mother, neither his childhood nor the prewar rural society may be regained; nor can he stay there, for that would now entail the loss of the postwar years spent in New York—a double bind in whose terrors all exiles live. In *Paradise Not Yet Lost (a/k/a Oona's Third Year)*, his new wife and their daughter initially appear to compensate him for the loss, and indeed his daughter allows him a surrogate experience of his own

[26] The most complete formulation of the influence of British Romanticism on the American avant-garde remains Sitney's *Visionary Film*, but his "Autobiography in Avant-Garde Film" is additionally valuable in tracing film autobiography to Wordsworth, as well as to Saint Augustine and Rousseau. Beyond the continuities he isolates, one further should be mentioned: the subgenre of Romantic poems that discover the possibility and process of their own composition during accounts of the impossibility of writing poems. *The Prelude* is the epic form of this, with Coleridge's "Frost at Midnight" its lyric equivalent. The structure completely subtends *Lost, Lost, Lost*, but is already visible in *Walden*, for example, in the inclusion of the short, organically edited films representing the road not taken.

childhood;[27] but he displaces his loss onto her, for whom, he predicts, the "fragments of paradise" caught in the film will eventually be as vague and irretrievable as are his of Lithuania, which, this time with his American family, he visits again. In *He Stands in a Desert* the voice-over lamentation is jettisoned, but the documentation of what is revealed as an astonishingly successful social life[28] still has the desperation of a man shoring against his ruin recollections of his moments in the life-styles of the rich and famous.

In these myths, loss is not simply the master narrative; it is the condition of their coming into being, and in this it registers a categorical difference between the film diary and the diary film. Reflecting the epistemological limits of photography, the former could register only what was present, while the contemplation of the fragments of what has become the past confronts the loss that is congealed in them. In this, they are all supplemental forms of the impossible footage, the absent center of the entire project, the footage of his childhood in Lithuania. Not only was this never shot but, since the introduction of mechanical reproduction would have destroyed the condition of premodernity, it is historically and logically inconceivable. The entire practice is constructed on and contingent on absence, a resuscitation of the Puritan diary of daily self-assessment driven by the search for an unattainable grace. Mekas will never catch up with himself to turn the ongoing diary footage immediately into a diary film without the intrusion of present consciousness over footage from the past. Thus, whenever a recompense for the originating loss appears, a new catastrophe must be entertained: hence the projection of the ravages of time onto Oona, still present to herself and her parents in *Paradise Not Yet Lost*.

Walden inaugurates this myth in a double argument with Tho-

---

[27] Mekas's strategy in this film is similar to Brakhage's use of his children in *Scenes from under Childhood* (1967–1970), and also to Gunvor Nelson's film about her daughter, *My Name is Oona* (1969).

[28] "The film consists of 124 brief sketches . . . of my film-maker friends such as Hans Richter, Rossellini, Marcel Hanoun, Adolfo Arrieta, Henri Langois, Cavalcanti, Kubelka, Ken Jacobs, Kenneth Anger, Kuchars, Breer, Willard Van Dyke, Frampton, etc. or just friends, such as John Lennon, Jackie Onassis, Lee Radziwill, John Kennedy Jr. & Caroline, Tina and Anthony Radziwill, Peter Beard, Andy Warhol, Richard Foreman, P. Adams Sitney, Yoko Ono, Raimund Abraham, Allen Ginsberg, George Maciunas, and countless others" (*Film-Makers' Cooperative Catalogue* 1989, 366–67). Mekas's decision to reserve from this film both the "personal" and the "abstract" material from its period is especially unfortunate and, as well as ensuring the discomforting obsession with the famous (especially John Lennon and the Kennedys), it reinstates the separation of public and private whose subversion otherwise marks his work's importance.

reau. In the dominant movement, Mekas reorganizes the terms of Thoreau's utopia, but in a subtext he reverts to them. For Thoreau, living in postindustrial America, Walden Pond provided solitude, with nature defined against community. But Mekas, recalling premodern Lithuanian village life, initially identifies the two according to the Wordsworthian redemptive trinity of friends, nature, and art; in his Walden the community is discovered in nature, either by reenvisaging Manhattan through the optic of its rural lacunae (notably Central Park) or in visits to artists who live outside the city. But counter to this runs the other movement that eventually recontains it, for even as Mekas discovers himself within the filmmaking avant-garde, he finally asserts his difference from it and makes a commitment to a differently construed practice, an individualism more like that of Thoreau. Since the textural richness of Mekas's *Walden* so intensely draws one's attention to its present, submerging the shape of this plot in the apparently paratactical, unmotivated disarray of daily life, it must be retrieved, the first movement in the detail of Mekas's own transcript (fig. 11.2),[29] and then more summarily.

The opening section establishes the thematic kernel the film will develop. Manhattan, where Mekas has lived deeply and sucked out "all the marrow of life," has been discovered as Walden; for him it is the place where art, friends, and nature coincide. The film announces what will emerge as its integral reflexivity, its documentation of the friendships and other aspects of the independent cinema that legitimate it and provide it with a context in which it will have meaning. The events of daily life are the construction of the institutions of the independent cinema, his friends are its agents, and all around is beautiful. Like Thoreau he may have been "walled in" in Manhattan, but it is everywhere enlivened by flowers, trees, sunsets, and other forms of nature. In the snow Mekas finds the element that allows him to see New York as Lithuania, while Bibbe Hansen, blonde and barelegged, plucking grass in the park, is the very image of a Lithuanian peasant girl.

After this summary introit, the film embarks on its major development. The events of 1964–1968 are, following the Thoreauvian model, condensed very roughly into an extended year of three phases, each occupying two reels: a spring that is followed through to fall, a winter, and another fall. In the first reel, after the opening

[29] This is reproduced from "First Draft Edition, *Diaries, Notes, and Sketches, Also Known as Walden*," the program for the first showings in 1969. Those notes indicate that it was a provisional version, and the film now in circulation differs substantially from it, but not in the opening section considered here.

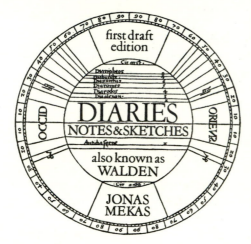

This film being what it is, i.e. a series of personal notes on events, people (friends) and Nature (Seasons) — the Author won't mind (he is almost encouraging it) if the Viewer will choose to watch only certain parts of the *work (film)*, according to the time available to him, according to his preferences, or any other good reason. To assist the Viewer in this matter, particularly in cases of repeated viewings (forgive the Author this presumption), the following Contents, a list of scenes and their time tables, reel by reel, have been prepared.

A note in the beginning says, that this is the First Draft of the Diaries. Why should the Author permit then, one may ask, the unpolished or half-polished edition to come out? His answer is, he thought that despite the roughness of sound and some parts of the images, there is still enough in them — he felt — to make them of some interest to some of his friends and a few strangers. In order to go to the next stage of polishing, he felt, he had to look at the footage as it is, many many more times, and gain more perspective to it — that's why this edition. There is another reason. A few months ago, suddenly he saw his room filling up with smoke — he couldn't even see the film cans — and only a very lucky coincidence stopped the fire next door which would have consumed five years of his work. So he gave himself word to bring out as soon as he can this First Draft version, and there he stands, and hopes that some of you will find some enjoyment in what you'll see.

December, 1969   The Author

REEL
00   DEDICATED TO LUMIERE
          DIARIES NOTES AND SKETCHES
          ALSO KNOWN AS WALDEN
          Close up of the Author
          IN NEW YORK WAS STILL WINTER
          Central Park, scattered snow
          BUT THE WIND WAS FULL OF SPRING
          naked branches in wind
          the Author playing accordion
          BARBARA'S FLOWER GARDEN
          Barbara planting flower seeds on the window sill
          Film-Makers' Cinematheque, 4th St.
          SITNEY IS FINGERPRINTED BY THE POLICE,
          AS DIRECTOR OF THE CINEMATHEQUE

1 min.   Sitney, CU of his hand
          I CUT MY HAIR, TO RAISE MONEY, HAVING
          TEAS WITH RICH LADIES
          the Author, showing his haircut, turning around
          daily expense notes
          SUNDAY AT STONES
          the Author, eating; also, David & Barbara Stone

2 min.   I WALKED ACROSS THE PARK. THERE WAS
          A PHANTASTIC FEELING OF SPRING IN THE AIR.
          apple blossoms
          a group of boys, in sport shirts, jumping up and down,
          in Central Park
          TONY CONRAD AND BEVERLY GRANT
          AT THEIR SECOND AVENUE HOME
          we see Tony Conrad and Beverly Grant in the doorway
          they look at the yard, at the trees

3 min.   PHOTOGRAPH THE DUST FALLING ON THE CITY,
          ON THE WINDOWS, ON THE BOOKS, EVERYWHERE
          the Author, in bed, can't sleep, turns around
          I THOUGHT OF HOME
          Central Park lake
          WALDEN

Chopin / street & subway noise

street & subway noise

11.2 Program notes for "first draft edition" of *Walden*.

11.3–11.18 First sequences of *Walden*; captions are Mekas's own words.

11.3 "Close-up of the Author"

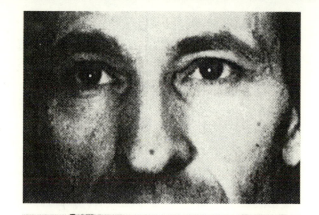

11.4 "Central Park, scattered snow"

11.5 "naked branches in wind"

11.6 "the Author playing accordion"

11.7 "Barbara planting flower seeds on the window sill"

11.8 "Film-Makers' Cinematheque, 4th St."

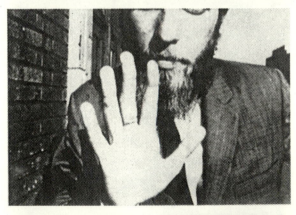

11.9 "Sitney, CU of his hand"

11.10 "the Author, showing his haircut, turning around"

11.11 "the daily expenses notes"

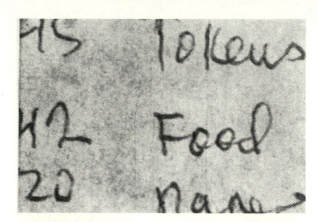

11.12 "the Author eating"

11.13 "also, David & Barbara Stone"

11.14 "apple blossoms"

11.15 "a group of boys, in sports shirts, jumping up and down, in Central Park"

11.16 "we see Tony Conrad and Beverly Grant in the doorway"

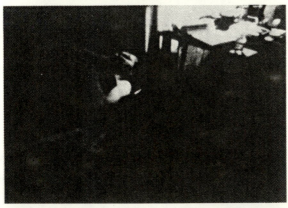

11.17 "the Author, in bed, can't sleep, turns around"

11.18 "Central Park lake"

sequence, the first of the weddings that punctuate each of the three sections appears, providing the occasion for the voice-over that equates home moviemaking and life. There follow visits with other filmmakers, artists, and intellectuals, Jerome Hill, P. Adams Sitney, the Stone family, Tim Leary, Gregory Markopoulos, Allen Ginsburg, and Hare Krishna hippies. The second part begins in midwinter with more scenes of New York filmmakers, a flashback to peace demonstrators seven years previously, *Film Culture* and Co-op business, winter hikes in the country, street scenes and Christmas parties, and a train ride and long visit to the Brakhage family in their snowy mountain home.

The Brakhages and their home movies are the center of the film, and also of its ethical system; in being received into their home and in sharing in their participatory, domestic filmmaking, Mekas is integrated into the ideal cinema. But since such a homecoming jeopardizes the position of Lithuania proper in his myth of his own life, it must also be problematic; in the next section, over images of folk-dancing Lithuanian émigrés, he recounts his various morbid fears and notes that he no longer remembers his dreams, and then asks: "Am I losing all that I had brought with me from the outside?" and cuts to a haunting Lithuanian folk song. The juxtaposition of the traces of the childhood Lithuania to the ideal form of its recreation is the film's crisis, and it is resolved by an acceptance of the compensation of the perfection of everyday life, even of life in the New World, and of the community of independent filmmakers. So in the third section, he returns to New York, to the milieu of the New American Cinema, recognizing it as Walden in the terms we have outlined. In discovering this home in cinema, he discovers an America, an individual reenactment of the origin of the nation.[30] But not completely; he also preserves his isolation, finally rejecting total assimilation into this community and the kind of filmmaking it has begun to practice.

In the last movement of the film, after returning from the Brakhages' home, he clarifies his own practice as one of personal perception defined not against Hollywood, but against the avant-garde, which is now revealed to be debased, commercialized, and sensa-

[30] Again I am reading Mekas through Cavell (1972), who remarks of Thoreau's move to Walden on Independence Day: "We know the specific day in the specific year on which all the ancestors of New England took up their abode in the woods. That moment of origin is the national event re-enacted in the events of *Walden*, in order this time to do it right, or to prove that it is impossible; to discover and settle this land, or the question of this land, once and for all" (8).

tionalized. The countertheme is dramatized in a longish sequence in which Adolfas directs scenes for *Hallelujah the Hills* for the benefit of a German TV crew making a documentary about underground film. It is also articulated discursively in a voice-over where, noting the lack of tragedy or drama or suspense in his images, Mekas claims that they are "just images for myself and a few others. One doesn't have to watch, but if one wants to, one can." This rejection of the organic art object and preference for the definitively amateur work, made for himself and "a few others," culminates in the last reel where, bitterly ridiculing and scorning what have become clichés of the underground, he returns to the photography of his daily life, asserting that he shoots only for himself, and ends the film with a woman friend on a beautiful autumn day in Central Park.

In discovering the New American Cinema as a compensation for the lost Lithuania, but then proposing within and against the underground film the obsessive revision of the fragments of his film diary, this narrative allegorically restates the interplay between the fragments of the past and the present contemplation of them that informs the process of composition. The same story of success and failure in the attempt to integrate life and film is told in the processes of exhibition and consumption, with the cinema implied and created by the film reproducing both the plurality and the infringements of the text. The refusal of sanctioned generic forms—the refusal to keep the private merely private and separate from the public—makes the rejection of the received cinemas all but inevitable. Neither the sequestered domesticity of the home movie on the one hand, nor on the other the marginal cinemas of the aesthetic avant-garde and the public cinemas of the film industry, can finally be a home for a film practice that refuses the rationalizations they each variously entail.

Bibliography

Abbot, H. Porter. 1984. *Diary Fiction: Writing as Action*. Ithaca: Cornell University Press.

Barthes, Roland. 1977. *Roland Barthes by Roland Barthes*. Trans. Richard Howard. New York: Hill and Wang.

Bruss, Elizabeth. 1980. "Eye for I: Making and Unmaking Autobiography in Film." In *Autobiography. See* Olney 1980.

Bürger, Peter. 1984. *Theory of the Avant-Garde.* Minneapolis: University of Minnesota Press.

Cameron, Sharon. 1985. *Writing Nature: Henry Thoreau's Journal.* New York: Oxford University Press.

Camper, Fred. 1986. "Some Notes on the Home Movie." *Journal of Film and Video* 38, no. 3–4:9–15.

Cavell, Stanley. 1972. *The Senses of Walden.* New York: Viking Press.

Chalfden, Richard. 1975. "Cinema Naivete: A Study of Home Moviemaking as Visual Communication." *Studies in the Anthropology of Visual Communication* 2:87–103.

Creeley, Robert. 1972. *A Day Book.* New York: Scribners.

Deren, Maya. 1960. "Cinematography: The Creative Use of Reality." *Daedalus* (Winter): 150–67.

———. 1965. "Amateur versus Professional." *Film Culture* 39:45–46.

Dorn, Ed. 1972. "From *The Day and Night Book.*" In *All Stars*, ed. Tom Clark. New York: Grossman.

DuPlessis, Rachel. 1985. "For the Etruscans: Sexual Difference and Artistic Production—The Debate over a Female Aesthetic." In *The Future of Difference*, ed. Hester Eisenstein and Alice Jardine, 128–56. New Brunswick: Rutgers University Press.

Eakin, Paul John. 1985. *Fictions in Autobiography: Studies in the Art of Self-Invention.* Princeton: Princeton University Press.

Emerson, Ralph Waldo. 1885. *Nature, Addresses, and Lectures.* Boston: Houghton Mifflin.

Film-Makers' Cooperative Catalogue. 1989. New York: Film-Makers' Cooperative.

Fothergill, Robert A. 1974. *Private Chronicles: A Study of English Diaries.* London: Oxford University Press.

Ginsberg, Allen. 1970. *Indian Journals.* San Francisco: City Lights.

———. 1972. *The Fall of America: Poems of These States.* San Francisco: City Lights.

Gusdorf, Georges. 1956. "Conditions and Limits of Autobiography." In *Autobiography. See* Olney 1980.

James, David E. 1989. *Allegories of Cinema: American Film in the Sixties.* Princeton: Princeton University Press.

King, Graham. 1986. *Say "Cheese!" The Snapshot as Art and Social History.* London: William Collins.

Lejeune, Philippe. 1987. "Cinéma et autobiographie: Problèmes de vocabulaire." *Revue belge du cinéma* 19 (Spring): 7–13.

———. 1989. *On Autobiography.* Minneapolis: Minnesota University Press.

Lowell, Robert. 1970. *Notebook, 1967–1968*. New York: Farrar, Straus, and Giroux.

MacDonald, Scott. 1980. "Surprise! The Films of Robert Huot: 1967 to 1972." *Quarterly Review of Film Studies* 5, no. 3 (Summer): 297–318.

———. 1984. "Interview with Jonas Mekas." *October* 29 (Summer): 82–116.

Mallon, Thomas. 1984. *A Book of One's Own: People and Their Diaries*. New York: Penguin.

Martens, Lorna. 1985. *The Diary Novel*. Cambridge: Cambridge University Press.

Mattheissen, F. O. 1941. *American Renaissance: Art and Expression in the Age of Emerson and Whitman*. New York: Oxford University Press.

Mekas, Jonas. 1962. "Notes on the New American Cinema." *Film Culture* 24:6–16.

———. 1969. "First Draft Edition, *Diaries, Notes, and Sketches, also known as Walden*." Program. Anthology Film Archives, New York.

———. 1972. *Movie Journal: The Rise of a New American Cinema, 1959–1971*. New York: Macmillan.

———. "The Diary Film." 1978. In *The Avant-Garde Film: A Reader of Theory and Criticism*, ed. P. Adams Sitney. New York: New York University Press.

Nussbaum, Felicity. 1988. "Towards Conceptualizing Diary." In *Studies in Autobiography*, ed. James Olney. New York: Oxford University Press.

Olney, James. 1980. *Autobiography: Essays Theoretical and Critical*. Princeton: Princeton University Press.

Rainer, Tristine. 1978. *The New Diary*. Los Angeles: Jeremy P. Tarcher.

Rosenwald, Lawrence. 1985. *Emerson and the Art of the Diary*. New York: Oxford University Press.

Sanderson, Alister. 1977. "The Diary Cinema of Howard Guttenplan." *Millennium Film Journal* 1, no. 1 (Winter): 107–20.

Sitney, P. Adams. 1977. "Autobiography in Avant-Garde Film." *Millennium Film Journal* 1, no. 1 (Winter): 60–106.

———. 1979. *Visionary Film*. New York: Oxford University Press.

Storr, Robert. 1986. "The Theoretical Come-On." *Art in America* (April): 159–65.

Stuckey, Charles F. 1984. "Monet's Art and the Act of Vision." In *Aspects of Monet*, ed. John Rewald and Frances Weitzenhoffer. New York: Harry N. Abrams.

Thoreau, H. D. 1971 [1845]. *Walden*. Princeton: Princeton University Press.

———. 1981 [1837–1844]. *Journal*, Vol. 1. Princeton: Princeton University Press.

———. 1984 [1842–1848]. *Journal*, Vol. 2. Princeton: Princeton University Press.

Tucker, Philip Hayes. 1982. *Monet at Argenteuil*. New Haven: Yale University Press.

Vertov, Dziga. 1984. *Kino-Eye: The Writings of Dziga Vertov*. Ed. Annette Michelson. Berkeley and Los Angeles: University of California Press.

Woolf, Virginia. 1953. *A Writer's Diary*. London: Hogarth Press.

12. Peter Moore

A Portfolio of Photographs

Selected by
Barbara Moore

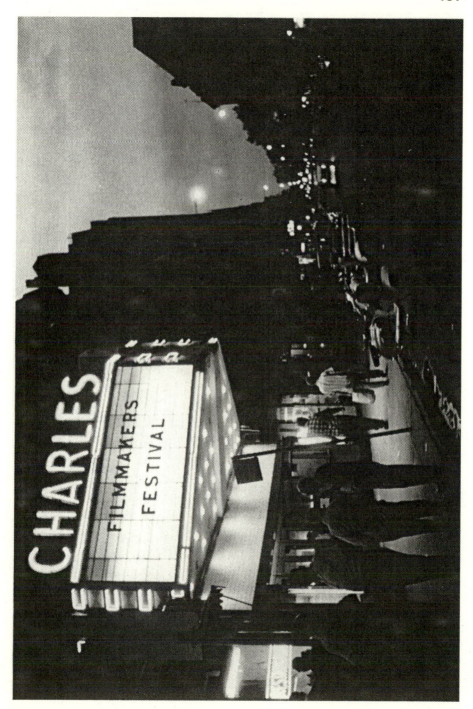

12.1 Charles Theater during the Film-Makers' Festival, 5 July 1962.

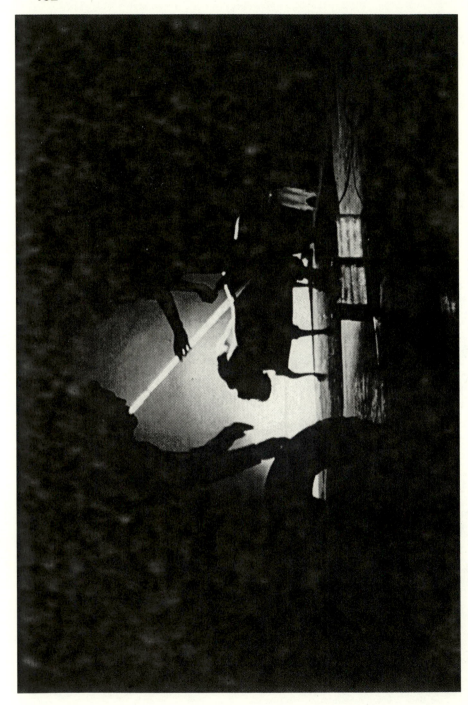

12.2 Robert Rauschenberg's *Map Room II* in the Expanded Cinema Festival, Film-Makers' Cinematheque, 2 December 1965: Alex Hay, Deborah Hay, Robert Rauschenberg.

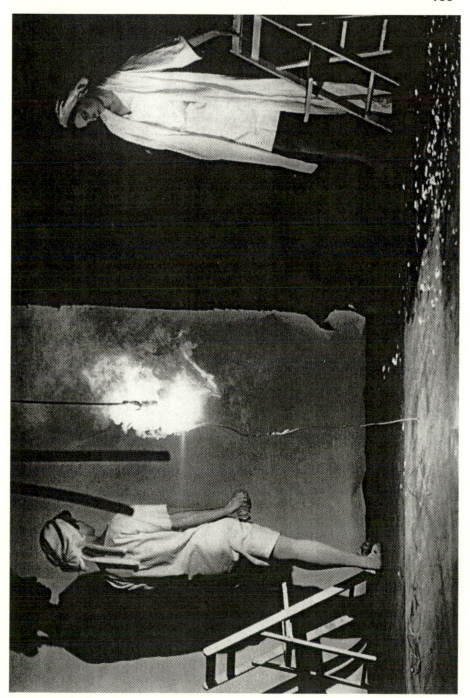

12.3 Robert Whitman's *Prune Flat* in the Expanded Cinema Festival, Film-Makers' Cinematheque, 17 December 1965: Simone Forti, Lucinda Childs.

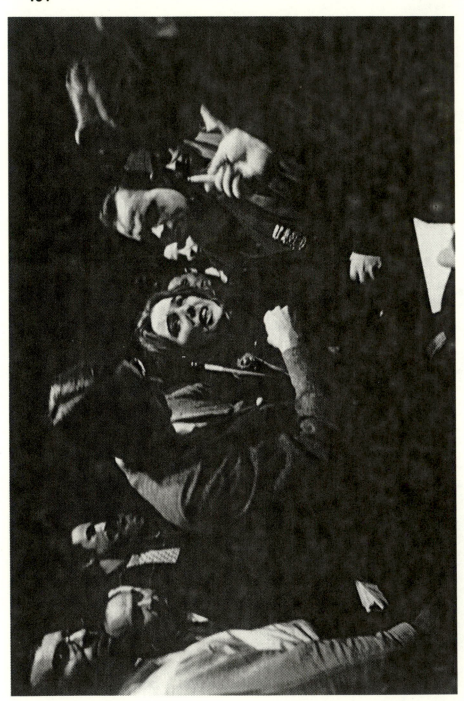

12.4 Charlotte Moorman being arrested after topless cello performance in Nam June Paik's *Opera Sextronique*, Film-Makers' Cinematheque, 9 February 1967.

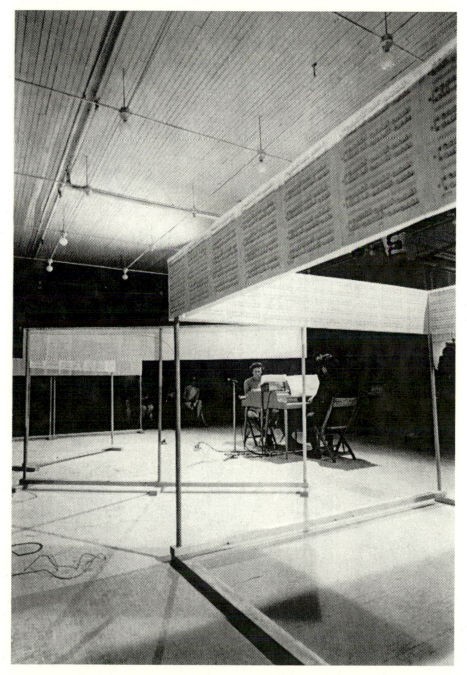

12.5 Philip Glass and Steve Reich performing Glass's "In Again Out Again," Film-Makers' Cinematheque, 19 May 1968.

12.6 Jonas Mekas with Yoko Ono and John Lennon, 9 June 1971.

12.7 George Maciunas's backyard, 80 Wooster Street, 29 June 1971. Clockwise from top: Andy Warhol, Fred Hughes, Yoko Ono, John Lennon, Pola Chapelle, Jonas Mekas.

12.8 Richard Foreman's "Paris—New York Telephone Call," West Broadway, 24 June 1972.

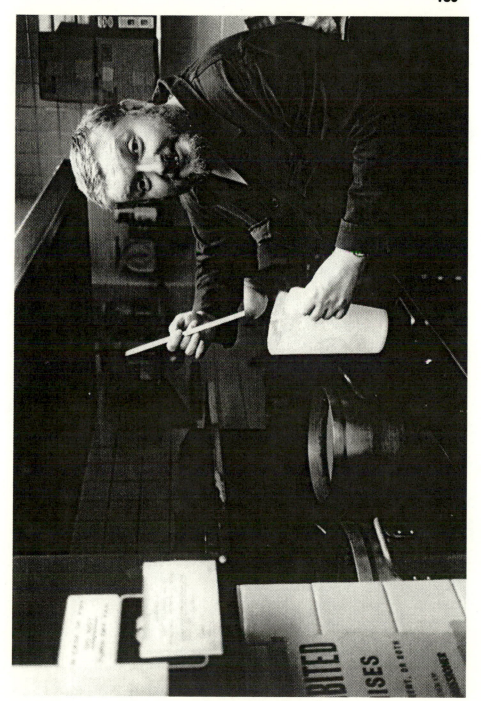

12.9 Peter Kubelka cooking after a Herman Nitsch performance at the Kitchen, 2 December 1972.

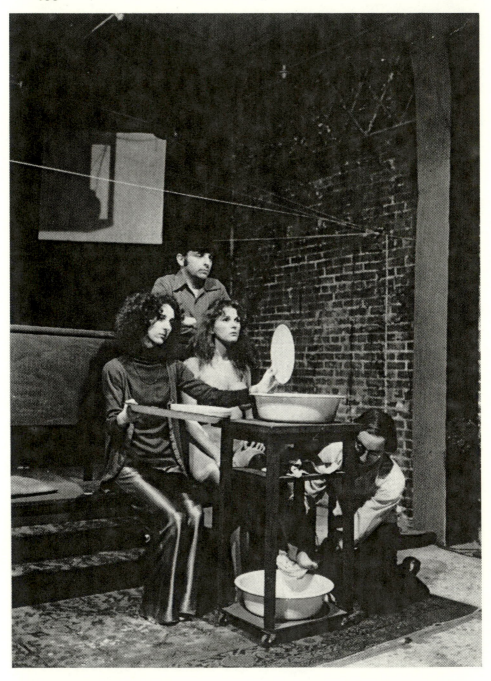

12.10 Richard Foreman's *Sophia = (Wisdom), Part 3: The Cliffs*, Anthology Film Archives, 80 Wooster Street, 26 January 1973.

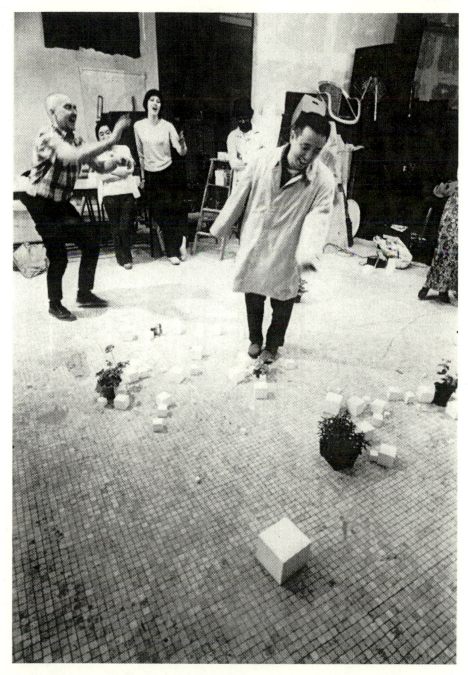

12.11 George Maciunas (left) and Nam June Paik (center) playing a game by Takako Saito, Flux Game Fest, Anthology Film Archives, 19 May 1973.

13. Maureen Turim   *Reminiscences,* Subjectivities, and Truths

AUTOBIOGRAPHICAL CINEMA, the cinema of the self, the diary film, personal cinema: these terms, widely used over the last thirty years and central to this volume on the film work of Jonas Mekas, will here be investigated differently. How does cinema, the great collective and mass-cultural art form, scale itself to the dimensions of a single self? How does an art-making process based on directing the camera out at the world invert its focus to reveal the person behind the camera? If the answer for many of the authors in this volume is evoked by the name Jonas Mekas, I wish to suggest that terms such as "diary film" and "personal cinema" evoked by Mekas constitute virtual oxymorons. They describe a process that is seemingly fraught with contradictions, and call into question just what the relationship is between film and memory, film and subjectivity, film and selfhood.

It is important to remember that the development of autobiographical cinema comes at a specific point in cinema history. It involves a process of rupture, in which the poetics of avant-garde cinema are conjoined with the embrace of "amateur" gauges of film stock as artistic tools for portraiture of the self. The cinematic autobiographer says not only "I want to tell my life through the cinema," but also, "enough of cinema as a mass medium and as an industrial and collective activity." Autobiographical cinema has therefore been conceived not as the story of any life, but as the story of the life of the artist. It is an artistic expression that more or less self-consciously highlights the artist in his or her subjective response to an environment and in his or her symbolic interiority.

Contradictions that bear theoretical ramifications, however, remain. Filming is different from looking in a mirror; how telling that the shot of the artist-filmmaker looking in the mirror obscures the filmmaker (a shot included in many film autobiographies, an example of which is Andrew Noren's *Adventures of the Exquisite Corpse. Part V: The Lighted Field*, 1987). The subject is hidden behind the camera itself. One can easily photograph oneself using a tripod, but in this case, filming oneself is possible only so long as the frame approximates the fixity of still photography. Recent autobiographical videotapes often adopt just this fixity of framing, in which the artist performs for the camera in a studio setting—for example, Lynn Hershman's *Binge*, 1988, which is dominated by a voiced commentary that laments the artist's inability to change or even move. Autobiography here is coupled with performance art.

For cinema, however, the question of autobiography has been *framed* differently, as a desire to render the filmmaker's life in the world and not in the studio. Yet one can not easily film one's body in motion and engaging in activities; representation of the self in the image depends largely on absence and metaphor. Film images are gathered, taken from outside the self, or by the other of the self. As the desire in film autobiography is to express the life of the self as subject (and so transform film), it is important to confront the constraints placed on such an undertaking from the outset by the cinema as apparatus. To state this theoretically, autobiography strains at the limits of cinema as an apparatus of representation when it strives for this level of mimetic reproduction. The other can record the self or the self can record the other and the world, but the self cannot simply capture or control its own filmic articulation.

One is forced to enlist other strategies to produce the filmic autobiography: either to engage the other to film the self (as for example when Maya Deren enlists Alexander Hammid to help her shoot *Meshes of the Afternoon*), to symbolize the self indirectly (also present in the dream-object imagery of *Meshes of the Afternoon*), or to mark one's presence in the filming through absence. It is this latter strategy, which in effect equates a subjective camera with the consciousness of the filmmaker, that is most significant to the formulation of the autobiographical film as it develops out of what has been called personal filmmaking.

This marking of presence through absence entails the following implicit enunciations: "I was there behind the camera. I chose this image. I chose this transformative process of registering the image to mark my presence as filmmaker. I inscribed myself through the ways I manipulated the camera." The image thus bears the traces of the subject creating and selecting it. When the filmmaker exposes himself or herself through such a process, it is, after all, figurative. We must recognize that we are then already in the realm of metaphor. To paraphrase two famous films that in fact explore both the strengths and the limits of such subjectivity on the part of a filmmaker, one is always a man or a woman with a movie camera; one can never simply leave one's will on film.[1]

Filming is also different from writing in the first person singular, except insofar as one has recourse to spoken and written language, as in a voice-over. To posit the "I" of first-person verbal narration other than through language, one is largely dependent on an equation of the "I" first-person pronoun with the eyes, with visual perception.[2] This is an equation whose homonymic status in English makes it especially attractive metaphorically, as Stan Brakhage's writings on his filmmaking illustrate (Brakhage 1963). Yet this charm inherent in sound similarity belies the gap between what the subject sees and who the subject is, or even who the subject construes himself or herself to be. To continue briefly with the example of Brakhage, his films do contain critical moments in which they mirror the self directly, but these moments are made possible only through external collaboration, as when his first wife, Jane, takes the camera at crucial moments to reveal Stan's reaction to their child being born, or his epileptic fit. More often they reflect the self metaphorically. Take for example the landscape shots in which light exposure is manipulated to create an apocalyptic vision in *Machine of Eden* (1970). The immediacy of seeing and recording, the subject "I" and the camera "eye," are collapsed into one another so that the subject, the filmmaker, becomes the effect of what he can make his camera see—or, to use Brakhage's own words in describing the first of the series of films he calls his autobiographies (the *Sincerity* reels, 1973–1980), "a graph of light equivalent to autobiographical thought process" (*Film-Makers' Cooperative Catalogue*, 1989, 51). Brakhage knows he is using metaphors, but he also sincerely believes in the equivalences they establish.

This sort of artist-autobiography borrows most heavily from cer-

---

[1] Dziga Vertov's *Man with a Movie Camera*, 1929, and Nagisa Oshima's *Battle of Tokyo, or the Young Man Who Left His Will on Film*, 1975.

[2] Cf. Bruss 1980. She makes some interesting observations on the differences between the filmic expression of stories derived from the author's past and linguistically based autobiography. The problem with her formulation is that her consideration of autobiography in film is limited to fictional films whose narratives have certain autobiographical components, such as Fellini's *8 1/2* and Truffaut's *400 Blows*. As such she is describing differences in focalization and identification that exist between literary fiction and literary autobiography; none of this is as specific to filmic enunciation as she holds. I am striving to articulate a more profound difference between the visual image and the first-person enunciation operative even in films that do attempt to collect images as just such expressions of the self "speaking."

tain principles of poetic cinema, a cinema that seeks an allegorical or metaphorical status for the image using montage as its tropology. Yet it also flirts with apparently diametrically opposed principles, those of direct cinema, a cinema that strives to record events unmediated by the processes of narration, elaborate prior-structuring, or restructuring montage. The paradox here is that the self and self-awareness are the "events" *least* accessible to filmic recording. The self is perhaps not an event or a series of events at all. The self is created in film through the mediation of the processes of narrative and symbolic representation, even if those processes rest on a phenomenology of vision.

It is with Lacanian psychoanalysis, with its emphasis on verbal enunciation, that the import of what I have just proposed attains its particular theoretical significance for film theory (Lacan 1977). I am tempted to propose that the psychoanalytic session is the ultimate act of autobiography because the self is remembered not simply in terms of a program of events and accomplishments, but as it is *heard* as a telling retelling. In the attempt to articulate the past, the subject gropes through and trips over the language that rules not only what he or she is, but how she or he can know anything about selfhood. Language has its advantages here as a medium of self-expression because language lends itself to revealing how the self as a concept is constructed in and through language. Insofar as a montage of images and voices substitute themselves for written language in the personal film, they transform the parameters of enunciation. We must look elsewhere for that to which we might otherwise listen if the retelling is to be as telling.

The literary autobiographer traditionally has cleaned up this act and adopted the formulas of a conventional wisdom of what constitutes a life in order to order what would otherwise be a symptomatic collage of failed and fragmented enunciations. For the autobiographer, language takes the form of narration. Failed and fragmented enunciations are respectively effaced and sutured, as narrations create a privileged form for the construction of the subject in history, for the writing of history is itself a process of narration. The filmic autobiographer in constructing filmic montage as narration to a certain extent duplicates the reordering of language as narrative, binding the sequences of imagery to a history-being-told, or if you will, argued.

Conversely, let us say one wants to try to imagine and reveal aspects of the self outside or beyond language, narrative, and history. Such a goal is in itself theoretically intriguing, though it also is riddled with the tragic history of the romantic quest and of primal nostalgia. There is perhaps no escaping history; there is certainly no direct access to the psyche. In acknowledging this, poetic cinematic autobiography would need to take account of its own processes of metaphorical rendering to recognize the ways in which it narrates. It could no longer simply offer its captured images as the truth of the self by some phenomenological appeal to the immediacy of their registration. Yet insofar as it makes self-conscious its form of articulation and does not naturalize its enunciative process, it provides the very markers of formal distance that undercut the directness required by the diary and personal revelation.

It is with this in mind that I wish now to turn to Jonas Mekas's *Reminiscences of a Journey to Lithuania*, which offers us the immediacy of recorded events as autobiography even while Mekas tempers this act with the poetics of memory and metaphorical renderings. The making of this film is preceded by historical interventions on Mekas's part that provide a context for understanding it, especially its third part, devoted to the muse of cinema, which serves as a conclusion to the first two parts, the meditation on being a displaced person and the chronicle of the journey to Lithuania.

If I return to the writings of Mekas, it is not to reveal a history never before told, but to examine this history differently. As with many other artists, Mekas's writings are often cited only as direct explanations of his praxis. If I tend to read the writings more symptomatically, it is to uncover what assumptions concerning the self-as-artist are voiced in these texts and consequently what assumptions concerning the relationship of filmmaking to lived experience form the nexus of Mekas's perspective.

As film critic for the *Village Voice* and editor of *Film Culture*, Jonas Mekas became a spokesperson for a movement with his call for a "personal cinema." He did not necessarily envision a solely autobiographical undertaking, at least initially. Personal cinema, a major component of what Mekas called the "New American Cinema," referred to low-budget, independently produced films of various lengths that conceived filmic expression differently from the repetitive and delimited narrative-theatrical codings of Hollywood cinema. Personal cinema was first and foremost to be understood as a poetic cinema, continuing and renewing the traditions of earlier filmic avant-gardes. Yet the term "personal" also evolved in Mekas's writings toward a notion of autobiography marked by images gathered to reveal the maker's life, his way of seeing, his thoughts and feelings. I would like to examine therefore the history of this evolution through which Mekas's conception of personal filmmaking came to be equated with a diaristic gathering of filmic images of the artist's life, which were then edited as reflections on the past and memory.

The focus on the person *behind* the camera (and behind the editing machine) as a defining characteristic of a film movement had deep historical and philosophical roots. Most immediate was the emphasis on the artist as unique individual in other artistic movements that dominated the American avant-garde culture in the preceding decade—Beat poetry and abstract expressionism. The Beat poets, like the Romantic poets who served as their inspiration, often wrote in the first person, either directly or implicitly. Free verse discarded poetic rhythmic and rhyming conventions in favor of more spontaneous rhythms characterizing a poet's individuality (although a certain stylistic conformity emerged). Humor could figure in Beat poetry as whimsical and light, but more often it was sarcastic and dark; the movement's greatest impact was in its expression of anger, alienation, and despair. Similarly, the abstract expressionist painter developed means of applying paint, composing abstract shapes, and selecting a palette that served as signatures as individualized as orthography. For many of the abstract expressionists, the goal was to externalize inner states as abstract graphic configurations considered to be the purest expression of those emotions. Thus the artist's emotional self was privileged in these works. Personal filmmaking extended certain of these artistic procedures to cinematic vision, to be framed by camera work and arranged by montage.

The ontological assumption of the personal cinema was that the filmmaker chose and juxtaposed images to reveal aspects of the self. The prerequisite of personal emotional investment was strong. Behind this ontology was the belief that cinema could reveal inner truths. The most of cinematic history had been ruled by other ontologies, one that privileged cinema's ability to record external realities, or conversely, its vocation as a storyteller able to embody collective fantasies, made this devotion to self-revelation a battle against various institutionalized cinematic practices. To turn cinematic expression away from its external or collective visions and its highly codified means of representation was a battle for the very definition of cinema itself. It amounted, if not literally, then at least figuratively, to reversing the direction of the image-taking so that the camera in a sense "turned around" to reveal the agent of its operation.

Advocates of personal cinema such as Mekas firmly believed they were seeking "true" cinema, in opposition to Hollywood's false dreams and its often even more false rendering of historical realities. Sometimes this opposition extended to include the European movements considered still commercial and too limited in their attempt to break Hollywood's rules. After 1961, Mekas became much more likely to vent his wrath at the new European cinema than at the studio productions of Hollywood, partly because the critique of commercial American cinema was taken for granted (Mekas 1972, 203–6, 252–54). This is not without irony, for the auteur theory and the stylistic freedom of new wave camera work and editing were close to some aspects of personal cinema. The new wave was seemingly more threatening because it was being embraced elsewhere as a revolutionary, alternative filmmaking practice. The struggle for recognition on the part of personal cinema seemed thwarted precisely because of the popularity of the European art cinema; Mekas's columns decrying the choices at the annual New York film festivals are evidence of how these films may in fact have been perceived as the real competition, the real problem. It must be noted as well that Mekas himself was often contradictory in his critical writing; not only did his positions evolve historically, but they also displayed ambivalences and inconsistencies. One week he would rant against the new wave's success, and the next praise certain films of Godard or Resnais (Mekas 1972, 57–58, 204–5). Whereas his definition of personal cinema at times broadened generously to include a wide range of films such as abstract, nonobjective films, rhythmic concrete cinema, and eventually, direct cinema and the formal and minimalist concerns of what came to be known as structuralist filmmaking, it would at times appear as a narrow delineation, limited to what he also termed the "Baudelairean cinema," characterized by expressionist poetics.

Thus Mekas's notion of personal cinema at a critical historical point lauded and favored the development of a certain artistic persona, one whose intense self-involvement and flamboyance provided the necessary material for projection within cinematic form. Emotionally intense images of inner states, such as those offered by Stan Brakhage and Kenneth Anger, could astound audiences with large-scale expositions of their extraordinarily dramatic selves. Myth, metaphor, and death loom as large as light, rhythm, and motion in such works. This is a measure of the Romantic and symbolist heritage that continued to define the very notions of artist and art in the wake of those nineteenth-century movements.

Yet here again, this championing of personal cinema evolved historically from an earlier reaction on Mekas's part against the very films that eventually were praised. In 1955, his article "The Experimental Film in America" spoke of the "markedly adolescent character" of the "young film poets" whose films were devoted to "personal lyricism." He also took a homophobic tack familiar to us in recent debates over the work of Robert Mapplethorpe when he claimed that "a conspiracy of homosexuality . . . is becoming one of the most persistent and most shocking characteristics of American film poetry today. In these films, the protagonists are consistently exposed to physical and mental assault; they are prey to the most ingenious forms of brutality, sadism and masochism. The perversion of sex seems to be accepted by these film poets (in their films) as a natural way of life" (Mekas 1970b, 17). Mekas even cites Hilton Kramer to bolster his condemnation of the homoerotic and sado-masochistic aspects that he claimed dominated the personal cinema in the mid-fifties. Further, he discounts any comparison between these works and such precedents as Rimbaud and surrealism in that "these films necessarily remain shallow and incomprehensible" (ibid.). Yet even this essay is riddled with contradictory impulses. This attack still recognized these films as part of an important movement, though morally suspect, asserting that "we can't deny a certain honesty to some of these films," which "even if they do not succeed in becoming works of art . . . still bear witness to the film poet's age, mentality and inner state (ibid.). This recognition is also apparent in the appended filmographies of what he calls "the most representative American film poets" (ibid.). Mekas would later term his renunciation of this article a "complete turnabout" from this early "Saint-Augustine-before-the-conversion piece" (itself an ironic metaphor, considering Saint Augustine's sexual politics *after* conversion).[3] His change seems to derive from his acceptance of a diversity of selves meriting expression and from a shift from his position in 1955 that "formal discipline" was a prerequisite for art, in favor of a position that could embrace what he earlier saw as "technical crudity" as a measure of a vital spontaneity.

Another crucial question for his early formulation of an aesthetics and ethics of personal cinema was his critical treatment of the films of women filmmakers, particularly Maya Deren. In the same 1955 essay that questioned the maturity of the younger generation, Mekas pejoratively dismissed Deren, by then one of the elder spokeswomen of avant-garde cinema. He termed her works "intellectual formalism" that resulted from "mechanical creation, without enough emotional content," and claimed that her "supposed depth" is "artificial." In this same article he claimed that "if the

---

[3] The disclaimer came with the republication of the essay in Sitney's anthology (1970).

man, the most frequent protagonist of American film poems, is presented as an unreal, frustrated dreamer, the woman here is usually robbed of both her true spirituality and her unashamed carnality. She is a white-dressed, unearthly, elusive symbol flowing dreamily along seashores (or sea-bottom) through bushes and upon hills (Deren, Harrington, Markopoulos, Broughton, Hugo, etc.)" (ibid.). To see Deren's female imagery this way involves a misreading of the complex permutations these figures undergo in her films. And though he cited the contribution of Marie Menken, for example, in creating avant-garde films, he failed to recognize that many of the first filmmakers to introduce abstract and personal filmmaking were women. He chose to concentrate instead on what he termed the "angry young men." The fierceness of this early attack on Deren was continued in an exchange between Deren and Mekas in the *Village Voice* between July 1960 and June 1961 in which Deren refused Mekas's casting of her on the side of orthodoxy and artistic law and order as traditionally defined, due to her denunciation of the " 'catch-as-catch-can and I hope the camera caught something' school of filming" (Deren 1965). Films that Mekas called early examples of personal cinema, such as Alfred Leslie and Robert Frank's *Pull My Daisy* and John Cassavetes' *Shadows,* Deren claimed, were in fact "more orthodox in structure and style" in their use of "semidocumentary structure" than her own film.

Part of what emerges in this highly polemical debate is the role of immediacy as a critical value for Mekas. The debate between Deren and Mekas implicitly also raises issues of the gendered subject: what happens to the notion of the personal cinema when the person behind the camera is a woman, and what happens to the representation of the other (and by extension, the world) within that which is offered as the personal vision of the self. Certainly the reconsideration of Deren's work by feminist film theory has indicated what Mekas's formulation of the personal cinema could not see— that which distinguishes her female protagonists from those of her male counterparts. Our current context has also allowed the reconsideration of homosexual artists expressing homosexual selfhood.

The present form of this debate in light of recent gender politics should give Mekas credit for recognizing that the personal cinema did indeed have certain tropes that were gendered, even if his analysis of those gendered tropes was symptomatic of gender prejudices. Inadvertently, perhaps, his observations indicated how certain tropes preoccupied the male protagonists of the personal cinema and rendered its females primarily as symbolic abstractions. Most significantly, we can now see how the "personal" was primarily a historically bound male perspective whose myths, heroics, and metaphors were conditioned by the consciousness of the male artists who sought to equate the camera with their own subjective eyes. We can be more suspicious of the equation of subjectivity with truth in the singular; we can see immediacy as a value that functions to naturalize that which in the subject is formed in history and is fundamentally ideological. If film artists found visual metaphors that expressed their subjective truths, we no longer find ourselves necessarily privileging that vision as the profound truth of the universe per se, or even as the truth of a singular and unique individual. We can now see subjectivities and truths as plural not only among subjects, but within a given subject, the self that is divided, and even in part unknown to itself.

Mekas's own films diverge from some of the pronounced aspects of the personal poetics he helped formulate in his writings; personal subjectivity writ on a grand scale gives way to the emergence of a quieter, more peaceful self. One factor in this shift is Mekas's interest in cinema verité and direct cinema—the French movement of documentary filmmaking that replaced the codes of documentary discourse with self-conscious immediacy of the camera as observer of and participant in the activities it recorded, and its American counterpart. Let us examine Mekas's often-quoted application of direct-cinema technique to the registration of the self formulated in his writing about his film *Diaries, Notes, and Sketches* (1968): "To keep a film (camera) diary, is to react (with your camera) immediately, now, this instant: either you get it now, or you don't get it at all. To go back and shoot it later, would mean restaging be it events or feelings. To get it now, as it happens demands the total mastery of one's tools (in this case, Bolex): it has to register the reality to which I react and also it has to register my state of feeling (and all the memories) as I react" (*Film-Makers' Cooperative Catalogue* 1975, 178). Here Mekas provides the explanation of how his camera work and his in-camera editing function as a means of obtaining a realism based on the exposition of emotional truth. The belief is that one can master the camera in such a way as to use it as an expression of all one's memories and feelings as one actually lives out an experience. The intrusion of the camera, its mediation and distortions, and indeed its limitations are in this view not a factor, or are overcome through mastery. If direct cinema took as its basis Barthes's zero-degree neutrality of voice, the version of direct cinema Mekas claims as his own is an almost magical transference of inner voice to external manifestations in the image made possible by a camera wielded as gesture.

In practice, ironically perhaps, in *Reminiscences*, the visual gestures are less grandiose than much of the poetic personal cinema, and more immediate in the sense that they strongly foreground the immanence of the moment in which footage was exposed. As a result, the images taken alone are often neutral. Their subjectivity is often a subjectivity of placement and phenomenological seeing. If the images often seem already remembered, already dreamlike, it is because of their fragmentation and their occasional rapidity of montage. Yet unlike French impressionist films, or Brakhage's films, which use such fragmentation and rapid montage as associational tropes that link images metaphorically, Mekas's films most often use them metonymically, to describe space and time without a specificity of emotion or even of thoughts. The specific subjectivity, the weight of memory, is in Mekas's work largely dependent on the voice, the written titles, the piano sonata and folk songs coloring the images we see. If Mekas's autobiography is very much a sound-image text in which images are colored as emotional memories, the images are subject to the controlling and defining articulations of the voice. Voice determines the manner in which the images are seen.

In the first section of the film, the meditation on being a displaced person, Mekas includes footage of two sorts: there are scenes of gatherings of immigrants and the streets of Brooklyn, documentary images of activities of those in exile, on the one hand, and on the other, images taken to experiment with the Bolex that Mekas tells us was his first camera, which, through their lighting and mise-en-scène, deviate from the codes of cinema verité documentary to pronounce themselves as the studied compositions of art photography. The voice-over plays a dominant role in situating and defining these images. The voice is speaking from the present, situating the images in the past. The subjective, poetic, casual quality of the voice wrenches these images from the presence as documentary evidence they might have had as records of an actual past and envelops them with the aura of memory. For example, the voice begins, "That early fall in 1957 or '58 we went to the Catskills"; the inability to date the event more precisely contrasts with the manner in which the images record the moments of the walk in question. The film image appears more precise, but in fact "speaks" only of figures in a landscape. The voiced memory is not sure of certain details, but it recalls emotions of a subjective landscape that the image alone cannot reveal. It tells us that this walk was a watershed event, the first time in which the last ten years, "the years of war, of hunger, of Brooklyn," receded, and Mekas for the first time experienced a "moment when I forgot my home. This was the beginning of my new home." The image meanwhile deviates from the voice ever so slightly, by shifting abruptly from "the early fall" to a snow-filled landscape, just as the voice locates the shift in emotional states in a precise and singular moment, the events of one day. The voice hesitates, stumbles, equivocates, and then repeats itself, instructively: "And almost in . . . *maybe* for the first time as we were walking through the woods that fa(—) that early fall day for the first time I did not feel alone in America." The ironies of this first interaction of voice and image are echoed throughout the film. The status of the recorded event and the remembered event within autobiography—the time of events and the time of consciousness—are, if not at odds, at least different.

That a close-up of a frayed rope dangling from a tree ends this segment of the first part of the film, as the voice says "I've escaped the ropes of time once more," supplements through metaphor both the actuality of the image and the discourse on temporality. Where does the metaphor come from? Does the image suggest it (the filmmaker saw this rope that early autumn day in the woods), or does the filmmaker invent the metaphor and insert the close-up back into the day (which after all has already been interrupted by the snow)? If we look closely we see perhaps that autumn in the Catskills is edited to join winter in what appears to be Central Park, and the rope dangles not in the mountains, but close by the buildings framing this space. If these discrepancies matter, it is because the celebration is precisely that of escaping the boundaries imposed by living in a given time and place, in a given history. The metaphor, like the woods before, is one in which we go "up and up, deeper and deeper." The filmmaker through montage controls time and renders it subjectively even as he seems to chronicle it.

This faith in montage is marked in the temporal sequencing of the rest of the first section, for temporally we flash back from this moment in 1957 or 1958 to recall each of the years 1950 (a street in Williamsburg, Brooklyn), 1951 (gatherings of displaced persons in Stony Brook and at Pier 21 in New York), and 1952 (railroad platforms accompanied by the story of Adolfas Mekas's return to Lithuania after being drafted, only to be rejected as crazy). In the middle of this flashback, the narration of the incidents of 1951 is interrupted by a return to 1950 and the acquisition of Jonas Mekas's first camera, illustrated by some footage of a self-portrait in the mode of the poetic filmmaker-artist autobiography discussed earlier. Yet here the voice-over tells us that this first film was meant to be a film "against the war" that would serve to remind an oblivious

America that there "were homes in the world where people couldn't speak, doors being kicked in at night, boots of soldiers and police somewhere where I came from." How the self-portrait footage was to engage in this political discourse is unclear, and this ambiguity was perhaps the reason the film was never completed (the word "never" appears enigmatically in this segment). However, in telling of the past, the project of the past is realized in the present; this film, *Reminiscences of a Journey to Lithuania*, will tell of that which was not told then.

Parentheses are opened and closed (by written titles) within this first part of the film, and white squares offset to the right of the frame against a black ground also act as punctuation not unlike parentheses. This punctuation does not coincide with the clear segmentation one finds represented in the image and the voice-over narration. Again we have discrepancies, here seeming to mark the weave of the filmic discourse, for all the material is already edited parenthetically, inserted, embedded. The marking at once increases awareness of this and heightens the ambiguity surrounding any structure we might take to be marked.

Even the feeling of belonging in America is contradicted throughout the first segment, and not just because what follows is meant to happen earlier. Mekas reads his images of immigrants as "displaced persons." Images that might otherwise convey opportunity, safety, contentment, and community are instead colored by a voice that refuses such interpretations. "They looked to me like sad dying animals in a place they didn't exactly belong to, in a place they didn't exactly recognize," he tells us, and continues, "We are still displaced persons even today. . . . The minute we left we started going home and we are still going home, I am still on my way home." If today is taken to be 1971, then the moment articulated in 1957 or 1958 as the moment in which America became home never took place, at least in the definitive manner in which it is first presented as having taken place. The effort to articulate an escape from the past can only succeed through forgetting the past, but Mekas reminisces incessantly. From the beginning he tells us "I was wondering myself that I could walk like this and not think anything about the last ten years"; in other words, the past is always there, as is thinking about it. The force of this autobiographical enunciation is that there is no escape from memory, despite all the play with time available to the filmmaker (or perhaps because of it).

Part 2, "100 glimpses of Lithuania," dated August 1971, chronicles the journey to Lithuania of the title; it actualizes physically the return that is the metaphor controlling the first part of the film.

Again the numbers that punctuate the images do not correspond simply to segments of the film imagery, though such segmentation exists apart from the numbers' intrusions. "Glimpses" here are not so easily numbered, but on the other hand the events depicted in this part are not so randomly glimpsed as this title might imply. Our gaze here is also one of a multiplicity of glimpses, figuratively speaking, for the camera bounces through a scene saccadically, jumping or racking focus from close-up to distance, or from whole to fragment, or from moment to different moment, as if to reassemble a larger picture by this fragmented collage of what otherwise might be seen as a more continuous whole. The glimpsing is not just nervous, it is provocative, meant to stimulate an active seeing.

All the events revolve around Mekas's return to his familial home and his reunion with mother, brothers and sister, and neighbors. The self is often depicted in the scene because the journey is made with his filmmaker brother and fellow émigré, Aldofas, who is so close to an alter ego here that he rarely figures in the commentary in this section. There is a chronology to the footage, from arrival to departure, and there is a structure of stories. The story of how Mekas fled his home when his role in producing an underground anti-Nazi paper was about to be discovered is told close to the beginning, cited again in the middle of the section, and completed toward the end. It is this story that haunts the return. This story is so profoundly political that it comes as a surprise that it is not matched by any political engagement in the present of Lithuania; the postwar period is repeatedly referred to as sad, but Stalin's name is never mentioned. Lithuanian nationalism is confined to folklore. These absences and positions may, however, also be evidence of what cannot be said in any other way in 1971 for fear of repercussions for the family remaining in a pre-*glasnost* Lithuania.

References to the collective-farming reorganization of the villages is given in visits of Mekas's brothers Petras and Kostas, who then take their brothers on a tour of the farms where they work. There is a playful contrast of modernization against held-over traditions. The older Lithuanian brothers jokingly toy with artifacts such as a sickle and hand plow, long since superannuated. They also joke with what it means to represent this through images as the truth of Lithuania to those overseas; the hay beds improvised for an evening of these long-ago discarded tools become their emblems for how the foreign other might misconceive their lives.

Yet it is in using these artifacts, and in seeing the aging mother, who still performs all tasks in the most traditional ways, that Mekas nearly achieves his objective of reliving memories, of meeting time, which stood still for him while he was in exile. Here is the evidence that the personal self (whose past was political) has become self-involved and even removed, distanced in his concerns. As Mekas has said, "You don't see how Lithuania is today; you see it only through the memories of a Displaced Person back home for the first time in twenty-five years" (Film-Makers' Cooperative Catalogue 1989, 363). Mekas seems aware of his self-indulgence on many levels, but of course self-indulgence is not something someone can escape by merely being aware of it. To know you are self-indulgent, to represent yourself as self-indulgent, is of course the most self-indulgent act of all. The film, though, does not simply end on the inability to recover the past or to make time stand still.

To a limited extent, there is also a search for the return of the political self. He becomes the substance of the transition to part 3, made by way of the trip to Hamburg to revisit the work camp and factory to which Mekas and his brother were deported when they were arrested attempting to reach Vienna. These sites are in fact presented in a manner not unlike that of the nostalgic visit to the familial home; Aldolfas lies on the grass where his bed in the camp would have been and Jonas revisits the workbench where he was punished for his slowness. Anger comes out in a direct address to an image of German children, whom he accuses of gawking at the foreigners. (They are probably looking at the camera.) "Run, children, run," Mekas says. "I hope you never have to run for your life." This anger seems strangely displaced onto children too young to remember the war.

The remainder of part 3 is the self-conscious celebration of an international artist-intellectual community. Four friends, Peter Kubelka, Hermann Nitsch, Annette Michelson, and Ken Jacobs, are canonized in recognition of their individual contributions to the cinema as they meet in Vienna. This act of religious sanctification expresses an autobiographical desire and tells as much about the self as any ending Mekas might have selected. He projects onto others his desire to find himself, to find a home, in his devotion to art and ideas; these images haunt us now as memories because the figures are so young, but they represent the only moments of the film in which memory is not in some way invading the images. Saints are after all icons, and sainthood seems to become the justification for the inclusion of these images. To turn your friends into icons, to use their accomplishments as mirrors of your own, has a pathos as autobiography. Is it any wonder that the film ends in a paranoid reading of a funeral pyre for a landmark, the fateful burning of a fruit market? It is not that governments are incapable of condemning us or our landmarks to an unjust death, but that here, without any evidence, the conviction is offered as its own proof.

The three sections then differ subtly in poetic form, corresponding to a difference in thematic investment in the pastness of the events. The first, devoted to the recovery and explanation of the past itself (old footage) reconstructed to reveal displacement, is the most structured.

The second part, seeking to recover the past in the present, becomes largely a symbolic and romanticized quest in which the superimposed daisies of memory presented in part 1 are reiterated through repeated shots of flowers and berries across the "hundred glimpses." These surround the figure of the mother, who is the most constant and obsessive image of all the "hundred glimpses," an obsession presented in the only translated song (just as "berries" is the only translated word). The song tells of someone who is far away: "Oh mother, how I long to see you again / I hope the long gray road will lead me home again." The mother is at the well, at the center of the earth. The newly named collective "togetherness" is superimposed on the mother's landscape, for her landscape is one where moose magically appear and grim reapers carry sickles reminding us of death. The glimpses, then, whose phenomenological investment is in the present, in observation, are ironically symbolic images. Not so much memories as *fantasies* of a center, they suffer the instability of the phantasm; no matter how obsessive the filmmaker, the fantasies cannot simply be possessed. One can locate this instability in merely physical displacement, but that would be to see the actual refugee experience as solely determinant in what is figured as a more primal longing.

The third part, then, poses as the answer for the obsessive, distressed subject. One can model oneself after those who are centered: in a world with no change (as is said of Kubelka), in childhood seeings and ecstasies (as is said of Jacobs), or by making culture into one's roots and one's life (as is said of Michelson). Certainly Vienna is not, nor was it during World War II, so stable as to lead one to envy life there; childhood vision is not so embracing, nor cultural investment so supportive. (If it were, artists and intellectuals would less frequently go to psychoanalysts, and they would be less prone to suicide.) The others are fantasies, as saints are myths. Mekas was arriving as a major critic and artist at the center of his culture, but the New York of the sixties and seventies allowed for no center. It promised only displacement. The last part of the film, then, is Mekas's awkward attempt to center himself in the humanist tradition. The texts of music hand-inscribed by monks, art in its most religious manifestation, is the constant, the value assigned to the world. We are no longer confronted by our continually decentered subjectivity; we have a canon to which we can hold.

This concept returns us to the history of Mekas's writings on personal cinema with which this essay began. If these writings constituted a claim for a cultural space in which an alternative cinematic practice, a more personal practice, could take place, they also simultaneously begin to establish an alternative canon. Now that the cinematic practice of personal cinema has been so established, we can afford to examine how it bore within itself not only prescribed notions of gender, but also a myth of the artistic persona. One aspect of my reading of *Reminiscences* sees it as the fulfillment of that myth. The artist creates a portrait of himself as a displaced person whose mother and past form the center to which he journeys as part of a quest for what is true of experience. Truth is found in what is most immediate, instinctual, emotional, as this can be embodied and imparted through privileging perception itself.

If the cinema as apparatus presents manifold difficulties for the creation of self-portraits and the writing of autobiography, one can see how it becomes the privileged medium for the type of reminiscence and truth Mekas seeks to uncover and reveal. Perception is the background on which memory is overlaid; the cinematographic renderings of moments considered present at the instants of their recording *become* memoirs when recollected through montage, a montage that includes a voice situating the emotions of the time. The voice carries the weight of pastness. It turns the phenomenology of experience into that of reminiscence.

We have to stop and examine the word "reminiscence." Though it, like memory, can mean the cognitive return of the past, it is just as often used to imply a stage removed from memory itself: memories put into literary form, the rough equivalent of the memoir, the writing of the past, though one not quite so formal or so reified as the autobiography. In fact, "reminiscence" can be used to indicate oral retelling, while memoir and autobiography suggest writing. Derrida has made much of the ontological privileging of speech over writing, by which speech is assumed to be "nonwritten" and therefore closer to experience. The choice of "reminiscence" then suggests an attempt to locate this film as more directly the outcome of both experience and its memory than any reference to writing might suggest. "Experience," "memory," "reminiscence," "memoir," and "autobiography" might be seen as stages of formalization of thought about events occurring to the self, and arranged in the order given above might suggest increasing degrees of "secondary revision." Freud used secondary revision to suggest the reordering processes that construct dreams-as-told out of dream imagery. Here I mean it as a parallel but more extensive process through which the significant moments (the signifiers) of personal experience are revised through the processes of memory and the processes of re-telling—that is, writing.

"Reminiscence" as used by Mekas evokes both the processes of memory and the reconstruction of memory inherent in the writing of memoirs. Through this double meaning (as indicated by its placement midway between experience and autobiography on the informal graph above), it enjoys a closer approximation to memory than other means of recording the past, except perhaps for the other term Mekas uses, "diary," which David James has analyzed as achieving this closeness differently (1989b). Unlike James, I do not follow Mekas in assuming this closer approximation to mean more than a difference in degree within a continuum. I instead emphasize the reconstruing and structuring that is not only inherent and deeply marked in reminiscing, but that is already a factor in memory and experience itself. For me, the cognitive and unconscious processes that constitute subjectivity do so even as we perceive, but especially and increasingly as we remember. What needs to be further investigated is the relationship of images to memory and the meaning of memory itself.

In an earlier work, on the coded subjectivity of the fictional flash-back, I found that the flashback works by taking advantage of a slip-page from our sense of "memory images" to images that are taken to represent memories (Turim 1989). At the foundation of our prac-tice of cinematic inscription of the past is the substitution of a con-structed image of the past for one we take to be an actual one, a memory. Flashbacks are nourished by an implicit equation of the eidetic image (visual recall) with memory images, and these in turn with the construction of images in fictions to represent memories appearing to fictive psyches. In other words, we believe we "see" the past in our memories and that visual images have a privileged access to the past. Yet the visual image offered as the actualization of a memory fills in with a visual plenitude, specificity, and whole-ness that which is more tenuous, complex, contradicatory, abstract, and multiple in the most vivid of visually reconstituted memories. Memory images are now understood through cognitive research to be reconstituted rather than simply stored and accessed as such in the mind. When we see a memory image in our "mind's eye," it is reformulated out of elements of information stored quite disparately; we reconstruct the visual images of our visual memories from traces that help us reestablish a scenography.

The most recent theory has the charm of accounting for the failures and errors of visual memory, the blending of memory images with fantasy, and what might be called changes in framing, focus, and masking that occur in the process of visual recall. In other words, the cinema's attempts mimetically to reproduce visual memory have been aimed short of the mark; they have assumed a visual retrieval system when the process is less automatic and more intriguing than that.

Knowing this, what interests me most (and I admit my fascination) in a film like *Reminiscences* is the gaps in the articulation of memory and experience: not those moments where Mekas can recover the past (be that past the experience of exile, the journey home, or the reunion with friends who find their salvation in art), but those instances in which the images and the voice fail to cohere, not only with each other but "internally" as intrinsically coherent articulations. Here is where I find the most invigorating reanimation of a poetics, perhaps that which Sidonie Smith has called "the poetics of autobiography." This allows us to see the physical journey back to Lithuania detailed as the "hundred glimpses" as a process of "rememorization" in which, as Marianne Hirsch (1990) has argued, the search to recover the past is available to the subject only in a fragmented submerging in and refiguration of a present that has changed. These fragmented images collaged together strike the viewer as a barrage of someone else's memory images; they do not mimetically depict memory, but their fleeting presence, at times rapid pace, and often fragmented view of events offer a kind of flooding of partially available information that at least suggests that memory is both illusive and active. This energetic imagery is coupled with long takes that not only supply the contrasting rhythms but substitute the movement across geographies metaphorically for the effort to drift back in time. The title *Reminiscences* tempts us to view the entire journey metaphorically, as a dream of memory.

This view of the film no longer sees part 3 as answering part 2, or part 2 answering part 1; it sees the questions raised in the figures of displacement as larger than the conclusions proffered in acts of recentering and accomplished through acts of mastery. *Reminiscences* suggests in its gaps and processes a poetics of our displaced and conflicted selves; at its best, it expresses more than it knows.

Bibliography

Barthes, Roland. 1968. *Writing Degree Zero*. Trans. Annette Lavers and Colin Smith. New York: Hill and Wang.

Brakhage, Stan. *Metaphors on Vision*. 1963. New York: Film Culture.

Bruss, Elizabeth. 1980. "Eye for I: Making and Unmaking Autobiography in Film." In *Autobiography: Essays Theoretical and Critical*, ed. James Olney. Princeton: Princeton University Press.

Deren, Maya. 1965. Letters in the *Village Voice*, 25 August 1960 and 1 June 1961. In *Film Culture* 39: 55–56.

Derrida, Jacques. 1976. *Of Grammatology*. Trans. Gayatri Spivak. Baltimore: Johns Hopkins University Press, 1976.

Film-Makers' Cooperative Catalogue. 1975. New York: Film-Makers' Cooperative.

———. *Film-Makers' Cooperative Catalogue*. 1989. New York: Film-Makers' Cooperative.

Hirsch, Marianne. 1990. "Maternity and Rememory." Paper presented at SUNY-Binghamton, New York, 8 February.

James, David. 1989a. *Allegories of Cinema*. Princeton: Princeton University Press.

———. 1989b. "Diary/Film/Diary Film." *Frame/Work* 2, no. 3: 21–23.

Lacan, Jacques. 1977. "Function and Field of Speech and Language." In *Ecrits: A Selection*, trans. Alan Sheridan, 30–113. New York: W. W. Norton.

Mekas, Jonas. 1970a. "A Call for a New Generation of Film-Makers." In *Film Culture Reader*, 73–75. *See* Sitney 1970.

———. 1970b. "The Experimental Film in America." In *Film Culture Reader*, 21–26. *See* Sitney 1970.

———. 1972. *Movie Journal: The Rise of a New American Cinema, 1959–1971*. New York: Macmillan.

Sitney, P. Adams, ed. 1970. *Film Culture Reader*. New York: Praeger.

Smith, Sidonie. 1987. *A Poetics of Women's Autobiography: Marginality and the Fictions of Self-Representation*. Bloomington: Indiana University Press.

Turim, Maureen. 1989. *Flashbacks in Film: Memory and History*. New York: Routledge.

14. Robert Breer   My Contacts with Jonas Mekas

MY CONTACTS with Jonas Mekas have mostly been confined to "state" occasions, however convivial they get to be sometimes: gatherings chez Mekas for medieval music and primeval food served up by Peter Kubelka, Film Co-op board meetings, award ceremonies, special screenings, openings. There has always been a certain formality between us, in contrast to the warm way he has treated my work in his columns over the years. I have referred to Jonas as a saint at times, with the hoped-for understanding that my definition does not exclude diabolical behavior. Though there is an open evangelical streak in Jonas, I have never seen piety as such.

There have been many contradictions in his stances, beginning with the now famous about-face on the worthiness of independent film. His hyperbole and inconsistencies have provided field days for his detractors and given pause to the faithful who might have been looking for an easy party line, but I think most people respect his insight and courage in supporting unpopular causes.

One of my first recollections of Jonas in the early sixties is how well he managed Amos Vogel's rejection of his bid to merge his fledgling Co-op with the then-prestigious Cinema 16. My memory of that awkward meeting includes the belated arrival of Ron Rice dressed as Charlie Chaplin. A little while later, Amos was to sell Cinema 16 to Grove Press and, with the help of his *Village Voice* column, Jonas's Film-Makers' Co-op became the only show in town.

Around that time, Jonas stopped me on the sidewalk one day to ask why the fall-out sequence in *Horse over Teakettle* reverses and becomes a fall-up sequence at the end. My ten-minute film had just had a midnight "world premiere" at the Charles Theater on Avenue B. I remember being impressed that he had paid that much attention and I was relieved when he gave it a favorable notice in the *Voice*.

On the other hand, my delight at having *A Man and His Dog Out for Air* booked to run with *Last Year at Marienbad* was only slightly dampened by Jonas's pointed caution in his column about the dangers to film artists who answer the siren call of commerce. This same caution, however, took a holiday during later negotiations between a commercial distributor and various members of the Co-op (including Jonas) to package "underground" films for general distribution, hoping to cash in on the notoriety of *Flaming Creatures* and Warhol. No deal was made, so far as I know. I think the perception of these films as "hot stuff" must have suffered from the steady increase of foreign "art" films in circulation.

Jonas's function as gadfly and polemicist was paying off in another area, though, by bringing serious critical attention to these films as art. Obvious personal bias aside, I find it difficult totally to dismiss Jonas's assertion in his column that the premiere of my film 69, though totally ignored at the time, was of equal importance to the opening of a show of new paintings by de Kooning, for instance. Whatever official resistance this type of claim met with, there were growing numbers of nonestablishment thinkers and writers and filmmakers getting interested. People like P. Adams Sitney and Annette Michelson, followed by (if I am correct about sequence) Noël Burch, Fred Camper, Noël Carroll, J. Hoberman, and others, began to give intellectual muscle to what eventually became a full-fledged movement.

Hollis Frampton and Jonas practiced what seemed to be breakthrough avant-garde child rearing by showing up at every gathering, day or night, with daughter Oona, first toddling, then running. I think of them when we do the same with Sally these days. On a grand scale and on a personal level, it would be difficult to overestimate Jonas's influence.

15. Michael Renov   *Lost, Lost, Lost*: Mekas as Essayist

*And so the opinion I give is to declare
the measure of my sight, not the measure of things.*
—Montaigne, *Essays*

*Of course, what I faced was the old
problem of all artists: to merge Reality
and Self, to come up with the third
thing.*
—Mekas, "The Diary Film"

IN THE CONCLUSION of a remarkably perceptive review of Jonas Mekas's *Lost, Lost, Lost* appearing soon after the film's 1976 release, Alan Williams suggests a relationship between the autobiographical project of this, the first volume of *Diaries, Notes, and Sketches*, and "the spirit of Montaigne and self-examination."[1] In so doing, Williams situates the work within an essayistic tradition whose roots, though traceable to Montaigne's three-volume *Essays* of the late sixteenth century, might be said to include certain writings of Nietzsche, Adorno, and, most recently, Roland Barthes. Indeed, the essay form, notable for its tendency toward complication (digression, fragmentation, repetition, and dispersion) rather than composition, has, in its four-hundred-year history, continued to resist the efforts of literary taxonomists, confounding the laws of genre and classification, challenging the very notion of text and of textual economy. In its heterogeneity and inexhaustibility ("with an 'amoeba-like' versatility often held together by little more than the author's voice" [Bensmaia 1987, ix]), the essayistic work bears with it a logic that denies the verities of rhetorical composition and of system, indeed of mastery itself.[2]

[1] Williams 1976, 62. Although Williams reviewed *Lost, Lost, Lost* soon after its release, he was already familiar with the third volume of the autobiographical project *Walden* (1968), filmed between 1964 and 1968.

[2] In an appendix to *The Barthes Effect: The Essay as Reflective Text*, Reda Bensmaia offers the historical and theoretical grounds for his claims for the essay as an "impossible" genre: "Among all the terms that relate to literary genres, the word

Knowledge produced through the essay is provisional rather than systematic; self and object organize each other, but only in a temporary way—"Nothing can be built on this configuration, no rules or methods deduced from it" (Good 1988, 4).

The Montaignean essay derives in part from disparate precursor forms—the confessional or autobiography as well as the chronicle—insofar as its codetermining axes, its concern for self and other ("the measure of sight" as well as the "measure of things" [Montaigne 1948, 298]), enact what Gerard Defaux has called the *Essays'* "twofold project." Descriptive and reflexive modalities are coupled; the representation of the historical real is consciously filtered through the flux of subjectivity. Neither the outward gaze nor the counter-reflex of self-interrogation alone can account for the essay. Attention is drawn to the level of the signifier ("let attention be paid not to the matter, but to the shape I give it" [Montaigne 1948, 296]); a self is produced through a plurality of voices, "mediated through writing, forever inscribed in the very tissue of the text" (Defaux 1983, 77).

This plurality of voices provides a clue to a fundamental if implicit presumption of the essayistic mode, namely that of indeterminacy. Neither locus of meaning—neither subject nor historical object—anchors discourse so much as it problematizes or interrogates it. This foundation of epistemological uncertainty has been widely theorized, initially by Montaigne himself, as in his essay

Essay is certainly the one that has given rise to the most confusion in the history of literature. . . . A unique case in the annals of literature, the Essay is the only literary genre to have resisted integration, until quite recently, in the taxonomy of genres. No other genre ever raised so many theoretical problems concerning the origin and the definition of its Form: an atopic genre or, more precisely, an *eccentric* one insofar as it seems to flirt with all the genres without ever letting itself be pinned down, the literary essay such as Montaigne bequeathed it to posterity has always had a special status. . . . [T]he Essay appears historically as one of the rare literary texts whose apparent principal task was to provoke a 'generalized collapse' of the economies of the rhetorically coded text" (Bensmaia 1987, 95, 96, 99). In my writing on the essayistic in film and video, I have chosen to resist the lure of genre, preferring instead to consider the essayistic as a modality of filmic inscription. The invocation of mode rather than genre sidesteps the difficulties raised by the latter's far greater historical stake in taxonomic certainty, as well as the presumption of thematic consistency attached to it. Conversely, the determining principle of resemblance for the mode is a formal or functional one. As Jacques Derrida notes, quoting a distinction framed by Gerard Genette: "Genres are, properly speaking, literary/or aesthetic/ categories; modes are categories that pertain to linguistics or, more precisely, to an anthropology of verbal expression" (Derrida 1980, 210). In the instance of the essayistic for film and video, formal, functional, and ideological commonalities converge as defining characteristics.

"On Repentance": "The world is but a perennial movement. All things in it are in constant motion. . . . I cannot keep my subject still. . . . I do not portray being, I portray passing. . . . If my mind could gain a firm footing, I would not make essays, I would make decisions, but it is always in apprenticeship and on trial" (Montaigne 1948, 3.2.610–11). That more contemporary essayist, Roland Barthes, claimed that the fragmentary or discontinuous writing of his latter works enacted a counter-ideology of form inasmuch as "the fragment breaks up what I would call the smooth finish, the composition, discourse constructed to give a final meaning to what one says, which is the general rule of all past rhetoric. . . . [T]he fragment is a spoilsport, discontinuous, establishing a kind of pulverization of sentences, images, thoughts, none of which 'takes' definitively" (Barthes 1985, 209–10).

Despite the epistemic distance separating Montaigne and Barthes, their respective writing practices enforce a shared refusal. If neither being-as-essence nor final determinations (neither first nor last causes) arise in the essays of Montaigne or Barthes, this reticence can be attributed in part to the protocols of (essayistic) writing they share. Essayistic practices achieve a degree of commonality not through thematic consistency (as is the case with genre) but through formal and ideological resemblances.

For the young Georg Lukacs, the essay was an "intellectual poem" whose first exemplar was not a literary trace but the life of Socrates. Unlike tragedy, whose end informs the whole of the drama, the life of Socrates and the essay form alike render the end an arbitrary and ironic moment. "The essay," declared Lukacs, "is a judgment, but the essential, the value-determining thing about it is not the verdict . . . but the process of judging" (Lukacs 1974, 18). Socrates as essayistic phenotype comes to stand for a method that is active, fragmentary, and self-absorbing—ever in pursuit of a question "extended so far in depth that it becomes the question of all questions" (14). In Reda Bensmaia's phrase, the essay is an "open-ended, interminable writing machine," for just as the real resists the strictures of representation (how to frame or carve out a historical personage or event without the loss of authenticity), so too are the fixity of the source and the subject of enunciation called into question. The interminability of the essay follows from the process-orientation of its activity, the mediation of the real through a cascade of language, memory, and imagination. Montaigne's "book of the self," the essay as autobiography, refuses any notion of simple or self-evident origins in a manner consistent with the Barthesian pronouncement: "I am elsewhere than where I am when I write" (Barthes 1977, 169).

In classical poetics, the coherence and the synthetic power of a work are the aesthetic manifestations of a rather different epistemological assumption, that of the unity and stability of the subject. Montaigne's refusal of being-as-stasis is one precursor of the more radical contemporary theoretical position that wishes to suggest otherwise: "In the field of the subject," writes Barthes, "there is no referent" (ibid., 56). As formulated in the latter works of that writer, the essay form is the textual manifestation of indeterminacy par excellence; heterogeneous and resistant to precise boundaries, it is metaphorizable as a Japanese stew, a broken television screen, a layered pastry. Consequently, the essay eschews grand design; Bensmaia (1987) characterizes its formal procedure as a "tactics without strategy" (51).

Little wonder that films such as *Lost, Lost, Lost* and the remainder of Mekas's *Diaries, Notes, and Sketches*, Raul Ruiz's *Of Great Events and Ordinary People* (1979), Chris Marker's *Sans soleil* (1982), Trinh T. Minh-ha's *Naked Spaces: Living Is Round* (1985), or the pair of television series produced by Jean-Luc Godard and Ann-Marie Mieville, "Six fois deux" (1976) and "France/Tour/Detour/Deux/Enfants" (1978)—all of which could be termed essayistic—have alternately intrigued and puzzled audiences and critics alike with their failure to conform to generic expectation or classical structuration.[3] In all cases, the works would appear to straddle certain of the antinomies that have defined the boundaries of film scholarship: fiction/ nonfiction, documentary/avant-garde, even cinema/video. Frequently, the critical appraisal of the taxonomically unstable film or video work returns to the name of the author: the television efforts of the seventies are an extension or revision of earlier Godard obsessions; *Naked Spaces* grapples with issues of Third World feminism and the limits of language as Trinh has done in previous film and literary efforts; *Sans soleil* is the summum of Marker's career as itinerant gatherer of images and sounds. And

---

[3] There is considerable elasticity inherent in my formulation of the essayistic, with the result that no enumeration of exemplary texts will suffice to name its borders. Of course, laws of membership and exclusion always pose a problem for aesthetic taxonomies, which must remain open and therefore "impure" sets. Certain principles of composition do, however, remain useful indicators of the essayistic enterprise for film and video as they have for literature. The "twofold project," descriptive and reflexive, enfolding self and other, the outward (documentary) glance coupled with the interrogation of subjectivity—these are the signs of a discursive practice termed essayistic. For further discussion of the essayistic for film and video, see Renov 1989.

Lost, Lost, Lost is the work of the chief polemicist and celebrant of the New American Cinema. The diary films of Mekas thus can be said to spring from (the) underground; the autobiographical renderings of an artist can only be art.

Yet it is my purpose to speak of Mekas as essayist, to claim for *Lost, Lost, Lost* and the other volumes of *Diaries, Notes, and Sketches* a discursive position shared by the aforementioned as well as by other essayistic works, a position mobile in its resistance to generic encirclement, one that traces a trajectory within and across the historical fields of the documentary as well as of the avant-garde. Far from being a mere quibble over scholarly classification, the discussion of Mekas's work within a documentary context yields several dividends: on the one hand, the relatively moribund critical discourse surrounding nonfiction is enlivened, its aesthetic horizons broadened; on the other, *Lost, Lost, Lost* is more easily delivered of its status as a key work of contemporary film historiography, a work that teaches us about history and about the limits within which the filmic inscription of history is possible. Finally, the placement of *Lost* within a documentary context is essential for the present enterprise in another way. There can be little doubt that Mekas's diary-film project offers one of the most exhaustive instances of self-examination in the history of the cinema. And yet, as has been established, the essayistic is notable for its enmeshing of two registers of interrogation—of subjectivity and of the world. It is my contention that *Lost, Lost, Lost* shares with Montaigne's *Essays* an unyielding attentiveness both to the measure of sight and to the measure of things. My greatest concern in what follows will therefore be for the shape and tactical dynamics of a *documenting* gaze and a desire—to retrace the visible and the historical—that impels the film.

The placement of *Lost* within the documentary tradition remains consistent with the genesis of Mekas's project. According to the filmmaker, the documentary intent of the earliest diary efforts constitutes *Lost*'s prehistory: "The very first script that we [Jonas and his brother Adolfas] wrote when we arrived in late 1949, and which was called *Lost, Lost, Lost, Lost*, was for a documentary on the life of displaced persons here" (MacDonald 1984, 84). Significantly, the kinship between the founding intention and the project's eventual outcome has remained generally unremarked. Indeed, virtually every critic who has written about *Lost, Lost, Lost* has focused on the emergence of an authorial voice that develops over the thirteen-year period covered by the three-hour film (1949–1963), a voice instantiated by a series of visible stylistic shifts.[4] Perhaps inevitably, this pattern is rendered teleological, an ascension toward a full-blown gestural style familiar from the work of Brakhage and others. The steadfastly observational camera of the first two reels devoted to the activities of the Lithuanian exile community becomes the sign of the artist as yet unaware of his true vocation. "When you were first starting to shoot here," asks MacDonald, "did you feel that you were primarily a recorder of displaced persons and their struggle, or were you already thinking about becoming *a filmmaker of another sort?*" (MacDonald 1984, 84 emphasis mine).

THE DOCUMENTARY DETOUR

In fact, this assumed pilgrimage toward artistic progress deserves further examination, as does the essayistic character of the film's textual mapping, but not before a brief consideration of the nonfiction realm to which *Lost, Lost, Lost* is here being consigned. What is necessary in this instance is a kind of critical disengagement from the received limits of the nonfiction film in order to comprehend its historical as well as its discursive parameters. Mekas himself talks about his early literary efforts undertaken in Lithuania in the mid-forties, his pursuit of a kind of "documentary poetry" that employed poetic means—of pace and prosody—to achieve largely descriptive ends. This hybridization of literary modes in itself echoes the essential dialogism of the essayistic enterprise. But, we are told

---

[4] See in particular MacDonald 1986, as well as his *October* interview with Mekas (1984). A more conceptually ambitious account of Mekas's career and achievements, contained in James 1989, continues to treat the development of an increasingly personal style through the *Diaries* as a kind of spiritual elevation, producing a filmic mode that "entirely fulfills [underground film's] aesthetic and ethical program" (100). This tendency to describe a progressive stylistic shift as a heightening or purification of form is a romantic notion traceable in the first instance to the filmmaker's own writings over several decades. To be sure, some notion of historical development is inescapable in the discussion of *Lost*, inasmuch as the film's image track appears to be structured chronologically. That irreversibility is, however, consistently undone by the voice-over, which ranges across time and memory speaking from a place of knowledge: "Paulius, Paulius—I see you. Remember, that day, that evening, that evening we all danced around a young birch tree outside of the barracks. We thought it will all be so temporary, we'll be all home soon." MacDonald (1986) suggests that the six reels of the film can be grouped as three couplets: the first pair focusing on the Lithuanian community in Brooklyn, the second on the formation of a new life in Manhattan and the beginnings of a new community around *Film Culture*, the last on the development of a cinematic aesthetic of spontaneity and personalism. Any critical engagement with the film must, in the first instance, comprehend this play of the progressive and the reversible.

in an interview with Scott MacDonald, this merger of the poetic and the nonfictional did not survive the move into cinema a few years later:

> When I began filming, that interest [documentary poetry] did not leave me, but it was pushed aside as I got caught up in the documentary film traditions. I was reading Grierson and Rotha and looking at the British and American documentary films of the '30's and '40's. I feel now that their influence detoured me from my own inclination. Later, I had to shake this influence in order to return to the approach with which I began. (MacDonald 1984, 93–94)

The notion of a return to origins is intrinsic to Mekas's filmic oeuvre. But the return is always itself a reworking, a movement of recuperation and renewal, in this case to a documentary poetics from which Mekas never entirely retreated. It is worth noting, for example, that the traditional documentary approach to which Mekas unfavorably refers, discernible in the fervent recording of expatriate activities in *Lost*'s early reels, is circumscribed and absorbed by the complex weave of the film's sound/image orchestration. We can only imagine the Griersonian intent of the raw footage, now dialogized by auditory elements (narration and music) and the film's rhythmic self-presentation; for the spectator of *Lost, Lost, Lost*, Mekas's departure is already contained within his return.

The reference to Grierson and Rotha in the interview quoted above is significant inasmuch as they were the chief polemicists for a vision of the documentary film as a tool for propaganda and social education during the embattled decades of depression and war. For Grierson, son of a Calvinist minister, the screen was a pulpit, the film a hammer to be used in shaping the destiny of nations. When Mekas's attachment to the Lithuanian exile community gave way to broader as well as more personal concerns and the engagement with formal questions, when the fixation on national identity subsided, it was historically as well as aesthetically apt that the Griersonian model should cease to hold sway. But a wholesale disavowal of the documentary tradition threatens to obscure the tangency between Mekas's literary and filmic practices of many decades' standing, embroiled as they have been in the materiality of everyday life, and certain currents of work in nonfiction. The diary-film project deserves its place in that filmic domain.

The documentary film has, since its beginning, displayed four fundamental, often overlapping tendencies or aesthetic functions; at some moments and in the work of certain cinéastes, one or another of these characteristics has frequently been over- or underfavored. They are stated here in the active voice appropriate to their discursive agency.

1. *To record, reveal, or preserve.* This is perhaps the most elemental of documentary functions, familiar since the Lumières, traceable to the photographic antecedent. In one of several of Mekas's efforts to parse the filmic firmament (this one circa 1961), the "Realist Cinema"—a category that bridges the fiction/nonfiction divide—is named as one of three general approaches to cinema, the one that most prizes the revelational potential of the medium:

> The third approach [the others being "Pure Cinema" and "Impure Cinema"] could be called Realist Cinema, and could be summed up as the tradition of Lumière. The film-maker here is interested primarily in recording life as it is. His personality, instead of creating a new reality, goes mainly into revealing the most essential qualities of the already existing reality, as it is seen at the moment of happening. Flaherty attempted it in *Nanook*, Dziga Vertov ("The Camera-Eye") devoted his life to it. (Mekas 1961, 12)

This emphasis on the replication of the historical real links anthropology and home movie since both seek what Barthes in his *Camera Lucida* has termed "that rather terrible thing which is there in every photograph: the return of the dead" (Barthes 1981, 9). The preservational instinct—resisting the erosion of memory, the inevitability of passage—is the motor force behind this, the first of documentary's aesthetic functions.

Mekas remains the visual chronicler throughout *Lost*. The stark black and white of certain images early on evokes the best of thirties documentary photography in its combination of precise compositional values and compelling subject matter: the arrival of displaced persons at the Twenty-Third Street Pier, the spare ramshackle of a Williamsburg front stoop or the round faces of the exiled young framed in tenement windows. But the specter of Méliès hovers nearby. Even in the midst of the most faithfully atmospheric renderings of place or person, one recalls the images with which the film commences: the brothers mugging playfully before the camera and Adolfas's magic tricks. Conjury and *actualité* are made to coexist.

Documentary has most often been motivated by the wish to exploit the camera's powers of revelation, an impulse rarely coupled with an acknowledgment of the mediational processes through which the real is transformed.[5] At times, as with Flaherty, the desire to retain the trace of an already absent phenomenon has led the nonfiction artist to supplement behavior or event-in-history with its imagined counterpart. The wish to preserve images of the traditional walrus hunt of the Inuit led Robert Flaherty to suggest the anachronistic substitution of harpoons for rifles in his *Nanook of the North*. In *Lost*, Mekas's voice-over narration speaks his desire for a recovery of the past (his obsessive witnessing of events is frequently accompanied by the spoken refrain "I was there"), even while the efficacy of such a return is repeatedly contested by the film's conflictual voices.[6] The spectator is constantly reminded of the distance that separates the profilmic event and the voiced narration written years afterward. Mekas's vocal inflections themselves enforce the separation, the words delivered with a hesitancy, a weary delight in their sonorous possibilities. Thus a discomfiting retrospection on an irretrievable past is mixed with a pleasurable if provisional control over its filmic reproduction.

Moreover, the sense of indeterminacy that has been suggested as a crucial ingredient of the essayistic comes to the fore in the choice of sound elements, particularly for several of the early sequences. Rather than reinforcing the pathos of loss and displacement evoked in the scenes that document the activities of the Lithuanian expatriate community, Mekas frequently chooses to play against or at oblique angles to the anticipated emotional response. Early scenes of Jonas walking the streets of New York, alone and dispossessed, gather great force from the plaintive Kol Nidre chant that accompanies them. The reference to the holiest of Hebrew prayers and its call to atonement on Yom Kippur Eve sounds the right liturgical note even while crossing cultural boundaries (and a particularly

[5] For a further discussion of the necessity and variability of mediation for the documentary film, see Renov 1986.

[6] The notion of a preservational obsession held in tension with its opposite, the need to release the past or deny its efficacy in the present through representation, provides a crucial underpinning for *Lost, Lost, Lost*. Another film to be situated within the realm of the essayistic, Chris Marker's *Sans soleil*, explores similar terrain through an equally variegated textual mapping of temporality and experience. Even while fragments from the filmmaker's past return obsessively—from his own films such as *La jetee* (1962) or *Le mystere Koumiko* (1964) or from Hitchcock's *Vertigo* (1958)—Marker celebrates their annihilation through a ritual destruction that in turn memorializes their loss; representation becomes that system through which retention and dissolution can be fused. "Memories must make do with their delirium, with their drift," says Marker in *Sans soleil*. "A moment stopped would burn like a frame of film blocked before the furnace of the projector." *Lost* and *Sans soleil* share a fascination for cinema's special admixture of presence and absence, a chemistry examined by generations of film theorists.

charged cultural boundary it is, given the troubled history of the Jewish Lithuanian population in this century). The resonances—and frequent dissonances—between sound and image consistently challenge the retrieval of untroubled or available historical meaning from documentary images.

"And I was there, and I was the camera eye, I was the witness, and I recorded it all, and I don't know, am I singing or am I crying?" These words accompany images from the early fifties—of placard-bearing Lithuanians, traditionally clad, marching along Fifth Avenue, protesting the Soviet occupation of their land, or of the impassioned oration of exiled leaders speaking to packed halls. The private and idiosyncratic character of the images enforces Mekas as the first reader of the text; his own uncertainty about the impact or affect engendered by his project demands that we too suspend our own certain judgments. On more than one occasion, *Lost* renders itself as undecidable—at the level of emotional response as well as of historical-interpretive activity.

Mekas's diary images document a variety of historical moments; in fact, *Lost* provides access to a *series* of histories that can be traced across the film. In the first instance, there is the discourse on the displaced person and the Lithuanian community that shares his or her exile in Brooklyn. But if the pictures of life—of work, recreation, family rituals—strain toward faithful evocation, the filmmaker's spoken refrain dissuades us from our apparent comprehension: "Everything is normal, everything is normal," Mekas assures us over the images of everyday life. "The only thing is, you'll never know what they think. You'll never know what a displaced person thinks in the evening and in New York." Occurring in the opening minutes of the film, this is the first lesson to be drawn from the *Diaries*, applicable to all forays into historiography through film. Historical meanings are never simply legible or immanent. Understanding arises from the thoughtful interrogation of documents (the real in representation) and the contradictions that are produced through their overlay. Mekas here reminds us of the irreparable breach between experience and its externalized representation, a notion implied by the film's very title. We are all of us lost in the chasm between our desire to recapture the past and the impossiblity of a pristine return—no one more so than Mekas himself.

The Lithuanian émigré experience, equivocal though our understanding of it may be, thus emerges as the first strand of *Lost*'s historiographic braid. It is, however, possible to trace a second preservational trajectory through the film's elaboration of a kind of postwar urban geohistory. Mekas's odyssey from Williamsburg to

Manhattan crisscrosses virtually every sector of New York—Orchard Street, East Thirteenth Street, Avenue B, Times Square, City Hall, Madison Avenue, Fifth Avenue, Park Avenue South, Washington Square, and the obsessive return to Central Park. There and elsewhere, Mekas finds himself inexorably drawn to the energy and tenacity of the picketers and the poets who agitate for their personal visions (fig. 15.1). The leaflet women of Forty-Second Street (appearing near the end of the fourth reel) who face public indifference on the coldest day of the year inspire Mekas's lyric testimonial, evinced at the level of word and image. "I was with you. I had to be. You were, you were . . . the blood of my city, the heartbeat. I wanted to feel its pulse, to feel its excitement. Yes, this was my city."

The cropped and canted composition of the leafleting trio celebrates at a historical—and stylized—remove; it also recalls the Three Graces on the Stony Brook beach near the close of reel 2, the trio of émigrés preserved in a moment of unselfconscious revelry (fig. 15.2). The leafleteers likewise anticipate the final instance of this figure at film's end—Barbara and Debby wading fully clothed, awash in the same sea as the original celebrant trio, two decades later (fig. 15.3). Each of the film's three sections thus contains near its close a strikingly composed female figure group. Far from performing a merely decorative function, these imaged women are

15.1 *Lost* as postwar urban geohistory. Mekas finds himself inexorably drawn to the energy and tenacity of the picketers and the poets.

15.2 The Three Graces on the Stony Brook beach. Lithuanian émigrés preserved in a moment of revelry.

15.3 The play of revision and erasure. "He remembered another day. . . . I have seen these waters before."

drawn from milieux particular to each stage of Mekas's life chronicle—from the Lithuanian nationalist period to the years of social activism to the consolidation of artistic identity. These dreamily eroticized avatars—part comrade, part goddess—are apt figures for a sensibility that obsessively couples the historical with the aesthetic. Endowed with a kind of grandeur, even monumentality (evoked through their framing and musical accompaniment), they bestow benediction on memory.

It is worth considering further the figural tableaux that conclude each of *Lost*'s three sections. Thick with classical and romantic allusions, their repetition is a marker of the autobiographical in the sense established by Jacques Derrida. In his analysis of Nietzsche's *Ecce Homo*, Derrida approaches the question of signature—and hence the attribution of the autobiographical—for literary and philosophical texts, particularly those that problematize self-presentation. He posits a dynamic borderline between the "work" and the "life," the system and the subject of the system, a "divisible borderline [that] traverses two 'bodies,' the corpus and the body, in accordance with laws that we are only beginning to catch sight of" (Derrida 1985, 5–6). This borderline—mobile, divisible—is a site of contestation, the place where the proper name or signature is staged. Thus the recurrence of the invested iconographic figure in *Lost, Lost, Lost* can be said to speak the artist's subjectivity even as it reproduces the concreteness of historical detail. As Mekas himself has remarked, "Therefore, if one knows how to 'read' them [the details of the actual], even if one doesn't see me speaking or walking, one can tell everything about me" (Mekas 1978, 193).

In his own writing, Mekas has tended to reduce the dynamism of the work/life borderline through his claim for the primacy of the subjective in the *Diaries*. "As far as the city goes, of course, you could say something also about the city, from my *Diaries*—but only indirectly" (ibid., 193). Indeed, New York is more than a passive wrapping for Mekas's personal odyssey. The fourteen-year period encompassed by the film coincides with a crucial period of thaw for America's cultural crossroads; New York, fast becoming the lodestone of art movements and accelerating social protest, is shown to experience a maturation in tune with the filmmaker's own.

But the surest focus of Mekas's witnessing throughout much of *Lost, Lost, Lost* is the constellation of creative pressures that produces the New American Cinema. The growth and development of that movement is the subject of a third history charted from the moment of this title card's appearance in the third reel: "Film culture is rolling on Lafayette Street." From the East Thirteenth Street

apartment that doubles as *Film Culture*'s headquarters to the New
Yorker Theater and its gathering of cinephiles to the Park Avenue
South offices of the Film-Makers' Co-op, these are the urban spaces
that frame the actions of the New Cinema's protagonists. What
they do there is much the subject of the film. But the altered aims
and methods of Mekas's creative drive testify to the historical development of the new aesthetic with equal cogency; a heightened
spontaneity of camera movement, flickering shot duration, and a
series of high-compression vignettes, the Rabbit Shit Haikus, are
the chief markers of this shift.

Lost thus documents a succession of events significant in the formation of a cultural moment that hold an equally crucial place in
the "discovery" of the artist's vocation. Exemplary instances include the collective efforts around the publication of *Film Culture*
from 1955 onward, the shooting of Mekas's first feature, *Guns of
the Trees* (1961), and the assault on the self-annointed arbiters of
documentary purism at the Flaherty Seminar. The footage from the
set of *Guns of the Trees* was, in fact, shot by Charles Levine; the
exploration of the artist's subjectivity, increasingly foregrounded in
the latter portions of *Lost*, is here suborned to the demands for a
physical witnessing, to cinema's preservational function. "It's my
nature now to record," says Mekas at the close of reel 4, "to try to
keep everything I am passing through . . . to keep at least bits of
it. . . . I've lost too much. . . . So now I have these bits that I've
passed through."

Mekas's preservational instincts serve to salvage the past for others as well. In this regard, Mekas may, in his later years, have come
full circle, from an attention to the needs of the extended family of
displaced persons to those of the nuclear family. His sense of the
historical or popular memory function of the diary films is expressed with appropriate tenderness in his "Film Notes" to *Paradise
Not Yet Lost, a/k/a Oona's Third Year* (1979): "It is a letter to Oona
[Mekas's daughter], to serve her, some day, as a distant reminder of
how the world around her looked during the third year of her life—
a period of which there will be only tiny fragments left in her memory—and to provide her with a romantic's guide to the essential values of life—in a world of artificiality, commercialism, and bodily
and spiritual poison" (Mekas 1980).

As we shall see, there is no contradiction between the elemental
documentary impulse, the will to preservation, and the exploration
of subjectivity; indeed, it is their obsessive convergence that marks
the essayistic work. It is, however, the irreconcilable difference between retention in representation and experiential loss that lends

urgency to the diary project, driving the filmmaker toward an unobtainable, ever-deferred resolution.

2. *To persuade or promote.* This is the dominant trope for many of the films of the Grierson group during the Empire Marketing Board period (*Night Mail* [1936], *Housing Problems* [1937]), and for a majority of state-supported works ranging from Dziga Vertov's *Three Songs for Lenin* (1934) to Santiago Alvarez's *Now!* (1965) or *Hasta la victoria siempre* (1967).[7] While Mekas remained for decades the most visible polemicist for the "new" or personal cinema through *Film Culture* and the "Movie Journal" column in the *Village Voice*, his filmmaking practice exhibits little of the rhetorical intent of a Vertov or an Alvarez. In his "Call for a New Generation of Film-Makers," appearing in *Film Culture* in 1959, Mekas issued a surrealist-inspired manifesto for an American avant-garde: "Our hope for a free American cinema is entirely in the hands of the new generation of film-makers. And there is no other way of breaking the frozen cinematic ground than through a *complete* derangement of the official cinematic senses" (Mekas 1959, 3). This directive is visibly executed in the last third of the film through the gestural style that received Mekas's critical endorsement. But the film exceeds the programmatic; its plurality outstrips polemics. As is the case with essayistic discourse generally, *Lost* is at odds with the kind of epistemological or affective certainty necessary for overt persuasion. Recall herewith the emotional ambivalence ("Am I singing or am I crying?") and the unhinging of interpretive stability ("You'll never know what they think"), both conditions ill-suited to the goal-orientation of propaganda. The gap of history and feeling that separates the images of 1949 from the voice that reassesses their meaning a quarter of a century later produces resonant or ironic effects rather than discursive streamlining. If there is a promotional impetus to be found in *Lost* it is for a life defined through a perpetual act of self-creation rather than for a particular political or aesthetic position.

3. *To express.* This is the rhetorical/aesthetic function that has consistently been undervalued within the nonfiction domain; it is, nevertheless, amply represented in the history of the documentary enterprise. While the Lumières' *actualités* may have set the stage for nonfictional film's emphasis on the signified, a historically conditioned taste for dynamic if not pictorialist photographic composition accounts for the diagonal verve of the train station at La Cio-

---

[7] Convents (1988) argues that the documentary film was recruited for the purposes of propagandizing colonialist efforts in Africa as early as 1897.

tat. Most sources agree that Robert Flaherty was the documentary film's first poet as well as itinerant ethnographer. Flaherty's expressivity was verbal as well as imagistic in origin; to the in-depth compositions of trackless snowscapes in *Nanook of the North*, one must consider as well the flair for poetic language ("the brass ball of sun a mockery in the sky"). The cycle of "city symphony" films of the twenties (*Man with a Movie Camera, Berlin: Symphony of a Great City, A propos de Nice*) declared their allegiance in varying degrees to the powers of expressivity in the service of historical representation. The artfulness of the work as a function of its purely photographic properties was now allied with the possibilities of editing to create explosive effects—cerebral as well as visceral. The early films of the documentary polemicist Joris Ivens (*The Bridge* [1928], *Rain* [1929]) evidence the attraction felt for the cinema's aesthetic potential, even for those artists motivated by strong political beliefs.

In his earliest attempt to categorize film types, Mekas had suggested that the "document film" encompassed both the "interest film" (newsreels, instructionals, films on art) and the "documentary film—realist, impressionist or poetical, the primary purpose of which is non-instructional (though teaching)" (Mekas 1955, 15–16).[8] Parker Tyler, a frequent contributor to *Film Culture*, suggested his own rather cumbersome category of poetic film, "the naturalistic poetry document," a grouping that included *The River* and *The Blood of the Beasts* (Tyler 1970, 173). Difficulties arise in such efforts to distinguish among film forms as ideal types, a problem reduced through attention to discursive function rather than to the erection of discrete categories.

It is important to note in the context of taxonomic confusion that certain works of the avant-garde canon (Brakhage's "Pittsburgh Trilogy" or Peter Kubelka's *Unsere Afrikareise*) share with mainstream nonfiction a commitment to the representation of the historical real. However, the focus of these pieces typically remains the impression of the world on the artist's sensorium and his or her interpretation of that datum (Brakhage's tremulous hand-held camera as he witnesses open-heart surgery in *Deus Ex*) or the radical reworking of the documentary material to create sound-image relationships unavailable in nature (Kubelka's "synch event"). Critical differences of emphasis such as these notwithstanding, the realm of

---

[8] Besides the "document film," Mekas's categorization of cinematic forms includes the film drama, the film poem, and the cinema of abstraction or "cineplastics."

filmic nonfiction must be seen as a continuum within which the Mekas diary films constitute a significant contribution. That a work undertaking some manner of historical documentation renders that representation in an innovative manner (in silence or soft focus, for example) should in no way disqualify it as nonfiction since the question of expressivity is, in all events, a question of degree. All such renderings require a series of authorial choices, none neutral, some of which may appear more "artful" or purely expressive than others. There can be little doubt that such determinations ("artful documentary" or "documentary art") depend on various protocols of reading that are historically conditioned.

One expressive vehicle common to Mekas's diary films deserves special mention: the use of the filmmaker's voice. Rich in performance values, Mekas's voice functions as an instrument of great lyric power—measured, musical in its variation, hesitation, and repetition. The incantatory tone reinforces *Lost*'s bardic quality, inaugurated by the epic invocation that is the filmmaker's first utterance: "O sing, Ulysses, sing your travels. . . ." The poetic use of language is strategically counterweighted, however, by the alternation of first and third person in the narration, never more effectively than at the film's conclusion: "He remembered another day. Ten years ago he sat on this beach, ten years ago, with other friends. The memories, the memories, the memories. . . . Again I have memories. . . . I have a memory of this place. I have been here before. I have really been here before. I have seen these waters before, yes, I've walked upon this beach, these pebbles—" Spectators are brought to their own recollections from a shared experience of some three hours' viewing; the young Lithuanian women on the beach at Stony Brook, captured in blissful dance, who recur as the leaflet women halfway through the film, are brilliantly recapitulated by the paired female figures at the film's end. We too have been here before. As with the poetic figure anaphora, so frequently invoked in the triplets of the Rabbit Shit Haikus and elsewhere ("the memories, the memories, the memories"), repetition proves to be not simple duplication, but a play of revision and erasure (see figs. 15.2 and 15.3).

4. *To analyze or interrogate.* If the question of expressivity has plagued discussions of documentary, the analytical function has been virtually ignored.[9] The imperative toward analysis (of the

[9] The many studies of reflexivity in cinema have focused on fictional works almost exclusively (e.g., the *Screen* debates on Brecht from the 1970s or Walsh 1981). Among the writings that do address this problem in the documentary context, the best may be Allen 1977, Kuhn 1978, and Ruby 1988.

enunciated and of the enunciative act) offers an intensification of and challenge to the record/reveal/preserve modality insofar as it actively questions nonfictional discourse—its claims to truth, its status as second-order reality. On what basis does the spectator invest belief in the representation? What are the codes that ensure that belief? What material processes are involved in the production of this "spectacle of the real," and to what extent are these processes rendered visible or knowable to the spectator? While many of these questions are familiar from the debates on reflexivity and the Brechtian cinema, applicable to fiction and nonfiction alike (the films of Vertov, Godard, and Straub and Huillet—essayists all—have most frequently inspired these discussions), their urgency is particularly great for documentary works, which can be said to bear a direct, ontological tie to the real.

As noted in the discussion of expressivity, nonfiction film is the result of determinate mediations or authorial interventions, some of which may be perceived as "style." The analytical documentary is likely to acknowledge that mediational structures are formative rather than mere embellishments. In *Man with a Movie Camera*, the flow of images is repeatedly arrested or reframed as the filmic fact is revealed to be a labor-intensive social process that engages camera operators, editors, projectionists, musicians, and audience members. Motion pictures are represented as photographic images in motion, variable as to their projected speed, duration, or screen direction: galloping horses are capable of being halted midstride, water can run upstream, smiling children can be transformed into bits of celluloid to be inspected at editor Svilova's workbench.

In the sound era, the breach between image and its audio counterpart has rarely been acknowledged; synchronized sound, narration, or music is meant to reinforce or fuse with the image rather than question its status. Such is not the case in Alain Resnais's *Nuit et brouillard* (1955) with its airy pizzicati accompanying the most oppressive imagery of Holocaust atrocities. Chris Marker's *Letter from Siberia* (1958) is another departure from the norm. The connotative power of nonlinguistic auditory elements (music, vocal inflection) is confirmed by the repetition of an otherwise banal sequence; the sequencing of images and the narration remain unchanged while the accompanying music and tonal values of the narrating voice create differing semantic effects. Every viewer is forced to confront the malleability of meaning and the ideological impact of authorial or stylistic choices that typically go unnoticed. In Straub and Huillet's *Introduction to "An Accompaniment for a*

Cinematographic Scene," a musical composition, Schoenberg's Opus 34, is "illustrated" by the recitation of Schoenberg's correspondence as well as by his drawings, photographs (of the composer and of the slain Paris Communards), archival footage of American bombing runs over Vietnam, and a newspaper clipping about the release of accused Nazi concentration camp architects. A process of interrogation is thus undertaken through the layering and resonance of heterogeneous elements. Schoenberg's music, the work of a self-professed apolitical artist, becomes the expressive vehicle for an outrage whose moral and intellectual dimensions exceed the parochial bounds of politics proper. Yet the collective coherence of the filmic elements remains to be constructed by a thinking audience. The analytical impulse is not so much enacted by the filmmakers as encouraged in the viewer.

The analytical impulse so rarely activated in mainstream nonfiction is strong in *Lost, Lost, Lost,* primarily due to the distance that separates the images, spanning more than a decade of the filmmaker's life, and the auditory elements, chosen years later, that engage them in dialogue. The relations between sound and image maintain a palpable tension throughout the film's duration, aided by the poignancy of silence. It is largely through the orchestration of acoustic effects (not least among them silence) that the film establishes its tonality. Despite the alterity of word and image, which occupy quite disparate planes of signification, conventional nonsync narrational techniques frequently attempt to sustain the impression of illustration, the visible enacting the spoken. In *Lost,* however, the breach between the seen and the heard remains irreparable; indeed, the sound elements themselves seem rarely to resolve into a "mixed" track—words, music, and effects remain discrete, virtually autonomous. From the clattering of subway trains to the plucking of stringed folk instruments to the subtle voicing of narration, each element retains its sovereign (that is, nonnaturalized) status.

Particularly through his spoken commentary, Mekas seized on the nonfiction film's ability to reassess human action even while revisiting it. Williams concluded his review of the film with a discussion of this aspect of its structure: "*Lost* is a particularly moving film because of the distance between the Jonas Mekas who shot— who wrote—the footage used in the work and the Jonas Mekas who assembled it in the 1970's. In this distance lies the material for powerful interactions between levels of experience" (Williams 1976, 62).

"WHEN I AM FILMING, I AM ALSO REFLECTING"

The reflexive character of the film, its will to analysis of self and events, returns us to the domain of the essayistic. While all documentary films retain an interest in some portion of the world *out there*—recording, and less frequently interrogating, at times with the intent to persuade and with varying degrees of attention to formal issues—the essayist's gaze is drawn inward with equal intensity. That inward gaze accounts for the digressive and fragmentary character of the essayistic, as André Tournon's assessment of Montaigne's *Essays* suggests: "Thought can abandon its theme at any time to examine its own workings, question its acquired knowledge or exploit its incidental potentialities" (Tournon 1983, 61).

Long before the appearance of his diary films, Mekas wrote admiringly of Alexandre Astruc's "camera stylo." Indeed, the work of Mekas, like that of Godard, Marker, and other prose writers turned filmmakers, offers important insight into the essayistic as a modality of filmic inscription. In a lecture on *Reminiscences of a Journey to Lithuania*, Mekas addressed the relationship between the diaristic in film and its literary counterpart; his reflections inform our consideration of filmic autobiography and of the defining conditions of historiographical pursuits more generally.

> At first I thought that there was a basic difference between the written diary which one writes in the evening, and which is a reflective process, and the filmed diary. In my film diary, I thought, I was doing something different: I was capturing life, bits of it, as it happens. But I realized very soon that it wasn't that different at all. When I am filming, I am also reflecting. I was thinking that I was only reacting to the actual reality. I do not have much control over reality at all, and everything is determined by my memory, my past. So that this "direct" filming becomes also a mode of reflection. Same way, I came to realize, that writing a diary is not merely reflecting, looking back. Your day, as it comes back to you during the moment of writing, is measured, sorted out, accepted, refused, and reevaluated by what and how one is at the moment when one writes it all down. It's all happening again, and what one writes down is more true to what one is when one writes than to the events and emotions of the day that are past and gone. Therefore, I no longer see such big differences between a written diary and the filmed diary, as far as the processes go. (Mekas 1978, 191–92)

Mekas's diaristic project is writerly at every turn, both because the process of inscription is foregrounded throughout and because, consistent with Barthes's description of the writerly in *S/Z*, *Lost* as

text approaches the status of the "triumphant plural, unimpover-
ished by any constraint of representation. . . . We gain access to it
by several entrances, none of which can be authoritatively declared
to be the main one; the codes it mobilizes extend *as far as the eye
can reach*" (Barthes 1974, 5–6). It is writing of a certain sort that
suffuses the film; the sense of sketch or palimpsest is retained
throughout, in contrast with, for example, the florid, unwavering
signature of Straub's Bach, whose piety engenders artistic as well as
moral certitude in *Chronicle of Anna Magdalena Bach* (1967). The
intermittently imaged snatches of written diary in *Lost* conjure for
us a process of self-inscription that is painfully, materially etched
(fig. 15.4). "October 3d, 1950," intones Mekas, from the distance of
decades. "I have been trying to write with a pencil. But my fingers
do not really grasp the pencil properly, not like they used to grasp
it a year, two years ago. From working in the factory my fingers
became stiff. They don't bend, they lost their subtlety of movement. There are muscles in them I haven't seen before. They look
fatter. Anyway, I can't hold the pencil. So I go to the typewriter and
I begin to type, with one finger." Apocryphal or not, this account of
graphological vicissitudes is corroborated at every turn of the text.
Typographic emendations are foregrounded in Mekas's imaging of
the diary pages. Significantly, it is the overstroke rather than the

I tried to sleep,

sed a round in my

exhausted, deep s

15.4 The process of self-inscription—painfully, materially etched.

erasure that prevails; the trace of each failed gesture remains legible beneath each correction. As so many theorists of the essay have noted, it is the process of judgment far more than the verdict that counts. Mekas is at pains to restore to his filmed diaries the physicality and sheer effort of their provenance.

The diary inserts thus reinforce our sense of the text as a handcrafted and provisional one, always subject to reconsideration. The provisional character of all filmed material in *Lost* is dramatically borne out by its occasional transfiguration in other volumes of *Diaries, Notes, and Sketches*. In addition, then, to the potential reassessment of each image by a narrating agency at great historical remove, these same images can be reinvested and reframed—in a manner consistent with Freud's notion of *nachtraglichkeit*, or deferred action.[10]

The triumphant plurality of which Barthes speaks results from the film text's temporal fluidity, the multiple styles and perspectives it mobilizes (mingling color with black-and-white film stock as well as footage shot by others) and its several historical foci. *Lost* mimes the richness of lived experience through its modulation of a range of filmic elements. It is the sheer extent and heterogeneity of Mekas's *Diaries, Notes, and Sketches* that is most responsible for producing the sense of Barthes's inexhaustible text.

But the heterogeneity of Mekas's oeuvre is distinguishable from Godard's unceasing referentiality, Straub's geologic stratification, and Marker's Borgesian labyrinths. While it is likely that, among these film practitioners, Mekas's diary format most approximates Montaigne's flight from final judgments, the writing practices of the two emerge from very different philosophical contexts. Montaigne's refusal of the preexisting limits of thought and literary protocol was vested in an intellectual skepticism that valorized reflection and the ceaseless revisionism it dictated. Mekas, on the other hand, responds to a tradition that embraces spontaneity over thought. The expansiveness of the diaries arises from the conviction that art and life are indissoluble.

---

[10] As discussed in Laplanche and Pontalis 1973, Freud's use of the term *nachtraglichkeit* is intended to convey the manner by which experiences, impressions, or memory traces are altered after the fact as a function of new experiences and are thus rendered capable of reinvestment, producing new, even unexpected effects of meaning. As Freud wrote to his confidant, Wilhelm Fliess: "I am working on the assumption that our psychical mechanism has come about by a process of stratification: the material present in the shape of memory-traces is from time to time subjected to a *rearrangement* in accordance with fresh circumstances—is, as it were, *transcribed*" (Laplanche and Pontalis 1973, 182–83).

The spontaneity of the new American artist is not a conscious or an intellectual process: it is rather his way of life, his whole being; he comes to it rather intuitively, directly.

The new artist neither chooses this spontaneous route himself nor does he do so consciously: it is imposed upon him by his time, as the only possible route. (Mekas 1960, 19)

That pronouncement, made in 1960, was slightly revised two years later, the emphasis having shifted from the involuntary (and apparently unknowable) source of art making to the art *process* and its institutional reception. This reassessment, responsive to the politicized environment of the New York art scene of the early 1960s, shares something of the rhetoric if not the material circumstances of the new Latin American cinema emergent at that moment. Mekas, however, spoke his refusal from the very nerve center of dominant culture rather than from its periphery; he wrote against the art establishment, not against the mass-culture colonizers. "I don't want any part of the Big Art game. The new cinema, like the new man, is nothing definitive, nothing final. It is a living thing. It is imperfect; it errs" (Mekas 1970, 88).

Diaries, Notes, and Sketches owes a great deal to the raw power of the improvisatory art Mekas championed at the time of those writings. Several sequences in *Lost* offer documentation of the people and activities of the Living Theater. In 1959, Mekas awarded the first Independent Film Award to John Cassavetes' *Shadows*; Drew Associates' *Primary*, which was said to reveal "new cinematic techniques of recording life on film," was the recipient of the third award. The 1962 essay "Notes on the New American Cinema" shares the spirit of the Willem de Kooning epigram it quotes in apparent admiration: "Painting—any kind of painting, any style of painting—to be painting at all, in fact—is a way of living today, a style of living, so to speak." (Mekas 1970, 88). Indeed, *Lost, Lost, Lost* shares something of the edgy immediacy of the art that prevailed in the moment of its shooting.

But *Lost* exceeds its roots in improvisation, in the capture of an uncontrolled reality, in a wished-for fusion of art and life. At last, it is through its character as essayistic work that the film yields its surplus. Vast in its purview, elliptical in its self-presentation, complex in its interpolation of historical substrata and textual voices, the film struggles with "the old problem"—"to merge Reality and Self, to come up with the third thing." But *Lost* resists the snares of resolution or completion, even in the dialectical beyond. Moreover, a belief in the revivification or recapture of experience in the crucible of art is actively disavowed, even if, as in Marker's *Sans soleil*, loss itself becomes ritual celebration.

In assessing the film four decades after its inception, the Lukacsian prescription might well apply. *Lost, Lost, Lost* will survive as a triumph of judgment independent of the world or psyche that it reveals. And "the value-determining thing about it is not the verdict . . . but the process of judging" (Lukacs 1974, 18).

Bibliography

Allen, Jeanne. 1977. "Reflexivity in Documentary." *Cine-tracts*, 1, no. 2 (Summer): 37–43.

Barthes, Roland. 1974. *S/Z*. Trans. Richard Miller. New York: Hill and Wang.

———. 1977. *Roland Barthes*. Trans. Richard Howard. New York: Hill and Wang.

———. 1981. *Camera Lucida*. Trans. Richard Howard. New York: Hill and Wang.

———. 1985. *The Grain of the Voice: Interview, 1962–1980*. Trans. Linda Coverdale. New York: Hill and Wang.

Bensmaia, Reda. 1987. *The Barthes Effect: The Essay as Reflective Text*. Trans. Pat Fedkiew. Minneapolis: University of Minnesota Press.

Convents, Guido. 1988. "Documentaries and Propaganda before 1914: A View on Early Cinema and Colonial History." *Framework* 35:104–13.

Defaux, Gerard. 1983. "Readings of Montaigne." Trans. John A. Gallucci. In *Montaigne: Essays in Reading*. Yale French Studies 64:73–92.

Derrida, Jacques. 1980. "The Law of Genre." *Glyph* 7:202–32.

———. 1985. "Octobiographies." Trans. Avital Ronell. In *The Ear of the Other*, 1–38. New York: Schocken Books.

Good, Graham. 1988. *The Observing Self: Rediscovering the Essay*. London: Routledge.

James, David. 1989. *Allegories of Cinema: American Film in the Sixties*. Princeton: Princeton University Press.

Kuhn, Annette. 1978. "The Camera I—Observations on Documentary." *Screen* 1, no. 2 (Summer): 71–83.

Laplanche, Jean, and Jean-Bertrand Pontalis. 1973. *The Language of Psychoanalysis*. Trans. Donald Nicholson-Smith. New York: W. W. Norton.

Lukacs, Georg. 1974. "On the Nature and Form of the Essay." In *Soul and Form*, trans. Anna Bostock, 1–18. Cambridge: MIT Press.

MacDonald, Scott. 1984. "Interview with Jonas Mekas." *October* 29 (Summer): 82–116.

———. 1986. "Lost Lost Lost Over *Lost Lost Lost.*" *Cinema Journal* 25, no. 2 (Winter): 20–34.

Mekas, Jonas. 1955. "The Experimental Film in America." *Film Culture* 3:15–20.

———. 1959. "A Call for a New Generation of Film-Makers." *Film Culture* 19:1–4.

———. 1960. "Cinema of the New Generation." *Film Culture* 21:1–20.

———. 1961. Introduction to "The Frontiers of Realist Cinema: The Work of Ricky Leacock (from an Interview conducted by Gideon Bachmann)." *Film Culture* 22–23:12.

———. 1970. "Notes on the New American Cinema." In *Film Culture Reader*, ed. P. Adams Sitney, 87–107. New York: Praeger Publishers.

———. 1978. "The Diary Film (A Lecture on *Reminiscences of a Journey to Lithuania*)." In *Avant-Garde Film: A Reader Theory and Criticism*, ed. P. Adams Sitney, 190–98. New York: New York University Press.

———. 1980. "Film Notes." In *Jonas Mekas*, ed. Judith E. Briggs. Minneapolis: Film in the Cities/Walker Art Center.

Montaigne, Michel de. 1948. *The Complete Works of Montaigne*. Trans. Donald M. Frame. Stanford: Stanford University Press.

Renov, Michael. 1986. "Re-Thinking Documentary: Toward a Taxonomy of Mediation." *Wide Angle* 8, no. 3–4:71–77.

———. 1989. "History and/as Autobiography: The Essayistic in Film and Video." *Frame/Work* 2, no. 3:5–13.

Ruby, Jay. 1988. "The Image Mirrored: Reflexivity and the Documentary Film." In *New Challenges for Documentary*, ed. Alan Rosenthal, 64–77. Berkeley and Los Angeles: University of California Press.

Tournon, André. 1983. "Self-Interpretation in Montaigne's *Essays.*" *Montaigne: Essays in Reading.* Yale French Studies 64:51–72.

Tyler, Parker. 1970. "Poetry and the Film: A Symposium, with Maya Deren, Arthur Miller, Dylan Thomas, Parker Tyler." In *Film Culture Reader*, ed. P. Adams Sitney, 171–86. New York: Praeger.

Walsh, Martin. 1981. *The Brechtian Aspect of Radical Cinema*. London: BFI Publishing.

Williams, Alan. 1976. "*Diaries, Notes and Sketches*—Volume I ('Lost, Lost, Lost')." *Film Quarterly* 30, no. 1:60–62.

16. Peter Kubelka   Dear Friends

When Jonas, in 1964, got me a grant of $10 a week, he helped me,
  when he brought me to New York and showed my films he became one of my fathers,
  when he beat me in a vodka drinking bout, he astonished me,
  when he kept my bicycle in his living room for years, friendship assumed a new meaning for me,
  when he established his diary style of views and glimpses, he forced me to put him into my category of special rascals like Buñuel, Brakhage, or Anger, whose work I have to envy,
  when I saw him prepare yogurt for his daughter, I understood why: out of a small container, he was cutting yogurt with a spoon and placing the slices one by one on a cool white plate, careful not to break them nor to destroy the consistency. Very slowly, very, very carefully. Such love in the preparation of each single bite I had witnessed only once before. It was in a Viennese early-morning market kitchen. "Imagine every piece as a bite in the mouth, don't just chop," the great cooking lady had said, as she cut the meat for the goulash.
  Jonas has realized that, whatever paradise there is, it should be here and now. Loving care is a key to it. Like Arlecchino, the never-resting lover, he moves and moves on and moves in.

SINCERELY,
PETER KUBELKA

17. Scott Nygren

Film Writing and the Figure of Death: *He Stands in a Desert Counting the Seconds of His Life*

FOR THOSE who know the recent history of losses within the film community, the number of people appearing in Jonas Mekas's *He Stands in a Desert Counting the Seconds of His Life* (1969–1985) who are now dead is overwhelming: Hollis Frampton, James Blue, John Lennon, Henri Langlois, Jerome Hill, George Maciunas, Andy Warhol, Willard Van Dyke, Hans Richter. The media image of John F. Kennedy is also implied through footage of Jackie and her children, invoking his assassination as a representation of loss in the domain of the political. The presence of death in this film is condensed into the hospitalization and extended illness of George Maciunas, which recurs throughout the reels, and the sequence of Hollis Frampton's funeral in Buffalo, placed near the end of the film. Although the funeral is followed by fireworks that celebrate the Brooklyn Bridge's birthday and by images of children playing, these images of regeneration and rebirth cannot erase the figure of death that weighs so heavily in this film.

Here I will consider death in *He Stands in a Desert* both as a Romantic figure that situates the author as subject of a lament in opposition to loss, and as an unstable figure that approaches absence as the basis of representation. Death figures the loss, not only of life but also of a national homeland. Accordingly I will also discuss the assertion (which appears twice in intertitles) that this is a "political film," and Mekas's exile from Lithuania as a central metaphor for his development of alternative institutions. The metaphor of exile is open to a specific rereading after recent events in Eastern Europe and invites a historical consideration of efforts to democratize an information economy.

Many of Mekas's familiar tropes from earlier films continue in *He Stands in a Desert*. As in his *Diaries, Notes, and Sketches (Walden)* (1968), intimate portraits represent the New York art scene as a community in which personal contacts defy the impersonal machinery of late-industrial bureaucracy. Early in the film at a dumpling party, George Maciunas argues a theory of the avant-garde as a theory of subversion and of doing new things, both artistic and political. Images of Allen Ginsberg at the New School in 1972, the Fluxus group on a Hudson River cruise in 1971, Richard Foreman calling from Paris to a pay-phone in Soho in 1972, and many other sequences of artists imagine a Romantic ideology of presence and improvisation against industrial depersonalization, as David James has described in the chapter on Mekas in his *Allegories of Cinema: American Film in the Sixties* (1989, 100–119).

Weddings and anniversaries, birthdays and celebrations of all kinds punctuate *He Stands in a Desert*, just as they do *Diaries, Notes, and Sketches*. Celebrations foreground family and children, and secondarily the old country, as in the sequence of Nick Perna's relatives celebrating their mother's and father's departure for Italy in 1970. Mekas's daughter Oona appears frequently, as in *Paradise Not Yet Lost (a/k/a Oona's Third Year)*, as an image of childhood and rebirth, of Romantic innocence and joy. *He Stands in a Desert* is framed by images of mothers and children. Julie Sitney and her baby in Central Park in 1969 is one of the first images we see, and Hollis Melton (Mekas's wife) with Oona is one of the last. The intertitle "Unity? Yes, my film has a unity—it's all spliced together" is followed by an image of breast-feeding, a juxtaposition that suggests that the biological continuity of generations is conceived as the structure of the film.

As in *Lost, Lost, Lost*, references to the history of cinema are plentiful. Portraits of other important filmmakers and film historians from Hans Richter and Henri Langlois to Elia Kazan, Willard Van Dyke, and Hollis Frampton ground Mekas's film language in personal contacts. The film begins with images of a fire in the streets of New York and of workers leaving a steel factory in Pittsburgh in 1971 that recall the earliest films of the Lumières. Later, a sequence at La Ciotat in 1974 is marked by the image of a passing train that quotes the Lumières, and by a plaque at the site that commemorates their role in film history.

Despite the continuation of tropes from earlier films, more strongly than any other Mekas has yet produced, *He Stands in a Desert* foregrounds cinematic writing as a structuring absence linked with loss and death. The forms of Mekas's work, from personal diaries that center the recording subject to portraits that celebrate the centeredness of the individualized other, ostensibly derive from the humanist logocentric tradition of male subjectivity and idealized female object. Indeed, most artists in Mekas's films are male (with important exceptions, including Carolee Schneeman in *He Stands in a Desert*, and the ghost of Maya Deren acknowledged in *Diaries, Notes, and Sketches* through the figure of her mother), while Hollis Melton and most women are positioned as child-bearing and erotic. Further, all the figures who die are male, and of the same approximate age, class, and background as the filmmaker, reflexively locating the self through a lament for the loss of its substitutes. It would be tempting to dismiss these aspects of Mekas's work as a reactionary nostalgia for the humanist centrality of the male speaking voice transposed to film and reified as visual imagery, but Mekas's texts are not this simple. Rather, it is precisely the retrieval of Romantic individualism in the context of Hollywood's industrially produced collective representations that makes possible Mekas's radical reinscription of cinematic language. Progressive and reactionary moves are intertwined in a fundamental break with the established dialectics of Western cultural formations that does not lend itself to easy analytic binaries such as Romantic versus materialist or individualist versus collective.

One of the persistent paradoxes of twentieth-century art has been the ironic interplay of humanist individualism against collective textual construction both in the dominant, mass-media forms of representation and in the alternative or avant-garde activities that circulate among small audiences. On the one hand, dominant practice is generated as a corporately produced system of narrative conventions, decentered from unitary subjective origins by the collaborative hierarchies of industrial organization. Yet these conventions foreground individual subjectivity through the centering of character and action characteristic of continuity conventions. As a result, apparent individualism is displaced to the domain of myth, and realist character development tends to be elided by social allegory and the melodramatic presentation of direct psychic figuration, as Fredric Jameson (1984) and Peter Brook (1976) respectively argue. The collective forms of representation that characterize the mode of industrial production reappear within film practice as the text's unconscious. The auteurist grouping of texts around the names of single directors, such as Ford, Hawks, and Welles, whom Jonas Mekas admired as a critic, perpetuates this individualist myth outside the film frame.

In contrast, so-called modernist or avant-garde work has tended throughout the century to foreground collective and decentered modes of representation, but through a production system that recuperates such radical practices within the figure of artist as subjective hero. The cubist fracturing of unified perspective, like the montage fracturing of continuity, tends to be reunified as the personal expression of Picasso or Léger. The problem for a critical analysis of the avant-garde is to explain how the association of humanist theory and production practices combines with the construction of radical texts that function primarily on nonhumanist grounds. The work of Jonas Mekas, like that of many other avant-garde artists, combines the rhetoric of humanist subjectivity with radical textual construction. The specificity of this conflict as worked out in given texts is what characterizes bodies of avant-garde work, and it prefigures the more deliberate postmodernist double-coding, as Jencks calls it, of classic and modernist values within the same text.[1]

Jonas Mekas presents himself through his films as an author, a diarist, celebrating the value of individual artists, their families, and their personal expression. Yet the figure of death undercuts the ideology of presence in *He Stands in a Desert* in a way that suggests how death, or loss, or absence has always figured directly in the formation of Mekas's strategies of film practice. From his earliest moments in this country, Mekas was recording what was lost to him as a displaced person after World War II and as an exile from Lithuania. *Lost, Lost, Lost* recovers this early period of his diary films, but it was only released after his signature style of rapidly composed single-frame sequences was established in *Walden* and *Reminiscences*. Although he always situates himself as a Romantic, his strategy of textual construction undercuts the ideological desire for presence that is claimed as a motivation for his work.

Derrida argues that part of what the ideology of presence represses is death. Writing, according to Derrida, is a structuring absence that cannot be accommodated within the illusionistic universality of full and present meaning.[2] Yet Mekas's work records how death and loss can function to generate a radical method of textual construction, despite the rhetoric of presence coexisting with this process. A deconstructive reading of *He Stands in a Desert* helps unravel this process, and recognizes how Mekas has generated a mode of cinematic writing that foregrounds writing as such, even while Romantic figuration throughout his critical and artistic work appears to deny the premises of writing in absence and death. An intertextual comparison with a more conventional type of film may

---

[1] Jencks 1986, 14. For a further discussion of the paradoxes of modernism, see Nygren 1989.

[2] Jacques Derrida discusses the imaginary identification of death, absence, and writing throughout his work; for instance, see his discussion of writing and violence in Derrida 1976.

help clarify what is at stake in Mekas's project. A similar reading could be attempted for Max Ophuls's *Letter from an Unknown Woman*, a film that also situates the Romantic figures of erotic opposition and death against the constructions of writing. Yet Ophuls represents these issues within the normative conventions of classical style, which recapitulates the ideology of presence through the effects of narrative transparency. It is precisely the ideological effects reproduced by classical norms that Mekas's signature style undercuts, to extend the foregrounding of writing to the cinematic apparatus itself.

A partial sequence of Mekas's development may be observed in the figures of the DP community in *Lost, Lost, Lost*, the recurrent New York snowstorms throughout Mekas's films, the positioning of the political, and his single-frame technique. The DP community is one of the first images recorded by Mekas on his arrival in the United States, yet it already prefigures his filmic return to his homeland in *Reminiscences*. The absence of Lithuania becomes a dominant motif throughout his work, not only directly as subject but indirectly as unconscious compositional strategy. Mekas has remarked that only after he had filmed so many snowstorms in New York, and recognized how his film image of the city created the appearance of much more snow than actually falls, did he realize that he had been recording those images as a memory of Lithuania. That determining absence, functioning through unconscious memory, then moves to the foreground as a direct subject of filmic address in *Reminiscences*, and is recalled throughout *He Stands in a Desert* by images of farms, snow, and Lithuanian bread. The last image of *He Stands in a Desert* is of Hollis Melton and Oona in the snow, and snow in Central Park is intercut early in the first reel with the intertitle "This is not a documentary film" and a close-up of Mekas's face. In other words, apparently improvisatory and documentary images of everyday life, parallel to the Lumières' *actualités*, are filled with significance through memory, through what is absent from the screen. Signification is not grounded in an indexical contact with the profilmic, but derives from the construction of the subject in the unconscious.

Midway through *He Stands in a Desert*, a key sequence on Jackie and Caroline Kennedy explains itself as fragments of an unfinished biography. A lock of hair, a poem's text that includes the word "nostalgia," a sound-track song about the decline of summer in "September . . . November," and photos of Jackie as a child are intercut as equivalences. In this array of fetishized indexical signs and verbal lament, an intertitle appears: "You keep a diary and the diary will keep you." Loss and fetishism are linked with representation and the subject in a way that summarizes other developments in the film, especially through the linking of memory with an evocation of the political domain.

Finally, Mekas's filmic strategy of rapid bursts of single-frame compositions, rhythmically interactive with the material within the frame, accomplishes the opposite of what it seems intended to do. In the name of bringing the filmmaker and the viewer closer to the spontaneous presence of immediate events, the single-frame technique instead incorporates visible absence in the form of the space between the frames into the recording process. At the moment of a closer approach to lived experience, the film visibly elides into a mode of writing, of structuring absence, that foregrounds precisely the "differance" that lies at the basis of all representation, and that a theory of writing emphasizes.

The doubleness of presence and absence, indirectly hinted at throughout Mekas's films, becomes the direct subject of address in *He Stands in a Desert*. Early in the film, Hollis Frampton is introduced through a story Frampton tells about being confused with Hollis Melton, Mekas's wife. This fable of signification and sexual difference turns on Frampton's protest, "I never broke up with Jonas!" Yet Frampton does break up with Mekas through death, while Hollis Melton as the mother of Oona is linked with the images of childhood and life that end the film. The double figure of life and death is linked through the single name Hollis, which circulates throughout the film, generating complex patterns of infancy and age, health and illness, birth- and death-day ceremonies. *Paradise Not Yet Lost*, Mekas's happiest film, recounts the figure of birth, renewal, and life that is recalled in *He Stands in a Desert*'s images of children, just as *Reminiscences* is recalled through the images of Lithuania. But only in *He Stands in a Desert* is the figure of death directly confronted as a basis of all representation, irretrievable loss linked with the ambiguous pleasure of the text, as Mekas comments in an intertitle about the images: "More real than the reality, gone by now."

The formation of the subject in Western discourse can be traced not only through the diary form but through biography and autobiography. In Mekas's films, the words "diary" and "biography" circulate through intertitles to assert a humanist interiority both for the filmmaker as author and for the others he records. In his work on the limits of biography, Tim Murray quotes Montaigne's "to philosophize is to learn how to die," and argues that the Western cogito has always been founded on death. Citing the baroque fascination with death and the intertwining of melancholia with philosophy, Murray (1989) suggests that death figured in the formation of the cogito as an imaginary erasure of social constraints. "He who knows how to die," as Murray quotes Montaigne, "knows freedom from constraint and subjection." Felicity Nussbaum (1989) further argues that the formation of the autobiographical subject in English literature is dependent on a series of divisions of gender, social class, and colonialist racism. Death and gender, in this formulation from literary history, function as other to position the cogito as male presence. For Lacanian analysis, death and gender coincide in the figure of castration at the site of the other, which in turn positions the subject of Western discourse. At its limits, Mekas's text encounters these formations of the cogito.

The linkage of the figures of life and death through the name Hollis is paralleled by the repositioning of the phrase "paradise not yet lost" as voice-over with the text "second angel sounded" from the apocalypse early in the second reel. The trace of the speaking voice and its desire for the imaginary presence of innocence and life through representation is juxtaposed to a text signifying an epistemological erasure, the end of a world or discursive system. One can also trace through *He Stands in a Desert* a linking of death with sexual reversal. Hollis Frampton's voice-over narrative about being confused with Hollis Melton through an identity of names is paralleled by the sexual cross-dressing at George Maciunas's wedding, which appears in the film just before the signifier of his death in the image of the Fresh Pond Crematorium. George's wedding ceremony in 1978 is celebrated by the bride and groom each stripping and dressing in the other's clothes, a visual exchange of costume that extends the confusion of naming in Hollis's story. Earlier in the film, following the sequence of Jerome Hill before his death intertitled "Last walk with Jerome," Mekas appears at a party pretending to cut off his nose, and then his finger. The figure of death in *He Stands in a Desert* is thereby elaborately linked with castration and the collapse of sexual difference. Cinematic writing or "differance" in Mekas's text is grounded in sexual "differance," or the collapse of individualist subjectivity into a play of gender signification, despite its apparent recuperation at the end of the film in the idealized image of Hollis Melton and Oona in the snow.

The dramatic end of *He Stands in a Desert* comes slightly earlier, as the long sequence of Hollis Frampton's funeral on 2 April 1984, in Buffalo, New York, is followed (after three intervening sequences) by the fireworks on 24 May 1983 that celebrate the one-hundredth birthday of the Brooklyn Bridge. Although the fireworks are then superimposed on the image of one of the many babies in the film, the baby is also linked back in time to the Brooklyn Bridge as an intertextual signifier of Frampton. Frampton had admired the Brooklyn Bridge, and recalled its depiction in paintings by Stella by incorporating it in such films of his own as *Surface Tension* (1968) and *Ordinary Matter* (1972). The elision of death by this intertextual figure again foregrounds the trace, or modes of writing, as a primary project of this film. Writing is situated between death and rebirth, between gender roles, and in the material encounter of camera and visual experience as the figure of cinema.

At the same time, Mekas situates *He Stands in a Desert* in a social context. Early in the film, he claims, in intertitles, that "this is not a documentary film. . . . This is a political film." At first this interjection may seem marginal or frivolous, but woven into the film it becomes a hinge between personal and public modes of address. In one sense, issues of social context seem unconnected to the figure of death that dominates intimate relationships within the film, and there is no need for such a connection to justify the autonomous operation of this discourse; parallel or conflicting discourses can be productive in a single text without being contained within a metanarrative unity. Yet in another sense, these two discourses not only connect but coincide. In the domain of desire, death raises the question of legacy or the transmission of art and community across generations, and leads to problems of institutionalization, of the regulation of authority, and of the reinscription of a social text. The figure of death here works to position institutional development as a mode of writing or of embedding social relations in history.

The "political film" intertitle appears twice, once linked with an image of a girl holding a large, round loaf of Lithuanian bread, and then with a bottle of wine that Mekas drinks in the vineyard in which it was produced. This ambiguous figure resonates throughout the film, linking Christian imagery with sexual difference and the specificity of place. The bread and wine of the Christian Eucharist that Mekas associates with politics is paralleled by numerous tropes drawn from Christian rhetoric. The Madonna and child, death and resurrection, and the biblical narratives of paradise and the apocalypse all generate figures in the film. Yet the fixed and idealized rhetoric of Christian archetypes is undercut by sexual and generational "differance," and by the embedding in memory that the specificity of place suggests. The *terroir*, or specific terrain in which grapes grow that contributes to the character of a wine, is associated with Lithuania as a memory of childhood and as an idealized female object. The politics of memory and nostalgia come to the surface, but are undercut by the visibility of territorialization as a process that functions both to embed and to resist the dominant discursive formations of Western culture.

In *Guns of the Trees* (1961), Mekas's art film feature that preceded his work on *Diaries*, protesters in Washington Square are seen carrying a sign that reads "Both Sides Are Wrong," a sign David James glosses as summarizing the film's "beat anti-politics" (James 1989, 105). In retrospect, this moment is open to rereading as a resistance to the binary polarization of "both sides." Rather than proposing an imaginary "anti-politics," the protest image seeks to introduce a radical break into the dominant dialectical model of social formations. In this impulse, Mekas was partially successful. Mekas's own commitments to alternative institutions are well known through his work on *Film Culture*, the New York Film-Makers Cooperative, Anthology Film Archives, and other activities without which the avant-garde film of the 1960s could not have existed or survived as we know it.

Yet later in *He Stands in a Desert*, we see images of Mohonk, where representatives of media arts centers held a preliminary meeting in 1973 that later led to the founding of the National Alliance of Media Arts Centers (NAMAC). These are preceded by a "last walk with Jerome," a complex temporal sequence of Jerome Hill, the filmmaker and financial angel who supported the early years of Anthology Film Archives. Implicit in these sequences are the politics of the media arts center movement and Mekas's controversial place within it. Coming from Eastern Europe, Mekas was highly suspicious of any dependence by artists on government support, which he saw as inevitably linked with restrictions on artistic practice. Other Mohonk participants, in contrast, saw artistic autonomy as protected by the panel process designed by the New York State Council on the Arts and later adopted by the National Endowment for the Arts (NEA), and considered public funding critically important support for alternative media institutions. They in turn were critical of the private-angel dependence that Mekas seemed to imply was preferable to public funding, as another alternative to corporate domination. This argument illuminates some of the unresolved contradictions inherent in current economic models for the support of innovative media arts. It also raises the question of how to apply methods of textual construction to questions of institutional practice.

The image of Mohonk in *He Stands in a Desert* is not alone in positioning arts funding as a central issue in contemporary politics. Woody Vasulka's videotape *The Commission* (1985) also addresses arts funding through its operatic narrative of Paganini as go-between for a newspaper editor's commission of a piece by Berlioz. The recent controversy over restrictions on NEA funding also clarifies what is at stake here: the Helms amendment to bar funding of supposedly offensive artworks has been eloquently criticized as an attempt to suppress the gay community's representation of the AIDS crisis. As with the Reagan administration's efforts to cut or eliminate funds for public broadcasting, the attempt to reduce sources of funding for the arts has the effect of enforcing the dominant ideology. In short, arts funding has become a figure of political power in an information economy.

Once Foucault had theorized the relationship of knowledge and power,[3] no question of funding for the arts, education, or communication could again be seen as isolated from central issues of authority and legitimation in a postindustrial society. These are problems that have preoccupied Lyotard's texts since *The Postmodern Condition* and *Just Gaming*.[4] The issue is neither the violation of idealist norms specific to certain segments of the population nor forced consumer support for products that a universalized concept of the public is assumed not to want. These shortsighted and imaginary problems are no more relevant here than they are for scientific and technological research, an arena in which this kind of struggle has a parallel history. The problem is rather how to develop consensus support for long-term investment in the innovation and diversity necessary for significant and legitimate cultural production, the problem prefigured by Mohonk and NAMAC.[5]

Mohonk as a figure of postmodernist political power in *He Stands in a Desert* is opposed by the politics of nostalgia that surround Mekas's images of Lithuania. *He Stands in a Desert* was released at the historical moment when Gorbachev first came to power, and long preceded Lithuania's declarations of independence. Yet Mekas's films already anticipate the contradictions between ethnic conflict and Soviet domination that are now following the decline of Stalinist dogma. The disintegration of totalitarian Communist regimes into ethnic violence between Hungary and Romania, between Armenia and Azerbaijan, and elsewhere reminds us that dictatorial power often justifies its suppression of human rights through its simultaneous suppression of an otherwise interminable

[3] See, for example, Foucault 1978.

[4] Lyotard 1984; Lyotard and Thébaud 1985.

[5] See Green 1980. Green has published partial summaries of this report as "Film and Not-for-Profit Media Institutions" (Green 1982) and "Film and Video: An Institutional Paradigm and Some Issues of National Policy" (Green 1984).

violence (see Keller 1990). In the United States, democratic institutions are more likely to cut across ethnic groups to decenter or partly limit the dominance of any single group. But the institutions of multicultural democracy that provide an alternative to Stalinist forced uniformity can easily remain unrealized in the rush toward ethnic nationalism. Current conflicts in Eastern Europe risk achieving local democratization through cultural isolationism, a partial achievement that can still make it impossible to participate effectively in an international economy.

In his diary films, Mekas was able to constitute a sense of self only in the context of the other, in a double-language situation of constant displacement and dislocation. Similarly, he constructed an image of community on the basis of exile. Alternative institutions for support of the avant-garde were founded by Mekas on the metaphor of death or irretrievable loss of Lithuania as a national home; avant-garde artists were another class of DPs, permanently in exile from American media hegemony. In light of the ethnic violence that has followed as one response to the democracy and independence movements in Eastern Europe, this equation of exile with nostalgia with artist could now be seen as problematic. The territorialized images of Lithuania in terms of Christianity and a maternal terrain in *He Stands in a Desert* suggest one form of absolutism in contrast to another, a regressive nostalgia in opposition to state control. It is this unresolvable conflict that Mekas seems to translate into an American context through his films and his institutional interventions. In these terms, angelic financing of the arts creates its own violence, which in isolation substitutes the arbitrary caprice of individualized wealth for the potentially arbitrary control of government support.

Yet the metaphor of exile was never simple or innocent. Exile introduced a radical break in social organization, not predictable from an interpretation of its origin as purely reactionary. As with Romantic figuration, which against Hollywood hegemony functioned to radicalize the text, the regressively nostalgic and idealized homeland became the figural means to reinscribe and partially radicalize the social institutions that surround the arts. Lithuania never served Mekas so well as when it was irretrievably lost. It remains to be seen if any independence, imaginary or real, can equally dislocate the institutional production of meaning, or whether national recognition will lead to an imaginary quest for idealist presence.

The problem here is one of shifting margins and mutual deconstruction. Ethnic specificity and private financing are productive as long as they remain at the margins and work against a dominant ideology of nationalist humanism; if they assume center stage, they can exert a tyranny of their own equal to that which they previously opposed. At present, arts financing in the United States is possible through either private or public means, and, although frequently minimal in its support of innovative or risky ventures, this mixed economic base has at times allowed one mode of support to offset the worst potential abuses of the other. Further, the ideological assumptions in each mode of financing invite deconstruction through positioning in relation to the other, and the more interesting question arises of how to reinscribe relationships between concepts of "private" and "public" to generate new, more productive modes of institutional organization.

Although these issues are not worked through in *He Stands in a Desert*, they nonetheless figure in the text. Because of Mekas's long-standing and pivotal role in the institutionalization of the avant-garde in the United States, and because of his controversial role in relation to NAMAC, images that evoke the politics of information surface in his film more directly than in most texts, avant-garde or not. As such, they are available to be read by those concerned with the postmodernist distribution of power in an international and multicultural information economy. Questions of private and public support of the arts are not unrelated to the figuration of the author within the text and to questions of who controls meaning. Reading out from the text demands that we consider how to restructure the institutions that support the production of meaning, consonant with what we now know about the decentering and multiplicity necessary for diversity and innovation within cultural production.

Mekas's films, especially *He Stands in a Desert*, ask their readers to consider the politics of information, and not only in the formalist terms that Noël Burch and others argue implicitly question the positioning of power within the text.[6] They also directly address institutional questions crucial to this moment in private and public history, and ask us to cross-read between personal and social formations of texts. If through death we confront the absence at the basis of representation, we are also in a position to relinquish ideological assumptions about the subject in a social context, and to consider how to reinscribe the relationships among institutions that support and produce meaning. If Mekas's text resists as well as proposes these questions, such contradictions in representation

---

[6] Regarding the relationship of formal analysis to politics and some of its critiques, see Burch 1979; Polan 1984; and Nichols 1989.

may in part be unavoidable traces of the text's position at a significant historical juncture.

Bibliography

Brook, Peter. 1976. *The Melodramatic Imagination: Balzac, Henry James, Melodrama, and the Mode of Excess.* New Haven: Yale University Press.

Burch, Noël. 1979. *To the Distant Observer.* Berkeley and Los Angeles: University of California Press.

Derrida, Jacques. 1976. "Writing and Man's Exploitation of Man." In *Of Grammatology,* trans. Gayatri Chakravorty Spivak, 118–40. Baltimore: Johns Hopkins University Press.

Foucault, Michel. 1978. *Discipline and Punish: The Birth of the Prison.* Trans. Alan Sheridan. New York: Vintage. Originally published as *Surveiller et punir: Naissance de la prison.* Paris: Éditions Gallimard, 1975.

Green, J. Ronald. 1980. *Media Arts Centers: A Report to the National Endowment for the Arts Media Arts Program.* Washington, D.C.: National Endowment for the Arts.

———. 1982. "Film and Not-for-Profit Media Institutions." In *Film/Culture: Explorations of Cinema in Its Social Context,* ed. Sari Thomas, 37–59. Metuchen, N.J.: Scarecrow.

———. 1984. "Film and Video: An Institutional Paradigm and Some Issues of National Policy." *Journal of Cultural Economics* 8, no. 1 (June): 61–79.

James, David. 1989. *Allegories of Cinema: American Film in the Sixties.* Princeton: Princeton University Press.

Jameson, Fredric. 1984. "Postmodernism; or, The Cultural Logic of Late Capitalism." *New Left Review* 146 (July–August): 53–92.

Jencks, Charles. 1986. *What Is Post-Modernism?* New York: Academy Editions.

Keller, Bill. 1990. "Russian Nationalists: Yearning for an Iron Hand." *New York Times Magazine,* 28 January, 18–50.

Lyotard, Jean-François. 1984. *The Postmodern Condition: A Report on Knowledge.* Trans. Geoff Bennington and Brian Massumi. Minneapolis: University of Minnesota Press. Originally published as *La Condition postmoderne: Rapport sur le savoir.* Paris: Les éditions de minuit, 1979.

Lyotard, Jean-François, and Jean-Loup Thébaud. 1985. *Just Gaming.* Trans. Wlad Godzich. Minneapolis: University of Minnesota Press. Originally published as *Au Juste.* Paris: Christian Bourgois, 1979.

Murray, Tim. 1989. "Translating Montaigne's Crypts: Melancholy and the Limits of Biography." Paper given at "Autobiographies, Visual and Verbal" conference, 22–24 September, State University of New York at Binghamton.

Nichols, Bill. 1989. "Form Wars: The Political Unconscious of Formalist Theory." *South Atlantic Quarterly* 88, no. 2 (Spring): 487–515.

Nussbaum, Felicity. 1989. *The Autobiographical Subject: Gender and Ideology in Eighteenth-Century England*. Baltimore: Johns Hopkins University Press.

Nygren, Scott. 1989. "Reconsidering Modernism: Japanese Film and the Postmodern Context." *Wide Angle* 11, no. 3:6–15.

Polan, Dana. 1984. " 'Desire Shifts the Differance': Figural Poetics and Figural Politics in the Film Theory of Marie-Claire Ropars." *Camera Obscura* 12 (Summer): 67–88.

18. David Curtis A Tale of Two Co-ops

THIRTY YEARS on we are faced by this paradox: in America, Jonas Mekas, architect of the Film-Makers' Cooperative and possessor of a vision of a different way of producing, distributing, and exhibiting film, is now immersed in the struggle to sustain Anthology Film Archives, a museum for an avant-garde elite. And while London's spectacular new Museum of the Moving Image (MOMI) has honored the Co-op idea by building a replica workshop–distribution center among its exhibits (or, more accurately, a nonfunctional, affectionate, three-dimensional caricature), the original, from which the museum borrowed much of its substance, is facing a fourth, possibly fatal rehousing crisis. It is perhaps inevitable that any cultural movement of worth will end up dry and dusty, on a museum shelf, but putting it there is surely not the business of artists, and would be a dubious reward for thirty years of struggle. Stan Brakhage's response to the dead weight of museum culture in Europe, summed up for him in the image of the Père Lachaise cemetery, is that of any healthy artist: "The grave-yard could stand for all my view of Europe, for all the concerns with past art" (*Film-Makers' Cooperative Catalogue* 1989, 41). So what has happened to Jonas's vision?

I should quickly admit that I am an admirer of Anthology, and I also had a hand in the creation of the MOMI exhibit, so I am fully implicated in the dimensions of this paradox. But the seriousness of the London Co-op's crisis suggests that this is a good moment to take a look at the institutions the avant-garde has invented for itself, to reflect on Jonas's role as inspirer and begetter, to consider the implications of the different paths chosen by the New York "original" and its London offspring, and finally, to suggest new priorities for the future.

Distribution of avant-garde film took place long before Jonas entered the scene. To introduce a sense of perspective, it is worth remembering that there was a "Co-op of Film Authors" in Warsaw in the 1930s, organized by Stefan and Francisca Themerson and their Polish avant-garde colleagues. But Jonas's co-op was unlike any that preceded it in its unique undertaking to distribute all works submitted to it, and not to engage in individual promotion. The 1989 catalogue is remarkably matter-of-fact about this: "Film-Makers

Cooperative is a film-rental library open to any film-maker wishing to place a print on deposit for a rental fee set by its owner. Films are accepted without any viewing or evaluation by the Cooperative" (*Film-Makers Cooperative Catalogue* 1989, 1). This is neither an invitation, nor a caution. The benefits of doing things this way are assumed to be self-evident.

But Jonas's own diary reminds us that this founding principle was achieved only after a bitter argument:

> 7 January 1961. We had a meeting of the [New American Cinema] Group at 414 Park Avenue South. Voted to establish our own cooperative distribution center. The only opposition came from Amos [Vogel]. He said, why do we need a new distribution center: Cinema 16 will distribute our films. I pointed out that recently he had rejected several important films, one being Brakhage's *Anticipation of the Night*. Amos said, it's up to him to decide what films can be distributed. He insisted that there is no place for two distribution centers, for the independent film. At which point some became pretty angry. Ron Rice was shouting at Amos, and Amos was shouting at us all. In any case, we now have a center of our own. No film will be rejected from it—that was the first point we all agreed upon. And we are going to run it ourselves. (Mekas 1982, 9)

As director of Cinema 16 and the New York Film Festival, Amos Vogel had achieved some success in selling the American avant-garde to European distributors and festivals, and represented the pragmatic "promote what you believe in" approach. In his riposte to the Co-op in his *Evergreen Review* article, "Thirteen Confusions," written when Jonas was also programming the Film-Makers' Cinematheque as a showcase for new work, Vogel accused the avant-garde of "Confusing Non-Selectivity with Art": "The NAC's proudly proclaimed policy of showing, distributing, and praising every scrap of film is self-defeating" (Vogel 1967, 131). Audiences denied the benefit of qualitative preselection, he suggested, will "stay away or stop renting films."

Even Brakhage, whose rejection by Vogel was one of the prompts to the founding of the Co-op, saw a problem in its nonselectivity. Protesting the presentation of the sixth Film Culture Award to Andy Warhol in 1964 and the Co-op's apparent surrender to hippiedom, he withdrew his films, writing to Jonas: "Your idea that Film-Makers' Cooperative/Cinematheque escapes 'Censorship' by 'accepting everything' is false: for finally I must 'censor myself'" (Brakhage 1982, 129).

But Jonas's principle of nonselection struck a chord elsewhere. London was visited in the mid-sixties by a stream of American film-

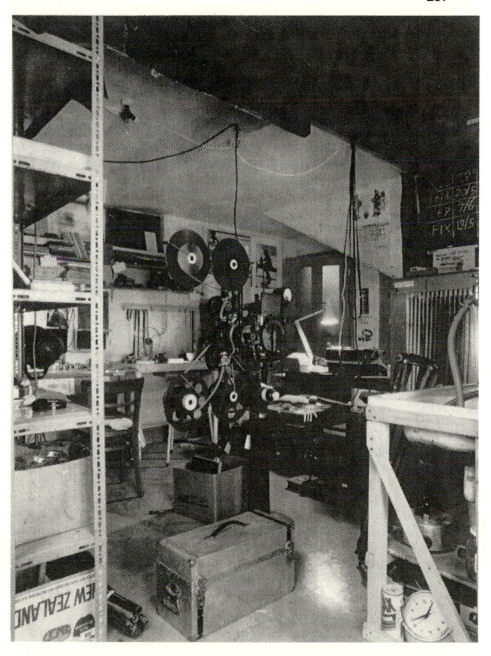

18.1 The Co-op exhibit at London's Museum of the Moving Image. Conceived by David Watson, David Curtis, and Charles Garrad; designed and installed by Charles Garrad.

makers, many of whom found their way to the screenings at the Better Books store at 94 Charing Cross Road, the London Co-op's birthplace. The store manager, Bob Cobbing, was a sound poet and film enthusiast, and he organized poetry readings, screenings, happenings, and even exhibitions between the book stacks and in the store's tiny basement. The program during the summer and fall of 1966 included screenings by Bill Vehr, Warren Sonbert, Andy Meyer, Peter Emmanuel Goldman, and the now London-based Steve Dwoskin. Their inevitable statement "My films are distributed by the Film-Makers Co-op" astonished us. We knew a few filmmakers (Peter Whitehead, Don Levy) who had one or two films placed with one distributor or another, but nobody whose work was distributed in its entirety, as we discovered Dwoskin's was, and no distributor prepared to accept what was unquestionably "difficult" work.

After one of the screenings, the decision was taken to set up a co-op. Through 1966 and 1967, the American films we saw included early works by Brakhage, Maya Deren, Ed Emshwiller, Kenneth Anger, and Marie Menken (which were already in commercial distribution in Britain); films from the West Coast brought over by Bob Pike, some of which the Co-op bought; and works by later visitors: Mike Snow, Gregory Markopoulos, Tom Chomont, and Stan Vanderbeek. What was striking to us—an audience of artists, writers, journalists, and filmmakers—was the assumption evident in all these films that making cinema could be a first-person-singular affair, and that film language could be complex and highly individual. By contrast, the films supported by the one source of public funding at the time, the British Film Institute's Experimental Film Fund, were very definitely cinema shorts, stepping-stones to cinema features. Symptomatically, recipients of BFI funding in the mid-sixties included the young Ridley Scott, Ken Russell, and Stephen Frears. The issue of censorship, and the desire to maintain control over every stage of the filmmaking process—not to allow others to determine what was acceptable—was important in the European context too, and strongly motivated the first generation of London Co-op filmmakers. Somewhat to Dwoskin and Cobbing's consternation, the London Co-op group included filmmakers more intent on making anti-Vietnam protest films and newsreels than art. Echoes of Jonas's *Flaming Creatures* trials resonated across the water. And English filmmakers were faced with prohibitive lab costs.

In a bid to establish self-sufficiency and autonomy, Malcolm LeGrice and his students from St. Martin's School of Art began in 1967 to build the Co-op's first film developing and printing machinery, and only later thought to acquire film editing equipment. With this act, initially more symbolic than practical (the Rube Goldbergian wooden film-developer leaked light and threatened to dissolve in its own chemical baths), the importance of the London Co-op to filmmakers was established, and the existence of film-printing equipment at the Co-op was to become fundamental to the emergence of the first distinctive English movement, the so-called structural materialism of the late 1960s and 1970s.

Twenty-five years later, the maintenance of this full range of equipment remains an important expression of the London Co-op's commitment to making filmmaking more accessible; filmmakers to whom the concept of "foregrounding the signifier by reprinting the image" has not the slightest interest still make their way to the Co-op workshop because it represents the possibility of making films even without a grant.

The egalitarian principle also presented the London Co-op with a number of problems. Initially, the Co-op interpreted its constitution as demanding that work should be shared equally by all members. It lived with the reality that some were more willing or skilled than others. An early crisis occurred, not in the work-intensive workshop, but in distribution, when Jonas offered the set of New American Cinema prints with which P. Adams Sitney had been touring in Europe, but on the understanding that Carla Liss, who had worked at the New York Cinematheque, was given responsibility for looking after them as a paid employee. Pragmatism triumphed over principle on that occasion, but years later, when deciding that paid employment should be the norm for key workers, the Co-op agreed that all appointments should be made subject to an interview and vote conducted by a meeting of the full membership, and that no post should be held for more than three years.

This eccentric interpretation of the egalitarian principle has in fact worked positively to ensure that the Co-op workshop is staffed by the peers of those who need it most, namely young filmmakers yet to establish themselves or filmmakers who have chosen to resist the compromise of teaching or working on the margins of the industry. By the time any worker has begun to set his or her mark too distinctly on the organization, the constitution obliges that worker to move on.

As a consequence, the Co-op sometimes appears to have a very limited collective memory; few workers have much sense of the struggles of their predecessors. "Wisdom" remains the responsibility of the membership. But this unique formula has meant that over the years, the Co-op has provided a sympathetic base for successive waves of filmmakers from most of the important British avant-garde movements: the structural materialists of the 1960s, the feminist filmmakers of the 1970s (though painfully; some split off to found the women-only group Circles), and (more distantly) gay filmmakers, the neo-Romantics associated with Derek Jarman, and the black filmmakers of the 1980s.

Moreover, as a filmmaker-led organization, the London Co-op was involved from the start in the shaping of the larger British independent sector. Filmmakers from the Co-op were among those who set up the Independent Film Makers Association (IFA) in 1974, a lobbying and information-gathering organization that included academics from the polytechnics and universities and filmmakers from the political wing, based in groups such as Amber Films in Newcastle and the Berwick Street Collective in London.

During the 1970s and 1980s, the IFA carried forward a number of important debates and negotiations, arguing with the British Film Institute for provision of workshops in the regions, and with the ACTT (the main film union) for recognition of the special needs and conditions of the sector, which led to the adoption by many funding organizations of a code of practice ensuring union recognition of an agreed minimum level of wages for publicly funded productions. The IFA also called for new sources of funding for the independent sector. There was hope in the mid-seventies, under the Labour government of the time, that a state-funded network of regional production resources might be set up as part of the government's proposed British Films Authority. A change of government meant that the British Films Authority never came into being, but many of these ideas were adapted for local implementation by the more radical of the surviving Labour-controlled local authorities, particularly the short-lived Greater London Council, which supported women's groups, and the new black film workshops emerging from the avant-garde, such as Sankofa and the Black Audio Film Collective. When, under the new Thatcher government, a fourth TV channel was proposed, the IFA successfully lobbied for a commitment from Channel 4 (as it became) to support programming of independent films of cultural and social value and small production groups across the country. The channel agreed to appoint a commissioning editor "sympathetic to work being done by independent filmmakers, and to provide funds for regional workshops."

Even more significant was the ACTT's "workshop declaration," which provided a framework for groups to bid to Channel 4 for funds to run workshop-style production centers, based on the much-debated model of an "integrated practice"; that is, operating within a philosophy that saw production, training, distribution, and exhibition as one indivisible process. The model of the Co-op was probably far from the ACTT's mind when it negotiated this agreement—the Co-op itself had no formal relationship with the union—but the adoption of this way of work by the Co-op, and the first wave of political workshops, Amber, the Berwick Street Collective, and Cinema Action, was evidence of its viability.

The egalitarian principle served the London Co-op's distribution and exhibition arms less well. In the market-led 1980s, an organization unable to sell was at a great disadvantage, as Vogel no doubt anticipated. But the important international collection held in distribution provided a steady income to a few; more importantly, it formed the basis for a tradition of strong programming at the Co-op's cinema, starting with Peter Gidal's term of office in the early 1970s and carrying on in an almost unbroken succession ever since. Somehow the egalitarian principle produced the right people at the right time, though an informal "apprenticeship" system may have had a hand in it. But the Co-op's various homes have always been geographically remote from London's West End, and its cinema therefore inevitably a place of pilgrimage. The issue of how to enlarge the public for avant-garde work has never been seriously addressed by the Co-op itself. It has been left to the public funding bodies, in this case the Arts Council and the BFI, to devise ways of promoting the art form and enabling artists to promote themselves. The Arts Council set up its Film and Video Artists on Tour plan in 1976 to encourage artists to introduce screenings of their own work personally, offering automatic subsidies to such shows, and supported the curating and touring of avant-garde programs by funding the Film and Video Umbrella, an agency dedicated to this purpose (rather as the American Federation of Arts stepped in to provide touring in the United States and abroad, occupying the vacuum left by the New York Co-op).

The message from Jonas that the London Co-op received via those visiting filmmakers in the early sixties—reinforced firsthand by the presence of expatriates such as Carla Liss, Steve Dwoskin, and Peter Gidal—it chose to apply not just to distribution, but to every branch of the organization, and even to the organization's management. The strength of this systematic application has been the organization's ability to keep in touch with the needs and ambitions of successive generations of filmmakers, and to be their voice to funding bodies and the world at large. To the funding bodies, the Co-op has proved an accurate barometer of the state of the avant-garde. The weakness of the system, which was the weakness of the New York original, was its inability to help individual filmmakers achieve the recognition they deserved, and to promote the art form.

When Jonas and the New American Cinema Group issued their "First Statement" in *Film Culture* in 1961, their vision of a new deal for filmmakers embraced every aspect of the film business, from script to screen. Making the case for a cinema of "personal expression," free from censorship and the "influence of producers, distributors and investors," they called for the setting-up of a cooperative distribution center, an investment arrangement with theatrical exhibitors (on Broadway lines), a pledge from successful members to invest a percentage of any profits in a hardship fund, and the negotiation of a new agreement with the film unions that would recognize low-budget work.

At the time, the NAC group was effectively a loosely defined trade association of low-budget feature filmmakers, whose membership was based on personal association, to be extended, presumably, by invitation, though the distribution arm was, following that fateful meeting, to be open to all. This built-in contradiction was dramatized by an early crisis. "Within a year," wrote P. Adams Sitney, "it was apparent that the Film-Makers' Cooperative could not bring in sufficient funds to keep a director working on a $25,000 budget; yet it could sustain the avant-gardists" (Sitney 1970, 71–72). (Even this sounds like an overestimation; it might have been wiser to claim "some income to some avant-gardists.")

The commercial success of Andy Warhol's *Chelsea Girls* in 1966 suggested for a moment that the Co-op could make real money for the few, but one swallow does not make a summer, as Vogel (1967) sourly noted, and Warhol followed many of the original signatories of the NAC statement in withdrawing his films from the Co-op shortly thereafter. In response to these moves, the Film-Makers' Distribution Center was set up in 1966 as a "theatrical" arm of the Co-op, with a limited range of promotional services, but still operating as an essentially responsive rather than aggressively promotional organization, with a predictable lack of impact. Jonas himself commented on its failure in an interview with English filmmaker and journalist John Ducane. "We discovered very soon that (to open up the market) we had to adopt all the practices of the commercial system—you immediately become involved in competition; it can't be done" (Ducane 1971, 49).

Jonas himself surprised the newly founded co-ops in Europe at this time by choosing to place his own films with the commercial capitalist system—initially Vaughan Films, run by a partner of NAC founding member Lionel Rogosin, and later CineGate, run by Jonas's old New York friends David and Barbara Stone, no doubt for the good commercial reason that they offered promotion to theatrical outlets and sales to TV, rather than a trickle of nontheatrical rentals.

When it looked as if Michael Snow was about to follow suit, Gidal began a frantic letter-writing campaign. "We had endless battles, and Michael Snow, who is not that political, finally understood it and said he'd made a big mistake letting [Annette] Michelson convince him to allow the Stones to have his work, because he realized it was divisive" (Rosenbaum 1983, 222). Only when the avant-garde had achieved the power that solidarity within its own structures would bring, Gidal argued, would it be possible to "make gains by making links." Gidal's example of the fruits of this policy was the successful series of avant-garde festivals held at the National Film Theater in 1970, 1973, and 1979. "These amazing experimental film festivals every five years where for ten days, day and night, you saw films by unknown, new, young, old filmmakers from 16 countries. The NFT could only allow itself to do that because the structure of experimental film had its own power, its own group of people, its own interest groups and funding" (ibid.).

The failure of the NAC group to make progress on the objectives set out in the First Statement seems to have carried through to the New York Co-op itself, although as Sitney points out, the interests of the founding group were those of feature filmmakers, not the no-budget avant-gardists now predominant in the catalogue. Why did this new constituency not try again? To be fair, there were signs of an attempt during the late sixties. The *Film-Makers' Newsletter* and its short-lived offshoot the *New Cinema Review* were attempts by filmmakers associated with the Co-op and the Cinematheque to represent the interests of a wider group, and to address the issues of funding, equipment availability, and exhibition. But by the end of the decade the focus of production for the avant-garde in New York had moved to the workshops of Millennium and the Collective for Living Cinema, and what was originally Jonas's vision of a single filmmaker-led organization, working to secure the avant-garde's interests over a wide area, was lost. Was the continuing link with the old NAC group the problem? (To this day, the Co-op is owned by NAC Group, Inc.)

Leaving the Co-op—now synonymous with distribution—to Leslie Trumbull, in whose dedicated hands it has remained for twenty-five years, Jonas himself concentrated initially on exhibition and the Cinematheque. The egalitarian spirit was still very much alive in him, and it transformed what was initially the simple requirement to promote the Cinematheque's new filmmakers' screenings into the major work, which was the "Movie Journal." In this, his weekly *Village Voice* column, he identified whole areas of over-looked and neglected cinema, and in the process redefined the pa-rameters of the avant-garde more effectively than most of the "heavyweight" critics and theorists in the field.

But Jonas was also already beginning to plan Anthology, the proj-ect that established the American avant-garde as a major cultural phenomenon, to be recognized and respected around the world. This involved him in precisely what the Co-op's egalitarian consti-tution prohibited—the selective promotion of individual filmmak-ers, and the construction of a pantheon to contain them. The pages of *Film Culture*, and the NAC international traveling exhibitions that Jonas and P. Adams Sitney curated, carried the project forward.

When Anthology opened, filmmakers in Europe and on the West Coast looked on with fascination and horror. To design and build an ideal cinema was a wonderfully mad ambition, but to have five people choose one hundred "essential" programs to run in it in per-petuity was entirely mad. The exclusion of any contemporary Eu-ropean avant-garde films (with the exception of the work of Peter Kubelka, himself one of the selectors) compounded the folly by making it appear deliberately insulting. In the seventies and eight-ies, Europeans drew comparisons between their own concept of the avant-garde as an international movement—made manifest by tribal meetings at the London, Knokke, and Hyeres/Toulon festi-vals—and New York's apparent determination to be seen as an ex-clusive, avant-garde elite, geared to participate, but never returning the invitation. But putting aside the complaints, it has become clear that Anthology's achievement is real and substantial. As a strategy for demanding that the art establishment take the avant-garde seri-ously, it has worked. American work of the sixties and seventies is now studied (for better or worse) in colleges; the Anthology core collection (or at least parts of it) has found its way into art galleries around the world. And the archive of films, documentation, and ephemera is an immensely valuable resource.

But Anthology plus an impotent distribution agency does not a co-op make. For the generation that followed Snow, Hollis Framp-ton, and Paul Sharits, the struggle to gain resources and recognition was not assisted by the Co-op or Anthology, not even to the extent that the London Co-op was able to help the second generation of English filmmakers—Lis Rhodes, Guy Sherwin, Tina Keane, John Smith—and a third and possibly a fourth generation. If Millennium came to occupy what could have been the Co-op's place as a film production and promotional agency, it was always in the shadow of

Anthology, and without the benefit of Jonas's driving force. There remains a job to be done.

If the Co-ops are to wrest back the initiative from Anthology and museum culture, they must sooner or later grasp the nettle of promotion, and with it the dangerous but promising territories of exhibition and sales. In other words, they must invent a way of squaring the fundamental egalitarian principle with their obligation to help filmmakers realize their commercial potential. They must also work to improve access for scholars, curators, and collectors. One practical step they could take (Jonas was ever-practical) would be to produce preview copies of their films on video. It is noticeable how much happier the art establishment is with video art than with film. Not because it is inherently more interesting than film; simply because it is easier to exhibit, to preview, and therefore to be familiar with. It is also noticeable that most young filmmakers now offer preview copies on video; it is only the avant-garde's grand old men and women who do not—and, of course, the Co-ops. Perhaps in this less fearful new generation will come a second Jonas, one with the energy, vision, and persuasive powers to take the Co-ops by storm and give them back their power.

Bibliography

Brakhage, Stan. 1982. "To Jonas Mekas." In *Brakhage Scrapbook: Collected Writings, 1964–1980*, ed. Robert Haller. New Paltz, N.Y.: Documentext.

Ducane, John. 1971. "New Cinema." *Time Out* (London), 5–11 November, 49–50.

Film-Makers' Cooperative Catalogue. 1989. New York: Film-Makers' Cooperative.

Mekas, Jonas. 1982. "From the Diaries." In *The American New Wave, 1858–1967*. Buffalo: Walker Art Center.

Rosenbaum, Jonathan. 1983. "Organizing the Avant-Garde: A Conversation with Peter Gidal." In *Film: The Front Line, 1983*. Denver: Arden Press.

Sitney, P. Adams. 1970. "The New American Cinema." In *Film Culture Reader*. New York: Praeger.

Vogel, Amos. 1967. "Thirteen Confusions." In *The American Cinema: A Critical Anthology*, ed. Gregory Battcock, 124–37. New York: E. P. Dutton.

19. Stan Brakhage   Jonas Mekas

MIDST the various film categories, most of which imitate the categories of other arts, there's the possibility of film journals and/or diaries: Jonas Mekas has cornered this shelf of filmic imagination. He is the only one who has had the patience to track his life and environs with clacking camera (most of his "writ" with light has been captured in brief bursts of camera and single-frame shooting—clackety-clack) across thirty-some years. Is this then the Samuel Pepys of film? Yes, but then no also—for he is something much more: he has single-hand-and-mindedly invented this whole field of consideration as an aesthetic of film. A number of filmmakers (some before Jonas, including myself) have recorded the daily living situations of their being, but none has chronicled the details, come what may, day by day across years, as has Jonas.

Some of the earliest memories I have of this man are of him, thin to gaunt's edge, lugging his Bolex in an innocuous-seeming laundry sack (to deceive thieves) down the streets of New York. Quite often, out would come the camera, quick, to his eye, and in a flurry of fingers a quarter-second's worth of single frames would be rattled off. Then back into the bag with the bulky camera and its telephoto lens, the drawstrings closing over it, and on his way. . . . Often his shooting would be preceded by a broad smile and flashing-of-eyes, in those days. But there were hard times coming, as there had been for him before; and I was to see him also photographing grim. But the catch-as-catch-can of his life's light he did, and does, continue to do.

These bits and pieces mostly gathered in quick minutes (out of his busy life of saving American independent film) were to be woven carefully together, cut by careful cut, accompanied by the sounds he had recorded or the music he most cared to have accompany them, along with his voice (the voice of one of Lithuania's most famous poets caught loose with emotion often and, as often as not, fraught with hard-as-nails thought) commenting on what has been or is or is-to-be seen. As an aesthetic procedure for editing, from every pure-film consideration, Jonas's "tack" is maddening: but it works! It works in the long run, which is to say that his films give the sense of life as it is lived and consciously re-membered ar-

chaeologically—as an archaeologist would put together the preserved bits and pieces of brick to get the foundations of the site or
as an anthropologist would organize and label the shards of bone to
suggest a human-long-gone but utterly imaginable through a
"story" wrung from microscopic examination and visually conjur-
able by the fancying eye.

I think that not enough has been said about Marie Menken's influence on Jonas's technique; one does not think about techne in
the grand wash and brilliant reflecting ripples of Jonas Mekas's
compendium work. Such nit-picking would be about like questioning the mechanism of the Mississippi River. But I would like to note
that Marie inspired Jonas across the sixties with those few films of
hers preserved (for whose preservation he is largely responsible) and
altered his style of photography (from that of his earlier *Lost, Lost,
Lost*) by the very example of her hand-held camera articulation—a
style he has made very much his own, and one that has grown
across the times', and his, continuum.

20. Lauren Rabinovitz Wearing the Critic's Hat: History, Critical Discourses, and the American Avant-Garde Cinema

The lack of clarity about their situation that prevails among musicians, writers, and critics . . . has immense consequences that are far too little considered. For, thinking that they are in possession of an apparatus that in reality possesses them, they defend an apparatus over which they no longer have any control and that is no longer, as they still believe, a means for the producers, but has become a means against the producers.—Bertolt Brecht

So that though I had intended . . . to become a "serious" film critic . . . very soon I discovered that my critic's hat was of no great use. Instead, I had to take a sword and become a self-appointed minister of defense and propaganda of the New Cinema.
—Jonas Mekas, *Movie Journal*

BERTOLT BRECHT posits an avant-garde that is at once a system of social, economic, industrial, technological, and aesthetic practices. But Brecht also warns the artist that he or she must purposefully intervene in that system in order to exercise avant-garde goals and power. It is not enough for artists to be concerned with artistic production when an avant-garde apparatus goes on fulfilling its sociopolitical function with or without the products each artist individually invents. Within the American postwar cinema, Jonas Mekas acted on Brecht's "call to arms." As a filmmaker-producer, critic, distributor, and exhibitor, Mekas attempted to invent the apparatus for a "new cinema," thereby justifying cinema itself as radical avant-garde practice. But once said apparatus was in place, did Mekas's defense of it become a wedge by which other producers were excluded and a means by which he was controlled? Did the American avant-garde cinema of the 1960s become in the 1970s and 1980s a conservative measure against radical cinema practices and discourse?

It has been difficult to answer or even to address such questions in their historical specificity, let alone theorize the political functions of an avant-garde cinema, when the American avant-garde cinema still remains such a narrowly defined subject within cinema studies. It exists primarily as the fetishized, exotic object championed largely through the formalist critical discourse in which Mekas participated more than twenty years ago. If formalist aestheticism served Mekas and others within the political struggles of the avant-garde in the late 1960s, it has long since assumed a conservative function, as convincingly argued by Peter Lehman's 1985 review essay on a decade of books that search for a recapturable past of avant-garde achievements.[1]

With little regard for how critical approaches are themselves part of the subject for study, many contemporary film historians are still too swayed by the discursive work of Mekas's cinematic past to read the critical activities of the avant-garde as discourse, a means for organizing, unifying, and regulating knowledge about avant-garde cinema. Even such exemplary studies as Lucy Fischer's *Shot/ Countershot: Film Tradition and Women's Cinema* (1989) and David E. James's *Allegories of Cinema: American Film in the Sixties* (1989), recent books that break with tradition and radically treat avant-garde cinema in new aesthetic and social contexts, still read avant-garde cinema "against the grain" of established textual categories without wholly investigating the social functions of textual categories themselves.

I propose that, instead, we analyze further the critical discourses of our recent past as an important means by which cinema's positions have been constructed within cultural practices, power relations, and other arts discourses. As Brecht suggests, the direction of

---

[1] Lehman, 1985. Lehman refers especially to the following: Lawder 1975; Sitney 1975; LeGrice 1977; Sitney 1978; and Cornwell 1979. Also see Lehman 1984.

radical political analysis must reach beyond inquiries into the individual subject and his or her textual products (the goals of formalist practice as well as of much recent psychoanalytically based criticism (Brecht 1964, 34–35). A new historical orientation would purposefully show how avant-garde cinema has been inscribed as a social site for, rather than a knowable object of, active cultural conflicts over language, power, and resistance. How an American avant-garde cinema was constructed and how Mekas participated in the practices and discourses of that construction become a complex "story" of the ways specific cinematic practices, meanings, and values were socially activated and circumscribed.

II

> *All artistic work, like all human activity, involves the joint activity of a number, often a large number of people. Through their cooperation, the art work we eventually see or hear comes to be and continues to be. The work always shows signs of that cooperation.*
> —Howard Becker, *Art Worlds*

> *Down with distributors! Until now the film-maker was always at the mercy of the distributor. If the distributor says your film is no good, it is no good; if he says your film is O.K., you are one step closer to obtaining a theatre. Or, as has been done so often, he takes your work and begins to chop it into pieces until it bleeds.*
> —Jonas Mekas, *Movie Journal*

For sociologist Howard Becker, the project of identifying the structure and structural relations within the art world is neither a reclamation of special individuals nor an attempt to perpetuate the framework for dramatically styled narratives of action, opposition, and final victory. Becker proposes the model of a cooperatively maintained and extended socioeconomic system for understanding the activities and the products of the art world. This system both defines the work of art and produces and authorizes the apparatus that sustains its component parts—artists as well as art objects. Within Becker's model, the "art world" is organized through its producers, its arts institutions and institutional gatekeepers, its critics and criticism. Its discursive practices are produced by and, in turn, produce aesthetic conventions and values, legal discourses and practices, the commercial exigencies of the economy, and cultural values and attitudes about conformity and individualism. As Jeffrey Ruoff has demonstrated in his analysis of Mekas's historical agency in the transformation of postwar avant-garde cinema into an art world, Becker offers a structural model of the art world in which avant-garde cinema was embedded and a means for studying its historical specificity.[2] Rather than theorize art or the avant-garde itself, Becker implies that any understanding of avant-garde cinema must be grounded in the social functions of the extended network or art world that sustains and defines what constitutes the avant-garde.

His approach departs significantly from the historiographic framework underlying those histories of American experimental cinema that have traditionally been concerned with close analysis of individual films (P. Adams Sitney's *Visionary Film*, David Curtis's *Experimental Cinema*, Malcolm LeGrice's *Abstract Film and Beyond*).[3] Tracing cinematic representation of intellectual, perceptual, and aesthetic matters, these histories chronicle an evolution of vanguard filmmaking after World War II that paralleled the dominant aesthetic direction (and economic ascendency) of American contemporary art. In order to preserve a modernist chain of command, they exclude the postwar cinema's connections to and breaks from any American cinema prior to World War II, especially avoiding mention of the earlier radical leftist cinema of the 1930s. In this way, Sitney, LeGrice, and Curtis inscribe an avant-garde without internal conflict and composed of regular, productive activity *independent* of the politics of an apparatus already in place. In particular, the Workers Photo and Film League, the John Reed clubs, Nykino, and Frontier Films all played significant roles in the apparatus—the production, distribution, exhibition, and critical discourse of an avant-garde cinema—in the 1930s. If the art world's shift from a radical leftist position in the 1930s to a conservative one in the 1950s has been fully discussed in at least two recent

---

[2] See chapter 24 below.

[3] Sitney 1974; Sitney's volume was revised for a second edition in 1979. See also Curtis 1971 and LeGrice 1977.

works of scholarship, formalist histories of avant-garde cinema (which remain text-centered) have refused to consider any analogous discursive and institutional realignments.[4] Instead, formalist studies offer narratives of how avant-garde cinema came to reside comfortably within the conventional boundaries of postwar modernist aesthetics and among the arts institutions that supported modernism.

Only recently have film historians begun to investigate the cultural and art-world contextualization of postwar avant-garde cinema. Both James's *Allegories of Cinema* and my *Points of Resistance*, take up the increased social disturbances of the late 1960s and how they polarized and divided the avant-garde cinema community into formalist and radical-political sides.[5] In this conflict, the formalist side increasingly promoted and produced structural film within the museums, galleries, and critical discourses of the art world. Generally considered the chief agent for the elevation of formalist critical standards, Annette Michelson actively wrote about avant-garde cinema for *Artforum* and other scholarly arts journals. Michelson, however, always understood the political significance of a discursively formalist cinema at a time when few New York intellectuals outside *Film Culture* thought avant-garde cinema was worthy of consideration.

Mekas's work of the 1960s was likewise connected to art-world struggles over its political self-consciousness. From Mekas's diary films to his intervention in the distribution and exhibition apparatus of experimental cinema to his participation in an American new wave commercial cinema, Mekas was fundamentally a political figure ("a minister of defense and propaganda") in the particular struggles of the historical period. His creation of Anthology Film Archives in 1970 as the most widely recognized cinema apparatus of the formalist ascendency was at the nexus of these struggles. The consequences of formalist domination and Anthology's critical elevation or canonization of those films most relevant in these terms (especially in its first decade) should be seen as the result of reconfigured power relations in the cinema avant-garde rather than the systemic suppression of political cinema, even if the latter appeared briefly to be one of its effects.

The critical and intellectual emphasis on formal artistry as the means for valorizing an entire system of avant-garde cinema grew

---

[4] See, for example, discussion of "art world" shifts in Guilbaut 1983 and Crane 1987.

[5] James 1989, 164–65; Rabinovitz 1991, 139–42, 170–78.

out of a discourse already circulating that privileged the identity of the author as the mark of artistic value. Both Sitney and Michelson, for example, specified filmmaker Maya Deren as the single important transatlantic link to the modernist tradition established in Paris in the 1920s, even though they agreed that her films were not specifically surrealist, that Deren herself denied any pleasure in the irrational, and that surrealist films may have had a limited influence on her.[6] Such statements of "authorial transcendence" over even their own biographical and cultural evidence for the authorial voice demonstrate the extent to which they are willing to carry their project. Unfortunately, by refusing to inscribe the author-filmmaker in a socially situated art world where surrealism was itself a dynamically evolving category connected to efforts at recouping power, Sitney and Michelson miss the ways that the critical construction and reception of Deren's films as surrealist may have "explained" the gap they create.

Deren's historical position—the "gap" she smooths over for Sitney and Michelson—becomes more politically coherent when one understands the contextualizing situation of surrealism as the prevailing aesthetic object of New York arts discourse in the middle and late 1940s. Writing and arguing for cinema's deserved place among the dominant aesthetic vocabularies, Deren did not work counterproductively to that aim by denying the irrational in her films and emphasizing her conscious control over form. Rather, she situated her work squarely within the current struggles among the European surrealists-in-exile. Painter Roberto Matta was challenging André Breton's leadership through his efforts to make surrealist automatism more compatible with conscious control of form. Deren's statements in behalf of "conscious control," which supported her friend and onetime collaborator Matta, as well as her absorption in the general argument, are about surrealism insofar as they locate an American experimental cinema inside contemporary fine-arts discourse. In this way, the critical discourse provided a position for receiving Deren's work from one's relationship to the surrealist films of the 1920s. It inscribed intertextual meanings to the dream imagery, the logic disturbances, and the concern for the subconscious that are at play in her films. But by simply forging continuity among modernist aesthetics, Sitney's and Michelson's analyses of Deren's work obfuscate these important dimensions to Deren's films, criticism, and role in organizing an avant-garde cinema apparatus. Whether or not Deren's films are surrealist depends on how

[6] Sitney 1974, 1–19; Michelson 1980, 48.

the historian recognizes the ways in which the social and economic circumstances of wartime New York City and the cultural language of authority in the postwar environment activated historical meaning.

III

The personal appearance system, bound by its own decorum, risks placing "meaning" quite totally within the brain of the author. . . . The resultant interpretive translations are nostalgic documentations, circumscribed by intention, remembrance and anecdote . . . [risking] an individualism of "secret singularities," outside history, without politics, and thus without effect.
—Patricia Mellencamp, "Receivable Texts"

Perhaps the only voices one can trust are those of the filmmakers themselves. Not when they are analyzing the meanings of their films (there, the truth of Matisse—the tongues of artists should be cut out—remains true), but when they speak about how the film was made, the processes, the procedures, the impulses, the attitudes, some of the reasonings, and a few other such matters which begin to help us understand the creative process of filmmaking and which begin to lay the first seeds of formal criticism.
—Jonas Mekas, *Movie Journal*

As early as the 1970s—that is, from the onset of a formalist critical "hegemony"—a few critics opposed the modernist purpose of reestablishing ties between an individual and a body of work based on evidence from the internal forms and relationships. The new generation of critics launched these attacks against the "public record" in such film journals as *The Velvet Light Trap, Screen,* and *Wide Angle* (and indirectly embracing *Camera Obscura*) and at such international conferences as the 1982 Center for Twentieth-Century Studies film-theory conference in Milwaukee on the avant-garde. They uniformly adopted highly specialized language and explicitly Marxist, feminist attitudes within forums that first challenged and then achieved dominant positions in professional film studies. They critiqued American avant-garde film history as a patriarchal discourse whereby formalist points of view celebrated individual historical roles and the overall importance of the male artist, revealing corrupt power hierarchies among avant-garde filmmakers.

For example, both Russell Campbell and Ellen Freyer noted and criticized the critical practices of avant-garde cinema while demanding redress and a more pluralist history. Campbell's "Eight Notes on the Underground" (1974) argued that sexist, elitist attitudes formed the basis for a preoccupation with formal novelty. Freyer (1974) asserted a more marked sociopolitical component in "Formalist Cinema," saying that the formalist sensibility veiled a conformist practice perpetuated by the New York cinema's white male leaders. Campbell and Freyer appear to have been especially motivated by the practices of Anthology Film Archives, an institution whose self-proclaimed goal was to collect masterpieces of cinema according to the rigidly formalist standards of its five-man selection committee. Anthology was increasingly singled out during the 1970s and 1980s for its exclusion of Shirley Clarke and Carolee Schneeman, in particular, and of women filmmakers generally.[7]

In 1978, Constance Penley and Janet Bergstrom provided a more radically extensive critique of Anthology Film Archives and the New York experimental cinema, deconstructing the avant-garde itself as a social system marked by political struggles. Published in *Screen,* Penley's and Bergstrom's "Avant-Garde: Histories and Theories" was an explicitly feminist analysis of dominant formalist discourse and practices.[8] Penley and Bergstrom examined the politics behind the canonization of films and filmmakers in Anthology Film Archives, Sitney's publication of *Visionary Film* (1974) and *The Essential Cinema* (1975), and John Hanhardt's museum catalogue *A History of the American Avant-Garde Cinema* (1976). The three books explicated films largely in the collection of Anthology Film

[7] For an exemplary as well as incisive critique of Anthology's selection practices, see Lehman 1985, 69–70.

[8] Penley and Bergstrom 1979, reprinted in Nichols 1985, 2:287–300.

Archives. Penley and Bergstrom contrasted Anthology's policy of formalist selection with that of most film archives, which attempt to collect as diverse a group of films as possible on the assumption that present critical standards will, in time, give way to others. They claimed the standardization among volumes based on Anthology's collection was particularly insidious since it caused other institutions to believe that an official canon existed (Penley and Bergstrom 1979, 123).

Penley's and Bergstrom's argument identified the mid-1970s publication of these three books as a point of consolidation for professional discourse that had begun in the late 1960s with cinema's entrance into the academy. Their analysis demonstrated how the process functioned politically, sustaining particular power relations and determining ideology. But they neglected how well placed and consolidated such a discursive practice was before it became further valorized within professional discourse. They did not examine the discursive roles played by the battery of nonacademic books published in the years (1967–1972) preceding Sitney's *Visionary Film*. The books on avant-garde cinema by Gregory Battcock, Sheldon Renan, Parker Tyler, David Curtis, and Jonas Mekas had singled out the same films (and often for the same reasons) for a canon of experimental cinema.[9]

It is significant, however, that they also wrote as representatives of the feminist collective editorial board of *Camera Obscura*, outlining as their new journal's goal the investigation of discourses and the ways in which the interplay of discourses is controlled. One could further organize a series of oppositions implicit in their essay, pitting feminism and antiphenomenological philosophy against the formalist avant-garde but also representing the West Coast against the East Coast and differences within French critical theories that may hark back to the earlier divisive struggles of 1968, their positions shaped by intellectual and political experiences in both Paris and Berkeley. By taking a stand against the ideological project of the New York discourse in the most influential international film-theory journal, Penley and Bergstrom framed an intellectual power struggle in which the new *Camera Obscura* became identified as an important site of opposition.

In 1985, Patricia Mellencamp extended Penley's and Bergstrom's analysis to the earlier group of publications as well as to more recent artist-centered, formalist examples.[10] Mellencamp argued that

---

[9] Battcock 1967; Renan 1967; Tyler 1969.

[10] Mellencamp 1985. The more recent titles under consideration included Michelson 1974; Gidal 1978; Cornwell 1979; and Sitney 1978.

the histories were corrupt because the authors adopted self-serving and multiple roles within an avant-garde cinema system. But contrary to her narrow standard for complaint, the history of the arts contains many instances where the professional functions of the artist, critic, and curator are neither separate nor distinct. The issue for concern should not be that the artist-critic's history subjectified the past and selectively recast films, events, and meanings, but how the artist's role in the apparatus extended beyond that of the producer and shaped knowledge. Such a shift refocuses the question to how structural relations within a particular historical practice construct knowledge about the avant-garde. It is necessary in these instances to consider how relationships between marginalized and dominant arts discourses activated, empowered, or silenced the very marginalized, repressed groups for whom Mellencamp and the others speak. Rather than examine intention as politics, we need to assess the politics of power relations in order to identify any historically constituted avant-garde.

All the above critiques of "institutionalized" discourse on experimental film are based on the appearances of books, a privileged form that may not always organize the critical practices of any avant-garde arts community. The tendency of scholars to emphasize books may be due as much to our own investment in publication and our desire, as scholars, to believe in the centrality of publication as to the public, privileged status of such discourse. If we depend solely on such published materials, public rhetoric is empowered, whereas private interpersonal relations and semiprivate discourse are rendered silent.

It is at the latter level rather than through public speech that most women (who are the primary concern in Campbell's, Freyer's, Penley's, Bergstrom's, and Mellencamp's critiques) participated in independent cinema. Their roles in new and sometimes temporary New York–based organizations from the middle 1950s to the late 1960s—organizations such as the Creative Film Foundation, the Golden Reel Film Festival, Cinema 16, the Independent Film Makers Association, the Film Council of America, and the Film-Makers' Distribution Center—were part of discursive struggles now partially silenced that should compete with the limited representations by *Film Culture*, the *Village Voice*, and other periodicals that forwarded Mekas's central role and identified experimental cinema's new status as a unified, self-sustaining network.

It is also important here to reconsider the position of formalism within not only competing discourses, but a wider range of discourse. Although avant-garde film expressivism of the 1960s overlapped with that of other art forms—jazz, experimental theater, Beat poetry, modern dance, vanguard painting—the production and reception of avant-garde cinema has rarely been understood within the social networks that encompass the other avant-gardes. James's *Allegories of Cinema* is instructive here for defining the avant-garde cinema of the 1960s more broadly within the cultural avant-garde, pointing the way to cultural practice as itself crisscrossed by conflicting, competing discourses.

IV

Jonas has many pockets . . . and all of them are open.
—Stan Brakhage

But there are really two Jonases—one very dedicated, the other a Machiavellian maneuverer, a history rewriter, an attempted pope. He has two passions: film and power. His greatest talent is to make people— some people—believe that he is what he is not.
—Amos Vogel

I don't talk about money, you know. Because I don't have any. But I'm willing to hustle for people I believe in.
—Jonas Mekas, *Movie Journal*

At stake is the need to consider avant-garde cinema generally, and Jonas Mekas and the formation of Anthology Film Archives in particular, within cultural models that allow for conflict and struggle. What is often lost, for example, in both formalist and feminist narratives of Anthology's ascendency is that it did not represent simply a new organization's rise to power and the accommodation of certain texts into elitist categories; rather, it reconfigured existing power relations in the New York independent cinema, and recuperated the radical potential of overtly political cinemas into safe, conservative categories.

Between 1955 and 1965, the configuration of an avant-garde cinema or independent film network in New York City had undergone successive shifts. One of the most significant among these was the

New American Cinema—a discursive and economic set of practices attempting to achieve commercial viability for independent films. In early 1966, Shirley Clarke, Jonas Mekas, and Louis Brigante set up a nonprofit cooperative for distributing independently made feature films to commercial art-film houses around the country. Modeled after and sharing office space with the Film-Makers' Cooperative, they set up similar guidelines for the Film-Makers' Distribution Center (FMDC). Initially successful both in the number of filmmakers who chose to participate in their catalogue and in economic terms, the FMDC reversed its fortunes within a few years.

Meanwhile, independent filmmakers themselves expressed increasing divisiveness over the goal of a commercial alternative cinema. Some filmmakers, such as Stan Brakhage, publicly denounced the FMDC and insisted on the "purity" of a separate, experimental cinema (Tomkins 1973, 32). When he angrily told Clarke that she was "nothing more than a commercial filmmaker," he was leveling his worst insult at her.[11] His position articulates an ideological crisis in the late 1960s regarding both the definition of the independent cinema and who would control it.

The struggle over two competing definitions was due as much to shifting economic and cultural forces in the arts as to the filmmakers' internal group politics. Avant-garde cinema was becoming an increasingly visible part of established culture institutions not only in New York City—where relations among colleges, museums, and marginal film organizations already existed—but across the country. Beginning in 1965, the new National Endowment for the Arts infused the nationwide arts economy with large sums of federal money; through the early 1970s, museums received 76 percent of all funds allocated to the visual arts by the NEA, whereas no more than 3 percent annually was typically given to individuals.[12] Following the federal government's lead, state arts councils were mandated and state funding agencies provided more widespread support for the arts. The New York State Council on the Arts, created in 1966, contributed $772,000 to the arts in 1966 but by 1976 annually provided $35.7 million. Twenty-two other states followed a similar pattern (Helms 1979). The academic expansion of cinema studies

[11] Personal interview with Shirley Clarke, Chicago, Illinois, 23 September 1981. Large portions of this interview appeared in Rabinovitz 1981.

[12] Netzer 1978, 66. For a general discussion of the massive economic expansion of the arts during this period, see Crane 1987, 2–9. For a discussion of further details of federal and state funding of the arts, see Banfield 1984; Berman 1979, Goody 1984.

also meant that educational institutions were now absorbing many of the filmmakers and critics of the avant-garde cinema.

Brakhage specified an orientation to avant-garde cinema wholly consistent with museums' and universities' accelerating practices for constituting cinema activities within noncommercial, arts-associated environments. In his 5 March 1970 "Movie Journal" column in *Village Voice*, Mekas decisively dramatized the situation:

> I know that the civil war of the nonnarrative and noncommercial film versus the commercial and narrative film has been clearly won. The existence of nonnarrative film forms in addition to narrative film has been established. Particularly one feels this when one leaves New York and visits the universities and small colleges. . . . Most serious learning institutions, museums, and art centers across the country have accepted the cinema in all its varieties. (Mekas 1972, 376–77).

Whereas the Film-Makers' Co-op experienced a sharp upsurge in university and museum rentals, the Film-Makers' Distribution Center could not generally find enough small art-film theaters able to compete with Hollywood and noncommercial outlets.

Mekas wanted to close the FMDC, while Clarke wanted more time to turn around the center's finances. In 1970, Mekas wrote to Clarke that it was necessary to close the FMDC in order to keep Co-op monies from being secured by creditors.[13] At the beginning of the summer, Mekas circulated a Co-op memo stating that he had personally incurred financial martyrdom in the FMDC's closing so that he would not endanger the Co-op (Tomkins 1973, 46). Despite his financial position, he publicly announced plans by the end of the summer to establish Anthology Film Archives for, as Calvin Tomkins wrote, "astonishingly enough, money had become available for another Mekas project" (ibid., 47). Completely dissociating himself from his former partners Brigante and Clarke and their goal of a commercial avant-garde, Mekas joined with a closed circle of political allies (including Brakhage) to enshrine films in an avowedly apolitical apparatus of formalist ideology. The founding of Anthology may thus be seen as the last ritual of an avant-garde elite in the midst of being threatened and overshadowed by the larger systems of museum and university practices. It represents an attempt to mirror the apparatus of museums and archives as a means for unifying and regulating the avant-garde cinema according to the

---

[13] Jonas Mekas, Letters to Shirley Clarke, n.d., 1970, Shirley Clarke Papers, Wisconsin Center for Film and Theater Research, University of Wisconsin–Madison and the State Historical Society of Wisconsin, Madison, Wisconsin.

larger models of structural and ideological relations. At another level, Mekas's move away from the discourse and practice of commercialism may also be seen as an effort to secure for himself and others a toehold of power among shifting institutional economic bases for avant-garde cinema.

By reorganizing the discussion about experimental cinema to accommodate competing discourses, notions of conflict, and larger cultural practices, one is better able to understand the social and economic relations that empowered or weakened the avant-garde cinema. Such conscious critical reorganization of purpose, strategies, and theory is a necessary component of any radical criticism that hopes not to succumb to the political power of past critical discourses. The historically significant power of formalist discourse is only reconstructed superficially in the present once one analyzes the articulation of and the structural relations among its subjects of victims and villains. But the instructional value for how a formalist American avant-garde cinema participated in, configured, and reconfigured social and economic relations remains.

What is unquestionably valuable here is the role of history for the political agendas of the present and immediate future. In an era where widespread outbreaks of rigorously applied censorship and conservative political standards are being tied to state funding for the arts, we must ask who controls the apparatus of the avant-garde and whom the avant-garde serves. If we ignore the state of power relations within which the avant-garde is figured and if we do nothing to change the situation, we will indeed have little left to do at all. It is time to rediscover that a critic's hat is generally of no great use unless one wears it as a self-appointed minister of defense.

Bibliography

Banfield, Edward C. 1984. *The Democratic Muse: Visual Arts and the Public Interest.* New York: Basic Books.

Battcock, Gregory, ed. 1967. *The New American Cinema.* New York: E. P. Dutton.

Berman, Ronald. 1979. "Art vs. the Arts." *Commentary* 68 (November): 46–52.

Brecht, Bertolt. 1964. *Brecht on Theatre.* Trans. John Willett. London: Methuen.

Campbell, Russell. 1974. "Eight Notes on the Underground." *Velvet Light Trap* 13 (Fall): 45–46.

Cornwell, Regina. 1979. *Snow Seen: The Film and Photographs of Michael Snow.* Toronto: Peter Martin Associates.

Crane, Diana. 1987. *The Transformation of the Avant-Garde: The New York Art World, 1940–1985.* Chicago: University of Chicago Press.

Curtis, David. 1971. *Experimental Cinema.* New York: Universe Books.

Fischer, Lucy. 1989. *Shot/Countershot: Film Tradition and Women's Cinema.* Princeton: Princeton University Press.

Freyer, Ellen. 1974. "Formalist Cinema: Artistic Suicide in the Avant-Garde." *Velvet Light Trap* 13 (Fall): 47–49.

Gidal, Peter. 1978. *Structural Film Anthology.* London: British Film Institute.

Goody, Kenneth. 1984. "Arts Funding: Growth and Change between 1963 and 1983." *Annals of the American Academy of Political and Social Science* 471 (January): 144–57.

Guilbaut, Serge. 1983. *How New York Stole the Idea of Modern Art.* Trans. Arthur Goldhammer. Chicago: University of Chicago Press.

Hanhardt, John G., ed. 1976. *A History of the American Avant-Garde Cinema.* New York: New York Federation of the Arts.

Helms, Roy. 1979. "State Funds Are Zooming: Twenty-Three States Top $1 Million for the Arts." *American Arts* 10 (December): 22–23.

James, David E. 1989. *Allegories of Cinema: American Film in the Sixties.* Princeton: Princeton University Press.

Lawder, Standish D. 1975. *The Cubist Cinema.* New York: New York University Press.

LeGrice, Malcolm. 1977. *Abstract Film and Beyond.* Cambridge: MIT Press.

Lehman, Peter. 1984. "The Avant-Garde: Power, Change, and the Power to Change." In *Cinema Histories, Cinema Practices,* ed. Patricia Mellencamp and Philip Rosen, 120–31. Frederick, Md.: University Publications of America.

———. 1985. "For Whom Does the Light Shine? Thoughts on the Avant-Garde." *Wide Angle* 7, no. 1–2:68–73.

Mekas, Jonas. 1972. *Movie Journal: The Rise of a New American Cinema, 1959–1971.* New York: Macmillan.

Mellencamp, Patricia. 1985. "Receivable Texts: U.S. Avant-Garde Cinema, 1960–1980." *Wide Angle* 7, no. 1–2:74–91.

Michelson, Annette. 1974. *New Forms in Film.* Montreux, Switzerland: n.p.

———. 1980. "On Reading Deren's Notebook." *October* 14 (Fall): 47–54.

Netzer, Dick. 1978. *The Subsidized Muse: Public Support for the Arts in the United States.* New York: Cambridge University Press.

Nichols, Bill, ed. 1985. *Movies and Methods.* Vol. 2. Berkeley and Los Angeles: University of California Press.

Penley, Constance, and Janet Bergstrom. 1979. "Avant-Garde: Histories and Theories." *Screen* 19, no. 3 (Autumn): 113–27.

Rabinovitz, Lauren. 1981. "Choreography of the Cinema: An Interview with Shirley Clarke." *Afterimage* 11, no. 5 (December): 8–11.

―――. 1991. *Points of Resistance: Women, Power, and Politics in the New York Avant-Garde Cinema, 1943–1971.* Champaign: University of Illinois Press.

Renan, Sheldon. 1967. *An Introduction to the American Underground Film.* New York: E. P. Dutton.

Sitney, P. Adams, ed. 1974. *Visionary Film: The American Avant-Garde, 1943–1978.* New York: Oxford University Press.

―――. 1975. *The Essential Cinema: Essays on the Films in the Collection of Anthology Film Archives.* New York: Anthology Film Archives and New York University Press.

―――. 1978. *The Avant-Garde Film: A Reader of Theory and Criticism.* New York: New York University Press.

Tomkins, Calvin. 1973. "All Pockets Open." *New Yorker,* 6 January, 31–49.

Tyler, Parker. 1969. *Underground Film: A Critical History.* New York: Grove Press.

21. Nam June Paik   Who Is Afraid of Jonas Mekas?

Who is afraid of Jonas Mekas?
I . . . Nam June Paik.
Why?
Because Mekas is far greater than I as a *video* artist.
Because the next stage of video art competition is who makes the best/most intelligent *two-way* videodisc.
I have thought about it for over two decades.
I did wring my poor brain like a squeezed towel for many sleepless nights.
Over the past decade I encountered only two interesting pieces using two-way video capability.
One is by Paul Krueger, who was shown at the Digital Vision show organized by Cynthia Goodman at the IBM Gallery a few years ago. You see yourself being changed a thousand different ways; certainly a *super* Freudian piece.
The other is a *Dog* piece by Paul Garrin, enfant terrible of the video scene on New York's Lower East Side. He divided the screen into two opposing spaces. One is an elegant cocktail party, and a watchdog is in front of this party. Dog is happily chewing the bone. . . . I see dog happy.
In the other side is the proleteriat of the nineties. I approach a little. . . . Dog . . . watches me. . . . I approach a little more . . . so dog: Brummm. . . . I approach more. . . . Dog gets madder . . . madder . . . howls . . . wang-wangs . . . and finally bites me.
Yet he is still inside the TV tube.
This piece was premiered in the Clocktower (with three other artists), and the show broke the Clocktower's ten-year attendance record. Certainly Paul made a brilliant two-way piece.

Yet Jonas Mekas will dwarf *all* the two-way video artists of today.
Because he has made history in the dense pack.
Mekas crammed his New York life from 1950 to 1990 into ten hours of single-frame odyssey. It starts with the anti-Stalin Lithuanian march and goes to the anti-Vietnam War march and is still

going on until the liberation of Lithuania and the New York visit of Landbergis (just before his presidency).

I was struck by two scenes.

One is of George Maciunas in his home with his father and mother. Later art historians will analyze this movie again and again to find why he became asthmatic.

The other is of Frances Starr, the former editor of the Something Else Press and a worker at the Cinematheque. On a very, very cold winter night around 2:00 A.M. I saw her trembling and shivering and hungry at the East Side Bookshop on St. Mark's Place. She did look intellectually pretty and tender. Obviously she did not have a place to go. I almost invited her to my Canal Street loft. But I did not because Shigeko was sleeping at Canal Street that night. I never saw her again; then suddenly I saw her twenty years younger in Mekas's movie: breakfast with Frances Starr.

Mekas's newsreel, especially its single-frame technique, is the most ideal artwork for the videodisc with its vast and convenient retrieval mode.

And this is landmark history. Nobody can copy it now, because nobody can reproduce the fifties. In the fifties Movietone newsreel (which sells for one thousand dollars per second) only crooks and villains and whores were on.

Real people, real underground fighters are all here in Mekas's films. Anybody can have good ideas; anybody can do it for three years. But he had patience . . . patience . . . and rewardless patience . . . forty years equals 120,000 days with a heavy Bolex. Expensive film and development! Only the *old* European culture's outfit could have done this. I envy him.

He will outpace me as a video artist soon.

22. Bob Harris   Video at Anthology

THAT VIDEO would be incorporated into Anthology Film Archives was inevitable; many compelling factors made it so. When, in the fall of 1974, Anthology reopened in Soho, at 80 Wooster Street, a sense of the openness and experimental vitality of the original cinematheque concept was combined with the highly refined aesthetic of Anthology's pure cinema collection. Consistent with the artistic lineage of the 80 Wooster Street building, and in keeping with the dominant aesthetic currents of the time, Anthology expanded its programming agenda to include poetry readings and a series of Flux concerts. In addition, a video program was inaugurated.

Soho in 1974 was at its creative and energetic peak, the locus of contemporary art activity in New York. Artists, drawn to the spacious, inexpensive industrial lofts, had begun living in the area in the latter half of the 1960s. By the early 1970s, most of the major midtown galleries had opened downtown branches, or moved there outright. Fueled by state arts funding, the alternative-space movement was underway. Created to meet the need for appropriate forums for emerging art forms, these new institutions, like the artists and galleries, moved to Soho for the lofts and the art-world vitality. Central to an aesthetic that would become associated with both the area and the particular historical period in contemporary art was an interest in interdisciplinary activity. A creative group with a profound influence on the evolution of this aesthetic (as it developed in Soho) was Fluxus. An intentionally fluid and malleable project, Fluxus has been best described in the following terms: "The locus of various trends—or, rather, of various arts. Music, theater, dance, literature, visual art, and even non-art factors inform Fluxus without forcing it, as they might force other forms of intermedia, to identify its principal roots. Unlike happenings, conceptual art, current performance art, visual poetry, and new forms of dance, music, and theater, Fluxus exists at a point equidistant from all the arts."[1] Coincidentally, through the real estate ventures of Flux artist and promoter George Maciunas, Fluxus played a significant role in So-

[1] Peter Frank, "Fluxus in New York," in *New York–Downtown Manhattan: Soho*, the catalogue for an exhibition at Akademie der Kunste, Berlin, 1976, 177.

ho's growth as a neighborhood of artists living in cooperatively owned lofts. The 80 Wooster Street building, incorporated in 1967 by Maciunas as the first Flux co-op, was the first artists' cooperative building in Soho. That same year, the Film-Makers' Cinematheque became one of the first Soho alternative art spaces when it began sporadically screening films at 80 Wooster Street, though this was interrupted by Buildings Department closings. The space was also being used by Richard Foreman's Ontological Hysteric Theater. It was in this fertile setting that video began at Anthology.

Mekas's choice of Shigeko Kubota, herself a Fluxus artist, video-maker, and close friend of George Maciunas, to develop and curate the video department is directly linked to the pervasive influence of Fluxus on Mekas and the entire downtown cultural climate, and to Kubota's association with Nam June Paik. Paik's Fluxus video-tapes and prepared television pieces constitute one of the quasi-mythical foundation pillars of video art. With Kubota, and by association Paik, the Anthology video program would inherit an eclectic aesthetic genealogy directly linked to the roots of video as art; it would be nonacademic, that is, from an art-making rather than an academic or curatorial background; it would be inclusive and open to all areas of video experimentation without being aligned with any specific ideological camp; and it would be serious-yet-playful in the Fluxus manner.

While the video program's existence within a film museum implied its institutionalization, the programming strategy stressed process and experimentation, and expressly sought diversity in viewpoints, styles, and attitudes. This fundamental commitment has remained unchanged, maintained by various strategies that assured that no single curatorial attitude, no aesthetic, philosophical, or regional bias would dominate. The primary criterion for screenings has been only a serious commitment to video as a medium of expression or communication. Accordingly, video copies of films have not been shown, nor have tapes whose primary purpose is the documentation of dance, theater, music, or other performance activity.

An important basic characteristic of the Anthology program was that, whenever possible, the videomaker would be present to introduce and discuss his or her work. Videomakers were encouraged to show works in progress, especially if they were willing to share information about the process of tape making and to enter into a dialogue with the audience. Shows of unfinished work reinforced the program's stance vis-à-vis video as a medium still in its formative stage. Curators from other institutions and independent curators were regularly invited to organize group shows, expanding the parameters of taste and expertise beyond those of Anthology's curatorial staff. Shows were organized to reflect regional character, styles, and activities, to create a dialogue around a given theme, or to focus on work from various minority groups. "Guest-curated" screenings have included work from Zagreb, Barcelona, El Salvador, Nicaragua, Great Britain, Canada, Southern California, Iowa, San Francisco, Providence, Chicago, and Buffalo, as well as work reflecting African-American, Asian, feminist, Latin American, and Native American sensibilities. "Open Screenings" were held regularly where anyone present could show his or her tapes, with the two-hour program duration evenly divided.

There was never any overt attempt on the part of Jonas Mekas, or anyone else within Anthology, to restrict or direct the activities of the video department. However, the range of programming possibilities was severely curtailed by the limited amount of space available for screenings. Anthology's 80 Wooster Street theater space was a small, narrow room with fixed, raked seats locked in a rigid, frontal, proscenium relation to the screen: a reasonably decent, intimate space for viewing films (even if the rattle of heat pipes constantly provided arrhythmic clatter during hours of Dovzhenko, Dreyer, Vertov, and Brakhage), but maddeningly inflexible for the presentation of work on a seventeen-inch or nineteen-inch screen, or for work with anything but a direct, frontal relation to its audience. Videomakers regularly seek to use the mobility of the monitor in an attempt to explore the sculptural and multiple-image possibilities of the technology, and to overcome the limitations of a single, intimate-scale monitor. At Anthology, the compromise solution to the space problems was an Advent Videobeam projector. The seven-foot diagonal screen was large enough to be seen from the back rows, but the substandard quality of the image cast video in an unnecessarily bad light. Attempting to present video as a large, projected image using the earliest, low-cost video projection technology only served to amplify video's greatest shortcoming: its lack of depth, definition, and subtlety of color. In the early 1980s, the purchase of six high-quality monitors and four playback decks with money from the New York State Council on the Arts allowed monitors to be placed throughout the space for smaller clusters of viewers. It also facilitated the presentation of multichannel works. However successful or unsuccessful these solutions might have been, video is ill served by the proscenium film theater. This problem has not been adequately addressed in any institution with which this writer is familiar, primarily because no one has made the necessary investment of space, money, and ingenuity to design a theater specifically for the public presentation of video, one adaptable to the full range of formal possibilities, from single-monitor tapes to multiscreen installations.

Video's countercultural genesis, its rejection of history, the tainted character of the parent medium (television), the diverse sensibilities and backgrounds of videomakers, the rapid and tumultuous shifts in the social and aesthetic climate during video's first fifteen years, have all profoundly affected the medium and the state of theory and criticism associated with it. Creative exploration of the new medium began in the late 1960s, in a milieu influenced by cybernetics, Zen, explorations of consciousness, and sociopolitical revolution. The utopian potential initially ascribed to the technology led to lofty expectations. Many believed the new medium would be quintessentially democratic (a quality that had been attributed to both cinema and photography at similar stages in their formative years), easily accessible to everyone by way of TV, with a limitless ability to store and disseminate information through interface with computers. Decentralizing the control of mass communication would allow "the people" to expropriate the powers of the communications network conglomerates. In the hands of the new videomakers, television would become a two-way exchange, activating receiver and sender equally. Numerous groups with philosophical links to radical political and cultural movements were formed to experiment with these possibilities. Electronic pioneers with a more aestheticized agenda investigated the image-generating principles of the technology, modifying television's logic to create tools that manipulate and transform images and synthesize wholly abstract forms. Yet another area of inquiry emerged by way of video's "real-time" immediacy: the feedback loop. From this mirrorlike electronic loop emerged a self-referential, self-conscious medium of psychological inquiry.

In the early 1970s, a series of important technological advances occurred over a short stretch of time. Small-format color systems were introduced, and soon thereafter came the three-quarter-inch cassette, time-base corrector, and computer-controlled editing system. In allowing vastly increased control over the process of making video, these new tools had a profound impact on the nature of the work produced. The early tapes had had a temporal sense and a look that was distinctly, and inherently, unlike TV, and since the early hardware choices were limited, images of equal quality were relatively accessible to all. The new technologies made near-mimicry of television possible, and radically inflated the potential costs of production. Technical sophistication became a new factor in the determination of quality, and the influence of broadcast television on video increased dramatically. Also in the early 1970s, financial assistance in the form of private, state, and federal grants became more available. The granting agencies, sharing the excitement over video's potential, were eager to support work in the new medium. The influx of money into an area too new to have any solidly entrenched ideological or individual power structures (up to this time, video had resisted such hierarchies in its attempts at decentralization and community-building) attracted artists from other disciplines, and contributed to the creation of an ever-larger and more influential class of bureaucrats and administrators. It would later be seen that these developments encouraged a shift toward higher and higher production values, and the corresponding gloss that high-tech work would inevitably obtain. The avant-garde became institutionalized at the expense of its bohemian roots. In barely ten years, video had gained a solid presence in the more progressive galleries, had demanded a full share of the funding distribution from granting agencies, had become established in modern-art museums, and was beginning to be taught in the academy.

To compare the development of "alternative" video to that of avant-garde film reveals some interesting dissimilarities. There has been a tradition of personal, experimental film art dating back to the formative years of cinema. The technology has remained sufficiently accessible, and work expressing the sensibilities of a single individual has continued to be produced. While such work has always existed at the extreme fringe of an industry-dominated medium, and the climate of support for such work has fluctuated, the precedent has been established for serious critical acceptance of creative filmmaking. With the independent filmmaking that began in America in the 1950s and flourished in the 1960s, a radical shift in sensibilities was needed to appreciate the new work. Such was the nature of Jonas Mekas's shift in advocacy from the serious, "intellectual" European narrative film to the freer, more formally innovative American avant-garde. Television, on the other hand, was the creation of a powerful postwar multinational industry. The paramount concern of these corporate interests was to maintain control over the technology they were developing. Therefore, when small-format equipment was introduced, making individual productions possible, there was virtually no artistic precedent within the medium against which the new work could resonate.

The American avant-garde film community of the early seventies was dominated by a powerful and influential modernist element.

The establishment of an institution such as Anthology Film Archives was a landmark achievement in the ascendancy of this aesthetic. The irony that the still raw and undeveloped medium of video, ostensibly lacking the maturity and elegance film had struggled to attain, should be placed in the house of "pure cinema" was apparent to many, and indeed heightened by the indifference of the Kubota/Paik/Fluxus rhetoric to modernist principles. Film and video were like rival siblings, with an intelligent, handsome, urbane, and literate elder, who had worked hard to obtain stature, and a scruffy, spoiled, comic-book-reading, upstart youngster, labeled a genius before the proof was at hand. Presumably, Mekas could have recruited a historian to devise a clear, "essentialist" model for video along the lines of the film anthology. The establishment of a "video selection committee" suggests such a desire. The committee consisted of Hollis Frampton, the only member of the modernist film hierarchy (as defined by Anthology's "Essential Cinema" collection), apart from Tony Conrad, to work seriously in video,[2] Gerald O'Grady, Douglas Davis, Shigeko Kubota, and Mekas himself. But the committee never met as a group, the curatorial decisions were left to Kubota, and the knotty problem of reducing the rampant diversity of a still-young medium through the filters of modernism was never formally confronted. Although numerous videotapes have directly and self-consciously engaged in defining and reflecting the medium's parameters, no specific core or cadre of videomakers has systematically devoted itself to the pursuit of modernist ideals. This may be partially attributed to the fact that, at the moment of video's arrival, the erosion of modernism's absolute grasp on the arts was well underway. The most definitive quality of video through its first twenty years was the lack of any single unifying definition. Born into a climate profoundly influenced by critical theory, burdened with instant status as a full-blown art form, thrust almost immediately into the historicizing nexus of gallery, museum, and academy, video has had countless histories and futures grafted onto it without being left to develop its own. The medium has been open territory, and, as with all frontiers, the playground of visionaries, mavericks, gunslingers, and strip miners as well as rooted, practical farmers. As modernism's influence faded, subsequent generations of videomakers charted their directions under the influence of increasingly diverse notions of art making. Perhaps re-

[2] Michael Snow has worked in video; "DE LA," his video installation featuring the "Central Region" machine, is his most important piece. He has also produced tapes. However, Snow, who has produced significant work in film, music, photography, painting, and sculpture, seems only peripherally interested in video.

flecting this resistance to the imposition of formalizing parameters on the aesthetic development of the medium, video at Anthology, even while maintaining its stature as one of the premier video showcases in New York, has yet to shed its outsider image and become settled. Resisting the comfort and complacency of a fixed aesthetic position, the program has thrived on the energy and vitality of risk, process, and cultural diversity.

23. Richard Leacock I Feel Passionate about the Film Journals of Jonas Mekas

I FEEL PASSIONATE about the film journals of Jonas Mekas!

Here is a filmmaker with a spring-driven camera who has developed his very own relationship with his camera and is artist enough to create sequences that are an extension of his personal vision. Why does he do it? Because he loves doing it. He does not have to be paid to do this! No political tyranny can stop him and no ideology can erase his humanity. No! I do not love all of it! But the things I do love are fabulous . . . a young woman walking in the rain on Fifth Avenue with her two little children . . . a friend dying . . . a rainstorm on Sixth Avenue . . . his mother blowing on the embers. . . . These are expressions of love—incomparable. A filmmaker who relates to his camera as a violinist to his instrument; a relationship that must be developed, nurtured, and continually practiced, that has no need for analysis by the beagles of academia.

As for a "movement," I am not so sure. When we (Bob Drew, Pennebaker, Maysles, me, others) were developing new ways of observing the world around us in the early sixties, I found the New York New Cinema (or whatever) to be an effete group of snobs, anchored along with the self-proclaimed "scholars" of academia, fiddling around with the myopic drivel of early Soviet cinema. Later, I overcame my hostility and became friends not only with Jonas, but with Brakhage and even Kubelka—but not with the movement. As an old-line EX-Communist, I had already become wary of movements.

Now I am out in the cold again. I am working in video-8! Not because it is cheap but because I love it!

Shhhh! So is Jonas!

24. Jeffrey K. Ruoff   Home Movies of the Avant-Garde: Jonas Mekas and the New York Art World

All artistic work, like all human activity, involves the joint activity of a number, often a large number, of people. Through their cooperation, the art work we eventually see or hear comes to be and continues to be. The work always shows signs of that cooperation.
—Howard Becker, *Art Worlds*

THE ART WORLD OF AVANT-GARDE FILM

Jonas Mekas has dedicated his life and work to the postwar avant-garde film community. In so doing, he collaborated in the construction of an art world, as this has been defined by sociologist Howard Becker: "Art worlds consist of all the people whose activities are necessary to the production of the characteristic works which that world, and perhaps others as well, define as art. Members of art worlds coordinate the activities by which work is produced by referring to a body of conventional understandings embodied in common practice and in frequently used artifacts. The same people often cooperate repeatedly, even routinely, in similar ways to produce similar works, so that we can think of an art world as an established network of cooperative links among participants" (Becker 1982, 34–35). The avant-garde film community may be thought of as an art world, a subset of the larger contemporary art world in the United States. As a critic, journal editor, polemicist, distributor, filmmaker, exhibitor, fund-raiser, archivist, and teacher, Mekas worked to build a community of filmmakers and an audience receptive to their art. Here I explore Mekas's contribution to the construction of the world of avant-garde film in the institutional frameworks of production, distribution, exhibition, and criticism.

Significantly, Mekas's own films bear witness to this process;

both in subject matter and in style, they call attention to the structure of the avant-garde film community, providing an excellent case study of the ways in which individual works show signs of the cooperation of the larger art world. In Mekas's cycle of diary films, originally called *Diaries, Notes, and Sketches*, the avant-garde film community and the New York art world emerge as the collective protagonist, and he maintains that his shooting style developed as a response to his own engagement in that community: "During the last fifteen years I got so entangled with the independently-made film that I didn't have any time left for myself, for my own filmmaking—between Film-Makers' Cooperative, Film-Makers' Cinematheque, *Film Culture* magazine, and now Anthology Film Archives" (Sitney 1978, 190). Covering his experiences in America from 1949 to 1984, Mekas's epic autobiography *Diaries, Notes, and Sketches* reworks the aesthetic of home movies into his own personal style, creating a new home for an artist in exile.

The avant-garde in both film and photography turned to home movies and snapshot photography in the 1950s and 1960s for new material. Photographers of the social landscape—Robert Frank, Diane Arbus, Garry Winogrand, Lee Friedlander—reworked the aesthetics of the snapshot within the context of the fine-art photograph. Like Jerome Hill, Bruce Connor, and Stan Brakhage, Mekas found in home movies an aesthetic form suitable for his own filmmaking, calling on our associations with home movies to infuse his films with nostalgia. Many of the scenes of his family and friends clowning for the camera are virtually identical to actual home-movie scenes. His casual, first-person voice-over narration recalls the spoken commentary that often accompanies home-movie screenings, which, as Fred Camper has noted, are, "as often as not, accompanied by the extemporaneous narration provided by the filmmaker, who usually doubles as the projectionist" (Erens 1986, 12). Mekas's voice-over commentary sounds spontaneous, with off-the-cuff remarks and grammatical mistakes retained for their conversational associations. However, his home movies are produced by, for, and about the avant-garde community; they document not his domestic or family life but the New York art world.

The avant-garde film community and the New York art world appear throughout *Diaries, Notes, and Sketches*: Ken Jacobs, Adolfas Mekas, Marie Menken, Gary Snyder, Gregory Markopoulos, Jerome Hill, Lou Reed, Harry Smith, Willard Van Dyke, Amalie Rothschild, Stan Brakhage, Bruce Baille, Gregory Corso, Leroi Jones, Peter Bogdanovich, Edouard de Laurot, Louis Brigante, Herman Weinberg, Tony Conrad, Ed Emshwiller, George Maciunas, Richard Foreman,

Robert Frank, Nam June Paik, Hollis Frampton, Norman Mailer, Hans Richter, Jim McBride, Richard Serra, Peter Kubelka, Annette Michelson, Andy Warhol, Allen Ginsberg, John Lennon, Yoko Ono, and P. Adams Sitney are only some of the most famous. Similarly, members of the international art-cinema world frequently make cameo appearances: Henri Langlois, Nicholas Ray, Roberto Rossellini, Marcel Hanoun, Carl Dreyer, Lotte Eisner, and Barbet Schroeder. At the end of *Lost, Lost, Lost*, Mekas hints that his personal search for community in the New World has been fulfilled by his involvement with the filmmakers of the avant-garde. *Diaries, Notes, and Sketches* outlines the cooperative network of social relationships of the emerging art world of avant-garde film. Richard Chalfen describes the symbolic function of ordinary home movies in similar terms: "The people who came together to be 'in' a home movie shall stay together in a symbolic sense, in a symbolic form, for future viewings. The home movie collection can be understood as a visual record of a network of social relationships" (Erens 1986, 107). Of all the experimental filmmakers, Mekas makes the most extensive use of the home-movie idiom. A greater understanding of ordinary home movies provides an important point of comparison for interpreting his films.

HOME MOVIES

Although in *Language and Cinema* Christian Metz defined cinema as a "total social fact," he nevertheless preferred to study only the specific cinematic codes in film language, the semiotics of cinema (Metz 1974, 9). Using home movies as my example, I suggest that cinematic codes should be studied in their broadest cultural contexts. In his essay *The Gift*, anthropologist Marcel Mauss writes of the total social fact, "Each phenomenon contains all of the threads of which the social fabric is composed. In these total phenomena, as we propose to call them, all kinds of institutions find simultaneous expression: religious, legal, moral, and economic" (Mauss 1954, 1). A holistic approach to culture is one of the distinctive features of anthropological studies of visual media. In his pivotal article "Margaret Mead and the Shift from 'Visual Anthropology' to 'the Anthropology of Visual Communication,' " Sol Worth outlines new directions in anthropological research, making a distinction between the use of images as data about culture and the interpretation of images as data of culture, between "using a medium and studying how a medium is used" (Worth 1980, 190).

The anthropology of visual communication studies visual artifacts not only as records of the world, but also as someone's statement about the world. In addition to making images, then, visual anthropologists interpret the image making of others. The most interesting research on home movies has developed out of Worth's paradigm: "[In the anthropology of visual communication] one looks for patterns dealing with, for example, what can be photographed and what cannot, what content can be displayed, was actually displayed, and how that display was organized and structured" (ibid., 191). Jay Ruby, Richard Chalfen, and Chris Musello, in their research strategies in the anthropology of visual communication, have followed Sol Worth's insights (Ruby 1982; Chalfen 1987; Musello 1980).

Anthropologists of visual communication have shown how family albums and home movies provide highly coded and selective information about the social lives of the individuals depicted. A clearly defined etiquette exists for the types of images made, the circumstances under which they are made and shown, and the persons and events represented. Chalfen has defined this form of expression, centered on the circle of intimacy, as the home mode of visual communication. Home moviemakers rarely edit their footage; the rushes are commonly shown in the chronological order in which they were shot. Other characteristics typical of the home movie include flash frames, over- and underexposure, swish pans, variable focus, lack of establishing shots, jump cuts, hand-held cameras, abrupt changes in time and place, inconsistent characters and no apparent character development, unusual camera angles and movements, and a minimal narrative line (Erens 1986, 16–17). These traits function perfectly well in their proper context; to their intended audience of family and friends, the significance of home movies is readily apparent, even though they may appear repetitive or banal to outsiders. Anthropologists of visual communication argue that visual documents do not provide a reliable or objective portrayal of social life. Similarly, avant-garde filmmaker Michelle Citron has noted the selective record contained in home movies: "When I asked my father for the home movies my request was motivated less by sentimental feelings and more by my unpleasant memories. I somehow expected the movies to confirm my family's convoluted dynamics. But when I finally viewed them after a ten year hiatus, I was surprised and disturbed that the smiling family portrayed on the screen had no correspondence to the family preserved in my childhood memories" (Erens 1986, 93–94). Citron incorporated this insight into her film *Daughter Rite* (1978) by contrasting optically printed sequences of her home movies with her spoken recollections of early childhood. Her memories contextualize the experiences preserved in her home movies.

In the research for his book *Snapshot Versions of Life*, Chalfen found that photographs produced in the home mode of communication depend heavily on contextual information—captions, dates, names, places, relationships. (I will show specifically how Jonas Mekas's diary films rely on contextual information familiar to art-world participants, information that he occasionally supplements for the viewer.) The study of culture and communication presupposes attention to such context. Chalfen's home image-makers often use rather nondescript photographs and movies as a springboard to a funny story or to a description of what was occurring at the time. "Anyone who has ever watched a group of people watching *their own* home movies or slides as the images appear on the home screen must have seen people 'involved' in a variety of ways; audience members frequently talk to one another, make various exclamations at the screen, tell stories, laugh, and sometimes cry, from sadness or happiness" (Erens 1986, 61). Similary, in "On the Invention of Photographic Meaning," Allan Sekula argues that photographs must be viewed in the context of their original rhetorical function, as part of the larger discourse in which they originated, in order their intended meaning to be understood (Sekula 1984).

Family photographs and home movies are not only the products of a mechanical device, but also the products of social relations. The social dimensions of production, distribution, and exhibition of family photographs and home movies define them as a specific mode of visual communication. As Coe and Gates note in their social and technological history of snapshot photography:

> Despite the technical advances which had been made in apparatus and materials, snapshooters at the beginning of the Second World War were covering much the same subjects as their predecessors at the end of the last century and, indeed, their successors today. Snapshot photography was primarily a leisure activity and basic patterns of human activity do not change as much as one would expect from the great material changes which have occurred. Thus the snapshot shows a continuing repetition of a few perennial themes, within which there can still be considerable variety. (Coe and Gates 1977, 15)

Material culture, such as family photographs and home movies, depends on an economy that affords leisure time and encourages consumption. Accordingly, then, home movies reflect the leisure activities of those who can afford both leisure and home movies. In the course of the twentieth century, the size of this group has grown, with a drop in the cost of mass-produced cameras and a rise in the disposable income of middle-class and working-class families (ibid., 40). Mekas's autobiographical films often incorporate a wide variety of typical leisure activities, which are both celebrated and undermined by the narrative structure. *Diaries, Notes, and Sketches* uses a solemn voice-over narration to counterpoint festive imagery, thereby suggesting the fragility of the visible world. Such an overwhelming of the presence of the imagery through voice-over reminiscence makes memory a central issue in his films.

Recent writers note the contradictions between the celebratory characteristics of home movies—birthday parties, weddings, holidays, vacations—and the realities of everyday family life. The home mode of visual communication rarely deals with personal trauma and family strife; divorces are as rare as weddings are commonplace. For ordinary home movies and family photographs, the social situations of production condition the range of subject matter. Nevertheless, viewers who are part of the intended audience of the home mode may read into the images just those emotions and incidents that the form systematically denies. The emphasis on celebration never really limits the free play of memory, for, as Citron's example indicates, the viewer cannot divorce domestic imagery from the associations of family history.

In David Galloway's novel *A Family Album*, the narrator considers the cultural significance of a family album. His meticulous description of the imaginary contexts of the photos' production and the way they are used sheds light on photography as an aspect of everyday life. He comments on how little we may actually know from a photograph, but also how much we may imagine. "When we consider the problem, the number of things not visible in this photograph bulks overwhelmingly large. Neither dreams nor fears are indicated here, though some are perhaps suggested. Nor are date, time, and place of death visible, though surely these are matters of considerable importance. We see neither the women this man will love, nor the ones he will cease to love, nor those to whom he will simply make love" (Galloway 1978, 50). Galloway foregrounds the essential poverty of photography; it gives the appearance of context while eliminating its substance. Novelists share with ethnographers an emphasis on experience as it is lived, remembered, and imagined by the subjects themselves.

Recently, theorists of the home mode of communication have come to recognize that this form contains such a highly selective slice of life that hopes for the discovery of broad visual cultural histories have been tempered by more realistic expectations. In Chris

Musello's words, "Viewers often cannot determine from a family photograph the range of contextual data necessary to interpret the events depicted, and they clearly cannot anticipate the range of significances attributed to the images by their users" (Musello 1980, 40). He concludes that as documents of everyday life, family albums share with oral histories a dependence on the vagaries of memory. To make sense of the home mode of visual communication, cultural anthropologists need "to grasp the native's point of view, his relation to life, to realize *his* vision of *his* world" (Malinowski 1922, 25). They need to consider their own use of home movies and snapshot photographs to understand both perspectives, to be participants and observers.

In traditional American families, with a division of labor across gender lines, the mother commonly holds the position of family cultural historian, preserving examples of children's accomplishments, writing letters, choosing and editing family albums. As the authors of *Middletown Families* note, "Women in Middletown seem to enjoy the maintenance of kinship ties more than men do; men are more apt to stress the obligations involved. The greater involvement of women in kinship activities appears at every turn" (Caplow et al. 1982, 223). More specifically, as Chuck Kleinhans suggests, "Whether through scrapbooks, photo albums, or home movies and tapes, it seems like women are often the historians of domestic space and activity" (Erens 1986, 34). Although the father may be the absent "voyeur" of family representation, the mother usually controls the subsequent editing and presentation of family life. For example, when my younger brother left home at eighteen, my mother began a major photographic inventory of the thirty years of our family existence, completing the family album, and providing individual copies to her five sons as they moved out of the home. Apparently, this rewriting and completion of family historiography at a later date in life is quite common: the unfinished business of parenthood and family consolidation. Recently, our home movies were transferred to videotape and, again, copies were made for the sons and their new families.

Roland Barthes's phenomenological study of photography, *Camera Lucida*, culminates with a meditation on a photograph of the author's mother as a child. For Barthes, this image distills the essence of photographic reproduction, the certainty that the depicted scene existed in the past, that it "has been." In this photograph, he sees an image of his mother just as she was for him. He refuses to reproduce this snapshot of his mother as a child for our scrutiny. "I cannot reproduce the Winter Garden Photograph. It exists only for

me. For you, it would be nothing but an indifferent picture"
(Barthes 1981, 73). He knows that for the outside viewer this photograph would have no meaning, no familiarity. It would be a mere
curiosity, another casual snapshot of an anonymous little girl. With
the passage of time, family snapshots and home movies become a
tenuous link to the past, often closely tied with childhood. Mekas's
repeated references to childhood in *Diaries, Notes, and Sketches*
make these associations available for the viewer. Many couples find
the birth of a child sufficient reason for the purchase of a still camera, a movie camera, or, increasingly, a video camcorder; the use of
these recording devices decreases with the passage of childhood.
Viewed as traces of a receding past and imbued with nostalgia,
home movies are typically regarded as among the most valuable
family possessions (Chalfen 1987, 75).

As with all cultural artifacts, the contexts of production, distribution, and exhibition of home movies are integrally bound up with
the movies' meaning. Through examination of the aesthetics, content, and circulation of home movies we learn of the assumptions
and goals of their users. By considering the home mode of visual
communication from the inside we may understand the profound
emotional investment families have made in their own snapshot
photographs and home movies. Their possession and dissemination
demonstrates a new form of kinship relations, where ties to others are wound in reels of moving images that fade with time, revi-
talized only by the redemptive power of memory. Without familiarity, we have no home, only movies, no family, only photographs.
Throughout *Diaries, Notes, and Sketches,* Mekas uses the kinship
associations of home movies to mark the consolidation of the
avant-garde film community.

HOME MOVIES OF THE AVANT-GARDE

Mekas's films share remarkable characteristics with ordinary
home movies: they take as their subject matter the everyday lives
of his family and friends. *Paradise Not Yet Lost*, the most domestic
of them, concentrates on Mekas's private experiences with his wife
Hollis and their child Oona, culminating with the celebration of
Oona's third birthday. Mekas's shooting style incorporates many of
the signature elements of home movies: flash frames, in-camera editing, rapid camera movements, abrupt changes in time and place,
variable exposure and focus, and jump cuts. And like home movies,
Mekas's films frequently depend on contextual knowledge; familiarity with the people and events depicted increases the viewer's

24.1 Anthology Film Archives Film Selection Committee, 1970: Ken Kelman, James Broughton, P. Adams Sitney, Jonas Mekas, Peter Kubelka.

emotional involvement. *Walden,* in particular, relies extensively on the viewer's knowledge of the New York avant-garde community of the 1950s and 1960s, while the Nicholas Ray sequence of *Paradise Not Yet Lost* depends on knowledge of American film. Similarly, in *He Stands in a Desert,* intertitles specifically invoke the world of avant-garde film: "Fluxus Hudson Trip July 1, 1971," "Jim McBride Leaves Town July 10, 1972," and "Hollis Frampton Buried August 2, 1984, Buffalo, NY."

As these examples indicate, to view a Mekas film is to participate in the avant-garde film community, to become a member of it, to share its struggles, to pay homage to the pioneers of film art. To some extent, all art invites this community involvement. As Patricia Erens notes in her case study of one family's home movies, "For all members in attendance, the movies provided a sense of solidarity and continuity, a renewed sense of 'family' and an increased commitment to the continuation of the annual get-togethers" (Erens 1986, 23). Mekas's films, however, make this invitation within the context of an art world. The extensive list of avant-garde

24.2 Staff of Anthology Film Archives, January 1980.

artists and filmmakers who appear in *Diaries, Notes, and Sketches* suggests the importance of this experience of community.

Mekas's home-movie aesthetic posits memory as the interpretive faculty for his films. Since his camera is so restless and the montage so rapid, the images he records are not experienced in the fullness of the present, but as memories. Memory thus restores the possibility of community and inscribes the individual in history, reforming the ties that bind groups together. *Reminiscences of a Journey to Lithuania* weds Mekas's documentary and avant-garde tendencies, bridging the new worlds of the expatriate community and the avant-garde film community in New York with the old world of Lithuania. In *Lost, Lost, Lost,* he speaks to his Lithuanian friends depicted in the images: "I see you, I see you, I recognize your faces, each one is separate in the crowd. . . . The only thing that mattered to you was the independence of your country. All those meetings,

24.3 Staff of Anthology Film Archives, December 1990.

all those talks, what to do, what will happen, how long, what can we do? Yes, I was there and I recorded it for others, for the history, for those who do not know the pain of exile." Thus, while these people are strangers to most viewers, we participate in the filmmaker's recognition of them years later, and we recognize ourselves as the others called on to bear witness to their struggles.

Mekas uses the chance phrase, the image recorded as if by accident, in a way seen by Fred Camper as characteristic of home movies. "Thus the home movie possesses a degree of randomness not present in more polished forms. It is indeed the combination of individual intentionality and lack of control that gives most home movies their particular flavor" (Erens 1986, 11). Mekas explores this technique most systematically in *Walden* through a pastiche of events, public and private, taking place in New York in the 1950s and 1960s: Hare Krishna celebrations, snowball fights, readings of Beat poetry, John Lennon and Yoko Ono's Christmas message, the Velvet Underground's premiere at Andy Warhol's Factory, phrases of Walt Whitman's poetry, meetings of the Film-Makers' Cooperative, antiwar protests, and P. Adams Sitney's wedding. Like the photographer Alfred Stieglitz, Mekas establishes a new iconography of the city, using a small-format hand-held camera. A voice-over in *Lost, Lost, Lost*—"There is very little known about this period of our protagonist's life. It's known that he was very shy and very lonely during this period. He used to take long, long walks. He felt close to the park, to the streets, to the city"—glosses the images of Mekas combing the streets of his new home, making it his own, while looking for traces of the past and signs of a possible future.

Mekas's direct voice-over address to the viewer contributes to his films' radically personal tone, undermining in every way the "Voice of God" ontology. In *Walden*, for example, he anticipates the audience response: "And now, dear viewer, as you sit and as you watch and as the life outside in the streets is still rushing, maybe a little bit slower, but still rushing from inertia, just watch these images. Nothing much happens. The images go, no tragedy, no drama, no suspense, just images for myself, and for a few others." This direct address displays the individuality of the narrator and calls forth the individuality of the viewer. Even more remarkably, in *Lost, Lost, Lost*, Mekas's voice-over directly addresses the aesthetic assumptions of his friends in the avant-garde film community. "I know I'm sentimental. You would like these images to be more abstract. It's OK, call me sentimental. You sit in your own homes but I speak with an accent and you don't even know where I come from. These are some images and some sounds recorded by someone in exile." These examples illustrate Becker's analysis of the role of audience expectations in artworks: "Artists create their work, at least in part, by anticipating how other people will respond, emotionally and cognitively, to what they do. That gives them the means with which to shape it further, by catering to already existing dispositions in the audience, or by trying to train the audience to something new" (Becker 1982, 200). Mekas challenges the prevailing aesthetic of abstraction and formal experimentation within the avant-garde community in favor of his own personal documentary style.

Overall, the films chronicle his involvement in the world of avant-garde film. One of the last sections of *Lost, Lost, Lost* records the attempt to screen Ken Jacobs's *Blonde Cobra* and Jack Smith's *Flaming Creatures* at the 1963 Robert Flaherty Film Seminar in Vermont. As Scott MacDonald notes, "Not allowed into the seminar, they sleep outside in the cold night (a wry reference to Flaherty's *Nanook of the North*) and the next morning commemorate their rejection with some ritual filmmaking" (MacDonald 1988, 12). Characteristically, Mekas also reports on this guerilla action in a 12 September 1963 column of his "Movie Journal" in the *Village*

Voice: "We took *Flaming Creatures* and *Blonde Cobra* to the seminar, two pieces of the impure, naughty, and 'uncinematic' cinema that is being made now in New York" (Mekas 1972, 95). Through these actions, Mekas makes explicit his allegiance to the avant-garde community.

ART WORLD INSTITUTIONS: FILM CRITICISM

Together with *Diaries, Notes, and Sketches*, Mekas's writings have been instrumental in the construction of an art world of avant-garde film. In his first editorial for *Film Culture*, he outlined his project for the years to come, forecasting the development of a new art world: "Like all art, cinema must strive towards the development of a culture of its own that will heighten not only the creative refinement of the artist but also—and pre-eminently—the receptive faculty of the public" (Mekas 1955, 1). In "The Experimental Film in America," he similarly linked the avant-garde film community to the cultivation of an audience. "Undoubtedly, one of the most important factors contributing to this change [in the growth of the American experimental film] is the increase in film education. The graduation of hundreds of students from University film classes, the work of the University of Southern California, The Museum of Modern Art Film Library, Hans Richter's Film Institute at CCNY, Cinema 16, The Film Council of America and a steadily growing film society movement were all responsible for bringing good films closer and deeper into our communities" (Mekas 1955, 16). A fully developed art world needs an audience capable of appreciating its products. In Becker's words, "Knowing the conventions of the form, serious audience members can collaborate more fully with artists in the joint effort which produces the work each time it is experienced" (Becker 1982, 48). *Film Culture* demanded a sophisticated readership, with articles by directors Orson Welles, Erich von Stroheim, and Hans Richter that derided the commercialism of the Hollywood film industry. Auteurism, championed by Mekas's friend and colleague Andrew Sarris in the pages of *Film Culture*, rescued the films of certain studio directors from commercial oblivion. A fifty-one page article published in 1963, "The American Cinema," formed the basis of Sarris's reevaluation of the classical Hollywood cinema (Sarris 1963, 1). In a 1957 editorial, Mekas bemoaned the state of film scholarship in America. "Recent visits to New York publishing houses revealed that the possibility of an audience for books on cinema is not even considered. Books are published—sentimental memoirs, company chronicles or popular pictorializations—but they are not what our colleges, universities and serious film students need" (Mekas 1957b, 1). Mekas recognizes that an art world of film, in addition to avenues of production, distribution, and exhibition, needs a critical discourse to validate these works, to cultivate a more sophisticated audience, and to provide methodologies of interpretation.

In his "Movie Journal" columns he promoted the avant-garde cinema in a number of different ways. He consistently validated film through references to other art forms, as in his 2 May 1963 column: "These movies are illuminating and opening up sensibilities and experiences never before recorded in the American arts; a content which Baudelaire, the Marquis de Sade, and Rimbaud gave to world literature a century ago and which Burroughs gave to American literature three years ago" (Mekas 1972, 85). He systematically criticized the resistance of the established newspaper and magazine critics to avant-garde film, writing in the 9 December 1965 column: "These smart and literary critics are ignorant of the fact that cinema, during the last five years (and through a series of earlier avant-gardes), has matured to the level of the other arts" (Mekas 1972, 218). He used his position at the *Village Voice* to advertise screenings, as in this 13 June 1963 column: "This Saturday at the Gramercy Arts Theatre (138 East 27th Street) at 7, 9, and 11 p.m., a new film by Gregory Markopoulos, *Twice a Man*, will have its first public screening. The showings are a benefit for the completion of the sound track of the film" (Mekas 1972, 86). *Lost, Lost, Lost* includes several shots of this premiere, signaled by an intertitle, "Premiere of *Twice a Man*."

Mekas regularly issued manifestos directly addressing the expanding art world, as in this 23 January 1969 column: "From my discussions with other independent film-makers the following few points have come out and I would suggest that the university film festival organizers take these points seriously, if they don't want to be boycotted" (Mekas 1972, 333). He himself served on the juries of these festivals and promoted film to the financial backers of the established art world, securing production funds for fellow filmmakers. In the 13 June 1971 "Movie Journal" column, in an interview with Harry Smith, Mekas stated, "I don't talk about money, you know. Because I don't have any. But I'm willing to hustle for people I believe in" (Mekas 1972, 420). In *Reminiscences*, we see Mekas in formal dress, his hair neatly combed, and the intertitle reads "Having tea with rich ladies." As Calvin Tomkins makes plain in his 1973 profile, Mekas was an important resource for avant-garde filmmakers. "Whatever their feelings about the underground, though, critics and filmmakers agree that its development and spectacular growth since 1960 are due in large part to the efforts of Jonas Mekas. Stan Brakhage, whom Mekas considers the most important filmmaker in America, states flatly that without Mekas's help and encouragement at least a third of his films would never have been made, and many other filmmakers could say the same thing" (Tomkins 1973, 32).

THE MAKING OF AN ART WORLD

Mekas has also been instrumental in the creation of exhibition and distribution outlets for avant-garde film. The founding of Anthology Film Archives in 1970 represented the final step in the construction of the art world of avant-garde film. "To persist, works of art must be stored so that they are not physically destroyed. To persist in the life of an art world, they must not only remain available by continuing to exist, they must also be easily available to potential audiences" (Becker 1982, 220). The manifesto of Anthology Film Archives outlined the founders' desire to preserve and promote a limited body of films, an act tantamount to the creation of a canon by the founders: Mekas, Sitney, Ken Kelman, James Broughton, and Peter Kubelka. While this act of film criticism with important institutional ramifications has been justifiably criticized by filmmakers and scholars, it further consolidated the place of film as a fine-art form in the United States.

In *Art Worlds*, Howard Becker offers the extreme example of a work of art entirely produced by one person. "Imagine, as one extreme case, a situation in which one person did everything: made everything, invented everything, had all the ideas, performed or executed the work, experienced and appreciated it, all without the assistance or help of anyone else. We can hardly imagine such a thing, because all the arts we know, like all the human activities we know, involve the cooperation of others" (Becker 1982, 7). Through a fictive situation, Becker makes his case for the networks of cooperation characteristic of the art world. And yet, in his example, we see many aspects of the avant-garde film world of the 1940s and 1950s. Filmmakers lacked distributors, audiences, and sources of financial support. Few universities offered courses in the art of film. The discourse of film criticism did not frame film primarily as an art form, as the projection of an individual artistic genius. As late as 1968, Annette Michelson, who subsequently trained many film scholars and participated in the consolidation of film studies in American universities, complained, "Neither the sophistication which has characterized the best literary criticism of our recent past nor the refinement of our current art criticism have begun to inform film criticism" (Michelson 1968, 67).

Earlier avant-garde filmmakers like Maya Deren were obliged to make maverick performances to bring their works to completion. As Sheldon Renan noted, "After making films, and being unable to get satisfactory distribution or exhibition, [Deren] rented the Provincetown Playhouse in New York's Greenwich Village, and exhibited them herself. She also distributed her films from her own home, publicized them with articles and lectures, and set up the Creative Film Foundation to provide cash awards and production money for experimental films" (Renan 1967, 212). Mekas followed Deren's example. On 2 May 1963, he wrote, "Cinema needs its own Armory Show" (Mekas 1972, 84). Like the photographer Alfred Stieglitz, whose Gallery 291 supported the European modernists exhibited at the 1913 Armory Show, Jonas Mekas presided over the transition of film to a fine-art form in the United States. According to Becker, "In a brief time, then, Stieglitz produced (on a small scale, to be sure) much of the institutional paraphernalia which justified photography's claim to be an art: a gallery in which work could be exhibited, a journal containing fine reproductions and critical commentary which provided a medium of communication and publicity, a group of mutually supportive colleagues, and a subject matter and style departing definitively from the imitations of painting then in favor" (Becker 1982, 341). In a similar way, Mekas integrated cinema into the contexts of the exhibition and criticism of the fine arts. He helped to organize his fellow filmmakers into a coherent community and facilitated the distribution of their films. Through his writings and lectures, he worked to create a receptive audience for film as an art form. In his own films, he bears witness to the artistic and political struggles entailed by the construction of the art world of avant-garde film. In the community of filmmakers who constitute the new art world, Mekas finds a shared language and commitment, a new home that he celebrates in his films.

Bibliography

Barthes, Roland. 1981. *Camera Lucida: Reflections on Photography*. New York: Hill and Wang.

Battock, Gregory, ed. 1967. *The New American Cinema*. New York: E. P. Dutton.

Becker, Howard S. 1982. *Art Worlds*. Berkeley and Los Angeles: University of California Press.

Caplow, Theodore, et al. 1982. *Middletown Families*. Minneapolis: University of Minnesota Press.

Chalfen, Richard. 1987. *Snapshot Versions of Life*. Bowling Green: Bowling Green State University Press.

Coe, Brian, and Paul Gates. 1977. *The Snapshot Photograph: The Rise of Popular Photography, 1888–1939*. London: Ash and Grant.

Erens, Patricia, ed. 1986. "Home Movies and Amateur Filmmaking." Special issue of *Journal of Film and Video* 38, no. 3–4 (Summer–Fall).

Galloway, David. 1978. *A Family Album*. London: John Calder.

Kazin, Alfred. 1951. *A Walker in the City*. New York: Harcourt, Brace, and World.

MacDonald, Scott. 1986. "Lost Lost Lost over *Lost Lost Lost*." *Cinema Journal*, 25, no. 2 (Winter): 21–34.

———. 1988. "Conspicuous Consumption: The 1987 Flaherty Film Seminar." *The Independent* 11, no. 2 (March): 12–17.

Malinowski, Bronislav. 1922. *Argonauts of the Western Pacific*. New York: Dutton.

Mauss, Marcel. 1954. *The Gift: Forms and Functions of Exchange in Archaic Societies*. London: Cohen and West.

Mekas, Jonas. 1955a. "Editorial." *Film Culture* 1:1.

———. 1955b. "The Experimental Film in America." *Film Culture* 3:15–20.

———. 1956. "Editorial." *Film Culture* 10:1–2.

———. 1957a. "Editorial." *Film Culture* 11:1–2.

———. 1957b. "Editorial." *Film Culture* 12:2–5.

———. 1957c. "Editorial." *Film Culture* 13:2.

———. 1957d. "Editorial." *Film Culture* 14:2–3.

———. 1957e. "Editorial." *Film Culture* 15:2.

———. 1958a. "Editorial." *Film Culture* 16:2.

———. 1958b. "Editorial." *Film Culture* 17:2.

———. 1958c. "Editorial." *Film Culture* 18:2.

———. 1960. "Cinema of the New Generation." *Film Culture* 21:1–20.

———. 1965. "Film-Makers' Cooperative Catalogue." *Film Culture* 37:1–70.

———. 1972. *Movie Journal: The Rise of a New American Cinema, 1959–1971*. New York: Macmillan.

Metz, Christian. 1974. *Language and Cinema*. The Hague: Mouton.

Michelson, Annette. 1968. "Review of *What is Cinema?*" *Artforum* 6, no. 10:67–71.

Musello, Christopher. 1980. "Studying the Home Mode: An Exploration of

Family Photography and Visual Communication." *Studies in Visual Communication* 6, no. 1 (Spring): 23–42.

Renan, Sheldon. 1967. *An Introduction to the American Underground Film.* New York: E. P. Dutton.

Ruby, Jay, ed. 1982. *A Crack in the Mirror: Reflexive Perspectives in Anthropology.* Philadelphia: University of Pennsylvania Press.

Sarris, Andrew. 1963. "The American Cinema." *Film Culture* 28:1–51.

Sekula, Allan. 1984. *Photography against the Grain: Essays and Photo Works, 1973–1983.* Halifax: Nova Scotia College of Art and Design.

Sitney, P. Adams, ed. 1975. *The Essential Cinema.* New York: Anthology Film Archives and New York University Press.

———. 1978. *The Avant-Garde Film: A Reader in Theory and Criticism.* New York: New York University Press.

Tomkins, Calvin. 1973. "All Pockets Open." *New Yorker,* 6 January, 31–49.

———. 1980. *Off the Wall: Robert Rauschenberg and the Art World of Our Time.* New York: Penguin Books.

Worth, Sol. 1980. "Margaret Mead and the Shift from 'Visual Anthropology' to 'the Anthropology of Visual Communication.'" *Studies in Visual Communication* 6, no. 1 (Spring): 15–22.

Appendixes

A. Jonas Mekas   Autobiographical Notes

Born: Sunday, 24 December 1922, just before sunrise.

Sign: Capricorn.

Place: Semeniškiai (a village of twenty families, about one hundred people), Lithuania—twenty miles from the Latvian border, fifteen miles from the town of Biržai, which has five thousand inhabitants.

Language: Lithuanian (Baltic, not related to Russian).

Parents: Elžbieta Mekas (born Jašinskas, 19 March 1887, died 12 February 1983), and Povilas Mekas (born 1869, died 1951), farmer and carpenter.

Other children in family: Elžbieta, born 24 December 1911, died 28 January 1985; Povilas, born 14 January 1914, died 6 March 1972, veterinarian; Petras, born 15 May 1915, agronomist; Kostas, born 20 November 1919, farmer; Adolfas, born 30 September 1925, filmmaker.

1928–1932 Takes care of cattle in the fields and forests.

1932 May–September, first grade at the primary school of Laužadiškis (four-mile walk).

1933 During the summer works as a shepherd; in the winter, continues school at Laužadiškis.

1934 Summer, cattle and field work; winter, school (third grade).

1935 Summer, cattle and field work; winter, school (fourth grade).

1936 In May, is graduated from primary school (four-grade school). Summer and fall, works as a hired hand in the neighboring village of Neciūnai. Sees his first movies (a Disney Mickey Mouse cartoon and a melodrama). Publishes first poems.

1937 Summer, field work; winter, fifth grade in Papilys (five miles away, mostly covered by bicycle). Edits school newspaper.

1938 In May, is graduated from the six-grade school at Papilys. Summer, field work. Fall, moves to Biržai, attempts to get into the gymnasium (high school); is rejected because too old. Gets angry; decides to stay in town. Spends winter and spring of 1939–1940 with private tutors trying to catch up.

1940 In May, passes examination into the sixth term of the gymnasium (jumps over five years of gymnasium). Summer, field work. Soviet army takes over Lithuania, declares Lithuania a Soviet Republic. Fall, gymnasium in Biržai. Lives in various homes, mostly on milk and bread.

1941 Gymnasium continues. In summer, takes a job as a salesman in a drugstore in Biržai.

1942 Gymnasium continues. Summer, German army takes over Lithuania. Joins staff of an underground newspaper. Begins to work for a local weekly paper, *Biržų žinios*.

1943 Is graduated from the gymnasium as the best student of the year. Becomes editor of *Biržų žinios*. In November, organizes with brother Adolfas the first dramatic theater in Biržai (under the guidance of Juozas Miltinis, director of the Theatre of Panevėžys; Miltinis was a roommate of Barrault during his theater studies, and a close friend of Jouvet). Studies acting under Alekna and Banionis. Travels with the Choir of Maironis, reading poetry.

1944 In January, moves to Panevėžys; works as an assistant editor of a semiliterary weekly, *Panevežio balsas*. In July, in order to escape imminent arrest by the Germans, obtains forged student papers and, with brother Adolfas, boards a train for Vienna. Is sent with Adolfas to Elmshorn, near Hamburg, to a forced-labor camp.

1945 In March, intending to reach Sweden (via Denmark, by secret refugee boat), escapes from Elmshorn. Is detained at the Danish border; hides for two months on a farm near Flensburg. Finds out about the end of the war a week after it ends. For two months lives in the displaced-persons camp at Flensburg. In August, leaves with Adolfas for Hamburg; stays at the Oschenzohl displaced-persons camp. At the end of August, by train, proceeds toward Bavaria. Stays for brief periods in Wuerzburg, Hanau, Tuebingen, Mannheim. Settles down in the DP camp at Wiesbaden. Begins to study philosophy at the University of Mainz.

1946 Studies at the University of Mainz. Edits *Camp News Bulletin*, a daily paper. Edits *Žvilgsniai*, a literary quarterly of the Lithuanian literary avant-garde in exile. Publishes a play for children based on fairy tales, *Trys broliai*, and *Iš pasaku krašto* (translations of international fairy tales for children).

1947 Moves to the DP camp at Kassel. Joins the actors' studio of Ipolitas Tvirbutas, a pupil of Stanislavski. Publishes *Knyga apie karalius ir žmones*, a book of literary sketches and poems in prose. Continues studies in Mainz; commutes between Kassel and Mainz.

1948 Publishes *Semeniškių idilės*, a book of poems, and has a story published in *Proza I*, a collection of short stories by four writers. Continues studies in Mainz. Writes a series of comic sketches for the Tvirbutas Theater.

1949 Moves to the DP camp at Schwaebisch Gmuend. 29 October, arrives in New York. Works at American Plastics Corporation, 567 Third Avenue, punching Coca-Cola signs (November), and at Bebry Castro Bed Company, Long Island (December). Lives in Williamsburg, Brooklyn.

1950 Works in a tailor's shop, ironing—Bancelli, 58–85 Maspeth Avenue (May); at a plumbing company on East Fourth Street, in Manhattan (June); at L. W. Machines as a machine operator, Johnson Street (July-August); cleaning ship parts, Forty-Fourth Avenue, Long Island (September). Lives in Maspeth. Buys a Bolex; begins filming Williamsburg and Lithuanian immigrants.

1951 Attends a few classes taught by Hans Richter at the Film Institute (City College). Contributes short stories to *Proza II*.

1952 Becomes program director of the Film Study Group (with Gideon Bachmann). Begins to work at Graphic Studios 126 West 22nd Street, first as messenger boy, later as cameraman. (Stays there until 1958.) Lives on Linden Street in Brooklyn.

1953 Moves to 95 Orchard Street, Manhattan. Edits Brooklyn footage (*Grand Street*, unfinished; in 1975 most of this footage is edited into *Lost, Lost, Lost*). Begins avant-garde film screenings at Gallery East, 7 Avenue A (September 1953– spring 1954). Organizes Film Forum series at Carl Fisher

Auditorium, New York City. Shoots *Silent Journey* (unfinished).

1955   Begins publishing *Film Culture* magazine (January). With Adolfas Mekas and Edouard de Laurot, shoots a parody of American experimental film (unfinished). The second edition of *Semeniškių idilės* (poetry) receives the Vincas Krėvė poetry award for 1955. Begins film column ("Film Diary") in *Intro Bulletin* (edited by Louis Brigante); continues writing it until 1957.

1956   Moves to 16 West 100th Street. Spends two months in Los Angeles.

1958   Begins the "Movie Journal" column in the *Village Voice* (12 November); continues it until 1976. Assists in organizing the New American Cinema Group; becomes secretary of the executive committee (September 1960). Shoots *Guns of the Trees*.

1961   Publishes second book of poetry, *Gėlių kalbėjimas*. Organizes the first New American Cinema Exposition at Spoleto, Italy. Becomes program director of the Charles Theater (until 1963).

1962   Organizes the Film-Makers' Cooperative. Assistant Director on *Hallelujah the Hills* (dir. Adolfas Mekas). *Guns of the Trees* wins first prize at Porretta Terme, Italy.

1963   Organizes screenings of independent and underground films at Bleecker Street Cinema and Gramercy Arts Theatre. Films *Film Magazine of the Arts*. Juror at Knokke–Le Zoute Third International Experimental Film Festival. Resigns when *Flaming Creatures* is excluded, and stages a protest that causes a national scandal in Belgium. Spends some time in Paris.

1964   Films *The Brig; Fool's Haikus; Flaherty Newsreel; Tiny Tim Newsreel; Award Presentation to Andy Warhol; Salvador Dali*. Arrested for screening *Flaming Creatures* and Genet's *Chant d'amour*; gets a two-month suspended sentence. Organizes Film-Makers' Cinematheque. Organizes New American Cinema Expositions (Paris, London, Stockholm, Munich, Amsterdam, Rome, etc.). *The Brig* wins first prize at Venice Film Festival, documentary section, and is shown at the New York Film Festival.

1965   Moves Film-Makers' Cinematheque to City Hall Cinema, and later to Lafayette Street. Spends two months in Cassis;

films Living Theater's *Frankenstein* and *Mysteries.* Films Kenneth King's *cup/saucer/two dancers/radio* and *Report from Millbrook.*

1966 Films *Hare Krishna* and *Notes on the Circus.* Receives Gold Star Award from Philadelphia College of Art "for his devotion, passion, and selfless dedication to the rediscovery of the newest art"; sends New American Cinema Exposition to South America. Works on the staff of the Adult Program, Great Neck Public Schools (1966–1967).

1967 Third book of poems *Pavieniai žodžiai,* is brought out in Chicago. Takes the second New American Cinema Exposition to Europe (Turin, Rome). Moves Cinematheque to West Forty-First Street. Visits Spain.

1968 First draft of *Diaries, Notes, and Sketches* is screened at Albright-Knox Gallery, Buffalo. Moves Cinematheque to 80 Wooster Street. Becomes film curator, the Jewish Museum (1968–1971).

1969 With Jerome Hill and P. Adams Sitney, begins work on creation of Anthology Film Archives at 425 Lafayette Street. Curates film screenings at Gallery of Modern Art.

1970 Becomes director of Anthology Film Archives (opens 1 December). Visits Hamburg, London, San Francisco.

1971 In Vilnius, Lithuania, *Poezija (Poetry)* is published. Visits Lithuania and Moscow in August. Films *Reminiscences of a Journey to Lithuania.* Visits Austria.

1972 Fourth book of poems, *Reminiscensijos,* published by George Maciunas/Fluxus. *Reminiscences of a Journey to Lithuania* premieres on Norddeutscher Rundfunk television, 12 February, and is also shown at New York Film Festival. Macmillan publishes *Movie Journal.*

1974 Marries Hollis Melton. Moves to 491 Broadway. Oona Mekas is born (3 November). Travels in Austria, Italy, France.

1975 Edits *Lost, Lost, Lost* (subsequently shown at the Berlin, London, and Amsterdam film festivals).

1976 Becomes movie critic for the *Soho Weekly News* (1976–1977).

1977 Receives Guggenheim Fellowship. Becomes member of P.E.N. (American chapter). Visits Lithuania; travels in Austria, Italy, and France. Teaches at the New School for Social Research.

1978 Edits *In Between* and *Notes for Jerome.* Teaches a course at MIT on autobiographical cinema.

1979 Acquires Second Avenue Courthouse building for Anthology Film Archives. Edits *Paradise Not Yet Lost.*

1981 Sebastian Mekas is born (9 December). Visits Sweden.

1983 Travels through Japan (December). Moves Anthology to 491 Broadway. Discontinues screenings at 80 Wooster Street. Works on renovation of the Courthouse building.

1984 Completes *Street Songs.* Visits Austria.

1985 Moves Anthology to the Courthouse building. Fifth book of poems, *Dienorasčiai (Diaries),* is published by Žvilgsniai, New York. Completes *He Stands in a Desert Counting the Seconds of His Life.*

1987 *City Lights Review* publishes translation of *Reminiscences.*

1988 Anthology reopens at the Courthouse in (October).

1989 Receives Brandeis University Creative Arts Award. Begins video diaries (Sony 8 mm).

1990 *Three Friends*—a book on George Maciunas, John Lennon, and Yoko Ono—is published in Tokyo. Edits *Scenes from the Life of Andy Warhol.* Visits Berlin and Stockholm. Conducts a one-month seminar on avant-garde film at Anthology for a group of visiting Lithuanian film students.

1991 *I Had Nowhere to Go— Diary of a Displaced Person* is published by Black Thistle Press. Edits *Dr. Carl C. Jung; or, Lapis Philosophorum* and *Scenes from the Life of George Maciunas.* Visits Japan.

B. Jonas Mekas   Filmography

Guns of the Trees (1960–1961)   75 minutes. B&W.
  Assisted by Adolfas Mekas and Sheldon Rochlin. Poetry inter-
  ludes written and spoken by Allen Ginsberg. Music by Lucia Dlu-
  goszewski. Folk songs by Sara Wiley, Caither Wiley, and Tom
  Sankey.
Film Magazine of the Arts (1963)   20 minutes. B&W/Color.
The Brig (1964) 68 minutes. B&W.
Award Presentation to Andy Warhol (1964)   12 minutes. B&W.
  Photographed by Jonas Mekas and Gregory Markopoulos.
Report from Millbrook (1965–1966)   12 minutes. Color.
  In a different form, the footage is also in *Walden*.
Hare Krishna (1966)   4 minutes. Color.
  Included in full in *Walden*.
Notes on the Circus (1966)   12 minutes. Color.
  Included in full in *Walden*.
Cassis (1966)   4–1/2 minutes. Color.
The Italian Notebook (1967)   14–3/4 minutes. Color.
Time and Fortune Vietnam Newsreel (1968)   4 minutes. Color.
Walden (1964–1969)   3 hours. Color.
  Filmed in 1964–1968; edited in 1968–1969.
  [Note: *Walden* was originally titled *Diaries, Notes, and Sketches,
  also known as Walden*. Mekas intended that subsequent selec-
  tions from his "diaries, notes, and sketches" would have similar
  subtitles; thus *Lost, Lost, Lost* was to have been *Diaries, Notes,
  and Sketches: Lost, Lost, Lost*, and so on. The confusion this
  caused, especially at film laboratories, caused him to abandon the
  general designation, and now all the films after (what is now
  known as) *Walden* have the specific title only. However, *Diaries,
  Notes, and Sketches* is often used to designate the overall project.]
Reminiscences of a Journey to Lithuania (1971–1972)   82 minutes.
  Color.
Lost, Lost, Lost (1949–1975)   2 hours 58 minutes. B&W/Color.
  Filmed in 1949–1963. Edited in 1975.
In Between: 1964–1968 (1964–1978)   52 minutes. Color.
  Filmed in 1964–1968. Edited in 1978.

Notes for Jerome (1966–1978)   45 minutes. Color.
Filmed in 1966, 1967, and 1974. Edited in 1978.

Paradise Not Yet Lost (a/k/a Oona's Third Year) (1977–1979)   96–1/2 minutes. Color.
Filmed in 1977. Edited in 1979.

Street Songs (1966–1984)   10–1/2 minutes. B&W.

cup/saucer/two dancers/radio (1965–1983)   23 minutes. Color.

Erick Hawkins: Excerpts from "Here and Now with Watchers"/Lucia Dlugoszewski Performs (1964–1983)   5–3/4 minutes. B&W.

He Stands in a Desert Counting the Seconds of His Life (1969–1985)   2–1/2 hours. Color.

Scenes from the Life of Andy Warhol (1965–1990)   35 minutes. Color.
Filmed in 1965–1982. Completed in June 1990.

Dr. Carl C. Jung; or, Lapis Philosophorum (1950–1991)   29 minutes. Color.
Filmed by Jerome Hill in 1950. Edited by Jonas Mekas in 1991.

Showcases I Ran in the
Sixties

1. Open House screenings at Charles Theater, Avenue B and East Twelfth Street, 1961–1963.

2. Screenings at Bleecker Street Cinema, 4 February to 8 April 1963, Saturday midnights. The managers of the theater, Marshall Lewis and Rudy Franchi, ordered the screenings discontinued because the low quality of the underground was ruining the reputation of the theater, they said.

3. Gramercy Arts Theatre, 138 East 27th Street, 1 July 1963 to 3 March 1964. The owner of the theater threw us out on the grounds that we were screening unlicensed and obscene movies.

4. New Bowery Theater, 4 St. Mark's Place, 24 February to 17 March 1964. Closed by police after seizure of *Flaming Creatures* on 17 March.

5. Writers' Stage Theater, 83 East Fourth Street, 7 March 1964. Closed on 14 March by the police after a screening of Genet's *Chant d'amour*. Film seized.

6. Washington Square Art Gallery, 530 West Broadway, 16 July to September 1964. Gallery closed; we had to leave.

7. New Yorker Theater, 30 November to 21 December 1964. Monday nights. Had to move out because New Yorker decided to use Monday nights for "rare classics."

8. Maidman Theater, 416 West Forty-Second Street, 18 January to 26 January 1965. Moved out after the owner or manager of the theater, seeing huge crowds coming to our shows, started raising the rental price.

9. City Hall Cinema, 170 Nassau Street, 25 January to 31 May 1965. Three days a week. Had to move out after the city decided to tear down the building.

10. Astor Place Playhouse, Lafayette Street, 4 June to November 1965. Four days a week, then daily. Moved out when the owner, seeing the crowds of customers, increased the price drastically.

11. Forty-First Street Theater, early 1967 to 30 August 1967. Daily screenings. Moved out after the rent of the theater was raised too high.

12. 80 Wooster Street, early 1968 to 30 July 1968. Daily screen-

ings. Closed by the police and Building Department "to complete the licensing" of the theater.

13. Methodist Church, West Fourth Street, 1 August to 25 August 1968. Mondays only. Temporary arrangement did not permit us to stay longer.

14. Bleecker Street Cinema, 25 August 1968. Moved out because of improper union projection of 16 mm films.

15. Jewish Museum, 1109 Fifth Avenue, 12 November 1968 to present. Tuesday evenings.

16. Gotham Art Theater, West Forty-Third Street, 31 January to 28 February 1969. Weekend screenings. Temporary arrangement. Not thrown out!

17. Elgin Theater, Eighth. Avenue and West Nineteenth Street, 26 January to 23 March 1969. Sundays, 11:15 A.M. only—not the happiest time. Temporary arrangement.

18. Gallery of Modern Art, Columbus Circle, 1 March to September 1969. Daily screenings (except Monday and Tuesday). Screenings stopped by me after a show of Stan Brakhage's *Window Water Baby Moving*, which the management of the gallery found obscene.

D. Jonas Mekas   Books Published

IN LITHUANIAN

Prose

Iš pasakų krašto (*From the Land of Fairy Tales*)
   (Wiesbaden: Giedra, 1946)
   Fairy tales of many lands, translated into Lithuanian.
Trys broliai (*Three Brothers*)
   (Wiesbaden: Giedra, 1946)
   A play for children based on Lithuanian fairy tales.
Knyga apie karalius ir žmones (*A Book about Kings and People*)
   (Tuebingen: Patria, 1947)
   A book of sketches and poems in prose.

Poetry

Semeniškių idilės (*Idylls of Semeniškiai*)
   (Kassel: Žvilgsniai, 1948)
Gėlių kalbėjimas (*Flower Talk*)
   (Chicago: Santara, 1961)
Pavieniai žodžiai (*Words Apart*)
   (Chicago: AM Fondas, 1967)
Poezija (*Poetry*)
   (Vilnius: Vaga, 1971)
Reminiscensijos (*Reminiscences*)
   (New York: Fluxus, 1972)
Dienoraščiai (*Diaries*)
   (New York: Žvilgsniai, 1985)
Juodi raštai ant aušros vartų (*Black Writing on the Gates of Dawn*)
   Unpublished poetry, 1985–1991.

IN ENGLISH

Movie Journal: The Rise of a New American Cinema, 1959–1971.
   (New York: Macmillan, 1972)
   Selected columns from the *Village Voice*.

I Had Nowhere to Go—Diary of a Displaced Person
  (New York: Black Thistle Press, 1991)
  Diaries, 1944–1954.

IN JAPANESE

Three Friends
  (Tokyo: Sha, 1990)
  On John Lennon, Yoko Ono, and George Maciunas.

Index